W9-CDH-790

Life Everlasting

LIFE EVERLASTING

DUANE S. CROWTHER

Salt Lake City, Utah

Library of Congress Catalog Card Number 67-25433

29th Printing, 1992

Lithographed in the United States of America
PUBLISHERS PRESS
Salt Lake City, Utah

All men know that they must die. And it is important that we should understand . . . our departure hence. . . . It is but reasonable to suppose that God would reveal something in reference to the matter, and it is a subject we ought to study more than any other. We ought to study it day and night, for the world is ignorant in reference to their true condition and relation. If we have any claim on our Heavenly Father for anything, it is for knowledge on this important subject.

—Joseph Smith
(*History of the Church*, Vol. VI, p. 50.)

November 10, 1961 September 5, 1966

This book is dedicated with eternal love to our daughter,

Laura Jean

who brought sweetness and joy into our home, and whose passing has been the motivation for this study.

ACKNOWLEDGMENTS

I WISH TO EXPRESS MY APPRECIATION TO THOSE WHO HAVE aided me in this project, for their help and suggestions have proven to be of great value. Ruth Gregory, Ronald DeMille, Dorothy Murphy, Mary Ellsworth, and Jaynann Payne provided a number of sources which were otherwise inaccessible to me. Sister Bertha Purser, librarian at the Logan L.D.S. Institute, was helpful in making certain rare materials available. My father, Don Q. Crowther, read and gave help on much of the manuscript. Loretta Merrill, Helen Porter, and Bruce Christensen have all spent countless hours reading proofs and helping the book towards publication. Their assistance and kindness are greatly appreciated. Thanks should also be expressed to those whose writings are cited herein for the pioneering they have done in preserving valuable accounts and for their courtesy in making them available for publication. Many others have continually expressed interest and given encouragement in the project, and I feel truly indebted to them for their friendship and concern.

Marvin Wallin and his associates at Bookcraft have given me much guidance in the preparation of this book. Their careful reading of the manuscript and many technical suggestions have proven invaluable and are greatly appreciated.

As I have searched into the messages of eternity I have drawn ever closer to my wife, Jean, and to my children, Don, Scott, Lisa and David. Their love and prayers in my behalf have brought me great joy. My wife is a "doer of the word, and not a hearer only," and she has spent dozens of hours typing and proofreading the manuscript, for which I am deeply thankful.

But most of all I give acknowledgement and thanks to my Father in heaven, who truly "gives good things to them that ask Him." May this book serve to give him honor and glory and to bring many souls into His eternal kingdom.

Duane S. Crowther

CONTENTS

INTRODUCTION

Could You Gaze Into Heaven

"Could you gaze into heaven five minutes, you would know more than you would by reading all that ever was written on the subject."[1] Thus the prophet Joseph Smith hurled the challenge, and set the goal, which many Latter-day Saints have accepted and achieved. They have seen into paradise! They have glimpsed the spirits in prison! They have seen the suffering of hell! They have seen the glory of the great resurrection day! Some have even beheld the glory of exaltation and God's celestial city! Joseph knew they could, and taught his followers so, saying, *"I assure the Saints that truth, in reference to these matters, can and may be known through the revelations of God in the way of His ordinances, and in answer to prayer."*[2]

Purposes of This Book

This volume is not a fanciful collection of consoling poetry and funeral phraseology. It is a careful analysis of the experiences of dozens of reliable individuals who have died and then returned to life, and of scores of others who have been visited by departed spirits. It is a gathering together of revelation after revelation telling of the glorious life which awaits the righteous. It is my personal witness that life continues beyond the grave, and that God allows mortal man to know many of the joys of the life to come!

The study found herein was designed to accomplish seven purposes:

1. To testify that life continues beyond death, that there is a continuation of individuality in the future worlds, that there exists a divine plan of salvation which gives meaning to life and death, and that the joys and rewards of eternity are

---

[1]HC 6:50. Oct. 9, 1843. Explanation of various footnote reference forms used in the introduction is given in the early footnotes of chapter 1.

[2]*Ibid.*, p. 51.

so glorious that man should valiantly labor to merit them in his life and in the life to come.

2. To bear witness and provide evidence that God has often revealed knowledge to the leaders and members of The Church of Jesus Christ of Latter-day Saints concerning the future estates of life.

3. To demonstrate that the information revealed by God in the last days is harmonious with the scriptures, and that the many revelations cited herein lend validity to each other because of their vast interrelationships.

4. To provide a pattern of understanding in order that those who receive manifestations and revelations on the themes treated herein may compare and link their experiences with others.

5. To clarify certain areas of ambiguity which exist in the teachings of many of the Saints concerning portions of the plan of salvation.

6. To give comfort to those who are troubled with uncertainties about death and that which follows.

7. To proclaim that there is a kind and just God who is guiding the earth and the lives, opportunities, and destinies of all who dwell upon it.

The Law of Witnesses

This book presents many items from three sources:

1. The revealed word of God as found in the scriptures,

2. The revealed word of God as expressed by His prophets, and

3. The revealed word of God as manifested to worthy members of the Church. It is a pioneering venture, for it goes beyond the oft-repeated quotations which have long been cited in the Church. It presents the eye-witness evidence of those who have actually visited the spirit world and can bear personal witness of the life beyond. Their words are not opinions and logic, but are factual observations. Their testimonies are complete. They are harmonious. They are true.

The reader will encounter many new ideas as he scans these pages. He will find these ideas grouped in clusters of supporting evidence in which one testimony verifies another. The Lord has set forth the divine law whereby truth may be identified, saying that *"in the mouth of two or three witnesses shall every word be established."*[3] The reader must judge the veracity of these witnesses and their testimony by that law, and by his own reception of the promptings of the Holy Ghost, for *"by the power of the Holy Ghost ye may know the truth of all things."*[4] The astute reader will discover that the personal manifestations cited do not conflict with the scriptures, nor with the words of the prophets. The revealed word of the Lord, through all its recipients, is a harmonious unity.

As in my other literary efforts to date, a constant effort has been made to present evidence rather than my personal opinion. Indeed, my personal views have been altered in a number of areas as I gathered and analyzed the evidence at hand. My views will only be expressed herein as a summary of the documentation presented. The reader is invited to cite Joseph Smith, Brigham Young, Orson Pratt, Joseph Fielding Smith and the host of others quoted herein rather than saying, "Brother Crowther says . . ." It is their insights as prophets, not mine as a compiler and analyst of their words, which is of value.

Personal Revelation the Key to Knowledge of Eternities

Joseph Smith taught that

> All men know that they must die. And it is important that we should understand the reasons and causes of our exposure to the vicissitudes of life and of death, and the designs and purposes of God in our coming into the world, our sufferings here, and our departure hence. What is the object of our coming into existence, then dying and falling away, to be here no more? *It is but reasonable to suppose that God would reveal something in reference to the matter, and it is a subject we ought to study more than any other. We ought to study it day and night, for the world is ignorant in reference to their true condition and relation. If we have any claim on our Heavenly Father for anything, it is for knowledge on this important subject.*[5]

---

[3]2 Cor. 13:1. See Deut. 19:15.

[4]Moro. 10:5.

[5]HC 6:50. Oct. 9, 1843.

He believed with all his heart that the members of the Church should know of the great themes of eternity, and longed to tell them more. He sounded the theme which this book has followed when he proclaimed, *"I advise all to go on to perfection, and search deeper and deeper into the mysteries of godliness."*[6] He set the standard when he said that "All I want is to get the simple, naked truth, and the whole truth."[7] And he told his followers how to do it, saying that "The best way to obtain truth and wisdom is . . . to go to God in prayer, and *obtain divine teaching."*[8] His admonition was to all the Church, and this book is a witness that the Saints—not just prophets and apostles, but stake presidents, bishops, temple leaders and workers, and faithful lay members of the Church—have heeded his challenge and obtained divine manifestations. They have followed the path Joseph outlined, that "When we understand the character of God, and know how to come to Him, *he begins to unfold the heavens to us, and to tell us all about it.* When we are ready to come to him, he is ready to come to us."[9]

Not as Doctrine

Brigham Young taught that "When any man publishes or preaches his peculiar views he should not say they are the views of the Church."[10] This book presents my views in the sense that they are based on the evidence available. As that evidence grows, my views grow and I grow. I write as an individual and not as an official spokesman for The Church of Jesus Christ of Latter-day Saints, and the concepts expressed herein are not official statements of Latter-day Saint doctrine. Undoubtedly the teachings expressed herein sometimes exceed in scope the Church's doctrines concerning the future life.

The items presented herein conform to the law of witnesses. I have checked them carefully. I believe them to be true. Certainly the study of these items is proper by the members of the Church, for "if there is anything virtuous, lovely,

---

[6]HC 6:363. May 12, 1844.

[7]HC 6:476. June 16, 1844.

[8]HC 4:425. Oct. 2, 1841.

[9]HC 6:308. April 7, 1844.

[10]Matthias F. Cowley, *Wilford Woodruff—History of His Life and Labors* (Salt Lake City, Utah: Bookcraft, 1964), p. 449.

or of good report or praiseworthy, we seek after these things."[11] The reader is invited to examine these accounts carefully, and, as Paul said, "Prove all things; hold fast that which is good."[12]

The evidence is historical, not clinical. The chemist or physicist will never hold the key to life after death unless it is revealed to them. That key lies in the accounts of those who have ventured into the spirit realm and then returned. Its meaning is found in the realm of religion, not of science. The things of the spirit are spiritually discerned.

How This Book Was Written

It is helpful to the reader to know an author and the story of a book. The material for this book has been gathered and contemplated for many years. Just as the doctrine of prophecy of the last days has long held my attention, I have also wanted to know what the future held on the other side of the veil. During my years as a missionary, during my labors as a graduate student in the Brigham Young University College of Religious Instruction, during my tasks as a Seminary instructor and principal, and during my years as a researcher and author, I have been interested in every source of information concerning the spirit life and man's future in the resurrected state. In 1963 and 1964, I began to gather information in earnest on these themes. But it was not until I learned that my daughter had leukemia, in early July, 1966, that I began to shape my materials into this manuscript. I have studied, written, prayed, and hunted for materials since that time with a hunger known only to those who have lost a loved one. The desire for knowledge of eternal truths is a compelling force, and it has provided me with motivation and determination.

It is my desire and expectation that many will find hope, understanding, and joy through the messages of this book. I believe that it will give the same comfort and solace to others in times of sorrow as the study gave to me at the time of the loss of my daughter.

Duane S. Crowther

[11]Article of Faith 13.
[12]1 Thess. 5:21.

CHAPTER I

ENTRY INTO THE SPIRIT WORLD

THROUGH THE CENTURIES MANKIND HAS MOURNED AND WEPT for departed loved ones without knowledge of their fate. They have reluctantly conceded their inability to peer beyond the veil of death. Mankind has stood, helpless, confused and afraid, before the unyielding certainty that all men must return to the dust of the earth. Questions concerning the future have cried out for a reply:

Does man continue to exist after death?

Does he maintain his identity and personality?

Where does he go? What does he do?

What does he look like?

What is it like to die?

These are questions mankind has posed through all the ages since the days of Adam. Neither scholars, philosophers, nor poets have been able to answer them. Indeed, the knowledge of mortals has not been sufficient to answer these profound queries.

Biblical Allusions to Spirit World Visits

The good news of Christ began to pierce this darkness of uncertainty and despair in the meridian of time. The promise of life beyond mortality was given by the Master, who proclaimed that "He that heareth my word, and believeth on him that sent me, hath everlasting life, and shall not come into condemnation; but is *passed from death unto life.*"[1] His promise, at first rejected as vain by the unbelieving, suddenly became a source of hope and joy to them as they saw that He truly had power to call men back from the grave. Imagine

---

[1]Jn. 5:24.

the wonder and amazement among the people as the Lord's power was manifested in restoring life to the son of the widow of Nain:

> Now when he came nigh to the gate of the city, behold, there was a dead man carried out, the only son of his mother, and she was a widow: and much people of the city was with her.
>
> And when the Lord saw her, he had compassion on her, and said unto her, Weep not.
>
> And he came and touched the bier: and they that bare him stood still. And he said, Young man, I say unto thee, Arise.
>
> And he that was dead sat up, and began to speak. And he delivered him to his mother.
>
> And there came a fear on all: and they glorified God, saying, That a great prophet is risen up among us; and, That God hath visited his people.
>
> And this rumour of him went forth throughout all Judaea, and throughout all the region round about.[2]

What excitement the surging crowds must have felt as they heard the young man describe his visit beyond the veil!

Several months later, just twenty-two miles away, Jesus again showed his power over death by recalling the departed spirit of the twelve-year-old daughter of a Jewish leader, Jairus:

> And, behold, there came a man named Jairus, and he was a ruler of the synagogue: and he fell down at Jesus' feet, and besought him that he would come into his house:
>
> For he had one only daughter, about twelve years of age, and she lay a dying. But as he went the people thronged him. . . .
>
> While he yet spake, there cometh one from the ruler of the synagogue's house, saying to him, Thy daughter is dead; trouble not the Master.
>
> But when Jesus heard it, he answered him, saying, Fear not: believe only, and she shall be made whole.
>
> And when he came into the house, he suffered no man to go in, save Peter, and James, and John, and the father and the mother of the maiden.

---

[2]Lk. 7:12-17.

> And all wept, and bewailed her: but he said, Weep not; she is not dead, but sleepeth.
>
> And they laughed him to scorn, knowing that she was dead.
>
> And he put them all out, and took her by the hand, and called, saying, Maid, arise.
>
> And her spirit came again, and she arose straightway: and he commanded to give her meat.[3]

Perhaps this young child was also permitted to tell the wondrous sights she had seen, for it was recorded that "her parents were astonished"—so much amazed, apparently, that Christ "charged them that they should tell no man."[4]

Two years later, the Savior again rebuked the bonds of death and called forth a man from the tomb who had been dead for four days. With Jesus' shout of "Lazarus, come forth," this beloved brother of Mary and Martha rose from his tomb and came forth "bound hand and foot with graveclothes."[5] Is it any wonder that the Master was able to tell his sister, "He that believeth in me, though he were dead, yet shall he live."[6] Imagine what tales Lazarus must have been able to tell of his experiences during his four days in the world of the dead!

Ponder also the account of her visit into the spirit world the woman Tabitha must have related after being called back to mortal life by the apostle, Peter. What, exactly, did she see as her body lay in the upper chamber during the hours the messengers ran from Lydda to Joppa and returned with their beloved leader?[7]

And what tales did Eutychus, the sleepy lad from Troas, who fell from the window, have to tell about his brief visit into the spirit world? He died as a result of the fall and was restored to life by the apostle Paul.[8] Were they stories like those of the son of the widow of Zarephath, who was called

---

[3]Lk. 8:41-42, 49-55.
[4]Lk. 8:56.
[5]Jn. 11:1-44.
[6]Jn. 11:25.
[7]Acts 9:36-42.
[8]Acts 20:6-12.

back to life by the prophet Elijah after spending precious minutes in the life beyond death?[9] Or were they an echo of the testimony of the Shunammite's son, whose spirit went beyond the veil, and then returned to his body? While he was dead his mother rode on a donkey more than fifty miles to bring back the prophet Elisha from Mt. Carmel so that the prophet could restore the boy's life.[10]

Though the Bible gives careful evidence of people returning from the dead, it gives us no record of their experience in the life beyond. It does, however, set an important precedent and establishes the plausibility of other accounts of those who have entered and then returned from the spirit realm. In the latter days, many have also journeyed into the world of spirits and have been permitted to return to mortality. Though many such experiences have gone unrecorded, yet many other spirit world visitations are on record and are available for study.

This book is an intensive study and analysis of these recorded experiences, together with the messages of the scriptures and of latter-day prophets, as they define the path man must travel from death to eternal life.

Reception Into the Spirit Realm

Being greeted and received by one's guardian angel is a familiar experience among those who have ventured beyond the confines of mortality. This was the reception of Peter Johnson, a Latter-day Saint missionary who went into the spirit world for an hour-and-a-half in early September, 1898:

> My spirit left the body; just how I cannot tell. But *I perceived myself standing some four or five feet in the air, and saw my body lying on the bed. I felt perfectly natural,* but as this was a new condition, I began to make observations. *I turned my head, shrugged my shoulders, felt with my hands, and realized that it was myself.* I also knew that my body was lying, lifeless, on the bed. While I was in a new environment, it did not seem strange, for I realized everything that was going on, and *perceived that I was the same in the spirit as I had been in the body.* While contemplating this new condition, something at-

[9] 1 Ki. 17:17-24.
[10] 2 Kin. 4:18-37.

> tracted my attention, and on turning around I beheld a personage, who said: 'You did not know that I was here.' I replied: 'No, but I see you are. Who are you?' *'I am your guardian angel; I have been following you constantly while on earth.'* I asked: 'What will you do now?' He replied: *'I am to report your presence, and you will remain here until I return.'*[11]

Witness the similar experience of Henry Zollinger, who was crushed by a hay derrick in August, 1920, and was in the spirit world for several hours:

> My spirit left the body and I could see it lying under the derrick and *at that moment my guardian angel, my mother and my sister Ann were beside me.* My mother died Jan. 31, 1918 and my sister at the age of four years. I saw that *her spirit was full grown in stature* and also seemed very intelligent.[12]

Heber Q. Hale, who went into the spirit realm on January 20, 1920, described how he saw his body as his spirit left it, his impression of the nearness of the spirit world, and recorded that he also was greeted immediately by a reception committee:

> *I passed but a short distance from my body through a film into the world of spirits.* This was my first experience after going to sleep. I seemed to realize that I had passed through the change called death and I so referred to it in my conversation with the *immortal beings*

---

[11]Peter E. Johnson, "A Testimony," *The Relief Society Magazine,* Vol. VII, No. 8, p. 451, August, 1920. Peter Johnson was stricken with malaria on August 8, 1898. During the following month he sank rapidly and his spirit finally left his body.

[12]Henry Zollinger, "My Experience In The Spirit World," unpublished manuscript in the possession of his wife, a resident of Providence, Cache Co., Utah. Brother Zollinger explains the occasion for his spirit world experience in this manner:

> On Aug. 7, 1920, I was moving a hay derrick under a live electric wire, the derrick pole caught on the wire and consequence was I received a shock that threw me in the air, then I fell under the derrick frame and the boys that were with me seeing the situation urged the horses up a few feet which left me pinned under the frame, until they received help.
>
> The boys who were with me were Henry Merchant, a hired man, LeGrande Stirland a brother-in-law and my two boys Lyman and Ray. They all said I was dead. LeGrande took my boys away from the terrible scene while the Merchant boy went to the nearest house to telephone for a Doctor and for help. I lay there about an hour before the Doctors Eliason and Wallace Budge came. They at once lifted me out from under the derrick and took me to the Utah Idaho Hospital.
>
> After LeGrande had got the children quieted down a little he came to see me again and he says he saw me breathe. He then took my hat to the creek and brought water and put it on my face and hands until the Doctors came. While my body was under the derrick and they thought me dead, I had an experience in the spirit world which I wish to relate.

with whom I immediately came into contact. . . . My first visual impression was the *nearness of the world of spirits to the world of mortality. The vastness of this heavenly sphere was bewildering to the eyes of a spirit-novice.*[13]

Another entrant into the spirit world who returned after a three-and-one-half hour stay to report her experience was Ella Jensen. Sister Jensen, then a girl of fifteen who had suffered with scarlet fever for several weeks, died and then returned to life on March 3, 1891. As she crossed through the veil she found herself in a long room where she encountered her deceased relatives and friends:

> As soon as I had a glimpse of the other world *I was anxious to go and all the care and worry left me.*
>
> *I entered a large hall.* It was so long that I could not see the end of it. It was filled with people. . . . I passed on through the room and met a great many of my relatives and friends. It was like going along the crowded streets of a city where you meet many people, only a very few of whom you recognize. . . . *Everybody appeared to be perfectly happy.* I was having a very pleasant visit with each one that I knew. Finally I reached the end of that long room. I opened a door and went into another room. . . .[14]

---

[13]Heber Q. Hale, "A Heavenly Manifestation by Heber Q. Hale, President of Boise Stake of The Church of Jesus Christ of Latter-day Saints," unpublished manuscript. Concerning the circumstances of his visit to the spirit world, President Hale wrote:

> Let me say by way of preface that between the hours of twelve and seven-thirty, in the night of Jan. 20, 1920, while alone in a room at the home of my friend W. R. Ronson in Carry, Idaho, this glorious manifestation was vouchsafed to me.
>
> I was not conscious of anything that transpired during the hours mentioned except what I experienced in this manifestation. I did not turn over in bed, nor was I disturbed by any sound, which indeed is unusual for me, whether it be called a dream, an apparition, a vision or a pilgimage of my spirit into the world of spirits, I know not, I care not. I know that I actually saw and experienced the things related in this heavenly manifestation and that they are as real to me as any experience of my life. For me at least, this is sufficient.

The film separating mortality from the spirit world, which has been seen by President Hale and others, is apparently that to which the deceased mother of Harriet Salvina Beal made reference when she escorted her daughter on a visit to the spirit world. Sister Beal wrote, "We then left the [earth] and floated through the air, side by side. When we came to a certain place Mother said to me, *'Now hold your breath until we pass the place as the air is too light for mortals!'* " (Cora Anna Beal Peterson, *Biography of William Beal,* unpublished manuscript in the possession of Ronald DeMille of Smithfield, Utah, p. 7.)

[14]LeRoi C. Snow, "Raised From the Dead," *Improvement Era,* Vol. XXXII, No. 12, pp. 973-974, October, 1929. "Ella" was actually a nickname for Mary Ellen Jensen, who was born August 3, 1876, and who ventured into the spirit world on March 3, 1891, after suffering from scarlet fever. She was called back to mortality after she was dead through the priesthood administration of President Lorenzo Snow and Rudger Clawson. See also the account of her return from the dead in *Young Women's Journal* 4:164-165.

Lorenzo Dow Young, brother to Brigham Young, was was shown the death process, the spirit world, and the celestial kingdom in a night vision. He described the nearness of the departed to their loved ones following their passing, but realized their inability to communicate their nearness as they watched their mortal remains and the sorrow of those left behind:

> I had a remarkable dream or vision. I fancied that I died. In a moment I was out of the body, and *fully conscious that I had made the change. At once, a heavenly messenger, or guide, was by me.* I thought and acted as naturally as I had done in the body, and *all my sensations seemed as complete without as with it.* The personage with me was *dressed in the purest white.* For a short time I remained in the room where my body lay. My sister Fanny (who was living with me when I had this dream) and my wife were weeping bitterly over my death. I sympathized with them deeply in their sorrow and desired to comfort them. *I realized that I was under the control of the man who was by me. I begged of him the privilege of speaking to them, but he said he could not grant it.* My guide, for so I will call him, said 'Now let us go.'[15]

Apparently those who die and are not to return to the mortal sphere have the responsibility of watching over their bodies until they are interred. This was the instruction given to Peter Johnson, and may explain why living relatives sometimes sense the presence of departed loved ones before and during the funeral.

> When we returned to the place where my body was lying, *I was informed with emphasis that my first duty would be to watch the body until*

---

[15]Lorenzo Dow Young, "Lorenzo Dow Young's Narrative," *Fragments of Experience,* (sixth book of the Faith-Promoting Series, Salt Lake City: Juvenile Instructor Office, 1882), pp. 27-28. Of his vision, which he received at Watertown, New York, about 1828, he later wrote:

> Call it a dream, or vision, or what I may, what I saw was as real to every sense of my being as anything I have passed through. The memory of it is clear and distinct with me to-day, after the lapse of fifty years, with as many changes.

It should be observed that many who venture beyond the veil of death are uncertain as to whether their spirit has left their body or whether they are receiving a dream or vision. A typical example is the case of the apostle Paul, who told of his visits to the "third heaven" and to "paradise." In his account he said these journeys were made, but commented, "Whether in the body, I cannot tell; or whether out of the body, I cannot tell, God knoweth." (2 Cor. 12:1-4)

> *after it had been disposed of,* as that was necessary knowledge for me to have in the resurrection.[16]

Entry Into the Spirit World a Joyful Experience

It is important to recognize that death is a blessing, a joyful experience, and often serves as a pleasant relief to those who were suffering in mortality. The many instances recorded of those who have left their bodies to enter the spirit world are almost completely void of allusions to difficulty or pain from the separation process. To the contrary, their experiences may by summarized in the statement of Ella Jensen, who related that

> *There was practically no pain on leaving the body in death* but the intense pain was almost unbearable in coming back to life. Not only this, but for months, and even years afterward, she experienced new aches and pains and physical disorders that she had never known before.[17]

Heber Q. Hale, while talking with his guides in the spirit world,

> Readily observed their *displeasure at our use of the word 'death' and the fear which we attach to it.* They use there another word in referring to the transition from mortality, which word I do not now recall, and I can only approach its meaning, as the impression was left upon my mind, by calling it the *'New Birth.'*[18]

Jedediah M. Grant, a counselor to Brigham Young in the first presidency of the Church, was twice allowed to venture

---

[16]Peter E. Johnson, *Relief Society Magazine, op cit.,* Vol. VII, p. 452. Knowledge of this procedure was made known to him because his guides in the spirit world saw fit to show him of what the remainder of the process for entry into the world of spirits consisted. This was to aid him to decide whether to remain or to return to mortality.

[17]LeRoi C. Snow, *Improvement Era, op cit.,* Vol. XXXII, p. 975. It should be observed that while passing from mortality into the spirit world is apparently an easy procedure, it may be far more difficult, and perhaps painful, for an adult spirit to enter the tiny body of an unborn child in its mother's womb at the time of birth into mortality.

[18]Heber Q. Hale, *op cit.* President Wilford Woodruff also understood death to be a birth into the spirit world. He taught that

> I cannot help but think that in every death there is a birth: the spirit leaves the body dead to us, and passes to the other side of the vail alive to that great and noble company that are also working for the accomplishment of the purposes of God in the redemption and salvation of a fallen world. (*Journal of Discourses* (Los Angeles, California: General Printing and Lithograph Co., 1961; Photo Lithographic Reprint of exact original edition published in 1882), Vol. XXII, p. 348. Further references to this source will be shown as JD 22:348. Jan. 29, 1882.)

into the spirit world as his death drew nigh. He recounted his experiences to the other counselor in the presidency, Heber C. Kimball, who retold Brother Grant's experiences at the funeral. President Grant had recounted his newly-gained knowledge of the superiority of the future to the present life in these words:

> Brother Heber, I have been into the spirit world two nights in succession, and, of all the dreads that ever came across me, the worst was to have to again return to my body, though I had to do it.[19]

In the funeral sermon President Kimball added his own comment that "Brother Grant said that he *felt extremely sorrowful at having to leave so beautiful a place* and come back to earth, for he looked upon his body with loathing, but was obliged to enter it again."[20]

It was perhaps, because of this experience of Jedediah M. Grant that President Brigham Young later said,

> I can say with regard to parting with our friends, and going ourselves, that I have been near enough to understand eternity so that *I have had to exercise a great deal more faith to desire to live than I ever exercised in my whole life to live.* . . .[21]

Lorenzo Dow Young, during his vision of the life hereafter, also felt great reluctance to leave the beauty of the future life and to again take up mortality:

> I could distinctly see the world from which we had first come. . . . To me, *it looked cloudy, dreary and dark. I was filled with sad disappointment, I might say horror, at the idea of returning there.* I supposed I had come to stay in that heavenly place, which I had so long desired

[19]JD 4:135. Dec. 4, 1856. Concerning the circumstances in which he heard President Grant's account, President Kimball said the following during the funeral sermon:

> I will not stoop to the principle of death. I could weep, but I will not. There is a spirit in me that rises above that feeling, and it is because Jedediah is not dead.
>
> I went to see him one day last week, and he reached out his hand and shook hands with me; he could not speak, but he shook hands warmly with me. . . . I laid my hands upon him and blessed him, and asked God to strengthen his lungs that he might be easier; and in two or three minutes he raised himself up and talked for about an hour as busily as he could, telling me what he had seen and what he understood, until I was afraid he would weary himself, when I arose and left him. (*Ibid.*, p. 135.)

See also the sermon of President Brigham Young at Brother Grant's funeral. JD 4:129-134.

[20]*Ibid.*, p. 136.

[21]JD 14:231. Sept. 16, 1871.

to see; up to this time, the thought had not occurred to me that I would be required to return.

I plead with my guide to let me remain. He replied that I was permitted to only visit these heavenly cities, for *I had not filled my mission in yonder world; therefore I must return and take my body. . . .*

We returned to my house. There I found my body, and it appeared to me dressed for burial. It was with great reluctance that I took possession of it to resume the ordinary avocations of life, and endeavor to fill the important mission I had received. I awoke and found myself in my bed. I lay and meditated the remainder of the night on what had been shown me.[22]

When the administration of President Lorenzo Snow restored Ella Jensen to life, her first words were, " 'Where is he?' We asked: 'Who, where is who?' 'Why, Brother Snow,' she replied. 'He called me back.' " They told her that he had gone. She said: "Why did he call me back? *I was so happy and did not want to come back.*"[23]

It appears that those who have hope of dwelling among the righteous in the next life may well anticipate that their death will bring them into a state of increased joy and happiness.

Reunion With Departed Loved Ones

One of the greatest blessings of passing through the veil is the privilege of again enjoying the company of relatives and friends who have previously died. The expectation of this blessing is a motivating force to all who seek a reunion with those who have preceded them, helping them to regard death with happy anticipation rather than fear.

The prophet Joseph Smith expressed his anticipation of such a joyful reunion when he said,

I have a father, brothers, children, and friends who have gone to a world of spirits. They are only absent for a moment. They are

---

[22]Lorenzo Dow Young, *Fragments of Experience, op cit.,* pp. 29-30. The cloudy and dark appearance of the earth may be explained by the vision of the prophet Enoch, who

Beheld Satan; and he had a great chain in his hand, and it veiled the whole face of the earth with darkness; and he looked up and laughed, and his angels rejoiced. (Moses 7:26)

[23]LeRoi C. Snow, *Improvement Era, op cit.,* Vol. XXXII, pp. 885-886.

> in the spirit, and we shall soon meet again. . . . *When we depart, we shall hail our mothers, fathers, friends, and all whom we love,* who have fallen asleep in Jesus . . . it will be an eternity of felicity.[24]

Almost all the accounts of those who are permitted to visit the spirit world contain references to happy reunions with previously departed loved ones. Often the family members come to welcome the entering individual, at times in a pre-arranged order. For instance, Peter Johnson reported that the guardian angel who met him

> Informed me, on returning, that we should wait there, as my sister desired to see me, but was busy just at that time. Presently she came. She was glad to see me and asked if I was offended because she kept me waiting. She explained that *she was doing some work* that she wished to finish.
>
> *Just before my eldest sister died she asked me to enter into this agreement:* That if she died first, she was to watch over me, protect me from those who might seek my downfall, and that she would be the first to meet me after death. If I happened to die first, she wished me to do the same for her. *We made this agreement, and this was the reason that my sister was the first one of my relatives to meet me.* After she arrived, my mother and other sisters and friends came to see me, and we discussed various topics, as we would do here on meeting friends. After we had spent some little time in conversation, the guide came to me with a message that *I was wanted by some of the apostles who had lived on the earth in this dispensation.*[25]

For many who do not have members of their immediate family awaiting them in the spirit world, the encounters with distant relatives are more casual. Such was the case with Ella Jensen, who reported,

> As I went through the throng, the first person I recognized was my grandpa, H. P. Jensen, who was sitting in one end of the room, writing. He looked up, *seemed surprised to see me* and said: 'Why! There is my granddaughter, Ella.' He was very much pleased, greeted me and, as he continued with his writing, I passed on through the room and met many of my relatives and friends. . . . *Some seemed*

---

[24]Joseph Smith, *History of the Church of Jesus Christ of Latter-day Saints,* (second edition; Salt Lake City, Utah: Deseret Book Company: 1959), Vol. VI, p. 316. Further references to this source will be shown as HC 6:316. This statement was a portion of the Prophet's famous King Follett Discourse, which he delivered at the funeral of King Follett on Sunday, April 7, 1844.

[25]Peter E. Johnson, *Relief Society Magazine, op cit.,* Vol. VII, p. 451.

to be in family groups. . . . Some inquired about their friends and relatives on the earth. Among this number was my cousin.[26]

The meeting with departed relatives often involves encounters with those who died so long ago as to be unknown to the spirit world entrant. Sister Jensen described to her mother her meeting of two such individuals:

> 'While in this large building in the spirit world, I met a woman who greeted me and said she was Aunt Mary and told me that she died while I was a baby.' The mother asked: 'Can you describe her?' The answer was: 'Yes, she was a tall woman with black hair and dark eyes and thin features.' 'Yes,' the mother answered, 'surely you have described your Aunt Mary.'
>
> 'I also met another woman there, who said she was my Aunt Sarah and had died just before I was born.' 'Will you describe her?' the mother asked. 'Yes, she was rather short and somewhat fleshy, with round features, light hair and blue eyes.' 'Why yes, Ella, that is your Aunt Sarah. You have described her perfectly.'[27]

Henry Zollinger recorded that "My mother then introduced me to the heads of five generations of my father's people, all of whom had believed the gospel."[28]

When one leaves mortal life to dwell in the world of spirits, he may expect to be integrated and absorbed into his own family beyond the veil.

Location of the Spirit World

Although the scriptures are silent concerning the location of the world of spirits, it becomes apparent from the revelations already cited in this chapter that the spiritual realm is not far removed from the world of mortals. Rather than being transported to some unknown, distant sphere, the spirits of the dead remain associated with this earth, but function in a dimension unseen by mortal eyes.

This has continually been the teaching of the prophets and leaders of the Church. Joseph Smith taught that

> The spirits of the just are exalted to a greater and more glorious

---

[26]LeRoi C. Snow, *Improvement Era, op cit.*, Vol. XXXII, pp. 973-974.
[27]*Ibid.*, pp. 979-980.
[28]Henry Zollinger, *op cit.*

work: hence they are blessed in their departure to the world of spirits. Enveloped in flaming fire, *they are not far from us.*[29]

Elder Parley P. Pratt, in his *Key to The Science of Theology,* was another Latter-day Saint leader who was among the first in the Church to teach that the spirit world was on this earth, though unseen to mortal eyes.

> As to its location, *it is here on the very planet where we were born;* or, in other words, the earth and other planets of a like sphere, have their *inward or spiritual spheres,* as well as their outward, or temporal. The one is peopled by temporal tabernacles, and the other by spirits. *A veil is drawn between the one sphere and the other,* whereby all the objects in the spiritual sphere are rendered invisible to those in the temporal.[30]

President Brigham Young also taught the close proximity of the spirit world to this earth:

> Where is the spirit world? *It is right here.* Do the good and evil spirits go together? Yes, they do. Do they both inhabit one kingdom? Yes, they do. Do they go to the sun? No. *Do they go beyond the boundaries of this organized earth? No, they do not.* They are brought forth upon this earth, for the express purpose of inhabiting it to all eternity. Where else are you going? Nowhere else, only as you may be permitted.[31]

In the same discourse he said,

> Here the inquiry will naturally arise, when our spirits leave our bodies where do they go to?
>
> I will tell you. Will I locate them? Yes, if you wish me to. They do not pass out of the organization of this earth on which we live, . . . where is the spirit world? *It is incorporated within this celestial system.* Can you see it with your natural eyes? No. Can you see spirits in this room? No. Suppose the Lord should touch your eyes that you might see, could you then see the spirits? Yes, as plainly as you now see bodies, as did the servant of Elijah. If the Lord would permit it, and it was His will that it should be done, you could see the spirits that have departed from this world, as plainly as you now see bodies with your natural eyes.[32]

---

[29]HC 6:52. This statement was included in the prophet's remarks on the demise of James Adams, given October 9, 1843.

[30]Parley P. Pratt, *Key To The Science of Theology,* (ninth edition; Salt Lake City, Utah: Deseret Book Co.), pp. 126-127.

[31]JD 3:369. June 22, 1856. See pp. 154-158 concerning separation of righteous and wicked spirits.

[32]*Ibid.,* pp. 367-368. It was the servant of Elisha, not Elijah, who was shown the spirits. See 2 Ki. 6:17.

And then to further clarify his point the prophet added:

> Is the spirit world here? *It is not beyond the sun, but is on this earth* that was organized for the people that have lived and that do and will live upon it.[33]

These early statements by prophets and apostles have been quoted often in the Church and form the basis for numerous similar statements by later L.D.S. leaders.

Increased Capacity of Spirit Beings

According to the teachings of Latter-day Saint leaders and theologians, the separation of the spirit from the mortal body will return the spirit to the full use of powers which were greatly limited during mortality. The mortal body has long been regarded as a limiting and retarding obstacle to the full functioning of the spirit's powers and capabilities, though a necessary tool in man's progress towards the resurrection. Orson Pratt taught, for instance,

> *Our happiness here is regulated in a great measure by external objects, by the organization of the mortal tabernacle;* they are not permitted to rise very high, or to become very great; on the other hand *it seems to be a kind of limit to our joys and pleasures, sufferings, and pains,* and this is because of the imperfection of the tabernacle in which we dwell; and of those things with which we are surrounded; but in that life everything will appear in its true colors; . . . This tabernacle, although it is good in its place, is something like the scaffolding you see round about a new building that is going up; *it is only a help, an aid in this imperfect situation;* but when we get into another condition, *we shall find that these imperfect aids will not be particularly wanted;* we shall have other sources of gaining knowledge, besides these inlets, called senses.[34]

One of the powers which spirit beings are expected to possess will be the capability for rapid movement from place to place. As Brigham Young explained,

> *The brightness and glory of the next apartment is inexpressible.* It is not encumbered with this clog of dirt we are carrying around here so that when we advance in years we have to be stubbing along and to be careful lest we fall down. We see our youth, even, frequently stubbing their toes and falling down. But yonder, how different!

---

[33]*Ibid.,* p. 372.

[34]JD 2:240, 244. Oct. 15, 1854.

> *They move with ease and like lightning.* If we want to visit Jerusalem, or this, that, or the other place—and I presume we will be permitted if we desire—there we are, looking at its streets. . . . If we wish to understand how they are living here on these western islands, or in China, *we are there;* in fact, we are like the light of the morning, or, I will not say the electric fluid, but its operations on the wires.[35]

On another occasion he taught,

> As quickly as the spirit is unlocked from this house of clay, it is free to travel with lightning speed to any planet, or fixed star, or to the uttermost part of the earth, or to the depths of the sea, according to the will of Him who dictates.[36]

Such powers of locomotion were observed in the actions of young Briant Stevens, who appeared to his father in a dream the night following his death from tetanus, February 3, 1887:

> At length he saw a light and in this light was little Briant, standing in the air, robed in snowy whiteness, with a face transfigured in its light and beauty. The boy smiled at him and moved his hands as if in loving recognition. *This ethereal form of Briant moved about in the room without effort. A single inclination of the shining head seemed to project the body in any desired direction.*[37]

Walter P. Monson, who died of a strangulated hernia and then returned to mortality, apparently sensed this ability of locomotion within himself when he passed beyond the veil:

> Then I awoke in *full possession of all my faculties* in another sphere of life. I stood apart from my body and looked at it. I noticed that its eyes were partly closed and that the chin had dropped. I was now *without pain,* and the *joy of freedom* I felt and the *peace of mind* that came over me were the sweetest sensations I had ever experienced. I *lost all sense of time and space. The law of gravitation had no hold upon me.*[38]

---

[35]JD 14:231. This discourse was delivered at the funeral of Aurelia Spencer, Sept. 16, 1871.

[36]JD 13:77. This discourse was delivered at the funeral of Daniel Spencer, Dec. 10, 1868.

[37]Kennon, "Briant S. Stevens," *Helpful Visions* (fourteenth book of the Faith-Promoting Series, Salt Lake City, Utah: Juvenile Instructor Office, 1887), pp. 35-36.

[38]Jeremiah Stokes, *Modern Miracles* (Salt Lake City, Utah: Bookcraft, Inc., 1945), pp. 78-79. Concerning the events which immediately preceded his entry into the spirit world, Brother Monson wrote,

> One evening just before Christmas while addressing an audience at the old Farmers' Ward chapel on South State Street, I was stricken with intense pain from strangulated hernia. That night I underwent an abdominal operation. My condition was so serious and my chances of living so slight that the doctors did not remove the

President Joseph F. Smith made reference to the increased powers of locomotion available to spirit beings with the statement that

> The disembodied spirit during the interval of the death of the body and its resurrection from the grave is not perfect, hence it is not prepared to enter into the exaltation of the celestial kingdom; but *it has the privilege of soaring in the midst of immortal beings,* and of *enjoying to a certain extent, the presence of God, not the fulness of his glory,* not the fulness of the reward which we are seeking and which we are destined to receive, if found faithful to the law of the celestial kingdom, but only in part.[39]

Just as we expect to enjoy increased powers for rapid movement from place to place, it is anticipated that we will also have the capacity to travel through time, or at least envision things as they were in the past or will be in the future. Brigham Young taught that

> If we want to behold Jerusalem as it was in the days of the Savior; or if we want to see the Garden of Eden as it was when created, there we are; and *we see it as it existed spiritually,* for it was created first spiritually and then temporally, and *spiritually it still remains.* And when there we may behold the earth as at the dawn of creation, or we may visit any city we please that exists upon its surface.[40]

Instances in the scriptures give evidence of the capacity to see into the past and into the future which is available to spirit beings. Moses, for example, "beheld the world and the ends thereof, and all the children of men which are, and which were created,"[41] and bore witness that he saw with his

---

afflicted section. They simply sewed up the wound, feeling that it was only a matter of a few hours at most before I would die.

Next morning when I awoke my family and others were kneeling about my bed and Bishop LeGrand Richards of the Sugarhouse Ward was praying for my recovery.

At midnight I was fully awake. I heard the Christmas chimes and felt the nurse taking my pulse and temperature. Suddenly, a coldness attacked my feet and hands. It moved up my limbs and up my arms towards my body. I felt it reach my heart. There was a slight murmur. I gasped for breath and lapsed into unconsciousness, so far as all things mortal.

For the account of his encounter with his daughter in the spirit world and his return to mortality see page 145 of this book.

[39]Joseph F. Smith, *Gospel Doctrine* (Salt Lake City, Utah: Deseret Book Co., 1919), p. 440.

[40]JD 14:231. Sept. 16, 1871. See Peter E. Johnson's travel forward in time, pp. 57-59.

[41]Moses 1:8. See also 1:27-29.

own eyes, "but not my natural, *but my spiritual eyes,* for my natural eyes could not have beheld. . . ."[42] Certainly the vision shown to Enoch, who saw "all things, even unto the end of the world,"[43] must have been perceived in like manner.

It appears that the brother of Jared must have enjoyed the privilege of beholding both the past and the future with the eyes of his spirit as he conversed with the Lord on Mt. Shelem. The scripture records that "the veil was taken from off the eyes of the brother of Jared. . . ."[44] and that "he could not be kept from beholding within the veil,"[45] therefore the Lord "showed unto the brother of Jared all the inhabitants of the earth which had been, and also all that would be; and he withheld them not from his sight, even unto the ends of the earth."[46]

Surely the ability to see into other eras of time is a choice power which is possessed by spirit personages. Though the opportunity to see with spiritual eyes is but infrequently enjoyed by mortal beings, all shall be able to enjoy this privilege when they pass beyond the limitations of their mortal bodies into the spirit realm.

It is believed that those who dwell in the spirit world enjoy the use of other powers and senses which are not available to mortal beings. Orson Pratt once said,

> When I speak of the future state of man, and the situation of our spirits between death and the resurrection, *I long for the experience and knowledge to be gained in that state,* as well as this. We shall learn many more things there; we need not suppose our five senses connect us with all the things of heaven, and earth, and eternity, and space; we need not think that we are conversant with all the elements of nature, through the medium of the senses God has given us here. *Suppose He should give us a sixth sense, a seventh, an eighth, a ninth, or a fiftieth. All these different senses would convey to us new ideas,* as much so as the senses of tasting, smelling, or seeing communicate different ideas from that of hearing.[47]

---

[42]*Ibid.*, 1:11.

[43]*Ibid.*, 7:67. See all of chapter 7.

[44]Ether 3:6.

[45]*Ibid.*, 3:19.

[46]*Ibid.*, 3:25.

[47]JD 2:247. Oct. 15, 1854. It is suggested that Orson Pratt's entire discourse be read so that the evidence he gives for his beliefs may be thoroughly understood. See also the teachings of President Charles W. Penrose in JD 24:94.

In this discourse he went on to describe some of these senses and powers which are to be characteristic of spirit beings, and commented on three in particular.

First, he described the greatly increased ability to remember which is possessed by spirit beings:

> We read or learn a thing by observation yesterday, and to-day or tomorrow it is gone, . . . some of the knowledge we receive here at one time becomes so completely obliterated, through the weakness of the animal system, that we cannot call it to mind, no association of ideas will again suggest it to our minds; it is gone, erased, eradicated from the tablet of our memories. *This is not owing to the want of capacity in the spirit;* no, but the *spirit has a full capacity to remember . . . it is not the want of capacity in the spirit of man that causes him to forget the knowledge he may have learned yesterday; but it is because of the imperfection of the tabernacle in which the spirit dwells;* because there is imperfection in the organization of the flesh and bones, and in things pertaining to the tabernacle; it is this that erases from our memory many things that would be useful; we cannot retain them in our minds, they are gone into oblivion. *It is not so with the spirit when it is released from this tabernacle. . . .* Wait until these mortal bodies are laid in the tomb; when we return home to God who gave us life; then is the time *we shall have the most vivid knowledge of all the past acts* of our lives during our probationary state.[48]

Elder Pratt spoke of a second power which man is to enjoy in the spirit world. He taught that in addition to increased memory ability, spirit beings are to enjoy greater powers of vision and will be able to see with all parts of their body:

> We become acquainted with light and color through the organization of our bodies. In other words the Lord has constructed the mortal eye and framed it in such a manner that it is capable of being acted upon by one of the elements of nature, called light; and that gives us a great variety of knowledge . . . *suppose that the whole spirit were uncovered and exposed to all the rays of light, can it be supposed that light would not affect the spirit if it were thus unshielded, uncovered, and unclothed?* Do you suppose that it would not be susceptible of any impressions made by the elements of light? *The spirit is inherently capable of experiencing the sensations of light;* if it were not so, we could not see. You might form as fine an eye as ever was made, but if the spirit, in and of itself, were not capable of being acted upon by the rays of light, an eye would be of no benefit. Then unclothe the

[48] *Ibid.*, p. 239.

> spirit, and instead of exposing a small portion of it about the size of a pea to the action of the rays of light, the whole of it would be exposed. *I think we could then see in different directions at once, instead of looking in one particular direction, we could then look all around us at the same instant.* . . . Then there would be a vast field opened to the view of the spirit, and this would be opened not in one direction only, but in all directions; . . . when this tabernacle is taken off; we shall look, not in one direction only, but in every direction. This will be calculated to give us new ideas, concerning the immensity of the creations of God, concerning worlds that may be far beyond the reach of the most powerful instruments that have been called to the aid of man. *This will give us information and knowledge we never can know as long as we dwell in this mortal tabernacle.*[49]

Heber C. Kimball also commented on the power of sight possessed by a spirit being, while telling of a vision of evil spirits which he saw in England:

> All at once my vision was opened, and *the walls of the building were no obstruction to my seeing,* for I saw nothing but the visions that presented themselves. Why did not the walls obstruct my view? *Because my spirit could look through the walls of that house,* for I looked with that spirit, element, and power, with which angels look; and *as God sees all things, so were invisible things brought before me,* as the Lord would bring

---

[49]*Ibid.,* pp. 242, 243, 244. It appears that a portion of this power was briefly granted to the prophet Joseph Smith when he saw "The Vision" of the three degrees of glory (D&C 76). An early convert to the Church, Philo Dibble, was present when Joseph and Sidney Rigdon emerged from the Johnson home after seeing the vision. He recorded,

> I arrived at Father Johnson's just as Joseph and Sidney were coming out of the vision alluded to in the book of Doctrine and Covenants, in which mention is made of the three glories. Joseph wore black clothes but at this time seemed to be dressed in an element of glorious white, and his face shown as if it were transparent, but I did not see the same glory attending Sidney. Joseph appeared as strong as a lion but Sidney seemed as weak as water, and Joseph noticing his condition smiled and said: 'Brother Sidney is not as used to it as I am.' (Philo Dibble, "Philo Dibble's Narrative," *Early Scenes In Church History,* (eighth book of the Faith-Promoting Series; Salt Lake City: Juvenile Instructor Office, 1882), p. 81.

It appears that Elder Dibble either did not record all of Joseph's comments or that a portion of his narrative was edited out. The following statement by a close neighbor of Elder Dibble's, Mrs. Sarah N. Williams Reynolds, of Salt Lake City, adds important information concerning the above experience:

> I was a close neighbor of Philo Dibble who visited me very often. He had been very familiar and intimately acquainted with the Prophet Joseph Smith, and took great delight in rehearsing his wealth of information concerning this acquaintance. Brother Dibble stated to me that the Prophet Joseph told him in connection with the others who were present in Father Johnson's home at the time the Vision was given to the Prophet Joseph and Sidney Rigdon, that (the Prophet speaking), *'My whole body was full of light and I could see even out at the ends of my fingers and toes.'* (N.B. Lundwall (comp.), *The Vision* (Salt Lake City, Utah: Bookcraft Publishing Co., n.d.), p. 11.)

things before Joseph in the Urim and Thummim. It was upon that principle that the Lord showed things to the Prophet Joseph.[50]

Orson Pratt referred to a third power possessed by spirit beings, the ability to obtain and consider many different ideas at the same time:

> There is a faculty mentioned in the word of God, which we are not in possession of here, but we shall possess it hereafter; that is not only to see a vast number of things in the same moment, looking in all directions by the aid of the Spirit, but also *to obtain a vast number of ideas at the same instant.* . . . I believe we shall be freed, in the next world, in a great measure, from these narrow, contracted methods of thinking. Instead of thinking in one channel, and following up one certain course of reasoning to find a certain truth, *knowledge will rush in from all quarters; it will come in like the light which flows from the sun, penetrating every part, informing the spirit, and giving understanding concerning ten thousand things at the same time; and the mind will be capable of receiving and retaining all.* . . .
>
> Here, then, is a new faculty of knowledge, very extended in its nature, that is calculated to throw a vast amount of information upon the mind of man, almost in the twinkling of an eye. How long a time would it take a man in the next world, if he had to gain knowledge as we do here, to find out the simplest things in nature? He might reason, and reason for thousands of years, and then hardly have got started. But when this Spirit of God, this great telescope that is used in the celestial heavens, is given to man, and he, through the aid of it, gazes upon eternal things, what does he behold? Not one object at a time, but a *vast multitude of objects rush before his vision, and are present before his mind, filling him in a moment with the knowledge of worlds* more numerous than the sands of the sea shore. Will he be able to bear it? Yes, *his mind is strengthened in proportion to the amount of information imparted.* It is this tabernacle, in its present condition, that prevents us from a more enlarged understanding.[51]

Passage into the world of spirits is thus anticipated by Latter-day Saints as the opportunity to regain many powers which have been limited during earth-life by the weaknesses of a mortal body. For the righteous who are privileged to dwell in paradise, entrance into the spirit world will also represent a victory over the devil and freedom from his temptations. President Brigham Young taught,

---

[50]JD 4:2. June 29, 1856.
[51]JD 2:246, 245. Oct. 15, 1854.

Joseph and the faithful who have died have *gained a victory over the power of the devil,* which you and I have not yet gained. So long as we live in these tabernacles, so long we will be subject to the temptations and power of the devil; but when we lay them down, *if we have been faithful, we have gained the victory so far;* but even then we are not so far advanced at once as to be beyond the neighborhood of evil spirits.[52]

Limitations of Spirit Beings

Separation from the mortal body will not only bring the return of lost capabilities, it will also impose certain limitations and difficulties which will affect the well-being of each inhabitant of the spirit realm. Elder Melvin J. Ballard recognized the importance of disciplining the body and the spirit together and taught the importance of repenting during mortal life rather than procrastinating the repentance process till the spirit life:

A man may receive the priesthood and all its privileges and blessings, but until he learns to overcome the flesh, his temper, his tongue, his disposition to indulge in the things God has forbidden, he cannot come into the Celestial Kingdom of God—he must overcome either in this life or in the life to come. But this life is the time in which men are to repent. *Do not let any of us imagine that we can go down to the grave not having overcome the corruptions of the flesh and then lose in the grave all our sins and evil tendencies.* They will be with us. They will be with the spirit when separated from the body.

It is my judgment that any man or woman can do more to conform to the laws of God in one year in this life than they could in ten years when they are dead. *The spirit only can repent and change, and then the battle has to go forward with the flesh afterwards. It is much easier to overcome and serve the Lord when both flesh and spirit are combined as one.* This is the time when men are more pliable and susceptible. We will find *when we are dead every desire, every feeling will be greatly intensified.* When clay is pliable it is much easier to change than when it gets hard and sets.

This life is the time to repent. That is why I presume it will take a thousand years after the first resurrection until the last group will be prepared to come forth. *It will take them a thousand years to do what it would have taken, but three score years to accomplish in this life. . . .*

I grant you that the righteous dead will be at peace, but I tell you that when we go out of this life, leave this body, *we will desire*

[52]JD 3:371. June 22, 1856.

> *to do many things that we cannot do at all without the body.* We will be seriously handicapped, and we will long for the body; we will pray for that early reunion with our bodies. We will know then what advantage it is to have a body.
>
> Then, *every man and woman who is putting off until the next life the task of correcting and overcoming the weakness of the flesh are sentencing themselves to years of bondage,* for no man or woman will come forth in the resurrection until they have completed their work, until they have overcome, until they have done as much as they can do . . . those who are complying in this life with these conditions are shortening their sentences, *for every one of us will have a matter of years in that spirit state to complete and finish our salvation.* And some may attain, by reason of their righteousness in this life, the right to do postgraduate work, to be admitted into the Celestial Kingdom, but others will lose absolutely the right to that glory, all they can do will not avail after death to bring them into the Celestial Kingdom.[53]

The Lord has taught that "Man is spirit. The elements are eternal, and spirit and element, inseparably connected, receive a fulness of joy. And *when separated, man cannot receive a fulness of joy.*"[54] Thus the separation of the spirit from the body is regarded as a period of imbalance and incompleteness—of anticipation and longing for the restoration of the body in the resurrection so that a fulness of joy may be obtained. President Joseph F. Smith, in his "Vision of the Redemption of the Dead," reported his observation while in the spirit world that *"the dead had looked upon the long absence of their spirits from their bodies as a bondage."*[55]

It appears that those who are in the spirit world, through their increased capacity for learning and understanding, are made acutely aware of their need to progress onward to yet another stage in the eternal plan. Though the spirit world represents a higher stage of progression than does mortal life,[56] yet those righteous spirits who go there must inevitably yearn to receive their resurrected bodies and enter into their exaltation to a far greater degree than do mortal beings.

---

[53]Melvin J. Ballard, "The Three Glories," as printed in N.B. Lundwall, *The Vision, op cit.*, pp. 46-47.

[54]*The Doctrine and Covenants of The Church of Jesus Christ of Latter-day Saints* (Salt Lake City, Utah: The Church of Jesus Christ of Latter-day Saints, 1921), section 93, verses 33-34. Other references to this book will be shown as D&C 93:33-34. See also D&C 45:17.

[55]Joseph F. Smith, *Gospel Doctrine, op cit.*, p. 475.

Meaning of Returning to the Presence of God at Death

The prophet Alma, while instructing his son, Corianton, made this statement concerning the death process:

> Now, concerning the state of the soul between death and the resurrection—Behold, it has been made known unto me by an angel, *that the spirits of all men, as soon as they are departed from this mortal body,* yea, the spirits of all men, whether they be good or evil, *are taken home to that God who gave them life.*
>
> And then shall it come to pass, that the spirits of those who are righteous are received into a state of happiness, which is called paradise, . . .
>
> And then shall it come to pass, that the spirits of the wicked, yea, who are evil . . . these shall be cast out into outer darkness. . . .[57]

Confusion has arisen concerning the meaning of being taken home to God as Alma has explained it. Some have mistakenly taught that following death, men go to stand before the judgment bar of God and are specifically assigned by God a place in either paradise or the spirit prison. This teaching is termed a "partial judgment" by those who voice the teaching. Yet the dozens of eye-witness accounts of those who have seen into the spirit world never speak of such an episode in the death process. True, the dead are assigned to specific places of abode in the spirit world, but their destination seems to be pre-determined, without the necessity of a direct confrontation with God and his bar of justice at this time.

Evidence that there is no immediate confrontation with God upon death is found, for instance, in the conversation between Elder Thomas A. Shreeve and his departed brother, Teddy, who had been dead for almost two decades. Elder Shreeve, a Latter-day Saint missionary who lay near death on

---

[56]President Brigham Young taught,

> When we pass into the spirit world we shall possess a measure of this power; not to that degree that we will when resurrected and brought forth in the fullness of glory to inherit the kingdoms prepared for us. The power the faithful will possess then will far exceed that of the spirit world; but that enjoyed in the spirit world is so far beyond this life as to be inconceivable without the Spirit of revelation. (JD 14:231, Sept. 16, 1871.)

[57]Al. 40:11-13.

board the steamer *Wakatipu* enroute from Australia to New Zealand in 1878, was visited by his younger brother in a dream.

> I saw the figure of a little child standing at the foot of the bed. *I looked closely and recognized my little brother Teddy, who had been drowned nearly twenty years before. I seemed to know that he had come from the spirit world,* and in my anxiety I sprang from the bed, and resting one knee upon the floor, I gazed intently at him. He stepped near me, and I took one little arm in my hand. Although a spirit, *he seemed palpable to my touch.* I said:
>
> 'I think you are my little brother Teddy; but it is so long since I saw you that I had almost forgotten how you looked.'
>
> Then the thought came into my mind that I must ask him some question. I said:
>
> *'Teddy, have you seen our Heavenly Father yet?'* He answered in the sweet voice of a child:
>
> *'No—but I shall see Him.'* . . . I asked again:
>
> 'Have you brought any message to me?'
>
> To this question he answered, 'Yes' . . . and his eyes looked straight into mine, and he came nestling into my arms. He lifted the forefinger of his right hand toward my face and said:
>
> 'Only be true!'[58]

To return to the presence of God apparently means to return to a condition in which one can behold Him if the occasion so requires. This is the intent of Orson Pratt's explanation when he stated,

> *To go back then, into the presence of God, is to be placed in a condition wherein his presence can be seen. It does not mean, in all cases, that people who return into his presence are immediately placed within a few yards or rods, or within a short distance of his person.* Is there any revelation to prove this? Yes, I have already quoted what the Lord said in relation to all these creations. He said that from the whole of them which he had made he had taken Zion to his own bosom. Now if he has taken Zion to his own bosom from all these numberless creations, *can they all be concentrated in a little spot of a few rods in diameter in order to get into his presence? Why no.* If each Zion did not occupy any more space than one particle of our globe, yet inasmuch as the worlds are more numberless than the particles of millions of earths like this,

[58]Thomas A. Shreeve, "Finding Comfort," *Helpful Visions, op cit.,* pp. 60-61.

> how could they all get into so small a space as to get near to the person of the Lord? They could not do it. *But suffice it to say the vail is removed, and no matter how distant a redeemed world may be, it will be in the presence of God.*[59]

In like manner President Brigham Young explained that the phrase "return to the presence of God" referred to the ability of spirit beings to see, hear, and understand spiritual things, rather than to a direct confrontation with Diety at the time of death:

> You read in the Bible[60] that when the spirit leaves the body it goes to God who gave it. Now tell me where God is not, if you please; you cannot. How far would you have to go in order to go to God, if your spirits were unclothed? Would you have to go out of this bowery to find God, if you were in the spirit? If God is not here, we had better reserve this place to gather the wicked into, for they will desire to be where God is not. The Lord Almighty is here by His Spirit, by His influence, by His Presence. I am not in the north end of this bowery, my body is in the south end of it, but my influence and my voice extend to all parts of it; in like manner is the Lord here.
>
> *It reads that the spirit goes to God who gave it. Let me render this Scripture a little plainer; when the spirits leave their bodies they are in the presence of our Father and God, they are prepared then to see, hear and understand spiritual things.*[61]

Many Know When Death Approaches

There is ample evidence that many who are about to die are given notification of their impending passage into the spirit world before the arrival of the actual time for them to pass through the veil. This notification may come through any of the normal channels of revelation and communication beyond the veil such as the visitation of spirit messengers, visions, dreams, voices, inspiration and promptings of the Holy Ghost, etc. Some are apparently able to diagnose the terminal nature of their illness or injury without the need of any call from beyond the veil. Others seemingly "sense" death, or feel a

---

[59]JD 16:365. Jan. 27, 1874.

[60]It would appear that President Young was referring to a Book of Mormon passage, Al. 40:11, rather than to a Biblical item.

[61]JD 3:368. June 22, 1856. See the teachings expressed by Heber C. Kimball on the theme of going to the presence of God at the time of death, in JD 3:112-113.

"strange foreboding" which tends to prepare them for their passage into the spirit world.

An example of the prior notification of approaching summons into the spirit world is found in Mrs. Wilford Reeder's account of the death of Ella Jensen. Mrs. Reeder had been watching at Ella's sick bed during the night:

> About three or four o'clock in the morning I was suddenly awakened by Ella calling me. I hurried to her bed. She was all excited and asked me to get the comb, brush and scissors, explaining that she wanted to brush her hair and trim her finger nails and get all ready, 'for,' she said, *'they are coming to get me at ten o'clock in the morning.'*
>
> I asked who was coming to get her. *'Uncle Hans Jensen,'* she replied, *'and the messengers. I am going to die and they are coming at ten o'clock to get me and take me away.'* . . .
>
> The parents were called and as they entered the room the daughter told them that her *Uncle Hans, who was dead, had suddenly appeared in the room, while she was awake, with her eyes open, and told her that messengers would be there at ten o'clock to conduct her into the spirit world.*[62]

Others are given longer to prepare than was Ella Jensen. For instance, Daniel Tyler, an early Saint, related the following concerning his grandfather's passing:

> After my grand-father was taken with his last illness, he told my parents that an angel appeared to him clothed in white, and *told him he would not recover, for his sickness was unto death.* Ten days later he died. To save ridicule, however, this vision was kept secret and only told me afterwards by my mother. . . . The vision of my grandfather seemed so strange that my parents hardly knew whether to

[62]LeRoi C. Snow, *Improvement Era, op cit.*, Vol. XXXII, p. 882. Ella told the following concerning the interval between the visit by the messenger and the time of her death:

> *I could see people from the other world and hear the most delightful music and singing that I ever heard. This singing lasted for six hours, during which time I was preparing to leave this earth, and I could hear it all through the house.* At ten o'clock my spirit left my body. It took me some time to make up my mind to go, as I could hear and see the folks crying and mourning over me. It was very hard for me to leave them, but as soon as I had a glimpse of the other world I was anxious to go and all care and worry left me. (*Ibid.*, p. 973.)

While speaking of the incident President Rudger Clawson added another item of interest:

> Sister Ella Jensen, in relating to me her very remarkable experience, said that during all the morning of our visit, and going back into the night, *the veil between this world and the other seemed to be growing thinner and thinner. She heard singing all through the house from the unseen world and seemed herself to be about to step into the spirit world.*

attribute it to imagination or a reality, as they could not question his sincerity, he having always been strictly reliable. I have never doubted, however, his having had the vision.

He walked half a mile to bid my parents good-by, although in poor health. On parting, my grand-father wept like a child, and said, *'This is the last I shall ever visit you while I live.'*[63]

At times the information concerning someone's death is revealed to another individual. Such was the case with Elder George Cannon, the father of the counselor to President Brigham Young—George Q. Cannon, who was shown the death of his wife, Ann Quayle, even before their marriage, and almost fifteen years before her death:

Long before his marriage the father of the family had a dream concerning the death of his wife, and when emigration was talked about, they both seemed to be aware that she would not live to reach Zion. Her relatives remonstrated with her for going with the Saints, but in reply she said to them, that though *she knew she never would live to reach the body of the Church,* she was determined to undertake the journey for the sake of her children, and she never shrank at the prospect before her. The manifestation that they had received proved to be true. They started for Zion, sailing from Liverpool in the ship 'Sidney,' Sept. 17, 1842, but she died and was buried in the ocean.[64]

On some occasions the individual who is about to die is given an understanding of the responsibilities he is to fulfill beyond the veil. Jacob Hamblin found this to be the case in the death of his Indian helper:

We left St. George to take the Moquis visitors home on the 18th of March, 1863. The party consisted of six white men and our Moquis friends. As I was leaving home, my Indian boy, Albert, met me, and I remarked to him that the peach trees had begun to bloom, and it would be warmer than it had been.

He replied, *'Yes, and I shall bloom in another place before you get back. I shall be on my mission!'* (He doubtless referred by this to a vision which he had of preaching to a multitude of his people.)

Said I, 'What do you mean by that?'

---

[63]Daniel Tyler, "Incidents of Experience," *Scraps of Biography* (tenth book of the Faith-Promoting Series; Salt Lake City: Juvenile Instructor Office, 1883), p. 23.

[64]Andrew Jenson, *Latter-day Saint Biographical Encyclopedia* (Salt Lake City, Utah: Published by the Andrew Jenson History Company and printed by the Deseret News, 1901), Vol. I, p. 44.

He replied, '*That I shall be dead and buried when you get back.*'[65]

After telling of his trip, Elder Hamblin added,

> I found on my return home that my Indian boy, Albert, was dead and buried, as he had predicted he would be when I left home.
>
> I supposed his age to be about ten years when he came to live with me; he had been with me twelve years making him twenty-two years old when he died. For a number of years he had charge of my sheep, horses and cattle, and they had increased and prospered in his hands.
>
> *Sometime before his death he had a vision, in which he saw himself preaching the gospel to a multitude of his people. He believed that this vision would be realized in the world of spirits.* He referred to this when he said that he should die before my return home, and be on his mission.
>
> He was a faithful Latter-day Saint; believed he had a great work to do among his people; *had many dreams and visions,* and had received his blessings in the house of the Lord.[66]

Often people receive a premonition of their death just a few minutes or hours before their passing. Wilford Woodruff recorded, for example, the premonition expressed by William Player as he assisted at the funeral of William Pitt, February 23, 1875:

> His funeral was attended by hundreds of people and there were several bands of music in attendance. Elder Woodruff was one of the speakers on that occasion. He mentions a peculiar circumstance which took place at that time. Brother William Player, then eighty years old, was one of the pall-bearers. The handle broke in his hand, and turning aside he leaned up against a post. His son, who was anxious about his father's condition, went immediately to his assistance, and when asked what the trouble was, said: '*My breath has given out, but I would like to follow my old friend to the grave, for I shall soon be in a similar condition myself. I wonder if as many will attend my funeral when I die?*' The father was taken home in a wagon, and in about four hours was dead. Elder Woodruff also preached at his funeral.[67]

Others are permitted to see the messengers who are to assist them into the spirit world or are given a glimpse beyond

---

[65]James A. Little, *Jacob Hamblin* (fifth book of the Faith-Promoting Series; Salt Lake City, Utah: Juvenile Instructor Office, 1881), pp. 81, 86-87.

[66]*Ibid.*

[67]Matthias F. Cowley, *Wilford Woodruff—History of His Life and Labors* (Salt Lake City, Utah: Bookcraft, Inc., 1964), p. 480.

the veil before their passing. These sights, however, are reserved for them alone and are not available to others. Such was the case with Brother Barber, who was mortally wounded by an anti-Mormon mob at the Whitmer settlement west of Independence, Missouri, in 1833:

> Several others of the brethren were also shot, and one, named Barber, was mortally wounded. After the battle was over, some of the brethren went to administer to him, but he *objected to their praying that he might live, and asked them if they could not see the angels present.* He said the room was full of them, and his greatest anxiety was for his friends to see what he saw, until he breathed his last, which occurred at three o'clock in the morning.[68]

It appears that this also happened with my own young daughter, Laura Jean, who conversed with those beyond the veil and was told that she would soon "wake up" in the spirit world:

> Laura Jean Crowther passed into the spirit world on September 5, 1966, at 2:10 p.m., just north of Cascade, Valley County, Idaho. Her death occurred as our family, together with JoAnn Woodruff, a friend, was returning to Utah after addressing a Richland Stake M-Men-Gleaner Conference at Fields Spring State Park in southeastern Washington.
>
> During the first two hours of our trip homeward that morning, Laura had been content to lie quietly on a makeshift bed in the back seat of our station wagon. During the Conference she had become ill with several symptoms of the acute Leukemia which she had had for about two months. As we traveled she dozed for a few minutes and then, while seemingly still slumbering, began to toss and turn and *carry on an animated conversation with an unseen being or beings.* We could only hear her part of the conversation, of course, but we heard her say in her sweet voice, *'I can't'*, and *'I don't want to'*. It seemed that she was eventually convinced of the necessity of her leaving mortality because she ceased to raise objections. She soon awoke, sat up, and said, *'Mother, I'm going to wake up soon.'* At the time we didn't realize the significance of what we heard, and we only helped her to lie back down, talked to her a moment, and then encouraged her to go back to sleep. A few moments later she hemmoraged a small quantity of blood from her mouth which alarmed us further and we began to search for a doctor. We traveled for almost two more hours before we found a doctor in McCall, Idaho. During this time she again hemmoraged blood and again roused

[68]Philo Dibble, *Early Scenes in Church History, op cit.*, p. 83.

herself from her lethargic slumber just long enough to reassure us by saying, *'Daddy, I'm going to wake up soon.'* Then she returned to her sleep or unconsciousness—we did not know which it was.

Dr. Nokes, who examined Laura in the emergency room of the hospital at McCall, was unable to help us and advised us to take her to one of the Boise hospitals where adequate blood and equipment were available. We drove about another twenty miles south to Cascade, where Laura suddenly sat up, and then her spirit quietly slipped from her body. We found ourselves only two blocks from the hospital there, where the attending doctor pronounced her dead.

It was not until after her passing that we were able to fully comprehend the meaning of her cryptic conversation and to grasp the reassuring intent of her twice repeated announcement, 'I'm going to wake up soon.'[69]

Evidence that many people are in some manner previously prepared for their death is frequently found. It does not appear, however, that all people receive such preparation. This blessing usually seems to be reserved for those who are called into Paradise, rather than into the spirit prison. It also appears to be based on personal needs rather than on worthiness alone. Indeed, it is difficult to determine why some individuals die suddenly and without warning, while others are notified of their approaching demise in advance. Suffice it to

---

[69]Duane S. Crowther, "Personal History," unpublished manuscript. Laura's statement about waking up soon is very similar, though opposite, to the words of the young daughter of President Joseph F. Smith shortly before her death:

> I cannot help but feel that the tenderest, sweetest and yet the strongest cord that bound me to home and earth is severed, my babe, my own sweet Dodo is gone! I can scarcely believe it and my heart asks, *can it be?* I look in vain, I listen, no sound, I wander through all the rooms, all are vacant, lonely, desolate, deserted. I look down the garden walk, peer around the house, look here and there for a glimpse of a little golden, sunny head and rosy cheeks, but no, alas, no pattering little footsteps. No beaming little black eyes sparkling with love for papa; no sweet little enquiring voice asking a thousand questions, and telling pretty little things, prattling merrily, no soft little dimpled hands clasping me around the neck, no sweet rosy lips returning in childish innocence my fond embrace and kisses, but a vacant little chair. Her little toys concealed, her clothes put by, and only one desolate thought forcing its crushing leaden weight upon my heart—*she is not here, she is gone. . . .*
>
> The morning before she died, after being up with her all night, for I watched her every night, I said to her, 'My little pet did not sleep all night.' She shook her head and replied, *'I'll sleep today, papa.'* Oh! how those little words shot through my heart. I knew though I would not believe, it was another voice, that it meant the sleep of death and she did sleep. . . . The star of my life and happiness seemed to have shone its last on earth, and my soul bowed into the dust. (Archibald F. Bennett, *Saviors on Mount Zion* (Salt Lake City, Utah: The Deseret News Press, 1950), p. 42.)

be said that the manner in which the selection is made is according to the will of the Lord, for "all things were created by him, and for him: And he is before all things, and by him all things consist."[70]

SUMMARY

1. Information concerning life in the spirit world is available from three reliable sources:
   - A. the words of Christ which are revealed in the scriptures,
   - B. eye witness accounts by numerous individuals who have entered the spirit world and then have returned to mortality, and
   - C. inspired statements by Latter-day Saint prophets.
2. The Bible sets a strong precedence for the teaching that man may return to mortal life after dying by recounting seven such instances. Dozens of similar experiences have been recorded in the latter-day era.
3. From the incidents cited in this chapter, certain things are indicated about the process of entering the spirit world:
   - A. the spirit encounters practically no pain when it leaves the body,
   - B. those who die can often see their physical body as they leave it,
   - C. those who die are immediately concious that they have changed conditions and abodes,
   - D. those who die are soon met beyond the veil by a specific welcoming committee, which often consists of their guardian angel and/or deceased relatives,
   - E. individuals entering the spirit world are under the control and direction of their guide(s),
   - F. death gives opportunity for reunions with departed friends and loved ones,
   - G. prearranged covenants concerning the order of greeting after death are honored in the spirit world,
   - H. while some spirit beings are aware that an individual is about to enter their realm, others are surprised to see them. Spirits inquire of newcomers about the situation of those still in mortality,

[70]Col. 1:16-17.

I. the spirit world is entered near the earthly location where the spirit leaves the mortal body,

J. the world of spirits is near the world of mortality,

K. as one enters the spirit world he leaves his worldly cares behind,

L. upon entering the spirit world one soon comes in contact with numerous other spirits. The spirit world is a social situation,

M. an early duty of those entering the spirit world is to watch over their physical body until after its burial. The knowledge thus obtained is apparently necessary for the resurrection process,

N. spirit beings regard the death process as "waking up" or as a "new birth."

4. Certain characteristics of spirit beings are indicated:

A. spirit beings retain bodily form, with head, arms, hands, etc.,

B. spirit beings retain the senses and sensations they knew as mortal beings,

C. spirit beings maintain a sense of touch and can feel one another,

D. it appears that spirit beings may dwell in family groups and are aware of relationships from generation to generation,

E. righteous spirits dwell "enveloped in flaming fire,"

F. spirit beings enjoy increased capacities such as

(1) the ability to move with the speed of lightning, including the ability to project the body by merely inclining the head,

(2) no restriction from the force of gravity,

(3) the ability to travel in time by visiting the spiritual remains of places as they existed in the past or by seeing them in visions,

(4) unlimited powers of memory,

(5) greatly increased power of sight through ability to see through all parts of the spirit body and ability to see in all directions at once, and to see through interfering objects.

G. spirit beings are also limited, for,

(1) much repentance and growth involves both the spirit and the body,

(2) without the body the spirit will be limited in overcoming certain faults,

(3) the spirit without the body cannot receive a fulness of joy.

5. The Paradise of spirits is regarded as being a joyful and gloriously beautiful place by those who have seen it. Without exception they have preferred to remain there rather than return to mortal life. The earth, in contrast, appeared cloudy, dreary, and dark.

6. Certain facts are indicated about the nature of the spirit world:

A. It is filled with brightness and glory,

B. it does not extend beyond the boundaries of the temporal earth.

7. To return to the presence of God at death does not necessarily mean that one will come in close proximity to Deity. Rather, spirit beings will be returned to a condition where they can behold Him through increased powers of vision and communication if the occasion so requires.

8. No evidence has been found that men actually stand before the judgment bar of God in a partial judgment at death. The assignment of spirit beings to their appointed abodes in the spirit world appears to be determined previous to one's entrance into the spirit realm.

9. Many mortals are notified and prepared for their approaching death by communication from those in the spirit world. Some are shown the duty or assignment they will receive beyond the veil.

CHAPTER II

FACTORS INFLUENCING MAN'S TIME OF DEATH

Days and Bounds of Man Determined by God

"TO EVERY THING THERE IS A SEASON, AND A TIME TO every purpose under the heaven."[1] Basic to man's faith in God is the recognition that God controls man's ultimate destiny. Although man is given[2] the privilege of agency and choice in the way he conducts the affairs of his daily life, yet it is an all-wise God who determines the time of man's birth and death and the circumstances of his mortal probation. Indeed, the Lord said,

> Thus did I, the Lord God, *appoint unto man the days of his probation*—that by his natural death he might be raised in immortality unto eternal life, even as many as would believe;
>
> And they that believe not unto eternal damnation.[3]

Job on one occasion queried, "Is there not an appointed time to man upon earth?"[4] Then he cried unto God this great truth:

> Man that is born of a woman is of few days. . . .
>
> *His days are determined, the number of his months are with thee, thou hast appointed his bounds that he cannot pass.*[5]

The Apostle Paul set forth a similar teaching in his discourse on Mars' hill, when he proclaimed,

> God that made the world and all things therein, . . . hath made of one blood all nations of men for to dwell on all the face

---

[1]Eccles. 3:1.

[2]The Lord said unto Enoch:

> Behold these thy brethren; they are the workmanship of mine own hands, and *I gave unto them their knowledge,* in the day I created them; and in the garden of Eden, *gave I unto man his agency.* (Moses 7:32.)

[3]D&C 29:43-44.

[4]Job 7:1.

[5]Job 14, 1, 5.

> of the earth, and *hath determined the times before appointed, and the bounds of their habitation.*[6]

The Prophet Alma also raised his voice to proclaim that *"God knoweth all the times which are appointed unto man."*[7]

To Joseph Smith the Lord commanded, "Hold on thy way, and the priesthood shall remain with thee; for their [Joseph's enemies] bounds are set, they cannot pass. *Thy days are known, and thy years shall not be numbered less."*[8]

Man Partially Able to Shape His Mortal Life Before Coming to Earth

If God holds control over the time, days, and bounds of men, how does He decide what circumstances each individual will experience during mortality? Does He carefully select the earth program of each individual or are men sent to earth without divine consideration of their mortal environment? Is it happenstance that one man is born during the dark ages while another comes to earth in the era of the restored gospel? Is it a quirk of fate that one man lives in a primitive African hut while another is born to sit in splendor on a European throne? Does God arbitrarily send one individual to earth in circumstances where he will never hear the gospel, while another is born into the home of a faithful bishop who will prepare him to live gospel truths? Is it the will of God that one man may leap and play while another is born a hopeless cripple? The scriptures leave these questions unanswered. Man, knowing of the infinite wisdom and mercy of God, must rely on His justice and His love through faith. By that power man must accept and believe that God has given each individual the program of birth, life circumstances, and death, which will be best designed to bring the individual the reward of celestial glory in the hereafter.

It does not appear that man has been without oppor-

---

[6]Acts 17:24, 26. Moses taught in a similar manner when he admonished Israel to

> Remember . . . when the most High divided to the nations their inheritance, when he separated the sons of Adam, *he set the bounds of the people* according to the number of the children of Israel. (Deut. 32:7-8)

[7]Al. 40:10.

[8]D&C 122:9.

tunity to participate in the determination of his earth circumstances. To the contrary, it would seem that some men, as pre-mortal spirit beings acting under divine supervision, were given the privilege of selecting the mortal circumstances and probation which would best satisfy their needs and which would aid them best in their search for eternal joy. It appears that pre-mortal agreements which men have made have shaped the course and time of their mortal probation. While writing concerning the great council[9] held before the creation of the earth, Elder John A. Widtsoe set forth this teaching as he said that

> In our preexistent state, in the day of the Great Council, *we made a certain agreement with the Almighty. The Lord proposed a plan, conceived by him. We accepted it.* Since the plan is intended for all men, we became parties to the salvation of every person under that plan. We agreed, right then and there, to be not only saviors for ourselves but measurably, saviors for the whole human family. *We went into a partnership with the Lord.* The working out of the plan became then not merely the Father's work, and the Savior's work, but *also our work. The least of us, the humblest, is in partnership with the Almighty in achieving the purpose of the eternal plan of salvation.*[10]

President Joseph F. Smith commented on the role the pre-mortal spirits played in the great council in heaven before the earth was created and emphasized that the spirits were not merely observers in this council but that they labored actively to properly shape and mold their own future:

> Our spirits existed before they came to this world. *They were in the councils of the heavens before the foundations of the earth were laid.* We were there. We sang together with the heavenly hosts for joy, when the foundations of the earth were laid, and when the plan of our existence upon this earth and redemption were mapped out. *We were there; we were interested, and we took a part in this great preparation.* We were unquestionably present in those councils. . . . We were, no doubt, there, and took a part in all those scenes; *we were vitally concerned in the carrying out of these great plans and purposes; we understood them, and it was for our sakes they were decreed* and are to be consummated.[11]

The prophet Alma, while telling of men in his day who

---

[9]See Job 38:4-7, Moses 4:1-4; Abra. 3:22-28; D&C 121:32.

[10]Archibald F. Bennett, *Saviors on Mount Zion, op cit.,* p. 11. See also Tit. 1:1-2.

[11]JD 25:57. Feb. 17, 1884.

were laboring in priesthood callings, told how their pre-mortal choices had enabled them to be called to the priesthood offices they were to hold in mortality at the foundation of the world:

> This is the manner after which they were ordained—*being called and prepared from the foundation of the world* according to the foreknowledge of God, on account of their exceeding faith and good works; *in the first place being left to choose good or evil; therefore they having chosen good,* and exercising exceeding great faith, are called with a holy calling.[12]

There is evidence that some pre-mortal spirits are able to choose their mortal parents and are able to request parentage who will be suitable to the level of activity they have decided to pursue. Apostle Orson Hyde taught that some pre-mortal spirits have been able to choose the family into which they are to be born, and have sought their own level here on earth:

> So, when those spirits come to take bodies, where will the noble and high order of them go? *Will they take bodies that have come through a low and degraded parentage? No, no more than the righteous man will take up his abode with the vile and wicked.* Where will he go? 'Why,' says that noble spirit, that is swelling with light and intelligence, 'I will take a body through an honorable parentage; *I will have a body that will correspond with my mind;* I will go to the place where purity and righteousness dwell.'
>
> *Where do the spirits of a lower grade go? Among the lowest, and uncultivated,* where the cultivation of the principles of virtue and integrity is in part or entirely neglected. In this way the sins of the fathers are answered upon their children to the third and fourth generation.
>
> *Do good spirits want to partake of the sins of the low and degraded? No; but they will stay in heaven until a way is opened for purity and righteousness to form a channel in which they can come, and take honorable bodies in this world, and to magnify their calling.*[13]

---

[12]Al. 13:3. Thus choices made in the pre-mortal life influenced their priesthood standing in mortality. According to Joseph Smith, the principle seems to apply to all priesthood bearers, for he taught that

> Every man who has a calling to minister to the inhabitants of the world was ordained to that very purpose in the Grand Council of heaven before this world was. I suppose that I was ordained to this very office in that Grand Council. (HC 6:364. May 12, 1844.)

[13]JD 2:116-117. Sept. 24, 1853.

An experience of Edward James Wood while president of the Canadian Temple lends weight to the teaching that some children are allowed to choose their parents before coming to earth:

> Several of the couples of the mission had been married for years and had never been blessed with children. I admonished them to join in this great movement [excursion to the temple] and they would receive the blessing they had hoped for and prayed for. Two such couples were with the caravan. In one of the sessions in the temple, President Wood *saw two spirits hovering over the congregation. He told all present that they were from the Spirit World and were anxious to come to the earth and take mortal bodies.* He promised the sisters in the room who had come for that special blessing would have their hearts' desires granted. *All had the experience of witnessing spirits from the unseen world come and stand in their very presence and even the angel's choir sang with joy.* In less than one year from that date, those two homes were blessed with babies.[14]

Additional evidence that children are not sent to earth by happenstance but are designated to be born into particular families is found in the spirit world experience of Henry Zollinger, who during the eight hours he was separated from his body, was taken from the spirit world area he had entered to another portion of God's creation:

> My guide then took me and showed me *the spirits of the children that would yet come to my family* if we would be faithful. *They were full grown but not in the same sphere as those which had lived upon this earth.*[15]

Other choices concerning mortal life were apparently available to the spirit children of the Father also. There is indication that pre-mortal spirits were allowed to choose the type of trials and hardships they would have to endure while on the earth. Consider the experience of Niels P. L. Eskildz, a Danish convert to the Church, who was seriously crippled and deformed when but ten years of age. The sixteen years which followed were a time of misery and despair for him. However, in the summer of 1862, just prior to his baptism, he received a revelation which helped him to understand many of the unexplained circumstances of his earth life:

---

[14]Melvin S. Tagg, *The Life of Edward James Wood, op cit.*, pp. 117-118. His sources: "Unpublished Writings of Myrtle Olsen," Cardston, Alberta. See also "Edward J. Wood, Record," 1952, Church Historian's Office. Also verified in an interview with Preston Nibley, May 29, 1959.

[15]Henry Zollinger, *op cit.*

> While engaged preparing his evening meal a glorious vision burst upon his view. It was not a single scene that he beheld, but a series of them. . . . He beheld as with his natural sight, but he realized afterwards that it was with the eye of the spirit that he saw what he did. His understanding was appealed to as well as his sight. What was shown him related to his existence in the spirit world, mortal experience and future rewards. He comprehended, as if by intuition, that *he had witnessed a somewhat similar scene in his pre-mortal state, and been given the opportunity of choosing the class of reward he would like to attain to. He knew that he had deliberately made his choice. He realized which of the rewards he had selected, and understood that such a reward was only to be gained by mortal suffering*—that, in fact, he must be a cripple and endure severe physical pain, privation and ignominy. *He was conscious too that he still insisted upon having that reward, and accepted and agreed to the conditions.*
>
> He emerged from the vision with a settled conviction, that *to rebel against or even to repine at his fate, was not only a reproach to an Alwise Father whose care had been over him notwithstanding his seeming abandonment, but a base violation of the deliberate promise and agreement he had entered into, and upon the observance of which his future reward depended.*[16]

Elder John Taylor was another who believed that spirits in their pre-mortal state were able to affect the course of their mortal life by means of choices and covenants which they made in the pre-existence. As he explained the past, present, and future status of faithful Latter-day Saint women he taught that in addition to some being able to choose their parents, some pre-mortal spirits were permitted to covenant with others to be their spouse, their children, and their guardian angel. His statement effectively summarizes the teachings of the others cited in this section:

---

[16]George C. Lambert, "A Modern Stoic," *Treasures In Heaven* (fifteenth book of the Faith Promoting Series, Salt Lake City, Utah: by the author, 1914), pp. 21-22. Brother Lambert's manuscript was read and approved by a reading committee composed of Elders George F. Richards, A. W. Ivins, and Joseph F. Smith, Jr. They acted under the direction of Joseph F. Smith, Anthon H. Lund, and Charles W. Penrose, the First Presidency.

The author's commentary concerning the attitude of the recipient of this vision is of interest:

> Whatever opinion others may entertain concerning the philosophy involved in this theory, is a matter of absolute indifference to Niels. He does not advocate it: he does not seek to apply it to any other case; but he has unshaken faith in it so far as his own case is concerned. Whether true or not, the fact remains that he has derived comfort, satisfaction, resolution and fortitude from it. He has ever since been resigned to his affliction, and, though never mirthful, is serene and composed and uncomplaining. He has always felt that the vision was granted to him by the Lord for a wise and merciful purpose—that he might, through a better understanding of his duty, be able to remain steadfast thereto.

Knowest thou not that eternities ago *thy spirit, pure and holy, dwelt in thy Heavenly Father's bosom, and in His presence, and with thy mother, one of the queens of heaven, surrounded by thy brother and sister spirits in the spirit world, among the Gods?* That as thy spirit beheld the scenes transpiring there, and thou grewest in intelligence, thou sawest worlds upon worlds organized and peopled with thy kindred spirits who took upon them tabernacles, died, were resurrected, and received their exaltation on the redeemed worlds they once dwelt upon. Thou being willing and anxious to imitate them, waiting and desirous to obtain a body, a resurrection and exaltation also, and *having obtained permission, madest a covenant with one of thy kindred spirits to be thy guardian angel while in mortality, also with two others, male and female spirits, that thou wouldst come and take a tabernacle through their lineage, and become one of their offspring. You also chose a kindred spirit whom you loved in the spirit world* (and who had permission to come to this planet and take a tabernacle), *to be your head, stay, husband and protector on the earth and to exalt you in eternal worlds. All these were arranged, likewise the spirits that should tabernacle through your lineage.* Thou longed, thou sighed and thou prayed to thy Father in heaven for the time to arrive when thou couldst come to this earth, which had fled and fallen from where it was first organized, near the planet Kolob. Leaving thy father and mother's bosom and all thy kindred spirits thou camest to earth, took a tabernacle, and imitated the deeds of those who had been exalted before you.

At length the time arrived, and thou heard the voice of thy Father saying, go daughter to yonder lower world, and take upon thee a tabernacle, and work out thy probation with fear and trembling and rise to exaltation. But daughter, remember you go on this condition, that is, you are to forget all things you ever saw, or knew to be transacted in the spirit world; you are not to know or remember anything concerning the same that you have beheld transpire here; but you must go and become one of the most helpless of all beings that I have created, while in your infancy, subject to sickness, pain, tears, mourning, sorrow and death. But when truth shall touch the cords of your heart they will vibrate; then intelligence shall illuminate your mind, and shed its lustre in your soul, and you shall begin to understand the things you once knew, but which had gone from you; you shall then begin to understand and know the object of your creation. Daughter, go, and be faithful as thou hast been in thy first estate.

Thy spirit, filled with joy and thanksgiving, rejoiced in thy Father, and rendered praise to His holy name, and the spirit world resounded in anthems of praise to the Father of spirits. Thou bade father, mother and all farewell, and *along with thy guardian angel, thou came on this terraqueous globe. The spirits thou hadst chosen to come and tabernacle through their lineage, and your head having left the spirit world*

> *some years previous,* thou came a spirit pure and holy. Thou hast obeyed the truth, and *thy guardian angel ministers unto thee and watches over thee. Thou hast chosen him you loved in the spirit world to be thy companion.* Now crowns, thrones, exaltations and dominions are in reserve for thee in the eternal worlds, and the way is opened for thee to return back into the presence of thy Heavenly Father, if thou wilt only abide by and walk in a celestial law, fulfill the designs of thy Creator and hold out to the end that when mortality is laid in the tomb, you may go down to your grave in peace, arise in glory, and receive your everlasting reward in the resurrection of the just, along with thy head and husband. *Thou wilt be permitted to pass by the Gods and angels who guard the gates, and onward, upward to thy exaltation in a celestial world among the Gods.*[17]

If an individual, while in the form of a pre-mortal spirit, has been able to choose his parents and relatives, then has he elected the time and general location of his birth and life activity? If he has been privileged to choose the nature of his mortal probation and the challenges which he must overcome, has he also chosen the length of his probation, and hence the time of his death?

A Time to Die

Although man does not fully understand how the time of his death is fixed, yet it is clear that mortals have such a time set for them. The author of Ecclesiastes taught that man has "a time to be born, and a time to die."[18] A significant passage concerning the healing of the sick, found in the Doctrine and Covenants, also speaks of the set time of death of an individual:

> It shall come to pass that he that hath faith in me to be healed, and *is not appointed unto death,* shall be healed.[19]

The righteous man, who gives due care to his physical being and fulfills his obligations to the Lord, may expect the privilege of remaining on earth to fulfill his life's mission and course and living the full extent of his appointed years. The Savior, for example, went unharmed in several situations where he suffered bodily attack because "his hour

[17]John Taylor, "The Mormon," (New York City, August 29, 1857), as cited in N. B. Lundwall, *The Vision* (Salt Lake City, Utah: Bookcraft Publishing Co., n.d.), pp. 146-147.

[18]Eccles. 3:2.

[19]D&C 42:48.

was not yet come."[20] But when his mission approached its culmination on the cross he then told his apostles, "The hour is come, that the Son of man should be glorified."[21]

A servant of the Lord may expect divine protection so that he may complete his authorized mission from the Lord and not be slain before his time. The prophet Abinadi was able to withstand the murderous advances of the wicked priests of King Noah with the warning,

> Touch me not, for God shall smite you if ye lay your hands upon me, for I have not delivered the message which the Lord sent me to deliver, . . . therefore, *God will not suffer that I shall be destroyed at this time.*[22]

His warning was strengthened by the "exceeding luster" with which his face shone, and his assailants shrunk back in fright. Yet after his mission was completed the protection ceased and Abinadi was martyred by fire.

In the Doctrine and Covenants we read of the Lord's promise to Lyman Wight that

> I will bear him up as on eagles' wings; and he shall beget glory and honor to himself and unto my name.
>
> That *when he shall finish his work I may receive him unto myself.* . . .[23]

The deathbed blessing of Joseph Smith Sr. upon the head of his son, Joseph the prophet, was a promise that his life would be preserved until his life's mission was completed:

> 'Joseph, my son, you are called to a high and holy calling. You are even called to do the work of the Lord. Hold out faithful and you shall be blest and your children after you. *You shall even live to finish your work.'* At this Joseph cried out, weeping, 'Oh! my father, shall I?' 'Yes,' said his father, '*you shall live to lay out the plan of all the work which God has given you to do.* This is my dying blessing upon your head in the name of Jesus. I also confirm your former blessing upon your head; for it shall be fulfilled. Even so. Amen.'[24]

---

[20]Jn. 7:30, 8:20.

[21]Jn. 12:23, 17:1, 13:1. The apostle Paul foresaw his approaching death in the same manner. See Acts 21:13.

[22]Mos. 13:3. See also the similar preservation of life granted to the sons of Helaman (Hel. 5:22-32) and to Nephi (1 Ne. 17:48-55).

[23]D&C 124:18-19.

[24]Lucy Mack Smith, *History of Joseph Smith by His Mother* (Salt Lake City, Utah: Bookcraft, 1958), pp. 309-310.

This promise was fulfilled, and Joseph's life was preserved until after he completed his mission and placed the responsibility for guiding the Church on the shoulders of the Twelve.[25]

Appointed Time of Death Changed by Pleas of the Righteous

There is evidence that the fixed time of death is not unalterable and that a number of factors can occasion a change in one's appointed death date. Apparently the requests of the righteous may prevail with the Lord to gain an extension of life in some instances. Witness the case of Hezekiah, king of Judah, who was told of his approaching death and then granted an extension of life:

> In those days was Hezekiah sick unto death. And Isaiah the prophet the son of Amoz came unto him, and said unto him, Thus saith the Lord, *Set thine house in order: for thou shalt die, and not live.*
>
> Then Hezekiah turned his face toward the wall, and prayed unto the Lord,
>
> *And said, Remember now, O Lord, I beseech thee, how I have walked before thee in truth and with a perfect heart, and have done that which is good in thy sight.* And Hezekiah wept sore.
>
> Then came the word of the Lord to Isaiah, saying,
>
> Go, and say to Hezekiah, Thus saith the Lord, the God of David thy father, *I have heard thy prayer, I have seen thy tears: behold, I will add unto thy days fifteen years. . . .*
>
> And this shall be a sign unto thee from the Lord, that the Lord will do this thing that he hath spoken;
>
> Behold, I will bring again the shadow of the degrees, which is gone down in the sun dial of Ahaz, ten degrees backward. So the sun returned ten degrees, by which degrees it was gone down.[26]

John the Revelator was another who asked that the time fixed for his death be altered. His request, "*Lord, give unto me power over death,* that I may live and bring souls unto thee,"[27] gained him the privilege of remaining on the earth till the coming of the Savior in the last days. Three of the Nephite Twelve sought the same privilege as the Apostle John and received the Lord's promise that

---

[25]For further documentation concerning the preservation of Joseph's life and transfer of responsibility to the Twelve, see the author's book, *The Prophecies of Joseph Smith* (Salt Lake City, Utah; Bookcraft, 1963), pp. 369-388.

[26]Is. 38:1-8. Hezekiah's despondency concerning his impending death and his praise of God concerning his extension of life is both beautiful and informative. See Is. 38:9-20. The Lord gave a similar blessing to Solomon; see I Ki. 3:14.

[27]D&C 7:2.

Ye shall never taste of death; but ye shall live to behold all the doings of the Father unto the children of men, even until all things shall be fulfilled according to the will of the Father, when I shall come in my glory with the powers of heaven.

And ye shall never endure the pains of death; but when I shall come in my glory ye shall be changed in the twinkling of an eye from mortality to immortality, and then shall ye be blessed in the kingdom of my Father.[28]

There is evidence that individuals in the world of spirits can influence the time of death of mortal beings. A manifestation given to Marie W. Weiss, wife of a German convert who in six years (from 1918 to 1923) gathered the names of over three thousand of his kindred dead and then spent many years laboring in the temples in their behalf, showed her that these spirits would seek permission for her husband to come and preach the gospel to them beyond the veil:

So grateful was he to the Lord for life, health and happiness that he volunteered for a short-term mission to the Northwestern States. The day before he was to return home from his mission, his wife in Salt Lake City had an unusual dream. *She saw a big, wide valley and in the valley a great concourse of people gathered and in earnest and animated conversation. At their head, evidently their leader, was a person dressed in the costume of an old-time schoolmaster.* A little farther away she saw her father-in-law, the father of her husband, Henry Weiss, who had died just after hearing of the Gospel from an Elder of the Church. The schoolmaster approaching said to him: *'We have heard that upon earth some labor has been performed in our behalf which will bring us great happiness. Can you tell us about it?'*

The father-in-law answered, 'I am sorry, but I cannot. I only heard of the Gospel once before I died. You should have my son, Henry Weiss, here as a missionary. He could tell you all about that.' *It was decided among the group to get up a petition asking for Henry Weiss to be called to the Spirit World on a mission to preach to his numerous kindred.*

When she awoke next morning she was deeply concerned as to the meaning of the dream. Her husband returned. He seemed in good health and two days after his arrival resumed his regular business and church duties. At the first opportunity, she related her dream to him. He said, 'It seems to refer to me, and I suppose it means that I should redouble my efforts to gather records of my relatives.'

But the family noticed that as the weeks went by he spent a

[28] 3 Ne. 28:7-8.

> great deal of time checking over all his records, seeing if any names had been omitted; and if all baptisms, endowments and sealings had been recorded and completed. He prepared a Book of Remembrance record of his life that was most creditable. . . .
>
> About six months after his return, his health was impaired and he suffered much pain. When at last he consulted a doctor, an x-ray picture showed that he was afflicted with cancer. An immediate operation was advised. When the operation was performed, the examination showed the cancer had already eaten its way through his stomach and infected the spine. But Henry Weiss, not knowing his serious condition, had high hopes of a speedy recovery. Only a few mornings later, on February 1, 1932, as a nurse adjusted his bed, he turned over on his side and in an instant he was dead.[29]

Spirit beings can also work for the continuation of the life of mortal beings, as was shown to Brother Alvin H. Patterson during his administration to Mrs. Samuel A. Cornwall, who lay near death from Bright's disease and dropsy. As Sister Cornwall later recorded,

> The administration was a miraculous manifestation of the power of the Lord. During the prayer of Brother Patterson, he paused for several seconds, *his eyes and mind centered upon something he saw above him.* And then, he resumed his supplication.
>
> The moment the last words of benediction were said, I felt the healing power of the Lord penetrate my whole being from head to foot. Immediately, I stood upon my feet and knew that my body had been cleansed from all affliction. I knew that I had been healed. Every vestige of the disease left me, and I was restored to perfect health.

---

[29] "The Hearts of the Fathers," unpublished manuscript in the possession of Sister Ruth Gregory, Smithfield, Utah. Following the death of her husband, Mrs. Weiss wrote,

> The interpretation of the dream is very clear to me now. My husband's father was the last who died in his family without having accepted the Gospel. The oldest man, dressed like a schoolmaster, was the earliest ancestor on our pedigree chart, who emigrated in 1620 from Silesia into Bavaria as a soldier and school teacher. The Gospel had to be preached to them and so they looked for someone in mortal life to be called on a mission over to the Spirit World to instruct them. My husband was the only one out of a big family of fifteen children to hear the Gospel message and accept it, and was ready to go over as a missionary to his father's household and preach to his kindred in the Spirit World the glad tidings of the Gospel.
>
> This is my testimony, that sometimes when my heart aches in longing for my husband, this dream is a solace and comfort to me, a source of faith and hope from which I get renewed strength to go forward. I can see clearly that he was the only one that was able to go and do this great and glorious work for his people.

The return of Peter E. Johnson to mortality because of the request of his progenitors in the spirit world that he return and perform their temple work for them should be recalled in this context. See p. 57-59.

When the administration was over, Brother Patterson, turning to mother, said, *'Have you lost a sister?'*

'Yes,' mother replied. *'My only sister.'*

'I thought so,' he continued, *'for I saw a beautiful young woman interceding with the heavens in behalf of your daughter.'*

This miracle happened about forty-six years ago and, although I am the mother of five children, four of whom are living, in all these years I have never had a recurrence of the disease.[30]

At times departed spirits may be influential in their own return to mortality, as was the case with Elder Brigham Smoot, a missionary who drowned in Samoa. The biography of Edward J. Wood gives the following account:

Probably the most remarkable experience of Elder Wood's first mission resulted from a missionary's disobedience to his mother's council. When Brigham Smoot left for his mission to Samoa, he promised his mother that he would not go swimming out in the sea. Only one day after his arrival in Samoa, he was persuaded by Edward to join the group for the usual bath at sea. As the new elder was wading out to sea, he slipped and fell into a deep hole in the reef. As he was unable to swim he soon dropped to the bottom of the hole. Edward had promised to be responsible for the new elder's safety, and noticing him absent, he began a frantic search. Brigham Smoot was soon found in the attitude of prayer at the bottom of the hole. His limp body was dragged from the hole and carried to the beach. Blood was flowing from his eyes, nose and mouth. Elder Wood said of his companion, 'He was perfectly life-

---

[30]Jeremiah Stokes, *Modern Miracles* (Salt Lake City, Utah: Bookcraft, 1945), pp. 107-108. In her statement, which was written and witnessed by her sisters on January 10, 1935, Mrs. Cornwall gave the following background for this experience:

When I was about twenty-one years of age, I was the recipient of a most remarkable blessing. I had suffered for nearly one and a half years with Bright's disease and during the time was under the care of Doctors Joseph Benedict and August Rauscher, both of whom are now dead. In spite of all that was done for me, I steadily grew worse until the last stages of the disease had developed, and dropsy had set in. My feet and limbs were so badly swollen that when I would press my thumb on my ankles it would sink in and the imprint would remain for some time. For days at a time I would be almost blind with the pain in my head and about my eyes. Both physicians told my parents that I could not live and that it was only a matter of a very short time until I would succumb.

At the request of my father, John Neff, then Bishop of the East Mill Creek Ward, and my mother, Ann Eliza Benedict Neff, Brother Alvin H. Patterson came to our home to join my father in administering to me. On this occasion there were present my parents, also Brother Patterson; my grandmother, Fidelia M. Benedict; my sisters, Marion B. Neff Stillman and Frances Neff Smith, all of whom are now dead. Two sisters, who are still living, were also there; namely, Mrs. Delia B. Spencer and Mrs. Esther E. Hixson.

> less and dead.' In vain the elders used all normal restorative measures. By this time a large crowd of inquisitive natives had gathered around. Their telling of a native boy who had previously drowned in the same hole brought no comfort to the worried missionaries. *Elder Wood said that at this time he felt inspired by the spirit that the only way his companion's spirit could re-enter his body would be to administer to him.* Accordingly the body of Elder Smoot was dressed in clean garments and a new suit of clothes. The superstitious natives warned against such treatment of the body, and thought it sacrilegious to tamper with life and death. Obedient to the inspiration, however, the body was anointed. While Elder Wood was sealing the anointing, he felt life come back to Elder Smoot's body. Shortly after the administration, Elder Smoot talked with the missionaries and bore solemn testimony to them. He told of how, in the spirit, he watched them recover his body from the hole, take it to the beach and try to restore it to life. *He also told of touching Elder Wood on the shoulder and telling him that the only way to bring life back into the body was to use the Priesthood which he bore.*[31]

In the latter days there have been numerous occasions when the faithful prayers and administration of priesthood bearers have altered the time of death of the afflicted.[32] In many instances faithful Saints have sought and received the restoration to health of their loved ones and have snatched the sick from the bonds of death. Examples of such administrations are so numerous as to be unnecessary in the present context.

Less known is the fact that Satan can also inflict mortals with sickness unto death, and that there are occasions when the righteous request for the extension of life must be accompanied with a rebuke of the Satanic power through priesthood authority. President Heber J. Grant told of such an experience in connection with the sickness of his daughter:

> When my wife died I took my oldest three daughters to Boston, New York and other places in the hope that the sorrow caused by the death of their mother might be forgotten. When we reached

---

[31]Melvin S. Tagg, *The Life of Edward James Wood,* Master's Thesis submitted to and accepted by the College of Religious Instruction, Brigham Young University, (Provo, Utah: by the author), pp. 36-37. The account is adapted from the "Samoan Mission Journal," a daily journal kept by Joseph Dean, then president of the mission, under date of June 18, 1889. The journal is now in the Church Historian's Office, Salt Lake City, Utah.

[32]For a discussion of the gifts of *faith to heal* and *faith to be healed* see the author's book, *Gifts of the Spirit* (Salt Lake City, Utah: Bookcraft, Inc., 1965), pp. 131-171.

Washington *two of them were taken ill with diphtheria.* They were as sick as any children I have ever seen. *The younger of the two was so low that her pulse beat only 28 times to the minute, and I felt sure she was going to die. I knelt down and prayed God to spare her life, inasmuch as I had brought my children east to relieve the terrible sorrow that had come to them; and prayed that I should not have the additional sorrow of taking one of my children home in a coffin. I prayed for her life, and shed bitter tears of humiliation.* While praying, the inspiration came to me that if I would send for the Elders who were then in Washington and have them administer to her, she would live. Some people say we cannot know for a certainty that we receive manifestations from the Lord. Well, I know that I was shedding tears of sorrow, fear and anguish, while I was praying, and I know that immediately thereafter I received the witness of the Spirit that my little girl should live, and I shed tears of unbounded joy and gratitude and thanksgiving to God, thanking him for the inspiration that came to me to send for the Elders that they might administer to my little girl.

Hiram B. Clawson and George Q. Cannon were in Washington at the time, and I sent for them. When George Q. Cannon laid his hands upon my daughter's head, to seal the anointing, wherewith she had been anointed, he made a statement that I have never heard before or since, in all my life, in any prayer. He said, in substance: *'The adversary, the destroyer, has decreed your death and made public announcement that you shall die; but by the authority of the priesthood of the Living God, we rebuke the decree of the adversary, and say that you shall live, and not die;* that you shall live to become a mother in the Church of Christ.' She did live to become a mother, and in the providences of the Lord her children are the great-grandchildren of the man who held the priesthood of God and gave her that blessing.[33]

---

[33]"Many Remarkable Cures and Other Instances of God's Power Attest That His Spirit Attends Church"—Address Delivered in the Tabernacle, Salt Lake City, Sunday, February 29, 1920, by President Heber J. Grant, *Deseret News,* April 24, 1920. President Grant went on to explain the way in which Satan had made public announcement of his daughter's death:

> I often thought of that blessing during the days and weeks that she was convalescing, and I wondered about the peculiar statement that the adversary, the destroyer, had publicly announced her death. As we were leaving the boarding house, the gentleman whose wife had been in charge there—he was a clerk in one of the departments at Washington—said to me: 'Mr. Grant, I have a joke on my wife. She believes in spiritualism, and when your little girls were taken sick she went to her medium. The medium went into a sort of trance and told her the following story:
>
> That she saw two little girls in her house; she saw the older one taken sick, very sick; then the other little girl became sick, nigh unto death; she finally saw the first little girl recover and the second little girl die. She then described how the child's body was put into a coffin and taken to a railroad station; then she described how the train traveled, carrying the body of that little girl, hundreds of miles to the west, through great cities, finally stopping in a large city where the body was transferred from one train to another. Going from Washington you know that there is a transfer from all trains at Chicago. Then she saw it cross two great rivers—the

Uninspired priesthood administration does not reflect the will of the Lord. Promises made in such a situation still carry the power of the priesthood, and may alter the time of death of the recipient, but not to his advantage and well-being. There may have been times when those who were appointed to die have been kept alive to suffer unnecessary pain and hardship, which was not the Lord's will. Commenting on this problem Elder Spencer W. Kimball said,

> *The power of the Priesthood is limitless but God has wisely placed upon each of us certain limitations.* I may develop Priesthood power as I perfect my life. I am grateful that even through the Priesthood I cannot heal all the sick. *I might heal people who should die.* I might relieve people of suffering who should suffer. I fear I would frustrate the purposes of God. . . .
>
> With unlimited power I might have healed my father and my mother. I might have never let them die.
>
> Would you dare to take the responsibility of bringing back to life your own loved ones? I, myself, would hesitate to do so. I am grateful that we may always pray: 'Thy will be done in all things for Thou knowest what is best.' *I am glad I do not have the decisions to make. We might consign loved ones to loss of faculties, loss of powers, terrible doom.*[34]

Administrations, where no direct guidance is received, should best be left that the will of the Lord be done, remembering the Lord's commandment and promise that

> The elders of the church, two or more, shall be called, and

---

Missouri and the Mississippi, although not named—she afterwards saw it traveling across the plains, and crossing mountains, mountains, always to the west, then saw it go south a little distance from Ogden to Salt Lake, although not giving the names—then the body was taken off the train and carried to a side hill to the place of burial; and as you know the burial place in Salt Lake City is on a side hill. But through the priesthood of the Living God, the decree of the adversary was rebuked, and my daughter lived.

President Brigham Young once made the statement that the planchette would tell ninety-nine truths and then put in one lie that would send you to hell if you believed it. Through the spiritualistic manifestation every detail was given on the trip which I have described. The adversary had publicly announced the death of this little girl, and that trip and the carrying of her body from Washington to Salt Lake City and burying it here on the side hill; but by the authority of the priesthood of God that false spiritualistic decree was rebuked. My daughter still lives and is the mother of four healthy children.

[34]Spencer W. Kimball, *Tragedy or Destiny,* Address to the Brigham Young University studentbody at Provo, Utah, December 6, 1955 (Provo, Utah: BYU Extension Division), pp. 7, 8.

shall pray for and lay their hands upon them in my name; *and if they die they shall die unto me, and if they live they shall live unto me.*[35]

Heber Q. Hale, who during his visit to the spirit world saw the departed and was shown why they died, emphasized that priesthood administrations must conform to the will of God:

> *When a man is stricken ill, the question of prime importance is not is he going to live or die. What matters whether he lives or dies so long as the will of the Father is done. Surely we can trust him with God.* Herein lies the special duty and privilege of administration by the Holy Priesthood namely: It is given the Elders of the church to divine the will of the Father concerning the one upon whose head their hands are laid. If for any reason they are unable to presage the Father's will, then they should continue to pray in faith for the afflicted one, humbly, conceding supremacy of the will of God, that His will may be done, in earth as it is done in Heaven.

Upon learning of the death of a close friend and the glorious mission which awaited him, President Hale received this sacred insight:

> Then flooding through consciousness came this awful truth: That the *will of the Lord can be done on earth as it is in heaven only when we resign completely to his will and let His will be done in us and through us.* On account of the selfishness of man in the assertion of the personal will as against the will of God, *many persons who might otherwise have been taken in innocence and peace have been permitted to live and have passed a life of suffering and misery and debauchery and crime, and have lived to their own peril.*[36]

Appointed Time of Death

Changed by Unrighteousness

It appears that those who commit sin may shorten the period of time they are allowed to remain upon the earth to less than their appointed period. The writer of Ecclesiastes warned, "Be not over much wicked, neither be thou foolish: *why shouldest thou die before thy time?*"[37]

Job also saw that sin might cause men to die before their

---

[35]D&C 42:44.

[36]Heber Q. Hale, *op cit.*

[37]Eccles. 7:17.

appointed time. He asked, concerning those who died in the days of Noah,

> Hast thou marked the old way which wicked men have trodden?
>
> *Which were cut down out of time,* whose foundation was overflown with a flood:
>
> Which said unto God, Depart from us. . . .[38]

The prophet Alma saw that Satan sought to draw the wicked into his spirit kingdom, and said, while speaking of the death of Zoram the anti-Christ, "We see that the devil will not support his children at the last day, but *doth speedily drag them down to hell.*"[39]

According to Brigham Young, the prophet Joseph Smith taught that premature death was also a means by which the Lord might protect those who had labored valiantly in His cause from forfeiting their exaltation by falling into temptation or apostasy:

> Before Joseph's death *he had a revelation concerning myself and others, which signified that we had passed the ordeal, and that we should never apostatize from the faith* of the holy gospel; 'and' said Joseph, *'if there is any danger of your doing this, the Lord will take you to Himself forthwith, for you cannot stray from the truth.'* When men and women have travelled to a certain point in their labors in this life, God sets a seal upon them that they never can forsake their God or His kingdom; for, rather than they should do this, *He will at once take them to Himself. Probably this is so with many of the elders who are taken from us,* and over whom many ignorantly mourn. I say, to God give thanks, for who knows but that had they lived there might have been trials to pass through which they could not overcome. It is all right, blessed be the name of the Lord.[40]

When Heber C. Kimball was subjected to a severe trial in his life he prevailed upon the prophet Joseph to inquire of the Lord in his behalf, and was given the following revelation through the prophet:

> Tell him to go and do as he has been commanded, and if *I see that there is any danger of his apostatizing, I will take him to myself.*[41]

---

[38]Job 22:15-17.

[39]Al. 30:60.

[40]JD 12:103. Nov. 17, 1867.

[41]Spencer W. Kimball, *Tragedy or Destiny, op cit.,* p. 11. (Quoted from Orson F. Whitney, *Life of Heber C. Kimball, op cit.,* p. 336.)

Wickedness is thus accepted as another reason why some individuals die before their appointed time and before completing their life's mission.

Many Die to Fulfill Spirit World Responsibilities

There is ample evidence, from both the teachings of Latter-day Saint General Authorities and from statements made by those who have returned to earth from beyond the veil, that many die to fulfill responsibilities in the spirit world. Apparently there is continuous need for service there, and those in leadership positions are empowered to call mortal beings through the death process just as Church leaders call people to labor in responsible positions here upon earth.

Brigham Young, on one occasion, commented on Joseph Smith's labors in the spirit world and said, *"He is calling one after another to his aid, as the Lord sees he wants help."*[42]

President Wilford Woodruff taught in a similar manner, and expressed the thought that a council must have been held on the other side at which the decision was made to call a larger number through the veil than was usually customary:

> Every Apostle, every Seventy, every Elder, etc. who has died in the faith as soon as he passes to the other side of the veil, enters into the work of the ministry, and there is a thousand times more to preach there than there is here. *I have felt of late as if our brethren on the other side of the veil had held a council, and that they had said to this one, and that one, 'Cease thy work on earth, come hence, we need help' and they have called this man and that man.* It has appeared so to me in seeing the many men who have been called from our midst lately.[43]

He then told of a significant experience which indicates both the power to call through the veil and the power of choice possessed by Church leaders in the spirit world:

> Perhaps I may be permitted to relate a circumstance with which I am acquainted in relation to Bishop Roskelley, of Smithfield, Cache Valley. On one occasion he was suddenly taken very sick—near to death's door. While he lay in this condition, President Peter

[42]Brigham Young, "Preaching To Spirits In Prison," *The Contributor* (Salt Lake City, Utah: The Deseret News Company), Vol. X, No. 9, p. 321. July, 1889.

[43]JD 22:334. Oct. 8, 1881.

> Maughan, who was dead, came to him and said: 'Brother Roskellye [sic], *we held a council on the other side of the veil. I have had a great deal to do, and I have the privilege of coming here to appoint one man to come and help. I have had three names given to me in council, and you are one of them. I want to inquire into your circumstances.'* The Bishop told him what he had to do, and they conversed together as one man would converse with another. President Maughan then said to him: *'I think I will not call you. I think you are wanted here more than perhaps one of the others.'* Bishop Roskelley got well from that hour. Very soon after, the second man was taken sick, but not being able to exercise sufficient faith, Brother Roskelley did not go to him. By and by this man recovered, and on meeting Brother Roskelley he said: 'Brother Maughan came to me the other night and told me he was sent to call one man from the ward,' and he named two men as had been done to Brother Roskelley. A few days afterwards the third man was taken sick and died. Now, I name this to show a principle. *They have work on the other side of the veil; and they want men, and they call them.*[44]

A similar occurrence took place in Canada in 1921 following an agreement between Alberta Stake President Edward J. Wood and Stake Patriarch Henry L. Hinman. They had promised that whichever of the two died first would return and tell the other about the work being performed in the spirit world:

> Another of the memorable occasions in the life of President Wood occurred in 1921. "Uncle" Henry L. Hinman, Stake Patriarch and last living personal witness of Joseph Smith the Prophet among the Canadian Saints, half-jokingly made an agreement with Edward Wood. The two men, while speaking of the spirit world, agreed that the first to die should return and tell the other about the work going on there. "Uncle" Henry died shortly thereafter.
>
> President Wood later told of an incredible experience wherein Henry L. Hinman actually kept his promise and returned for a final visit with his friend. He woke up one night and *saw Uncle Henry standing in the doorway of his bedroom.* His first thought was that the departed Patriarch had come for him, so he got up and greeted his spirit visitor. *President Wood recalled noticing his own body still in bed and wondered what his wife would think when she found out he had left his body.* Mr. Wood asked Uncle Henry if he had seen his favorite Bible prophet, Elijah, yet. The answer was that *he had been too busy and had not had time to go where Elijah was.* In explaining the nature of his busy life in the spirit world, he told President Wood that *he*

---

[44] *Ibid.*

was engaged in missionary work. He told of six men who had just been called to assist in the work there. Three of the six were still living and acting on the Alberta Stake High Council. This puzzled President Wood very much, and he thought he had better try to write down the names of the three lest he forget them. He went to his bedside table and, *although he remembered the names, he could not write them.* This he said he could not understand, but as he turned to speak further with his visitor he saw him pass through the door and leave. Upon 're-entering his body' he woke his wife and told her of his visitor, but he could not then remember which three of his High Council had been called.

Soon after this experience, the Stake President was called to administer to one of his High Councilmen, Willard G. Smith. *Near the sick man's bed he said he saw written the words, 'This is one of the men.'* Mr. Smith said to him, 'You know all about this—that I am going to pass on—I want you to get my children together to finish my temple work.' He died the next day. Nearly two weeks later, as the Stake President entered the home of Ephraim Harker, another of his High Councilmen, *he said he heard a voice say, 'This is another of those three men.'* He died soon thereafter. Another week passed and President Wood went to the hospital to visit another High Councilman, John Heninger. *He said he knew by inspiration that this man was the last of the three.* President Wood hesitated as he was about to administer to him. Mr. Heninger said, 'I am going to leave right away and you already know it, don't you?' President Wood blessed him, but not that he would recover. He died during the same week. Said President Wood of these experiences, 'It is a wonderful vision and assurance of the identity of the spirit apart from the body.'[45]

During his visit to the world of spirits, President Heber Q. Hale saw that

> To a righteous person, birth into the spirit world is a glorious privilege and blessing. *The greatest spirits in the family of the Father have not usually been permitted to tarry longer in the flesh than to perform a certain mission.* They are then called to the world of spirit where the field is greater and the workers fewer. This earth career, therefore, may be longer or shorter as the Father wills.[46]

It can be seen that the work of the Church in the spirit world must take precedence over the Church organized among mortals. Those in positions of authority beyond the veil apparently can summon mortals through the death process to aid them, and can even affect and alter the pre-appointed time of an individual's death.

---

[45]Melvin S. Tagg, *The Life of Edward James Wood, op cit.*, pp. 90-92.
[46]Heber Q. Hale, *op cit.*

Some Mortals Given Life or Death Option

Some mortals, who are on the verge of death due to serious illness or accident, are permitted to enter the spirit world briefly and then make their own decision as to whether they should continue their mortal life or die. This was the choice given in 1838 to the wife of Wilford Woodruff, Phoebe Whittemore Carter Woodruff, as was recorded by her husband:

> December 3rd found my wife very low. I spent the day in taking care of her, and the day following I returned to Eaton to get some things for her. She seemed to be sinking gradually, and in the evening *the spirit apparently left her body, and she was dead.* The sisters gathered around, weeping, while I stood looking at her in sorrow. *The spirit and power of God began to rest upon me until, for the first time during her sickness, faith filled my soul, although she lay before me as one dead.*
>
> I had some oil that was consecrated for my anointing while in Kirtland. I took it and consecrated it again before the Lord, for anointing the sick. I then bowed down before the Lord, prayed for the life of my companion, and in the name of the Lord anointed her body with the oil. I then laid my hands upon her, and in the name of Jesus Christ *I rebuked the power of death and of the destroyer, and commanded the same to depart from her and the spirit of life to enter her body. Her spirit returned to her body, and from that hour she was made whole;* and we all felt to praise the name of God, and to trust in Him and keep His commandments.
>
> While I was undergoing this ordeal (as my wife related afterwards) her spirit left her body, and *she saw it lying upon the bed and the sisters there weeping. She looked at them and at me, and upon her babe;* while gazing upon this scene, *two persons came into the room, carrying a coffin, and told her they had come for her body. One of these messengers said to her that she might have her choice—she might go to rest in the spirit world, or, upon one condition, she could have the privilege of returning to her tabernacle and of continuing her labors upon the earth.* The condition was that if she felt she could stand by her husband, and with him pass through all the cares, trials, tribulations, and afflictions of life which he would be called upon to pass through for the gospel's sake unto the end, she might return. When she looked at the situation of her husband and child she said, 'Yes, I will do it.' *At the moment that decision was made the power of faith rested upon me, and when I administered to her, her spirit reentered her tabernacle, and she saw the messengers carry the coffin out the door.*[47]

---

[47]Wilford Woodruff, *Leaves From My Journal* (third book of the Faith-Promoting Series, Fourth edition, The Deseret News, 1909), pp. 59-60.

Marriner W. Merrill, who was badly injured in an accident in Richmond, Cache County, Utah, in the early 1860's, was given a choice of life or death, and chose to remain in mortality. He later became President of the Logan temple and an apostle. His son told of his accident and spirit world experience:

> Indians were never very troublesome in Cache Valley and the country north, yet at times threatening situations arose. It was during one of these occasions that Father and a number of other men from northern Cache Valley were called to go to the protection of the settlers further north.
>
> A heavy rain fell just before their departure which made the roads and the countryside extremely muddy and slippery. As Father took a detour, he had gone out a short distance from the company when his horse slipped and fell with Father under him. When the other men of the party reached the scene Father was motionless and from all appearance, dead.
>
> *Father relates that his spirit left his body and stood, as it were, in the air above it. He could see his body and the men standing around and he heard their conversation. At his option he could re-enter his body or remain in spirit. His reflection upon his responsibility to his family and his great desire to live caused him to choose to enter his body again and live.* As he did so he regained consciousness and experienced severe pains incident to the injuries which he had suffered from the accident.[48]

Peter E. Johnson, who entered the spirit world while fulfilling a mission for the Church, was also given the option of life or death. His experience is remarkable because the privilege of his being able to make the choice was obtained at the insistance of his deceased progenitors, who were extremely desirous that he remain on earth to perform genealogy and temple work for them. As in other instances where a choice was made available to the spirit world entrants, Elder Johnson was allowed to see the feelings of others left on earth before making his decision. The following is his account of the conversation he held with certain apostles beyond the veil:

> As soon as I came into their presence, *I was asked if I desired to remain there.* This seemed strange, for it had never occurred to me that we would have any choice there in the spirit world as to whether we

[48]Bryant S. Hinckley, *The Faith of Our Pioneer Fathers* (Salt Lake City, Utah: Deseret Book Co., 1959), p. 183.

should remain or return to the earth life. *I was asked if I felt satisfied with conditions there. I informed them that I was, and had no desire to return to the fever and misery from which I had been suffering while in the body. After some little conversation this question was repeated, with the same answer.* Then I asked; 'If I remain, what will I be asked to do?' I was informed that I would preach the Gospel to the spirits there, as I had been preaching it to the people here, and that I would do so under the immediate direction of the Prophet Joseph. . . .

I was again asked if I desired to remain. This bothered me considerably, for I had already expressed myself as being satisfied. I then inquired why it was that I was asked so often if I was satisfied and if I desired to remain. *I was then informed that my progenitors had made a request that if I chose I might be granted the privilege of returning, to again take up my mortal body, in order that I might gather my father's genealogy and do the necessary work in the temple for my ancestors.* As I was still undecided, one of the apostles said: 'We will now show you what will take place if you remain here in the spirit world; after which you can decide.'

When we returned to the place where my body was lying, I was informed with emphasis that my first duty would be to watch the body until after it had been disposed of, as that was necessary knowledge for me to have in the resurrection. I then saw the Elders send a message to President Rich, at Chattanooga, and in due time all preparations were made for the shipment of my body to Utah. One thing seemed peculiar to me, that *I was able to read the telegram as it ran along the wires as easily as I could read the pages of a book.* I could see President Rich, when he received the telegram in Chattanooga. He walked the floor, wringing his hands, with the thought in his mind: 'How can I send a message to his father?'

The message was finally sent, and *I could follow it on the wire.* I saw the station and the telegraph operator at Price, Utah. I heard the instrument click as the message was received, and saw the operator write out the message and send it by phone from Price to Huntington. I also saw clearly the Huntington office and the man who received the message. I could see clearly and distinctly the people on the street. *I did not have to hear what was said, for I was able to read their thoughts from their countenances.* The message was delivered to my aunt, who went out with others to find my father. In due time he received the message. He did not seem to be overcome by the news, but began to make preparations to meet the body.

I then saw my father at the railroad station in Price, waiting for my body to arrive. Apparently he was unaffected; but when he heard the whistle of the train which was carrying my body, he went behind the depot and cried as if his heart would break. While I had been accompanying the body en route, I was still able to see what was going on at home. The distance, apparently, did not affect my vision. As the train approached the station I went to my father's side, and, seeing his great anguish, *I informed my companion that I would return. He expressed his approval of my decision and said he was pleased with the choice I had made.*

By some spiritual power, all these things had been shown to me as they would occur if I did not return to the body. Immediately upon making this choice or decision, my companion said: "Good, *Your progenitors will be pleased with your decision.*" I asked the question why and *I was told that it was their desire that I should return to the body.*[49]

It appears that one must have special permission from Church authorities beyond the veil to return to earth after once passing into the world of spirits. Having received permission was mentioned by the wife of David Lynn Brooks, who returned to visit her bereaved husband two years after her death which occurred May 26, 1945. Elder Brooks recorded,

I went in the house, turned out the lights and lay down on the studio couch to relax for a few minutes. I had no sooner relaxed when I heard a voice, the voice of my wife, she was praying. Oh! how wonderful to hear that beautiful voice which I recognized the minute she spoke. At the close of the prayer I was so tense I hardly dared breathe for fear of disturbing this beautiful experience. Immediately I saw a dim light filling the room, it was not a brilliant light but a soft light, then it began to part in the center like a curtain. As it parted, I saw in the opening the most beautiful sight in all the world, my lovely wife. She stood about four or five feet away from me and made no attempt to come closer. She spoke to me and said, 'Lynn, *I have seen your sorrow and grief* but it won't be long until you will be with me, that we might again enjoy each others' companionship and love; I have wanted to come to you before this, but *only tonight was I given permission by the priesthood to visit with you.'* She told me that my grief had made her sad and that I should try to be happy and *whenever I needed her, I should knock or pray and she would be with me, although I may never see her* again until I come into the world of spirits. She then invited me to look into the spirit world, and asked what I could see. *I told her I could see a group of people seated in a room or hall at a table or at desks with note pads and pencils. She then asked, 'Do you know who these people are?' I told her I didn't recognize any of them. She then asked me if I remembered the people we had done the temple work for in 1929 and 1930. She and I had worked the entire winter gathering genealogy of her people and then we did the temple work for them. She then told*

[49]Peter E. Johnson, *Relief Society Magazine, op cit.,* Vol. VII, pp. 451-453.

> *me she had been called by the priesthood to teach the gospel to those people and that she was very happy doing that work.* She then told me not to mourn, that *she was always close by.* She bade me goodbye. The light gathered from the two sides and was then gone. As soon as the vision closed, I was on my feet, tears streaming down my cheeks in torrents. This time, they were tears of joy; no sorrow now.[50]

It appears that some who enter the spirit world before their time are not privileged to choose between life and death. Rather, they are required to return and let their lives run their course. This was so in the case of Alpheus Cutler, who returned from the spirit world and later apostatized from the Church. He formed the apostate "True Church of Latter-day Saints." Years later he bore this testimony to his grandson, Abraham A. Kimball, who recorded it as follows:

> I know that Joseph Smith was a prophet of God, and I know that Brigham Young is his legal successor, and I always did know it. But the trouble with me was I wanted to lead, and could not be led. I have run my race and sealed my doom, and I know what I have got to meet.
>
> *I died once, and was dead for some length of time. My spirit left my body and went to the land of spirits. I saw the crown that I should wear if I remained faithful, and the condemnation I should receive if I did not. I begged to remain, but was informed that I must return and warn the people to repent, as my work on earth was not yet done.*
>
> After my spirit returned to my body, those around discovered the appearance of life. The first words that I spoke were to Sidney Rigdon, who was stooping over me. I called upon him to repent of his sins, or he would be damned.

---

[50]Personal Records of David Lynn Brooks, Morgan, Utah. Heber Q. Hale also learned that one must have special permission from Church authorities beyond the veil to return to earth after once passing into the world of spirits. He reported his encounter with the recently deceased president of the Church, Joseph F. Smith, who obtained this permission for him:

> The group was engaged in earnest conversation. One of their number parted from the rest and came walking down the path. I at once recognized my esteemed *Pres. Joseph F. Smith. He embraced me as a father would his son,* and after a few words of greeting, quickly remarked 'You have not come to stay,' which remark I understood more as a declaration than an interrogation. For the first time I became fully conscious of my uncompleted mission on earth and *as much as I would have liked to remain, I at once asked Pres. Smith if I might return. 'You have expressed a righteous desire,' he replied, 'and I will take the matter up with the authorities and let you know later.'*

Brother Hale told how they then separated and later met, when he received permission to return to mortality:

> Pres. Smith informed me that *I had been given permission to return* and complete my mission on the earth which the Lord had appointed me to fill.

My grandfather paused here, but continued by saying: 'I want you to go back to your father, taking your brother Isaac with you, as I know he is a good man, and remain steadfast to "Mormonism."

'Let what may turn up, *never yield the point; for it will save and exalt you in the kingdom of God.'*

He wept like a child after saying this. He then said to me: 'One favor I wish to ask of you, namely, that you will not divulge this confession to those whom I lead while I live.'[51]

Other Factors Affecting Time of Death

Just as the prayerful requests of the righteous, the evil deeds of the wicked, organizational needs in the spirit world, and the personal choice of the seriously ill or injured may cause one to die at other than his appointed time, yet other circumstances may cause untimely death. War, plagues, accidents, and murders all take their toll, and it is difficult to assume that all who thus die are passing through the veil in the time and manner previously appointed.

President Brigham Young believed that many of the diseases and plagues of the earth caused individuals to die before their appointed time, and said,

> It is not the design of the Father that the earthly career of any should terminate until they have lived out their days; and *the reason that so few do live out their days, is because of the force of sin in the world and the power of death over the human family. To these causes, and not to the design of the Creator, may be attributed the fact that disease stalks abroad,* laying low the aged, middle-aged, youth, and infants, and the human family generally by millions.[52]

In his discourse, "Tragedy or Destiny," Elder Spencer W. Kimball observed that

> There have been hundreds of thousands of young men *rushed prematurely into eternity through the ravages of war.* . . I am confident that there is a time to die. I am not a fatalist. *I believe that many people die before 'their time' because they are careless, abuse their bodies, take unnecessary chances, or expose themselves to hazards, accidents and sickness.*[53]

---

[51]Abraham A. Kimball, "Finding A Father," *Gems For the Young Folks* (fourth book of the Faith-Promoting Series; Salt Lake City, Utah: Juvenile Instructor Office, 1881), pp. 16-17.

[52]JD 14:230. Sept. 16, 1871.

[53]Spencer W. Kimball, *Tragedy or Destiny, op cit.*, p. 3.

The Lord implies that the sick that "have not faith to be healed" may either live or die unless their passing is actually determined by their being "appointed unto death."[54] Of this passage in the Doctrine and Covenants Elder Kimball commented, "If not 'appointed unto death' and sufficient faith is developed, life can be spared. *But if there is not enough faith many die before their time.*"[55]

President Heber Q. Hale, who conversed with numerous spirit beings during his entry beyond the veil, became aware that some individuals die before their time because of their own external circumstances rather than from a divine summons to the spirit world, and wrote,

> Many die because they have no faith to be healed. Others yet live along and pass out of the world of mortals without any special manifestations or action of the divine will.[56]

It appears that sometimes individuals die because they are observers or participants in important events rather than that their appointed time of death is near. On occasions dozens, or even hundreds and thousands, have died in fulfillment of divine edicts and prophecies, yet most of those who died seemingly had little to do with the problems at hand. When Elijah called down fire from heaven which consumed two groups of Israelite soldiers,[57] was God vindicating the word of his prophet or was He calling home the hundred men at their appointed time of death? When Gideon and his three hundred men surprised the Midianite hosts and frightened them so that they slew one another in the darkness until 120,000 lay dead,[58] was this the fulfillment of the Lord's promise to Gideon or were the slain Midianite soldiers being called to die at their appointed moment? When 185,000 troops of the Assyrian king Sennacherib suddenly died overnight during their seige of Jerusalem,[59] was the Lord answering king Hezekiah's prayer for salvation[60] or summoning the 185,000 soldiers through the veil at their appointed time of death?

---

[54]See D&C 42:43, 44, 48.
[55]Spencer W. Kimball, *Tragedy or Destiny, op cit.*, p. 6.
[56]Heber Q. Hale, *op cit.*
[57]2 Ki. 1:9-12.
[58]Jud. 7, 8:10.
[59]Is. 37:36.
[60]Is. 37:15-20.

Yet another factor enters into the picture as the matter of untimely deaths is considered. It appears that God, in His wisdom, is able to know if an individual needs to remain on earth for an extended period to gain further knowledge and experience, or if a brief appearance on earth for the purpose of obtaining a body is sufficient. Some pre-mortal beings are so advanced, apparently, that their eternal progression is best accomplished by having them linger on earth only a few days or months, and then allowing them to progress further by death and re-entry into the spirit realms. Before coming to earth they have already progressed past the normal level of earth activity, and they have little need for the experiences of earth life. Joseph Smith said,

> *The Lord takes many away even in infancy, that they may escape the envy of man, and the sorrows and evils of this present world; they were too pure, too lovely, to live on this earth;* therefore, if rightly considered, instead of mourning we have reason to rejoice as they are delivered from evil, and we shall soon have them again. . . . *The only difference between the old and the young dying is, one lives longer in heaven and eternal light and glory than the other, and is freed a little sooner from this miserable, wicked world.*[61]

Observations Concerning When and Why Men Die

In this chapter it has been shown that God rules in the affairs of men. He determines the time and location of man's birth, the major mortal experiences which will confront him, and appoints the time of his death. There is evidence which indicates that spirits in the pre-mortal stage of life may have had opportunity to make choices in these areas for themselves and then submit their proposals for divine ratification. This seems reasonable: it is compatible with the method of operation which is often used to best advantage by loving parents; it conforms to the procedure found in God's Church which is instituted to teach man the ways of eternity. However, little is known concerning the extent of man's agency in the pre-mortal existence in relation to the divine will and rule of God. Thus man is without full understanding of the manner in which his life is shaped and is compelled to rely, through faith,

---

[61]HC 4:553-554. Mar. 20. 1842. For further information on the fate of little children who die see pp. 83-86, 252-256.

on the love, justice, mercy, and parental concern of his Heavenly Father. As the Savior taught,

> Which of you by taking thought can add one cubit unto his stature?
>
> And why take ye thought for raiment? Consider the lilies of the field, how they grow; they toil not, neither do they spin. . . .
>
> Therefore take no thought, saying, What shall we eat? or, What shall we drink? or, Wherewithal shall we be clothed?
>
> (For after all these things do the Gentiles seek:) for *your heavenly Father knoweth that ye have need of all these things.*
>
> But *seek ye first the kingdom of God, and his righteousness; and all these things shall be added unto you.*[62]

Death is inseparable from life; it is the culmination of the life process. God is aware of man's needs in life and He is aware of his needs for death.

Just as some men are able to shape and develop their lives, there is evidence that they can also shape their death. It appears that to those who have labored valiantly and righteously to further God's eternal program, the Father grants protection against danger, He strengthens their faith so that they may be healed, He prolongs their life so they may fulfill their earth missions, or hastens their death in order that they may labor beyond the veil. He heeds the prayers of the faithful in their behalf, and on occasion, He even allows them the choice between life and death. Through the close bonds of understanding and communication with God which they establish, they are able to know and comprehend the divine will and are able to control and shape their life, fate, and eternal destiny as they deserve in righteousness. The decision that they be called through the veil is carefully weighed and considered in the eternal councils before they are summoned to a new phase of life.

In contrast, there are hosts of other people who have become stagnant in their mortal progression. They live life from day to day, never growing or changing in their relationship with God. Though God is aware of them and is concerned

[62]Mt. 6:27-28, 31-33.

for them, they are not the valiant laborers in his kingdom. They have risen to the level of existence which satisfies their daily needs—they will accept life, and death, as it comes. They react to external conditions, but fail to act of their own volition to improve their relationship with God. The status of the earth is unaffected by their presence and conduct. By eternal standards their standing before God will not be altered whether they die tomorrow or twenty years in the future. Can it be this group who, in death as in life, drift into the spirit world without summons as some external factor in their environment affects them? Do they die from sickness before their time because of lack of faith to be healed? Or do they die in accidents or war because of lack of desire to seek and inability to obtain divine guidance and protection? They approach mortal life with disinterest and unconcern and fill no real mission here; they will carry the same attitude into the spirit world, and have little effect on the divine program there. Who can say whether they die at their appointed time, or go into the spirit world as a matter of personal happenstance, without divine calling? And what difference does their time of death make to them in the eternal program? None, apparently. What does it matter if they die twenty years before their time? Perhaps different friends will mourn for them, but in the eternal relationship the time is negligible, and "all do not die at once, and this mattereth not; all is as one day with God, and time only is measured unto men."[63]

Yet a third group exists. There are those who are wicked and who seek to destroy the work of God. These are called to the associations of the wicked in the spirit world by Satan or are cast from the earth by God to dwell in the presence of Lucifer. Because of their wickedness and the master whom they choose to obey, such beings often forfeit the privilege of completing their appointed earth span and die before their time.

All men must die.[64] No good is accomplished by uninspired speculation as to the reason why certain individuals

[63]Al. 40:8.

[64]Al. 12:27; 2 Ne. 9:4, 6.

died. Especially in the case of the dead should one heed the Savior's warning, "Judge not, that ye be not judged,"[65] lest they challenge him at the judgment bar of God.[66] Yet when one who is dearly beloved is stricken and approaching death, it is right and proper that his family seek revealed confirmation that it is his appointed time, and that his death is in accordance with the divine will. The Holy Ghost is the Comforter, and in this circumstance, perhaps more than any other, can His comforting influence and reassurance be felt.

President Heber J. Grant recorded his search for this spiritual confirmation in behalf of his daughter at the time of her mother's death:

> *I was thoroughly convinced in my own mind and in my own heart, when my first wife left me by death, that it was the will of the Lord that she should be called away. I bowed in humility at her death.* The Lord saw fit upon that occasion to give to one of my little children a testimony that the death of her mother was the will of the Lord.
>
> About one hour before my wife died, I called my children into her room and told them that their mother was dying and for them to bid her good-bye. One of the little girls, about twelve years of age, said to me: 'Papa, I do not want my mamma to die. I have been with her in the hospital in San Francisco for six months; time and time again when mamma was in distress, you have administered to her, and she has been relieved of her pain and quietly gone to sleep. I want you to lay hands upon my mamma and heal her.'
>
> *I told my little girl that we all had to die sometime, and that I felt assured in my heart that her mother's time had arrived.* She and the rest of the children left the room.
>
> I then knelt down by the bed of my wife (who by this time had lost conciousness) and I told the Lord I acknowledged his hand in life, in death, in joy, in sorrow, in prosperity, or adversity, I thanked him for the knowledge I had that my wife belonged to me for all eternity, that through the power and authority of the priesthood here on the earth that I could and would have my wife forever if I were only faithful as she had been. But I told the Lord that I lacked the strength to have my wife die and to have it affect the faith of my little children in the ordinances of the gospel of Jesus Christ; and *I supplicated the Lord with all the strength that I possessed, that he would give to that little girl of mine a knowledge that it was his mind and his will that her mamma should die.*

[65]Mt. 7:1.

[66]See Moro. 10:27; Ro. 14:10.

Within an hour my wife passed away, and I called the children back into the room. My little boy, about five and one-half or six years of age, was weeping bitterly, and the little girl twelve years of age took him in her arms and said: 'Do not weep, Heber; *since we went out of this room, the voice of the Lord from heaven has said to me, In the death of your mamma the will of the Lord shall be done.*'[67]

Two years later, upon the death of his son, President Grant again recorded how the Comforter had labored in his behalf to help him understand the Lord's will:

I had been blessed with only two sons. One of them died at five years of age and the other at seven.

My last son died of a hip disease. I had built great hopes that he would live to spread the Gospel at home and abroad and be an honor to me. About an hour before he died I had a dream that *his mother, who was dead, came for him, and that she brought with her a messenger, and she told this messenger to take the boy while I was asleep.* In the dream I thought I awoke, and I seized my son and fought for him and finally succeeded in getting him away from the messenger who had come to take him, and in so doing I dreamed that I stumbled and fell upon him.

I dreamed that I fell upon his sore hip, and the terrible cries and anguish of the child drove me nearly wild. I could not stand it, and I jumped up and ran out of the house so as not to hear his distress. I dreamed that after running out of the house I met Brother Joseph E. Taylor and told him of these things.

He said: 'Well, Heber, *do you know what I would do if my wife came for one of her children—I would not struggle for that child; I would not oppose her taking that child away. If a mother who had been faithful had passed beyond the veil, she would know of the suffering and the anguish her child may have to suffer. She should know whether that child might go through life as a cripple and whether it would be better or wiser for that child to be relieved from the torture of life. And when you stop to think, Brother Grant, that the mother of that boy went down into the shadow of death to give him life, she is the one who ought to have the right to take him or leave him.*'

I said, 'I believe you are right, Brother Taylor, and if she comes again, she shall have the boy without any protest on my part.'

After coming to that conclusion, I was awakened by my brother, B. F. Grant, who was staying that night with us. He came into the room and told me that the child was dying. I went in the front room and sat down. There was a vacant chair between me and my wife

[67]Bryant S. Hinckley, *Heber J. Grant, Highlights in the Life of a Great Leader* (Salt Lake City, Utah: Deseret Book Co., 1951), pp. 243-244.

who is now living, and *I felt the presence of that boy's deceased mother sitting in that chair.* I did not tell anybody what I felt, but I turned to my wife and said, "Do you feel anything strange?'

'Yes, I feel assured that Heber's mother is sitting between us, waiting to take him away.'

Now, I am naturally, I believe, a sympathetic man, I was raised as an only child with all the affection that a mother could lavish upon a boy. I believe that I am naturally affectionate and sympathetic and that I shed tears for my friends—tears of joy for their success and tears of sorrow for their misfortunes. But I sat by the deathbed of my little boy and saw him die, without shedding a tear. *My living wife, my brother, and I upon that occasion experienced a sweet, peaceful, and heavenly influence in my home, as great as I have ever experienced in my life. And no person can tell me that every other latter-day Saint that has a knowledge of the Gospel in his heart and soul can really mourn for his loved ones, only in the loss of their society here in this life.*[68]

To the Latter-day Saint who knows and understands the eternal gospel program the death of a righteous loved one is regarded as an opportunity for the departed one to grow and progress towards his eternal goal. Though they weep for the lost companionship of their dear one,[69] faithful Church members react to death as did President Grant:

I never think of my wives and my dear mother, my two boys, my daughter, my departed friends, and my beloved associates as being in the graveyard. I think only of the joy they have in meeting with father and mother and loved ones who have been true and faithful to the Gospel of the Lord Jesus Christ. My mind reaches out to the wonderful joy and satisfaction and happiness that they are having, and it robs the grave of its sting.[70]

Dying Unto the Lord

In his King Follett discourse the prophet Joseph Smith said,

What have we to console us in relation to the dead? *We have reason to have the greatest hope and consolation for our dead of any people on the earth; for we have seen them walk worthily in our midst, and seen them sink*

---

[68]*Ibid.*, pp. 246-248.

[69]They should do so:

Thou shalt live together in love, insomuch that thou shalt weep for the loss of them that die, and more especially for those that have not hope of a glorious resurrection. (D&C 42:45. See also 1 Thess. 4:13)

[70]Bryant S. Hinckley, *Life of a Great Leader, op cit.*, pp. 248-249.

> *asleep in the arms of Jesus; and those who have died in the faith are now in the celestial kingdom of God.* And hence in the glory of the sun.
>
> You mourners have occasion to rejoice, speaking of the death of Elder King Follett; for your husband and father is gone to wait until the resurrection of the dead—until the perfection of the remainder; for *at the resurrection your friend will rise in perfect felicity and go to celestial glory, while many must wait myriads of years before they can receive the like blessings; and your expectations and hopes are far above what man can conceive.*[71]

This he spoke of one who had died in the Lord and would enjoy the privileges of the paradise of spirits and of the first resurrection. In the last days the Lord has revealed the contrasting status of those who do and those who do not die unto Him:

> *It shall come to pass that those that die in me shall not taste of death, for it shall be sweet unto them;*
>
> *And they that die not in me, wo unto them, for their death is bitter.*[72]

On another occasion he revealed the great promises he held for those who die in Him:

> *Blessed are the dead that die in the Lord,* from henceforth, when the Lord shall come, and old things shall pass away, and all things become new, they shall rise from the dead and shall not die after, and shall receive an inheritance before the Lord, in the holy city.[73]

Paul implied to the Saints in Rome that the Church members who lived to serve the Lord were those who would also die unto him:

> For none of us liveth to himself, and no man dieth to himself.
>
> *For whether we live, we live unto the Lord, and whether we die, we die unto the Lord: whether we live therefore, or die, we are the Lord's.*
>
> For to this end Christ both died, and rose, and revived, that he might be Lord both of the dead and living.[74]

Yet in the final analysis the criterion which separates those who die unto the Lord and those who do not seems to be the degree of righteousness involved. As Paul taught,

---

[71]HC 6:315. April 7, 1844.
[72]D&C 42:46-47.
[73]D&C 63:49.
[74]Ro. 14:7-9.

> O death, where is thy sting? O grave, where is thy victory? *The sting of death is sin. . . .*[75]

More concerning the spirit world fate of the righteous and the wicked will be found in chapters III, V, and VI.

SUMMARY

1. Man's time and place of birth, his major life circumstances, and his appointed time of death, are determined by God.
2. There is evidence that pre-mortal spirits may be permitted to choose, subject to the approval of God, their earth parents, their marriage partner, their children and their guardian angel before coming to earth. In doing so they apparently select a social and moral level which is compatible with their own level. It is implied that they have the privilege of choosing the time they come to earth.
3. There is evidence that pre-mortal spirits may be permitted to choose the reward they desire and the course of earth activity and experience which will enable them to gain the reward they select.
4. There is a specific time appointed for every man to die. Though this time is apparently fixed before he comes to earth, there is evidence that it may be reconsidered and subject to revision during his mortal lifetime.
5. The Lord protects those who are laboring valiantly in His cause so that they are able to complete their life mission before dying. However, He oftens calls them through the veil soon after the completion of their work.
6. Apparently many people die at other than their appointed time, because of
    - A. The pleas of the righteous that their lives be lengthened or shortened,
    - B. Unrighteousness which allows man to be called down to hell by Satan or causes the Lord to banish him from mortality as He did the wicked in the days of Noah,
    - C. The danger of sin or apostasy among Saints who would otherwise have merited the celestial kingdom. The Lord has promised He would call some individuals through the veil rather than allow them to lose their exaltation,
    - D. A call from beyond the veil due to the need for their services in the labors of the spirit world,

---

[75] 1 Cor. 15:55-56.

E. Their choice to remain in mortality, for the opportunity to choose between life and death is given to some who stand at the brink of death,

F. The desire of deceased relatives who request that an individual be allowed to continue in mortality to labor in their behalf,

G. Lack of faith to be healed or inability to secure the protecting influence of the Holy Spirit, thereby allowing external factors rather than divine summons to control man's time of death. Apparently many die, not because of any manifestation or action of divine will, but because they are associated by circumstance in accidents, wars, earthquakes, pestilence, etc.

H. The God-directed privilege of choice spirits who have already advanced beyond the level of earth life to by-pass the strife and sorrow of mortality through death in infancy or early childhood.

7. Satan also has power to cause sickness unto death or accident. His power may be rebuked through the authority of the holy priesthood.

8. Uninspired priesthood administrations which are not in accordance with divine will may alter the life course or time of death of the recipient in a manner at variance with his mortal and eternal well-being. In administrations where no specific prompting is given the ordinance should take the form of a request that the will of the Lord be done.

9. There is evidence that those who go into the spirit world must secure permission from Church authorities there before they can return to mortality.

10. The power to summon individuals through the veil is not held by God alone, but may be delegated to spirit world Church authorities who are authorized to summon mortal beings into the spirit realms to aid them in their labors.

11. Certain facts are known about the nature of spirit beings:

    A. They experience the sense of touch and embrace one another, etc.,

    B. They can see into the future and visualize things as they "may be," as well as "will be,"

    C. They can read the thoughts of mortals by merely looking at their countenances,

D. They can influence the actions of mortals by their requests in the world of spirits.

12. The reason people die and whether or not they died at their appointed time and fulfilled their life mission is often unknown to others. Men should refrain from judging their fellow man in death as in life.

13. Faithful Latter-day Saints are entitled to know if the approaching death of a loved one is according to the will of God through the ministration of the Holy Spirit. That Being also serves as a Comforter in times of sorrow and death.

14. Those who die unto the Lord are promised by Him that their death shall be sweet. The death of those who do not die unto the Lord shall be bitter. The sting of death is sin.

15. Though Latter-day Saints should weep for the loss of companionship of departed loved ones, they should also find joy in the knowledge that the dead individual has been permitted to progress to a more advanced sphere and enjoys far greater capacities than he did in mortality.

CHAPTER III

THE PARADISE OF THE RIGHTEOUS

Various Meanings of Term "Paradise"

THERE IS CONFUSION IN THE THEOLOGICAL CIRCLES OF CHRIS-tendom concerning the term "paradise." Latter-day Saints differ with the protestant world in their understanding of the term, and they feel that they have greater insight into the true meaning of the word. The sectarian concept that man, upon death, goes directly to his final resting place in either heaven or hell, causes them to regard the term "paradise" as synonymous with "heaven." Latter-day Saints understand that there is an intermediate dwelling place where one's spirit resides between death and the time he is assigned to his final resting place. To them "paradise" is a reference to either all or the righteous portion of that intermediate place.

As the Savior hung on the cross he conversed with the two thieves who shared his crucifixion. One of them, still defiant in death, hurled the challenge, "If thou be Christ, save thyself and us." His companion, however, rebuked him, and said unto Jesus, "Lord, remember me when thou comest into thy kingdom." The Savior replied, "Verily I say unto thee, To day shalt thou be with me in paradise."[1]

According to the Protestant theologian, He was promising the thief that he would be able to go to heaven when he died. Yet the Savior did not go to heaven that day. Indeed, three days later he told Mary Magdelene,

> *Touch me not; for I am not yet ascended to my Father:* but go to my brethren, and say unto them, I ascend unto my Father, and your Father; and to my God, and your God.[2]

---

[1]Lk. 23:43. See Joseph Smith's explanation of this passage in HC 5:424-425.
[2]Jn. 20:17.

Where did He go as his body lay in the tomb? Peter gave the answer, saying that Christ was "Put to death in the flesh, but quickened by the Spirit: By which also he went and preached unto the spirits in prison. . . ."[3]

Nothing is known concerning the attitude and deeds of the thief who hung on the cross. It would seem, however, if he were a thief whose deeds were worthy of crucifixion, that he would not find himself among the righteous when he entered the world of spirits. If this is true, then the Savior was using the term "paradise" in the general sense which includes all of the world of spirits. If, by some unknown means, however, the thief merited entrance into the righteous portion of the spirit world, then he went with Jesus into that portion of the spirit realm which bears the specific title, "paradise."

In summary, the term "paradise" is used in three ways:

1) meaning heaven, or the final resting place of the righteous in sectarian terminology. Latter-day Saints understand this usage but choose not to use it themselves.

2) meaning the entire world of spirits, including all who have lived on the earth and then died. Jesus, in his statement to the thief, apparently used the term with this meaning.

3) meaning the habitation of the righteous within the spirit world.

This chapter is a consideration of paradise in the third sense of the word—the spirit dwelling place of the righteous.

Descriptions of Paradise

Vivid descriptions of paradise have been made by those who have visited the spirit world and then have been permitted to return to earth. They have described in great detail the glorious sights they have seen. To record the many different sights of the spirit world is as difficult as to portray the entire range of vistas available in the mortal world, for there are many accounts of different portions and areas. Yet patterns exist in the cumulative accounts from which interesting generalities may be drawn.

---

[3] 1 Pet. 3:18-19.

Plants and Trees

One recurrent theme is the presence of many trees, shrubs, and rich foliage. President George Albert Smith described in this manner these trees and the beautiful lake which he saw in the spirit world in vision or in the spirit:

> I found myself standing with my back to a *large and beautiful lake,* facing a *great forest of trees.* There was no one in sight, and there was no boat upon the lake or any other visible means to indicate how I might have arrived there. I realized, or seemed to realize, that I had finished my work in mortality and had gone home. I began to look around, to see if I could not find someone. There was no evidence of anyone living there, just those *great, beautiful trees* in front of me and the *wonderful lake* behind me.
>
> I began to explore, and soon I found a *trail through the woods* which seemed to have been used very little, and which was *almost obscured by grass.* I followed this *trail,* and after I had walked for some time and traveled a considerable distance through the forest, I saw a man coming towards me.[4]

Elder Jacob Hamblin, who ventured into the spirit world in the summer of 1858, said,

> The place where I was, seemed very desirable to remain in. It was *divided into compartments by walls,* from which appeared to grow out *vines and flowers, displaying an endless variety of colors.*[5]

---

[4]Preston Nibley (comp), *Sharing the Gospel With Others, Excerpts from the Sermons of President Smith* (Salt Lake City, Utah: Deseret Book Co., 1948), p. 111. President Smith told of the way he entered the spirit world in this manner:

> A number of years ago I was seriously ill, in fact, I think everyone gave me up but my wife. With my family I went to St. George, Utah, to see if it would improve my health. We went as far as we could by train, and then continued the journey in a wagon, in the bottom of which a bed had been made for me.
>
> In St. George we arranged for a tent for my health and comfort, with a built-in floor raised about a foot above the ground, and we could roll up the south side of the tent to make the sunshine and fresh air available. I became so weak as to be scarcely able to move. It was a slow and exhausting effort for me even to turn over in bed.
>
> One day, under these conditions, I lost consciousness of my surroundings and thought I had passed to the Other Side. (pp. 110-111.)

[5]Jacob Hamblin, *Jacob Hamblin, op cit.,* p. 58. Elder Hamblin prefaced the account of his entry into the spirit world by writing:

> During the summer of 1858, when I was at my home on the Santa Clara, one morning about 9 o'clock, while engaged in cutting some of the large branches from a cottonwood tree, I fell a distance of twenty or thirty feet to the ground. I was badly bruised, and was carried to my house for dead, or nearly so.
>
> I came to my senses about 8 o'clock in the evening, and threw off from my stomach quite a quantity of blood. I requested the brethren who were standing

Heber Q. Hale also commented on the beautiful colors of the foliage and saw that there were attractive parks there:

> *The vegetation and landscape was beautiful beyond description: not all green, as here, but gold with varying shades of pink, orange, and lavender, as the rain-bow. A sweet calmness pervaded everything.* . . . I moved forward, covering an appreciable distance and consuming considerable time viewing the wonderful sights of *landscape, parks, trees and flowers* and meeting people, some of whom I knew, but many thousands of whom I did not recognize as acquaintances. I presently approached a small group of men standing in *a path lined with gorgeous trenches of flowers, grasses and shrubbery, all of a golden hue, marking the approach to a beautiful building.*[6]

President Jedediah M. Grant commented on the beautiful flowers he saw while visiting paradise:

> I have seen good gardens on this earth, but I never saw any to compare with those that were there. I saw *flowers of numerous kinds,* and some with from fifty to a hundred different colored flowers growing upon one stalk.[7]

Apparently in the midst of this beautiful foliage and shrubbery is the tree of life, for the Lord has revealed that it stands "in the midst of the paradise of God."[8]

---

around to administer to me, and they did so. *From the time I fell from the tree until then was lost to me, so far as earthly matters were concerned.*

During the time my body lay in this condition, it seemed to me that *I went up from the earth and looked down upon it, and it appeared like a dark ball.* (pp. 57-58.)

[6]Heber Q. Hale, *op cit.*

[7]JD 4:136. Dec 4, 1856. Flowers were also seen in the spirit world by the young daughter of Emma and Kee Delgarito, who was called back from the dead through the administration of the elders:

> On arrival, after the long worrisome bus ride, her [Mrs. Delgarito's] first thought was to inquire if there might be some Mormon Elders in the area and in a short time two young men were located and were happy to go with her to the hospital. As the three walked into the room where the girl lay the nurse in attendance was just in the act of drawing the sheet up over her face. Emma ran to the bedside and attempted to take the sheet away but was restrained with the words, 'Your daughter just passed away.' Emma cried, 'But I brought these men to administer to her, she must not die.' Against the wishes of the attendant the covering was taken from the little face and the Elders gave her a wonderful blessing wherein they promised that she would live. Gradually the eyelids began to twitch, then fluttered open and the child recognized her mother. She looked at the missionaries and said, 'These are the men who brought me out of *the meadow where the flowers were growing.'* Her mother asked, 'What meadow do you mean, darling?' She answered, *'I was running through a meadow filled with beautiful flowers. These men caught up to me, took my hand and brought me back.'* Emma knew that she had witnessed a miracle, her small daughter had been literally brought back from the spirit world. (*Life Story of Parley Thomas Richins and Fannie Judd,* p. 12. A copy of this manuscript is in the possession of Sister Ruth Gregory, of Smithfield, Utah.)

[8]Rev. 2:7. See also 1 Ne. 15:35-36.

It would seem that there is no change of seasons in paradise. At least a portion of the spirit world description left by 19-year-old Merrill Neville, who passed into the spirit world in January, 1917, was that "it was always springtime over there."[9]

Buildings

Heber C. Kimball, in telling of Jedediah M. Grant's testimony of the spirit world, said that

> He also spoke of the buildings he saw there, remarking that the Lord gave Solomon wisdom and poured gold and silver into his hands that he might display his skill and ability, and said that *the temple erected by Solomon was much inferior to the most ordinary buildings he saw in the spirit world.*[10]

David P. Kimball, fourth son of President Heber C. Kimball, received a number of visions and manifestations during the seven days in November, 1881, when he wandered, lost and without food or water, on the Salt River desert in Arizona. Among them was a vision of the spirit world in which he saw many of the deceased Saints. Then

> This scene vanished, and I was then taken in the vision into a *vast building, which was built on the plan of the Order of Zion.* I entered through a south door and found myself in a part of the building which was unfinished, though a great many workmen were busy upon it. My guide showed me all through this half of the house, and then took me through the other half, which was finished. *The richness, grandeur and beauty of it defied description. There were many apartments in the house, which was very spacious, and they differed in size and the fineness of the workmanship, according to the merits on earth of those who were to occupy them.* I felt most at home in the unfinished part, among the workmen. *The upper part of the house was filled with Saints,* but I could not see them, though some of them conversed with me, my father and mother, Uncle Joseph Young and others.[11]

---

[9] "Manifestation About Building of Temples," *Deseret Evening News,* May 18, 1918. According to the account, Merrill Neville died and then summoned his sister into the spirit world where he gave her a number of messages to bring back to his family. His sister, May, returned to life, delivered the messages, lived another ten days, and then died once again.

[10] JD 4:136. Dec. 4, 1856.

[11] O. F. Whitney, "A Terrible Ordeal," *Helpful Visions* (fourteenth book of the Faith-Promoting Series; Salt Lake City, Utah: Juvenile Instructor Office, 1887), p. 13. Harriet Salvina Beal also reported seeing an unfinished building in the account of her journey into the spirit world:

Merrill Neville, in his account of the spirit world, also commented on buildings there:

> He told her that his grandparents had met him when he died, and he was with them now. They had a beautiful home, and were preparing a beautiful home for his mother and her family.[12]

While a visitor in paradise, Heber Q. Hale saw a beautiful temple with golden domes:

> I moved forward feasting my eyes upon the beauties of everything about me and glorying in the indescribable peace and happiness that abounded in everybody and through everything. The farther I went the more glorious things appeared. While standing at a certain vantage point, I beheld a short distance away a *wonderfully beautiful Temple, capped with golden domes, from which emerged a small group of men dressed in white robes who paused for brief conversation. These were the first I had seen thus clad.*[13]

Organized, Industrious People

Jedediah M. Grant carefully described the organization of the people in the paradise of spirits, and told of their family relationship there:

> 'But O,' says he, 'the order and government that were there! When in the spirit world, I saw the order of righteous men and women: beheld them organized in their several grades, and there appeared to be no obstruction to my vision: I could see every man and woman in their grade and order. I looked to see whether there was any disorder there, but there was none; neither could I see any death nor any darkness, disorder or confusion! He said that the people he there saw were organized in family capacities; and when he looked at them he saw grade after grade, and all were organized and in perfect harmony. . . . 'To my astonishment,' he said, 'when I looked at *families there was a deficiency in some,* there was a lack, for

---

"After some time we came to a beautiful building, very large but as yet unfinished. We seemed to light very easily on the porch that was around the large building as far as I could see. . . .

"Mother then led me into a most beautiful bed-room which was very large. The workmanship of the room was beautiful as was also the rest of the building what I could see, although it was as yet unfinished. The floors of the bed-room, were as of gold and on the floor playing was our little darling William Francis that we buried on the plains. And with him were the twins. . . . Lovely beds were in the room. . . ." (Cora Anna Beal Peterson, *Biography of William Beal* (unpublished manuscript in the possession of Ronald DeMille, Smithfield, Utah), p. 8.

[12]"Manifestation About Building of Temples," *Deseret Evening News,* May 18, 1918.

[13]Heber Q. Hale, *op. cit.*

I saw families that would not be permitted to come and dwell together, because they had not honored their calling here.'[14]

President Heber Q. Hale witnessed the same order among the people in paradise as he visited them:

> The people I met there, did not think of [themselves] as spirit but as men and women, *self-thinking, and self-acting individuals, going about important business in a most orderly manner.* There was perfect order there, and *everybody had something to do* and seemed to be about their business.[15]

Elder Peter E. Johnson also commented on the highly organized society in paradise and said that their work seemed very similar to that done on earth:

> While I was in the spirit world *I observed that the people there were busy, and that they were perfectly organized for the work they were doing.* It seemed to me a continuation of the work we are doing here—something like going from one stake to another. *There was nothing there that seemed particularly strange to me; everything being natural.*[16]

It would appear that there is a happy, friendly spirit throughout the righteous portion of the spirit world, and that the same social amenities known on earth are enjoyed there. As the prophet Joseph Smith observed, the spirits of the dead "now exist in a place where they converse together the same as we do on the earth."[17] In the same theme, President Brigham Young said,

> Spirits are just as familiar with spirits as bodies are with bodies, though spirits are composed of matter so refined as not to be tangible to this coarser organization. They walk, converse, and have their meetings.[18]

Spirit World Fashions

It appears that there is a divergence of dress in the world of spirits, just as there is on earth. President Heber Q. Hale commented that

> The millions that I had previously seen were dressed, of course, but

[14]JD 4:135-136. Dec. 4, 1856.
[15]Heber Q. Hale, *op cit.*
[16]Peter E. Johnson, *Relief Society Magazine, op cit.*, Vol. VII, p. 455.
[17]HC 6:311. April 7, 1844.
[18]JD 3:371-372. June 22, 1856.

> were dressed variously. The soldiers, for instance, were dressed in uniforms.[19]

It should be noted, however, that he was seemingly referring to those he had seen who were not classified among the righteous spirits dwelling in paradise. There is evidence that the righteous in that portion of the spirit world choose to dress in white. John the Revelator, who saw the spirits of the righteous dead who had been slain for their testimony of Jesus, said that they were given white robes:

> I saw under the altar the *souls of them that were slain for the word of God, and for the testimony which they held.*
>
> And they cried with a loud voice, saying, How long, O Lord, holy and true, dost thou not judge and avenge our blood on them that dwell on the earth?
>
> *And white robes were given unto every one of them;* and it was said unto them, that they should rest yet for a little season, until their fellowservants also and their brethren, that should be killed as they were, should be fulfilled.[20]

Indeed, appropriate clothes are prepared for new arrivals in paradise before they pass through the veil, for Elder Hale witnessed their preparation:

> As I was approaching the place where I had entered, my attention was attracted to a small group of women preparing what appeared to be wearing apparel. Observing my inquiring countenance, one of the women remarked, 'We are preparing to receive Brother Phillip Worthington soon.' . . . As I gasped his name in repetition I was admonished, 'If you knew the joy and glorious mission that awaits him here you would not ask to have him longer detained on earth.'[21]

---

[19]Heber Q. Hale, *op cit.*

[20]Rev. 6:9-11.

[21]Heber Q. Hale, *op cit.* Phillip Worthington died two days later, on Jan. 22, 1920. President Hale was summoned to Boise by telegram and preached his funeral sermon January 23rd.

Elder Hale's report of the women finds support in the words of President John Taylor:

> When we go to the spirit world, we go naked, as we came into the world, or *if we get any clothing it is as much by our dependence upon others as when we were born into this world.* (Matthias F. Cowley, *Wilford Woodruff, op cit.,* p. 541. See Job 1:21.)

When Harriet Salvina Beal told of the return of her mother from the spirit world she said that

> "I asked her where she got that dress she was wearing as it was not the one she was buried in and she answered, 'The Lord gave it to me.' " (Cora Anna Beal Peterson, *Biography of William Beal, op cit.,* p. 7.)

Apparently there are exceptions to the rule that all are dressed in white in paradise. It seems that some are allowed to dress in different fashion so that they may be recognized by new entrants into the spirit realm. This took place in the case of Hans Jensen, who dressed in the fishing clothes in which he died in order to be recognized by his niece, Ella Jensen:

> *The people were all dressed in white or cream,* excepting Uncle Hans Jensen, who had on his dark clothes and long rubber boots, the things he wore when he was drowned in the Snake River in Idaho.[22]

The descriptions of those who have received visitors from paradise universally describe the spirit's clothing as being a robe and being white. Thus Thomas A. Shreeve recorded that

---

A dream granted to Wilford Woodruff on March 15, 1848, depicted other apparel being prepared:

> I saw Joseph and Hyrum and many others of the Latter-day Saints who had died. The innumerable company of souls which I saw seemed to be preparing for some grand and important event which I could not understand. Many were engaged in *making crowns for the Saints.* They were all dressed in white robes, both male and female. (Matthias F. Cowley, *Wilford Woodruff, op cit.,* p. 328.) See also JD 2:68-69.

[22]LeRoi C. Snow, *Improvement Era, op cit.,* Vol. XXXII, p. 974. President Rudger Clawson, who was intimately acquainted with Sister Jensen's experience, wrote the following concerning this aspect of what she saw:

> Sometime before this advent into the spirit world her Uncle Hans, who lived in Brigham City, counseled with me as president of the Stake as to the propriety of moving into the Snake River country, Idaho, to engage in salmon fishing. His idea was that if he was successful he could ship salmon from the north to Brigham City at a good profit and thus benefit himself financially. He needed the help that such a business would bring him.
>
> I said if it was his wish to engage in that business it was all right with the stake presidency and a matter entirely for him to decide for himself.
>
> Later he left for the north and at once turned his attention to salmon fishing. One morning he went from the home where he was staying, clothed in a jumper and overalls, with gum boots to fish; but he never returned. His oldest brother, Jacob Jensen, came to me greatly alarmed, said that no word had been received from Hans for some time and nobody seemed to know where he was. He was greatly excited about it and feared that his brother had been drowned in the Snake River.
>
> Jacob organized a posse of men and at once instituted a search covering a period of some two or three weeks, at the Snake River, but their efforts were fruitless. No trace could be found of Hans and he was never again heard from until his niece, Ella Jensen, met him in the spirit world. She said that he was dressed in a jumper and overalls with gum boots. The mystery was solved.
>
> There seemed to be no doubt thereafter that Hans Jensen was drowned in the Snake River. It is said that when the dead manifest themselves to the living they usually appear as they were last seen on earth so that the living will recognize them. If that be true, it accounts for the strange habit that her uncle was wearing. (*Ibid.,* p. 978.)

"a personage *clothed in a white robe* entered the room."[23] Lorenzo Dow Young reported that his guide into the spirit world "was *dressed in the purest white.*"[24] When Briant Stevens returned to his father he was *"robed in snowy whiteness."*[25]

It would seem that the clothing of the spirits in paradise is the same as that of angelic beings who have progressed to a higher level. Descriptions of their robes is more complete. For instance, Joseph Smith described the angel Moroni in detail, saying that

> He had on a *loose robe of most exquisite whiteness.* It was a whiteness beyond anything earthly I had ever seen; nor do I believe that any earthly thing could be made to appear so exceedingly white and brilliant. *His hands were naked, and his arms also, a little above the wrist; so, also, were his feet naked, as were his legs, a little above the ankles. His head and neck were also bare. I could discover that he had no other clothing on but this robe, as it was open, so that I could see into his bosom.*
>
> Not only was his robe exceedingly white, but his whole person was glorious beyond description.[26]

An angel who appeared at the dedication of the Kirtland Temple was described as being "a very tall personage, black eyes, white hair, and stoop-shouldered; *his garment was whole, extending to near his ankles; on his feet he had sandals.*"[27]

There is also evidence that heavenly beings are sometimes dressed in temple robes. Elder Alonzo A. Hinkley received three visitors from beyond the veil dressed in this manner shortly before his departure into the world of spirits:

> Shortly before Elder Hinckley's death, his daughter, Afton, was with him in his home in Salt Lake City. The family had gone out. Everything was quiet, there was an indescribably sweet influence in the house. She supposed her father was asleep and after some little time she went to his room. When she appeared at the door, he said, 'Come in, I have had a wonderful afternoon. *Three heavenly messengers dressed in the robes of the Holy Priesthood have been my visitors.' He spoke of them teaching him to sing a hymn.* At that juncture, the family began to appear and he never mentioned the matter again.[28]

---

[23]Thomas A. Shreeve, *Helpful Visions, op cit.*, p. 59.

[24]Lorenzo Dow Young, *Fragments of Experience, op cit.*, p. 27.

[25]Kennon, *Helpful Visions, op cit.*, p. 36.

[26]JS 2:31-32.

[27]Orson F. Whitney, *Life of Heber C. Kimball, op cit.*, p. 103.

[28]Bryant S. Hinckley, *The Faith of Our Pioneer Fathers* (Salt Lake City, Utah: Deseret Book Co., 1959), p. 236.

Mortal Children Who Die Are Adult Spirits

It is the understanding of Latter-day Saints that premortal spirits have reached adulthood before coming to earth. If, after they come into mortality, they die before their mortal body has reached maturity, their spirit once again resides in adult form, though the body they have laid in the grave is that of a child. This fact is attested by those who have seen the spirits of deceased children in paradise.

Henry Zollinger, for instance, saw his departed sister (who had died as a four-year-old), and reported that "her spirit was full grown in stature and also seemed very intelligent."[29] President Heber Q. Hale made a similar discovery:

> I was surprised to find there *no babies in arms.* I met the infant son of Orson W. Rawlins, my first counselor. I immediately recognized him as the baby who died a few years ago, and yet *he seemed to have the intelligence, and in certain respects, the appearance of an adult,* and was engaged in matters pertaining to his family and its genealogy. My mind was quite contented that mothers will again receive into their arms their children who died in infancy and will be fully satisfied; but the fact remains that *entrance into the world of spirits is not [into] an inhabition of growth, but the greater opportunity for development. Babies are adult spirits in infant bodies.*[30]

President Joseph F. Smith explained that the spirits of departed children could either be seen by mortals in child form for purposes of recognition or could be manifest in adult form if they came as special messengers:

> *The spirits of our children are immortal before they come to us, and their spirits, after bodily death, are like they were before they came.* They are as they would have appeared if they had lived in the flesh, to grow to maturity, or to develop their physical bodies to the full stature of their spirits. *If you see one of your children that has passed away it may appear to you in the form in which you would recognize it, the form of childhood; but if it came to you as a messenger bearing some important truth, it would perhaps come* as the spirit of Bishop Edward Hunter's son (who died when a little child) came to him, *in the stature of full-grown manhood,* and revealed himself to his father, and said: 'I am your son.'
>
> Bishop Hunter did not understand it. He went to my father and said: 'Hyrum, what does that mean? I buried my son when he

[29]Henry Zollinger, *op cit.*
[30]Heber Q. Hale, *op cit.*

> was only a little boy, but he has come to me as a full-grown man—a noble, glorious, young man, and declared himself my son. What does it mean?'
>
> Father (Hyrum Smith, the Patriarch) told him that the Spirit of Jesus Christ was full-grown before he was born into the world; and so *our children were full-grown and possessed their full stature in the spirit, before they entered mortality, the same stature that they will possess after they have passed away from mortality,* and as they will also appear after the resurrection, when they shall have completed their mission.[31]

There are a number of instances where the spirits of departed children have appeared in the form of children to those who would be able to best identify them in that manner. Jedediah M. Grant, for example, saw his daughter as a tiny baby while in the spirit world:

> He saw his wife; she was the first person that came to him. He saw many that he knew, but did not have conversation with any except his wife Caroline. She came to him, and he said that she looked beautiful and *had their little child, that died on the Plains, in her arms,* and said, 'Mr. Grant, here is little Margaret: you know that the wolves ate her up, but it did not hurt her; here she is all right.[32]

In like manner Elder Thomas A. Shreeve was able to recognize his little brother who appeared as a small child, apparently to facilitate recognition after a separation of almost two decades:

---

[31]Joseph F. Smith, *Gospel Doctrine, op cit.,* p. 455. Pertinent to the account of the appearance of Bishop Hunter's son was a previous communication by Patriarch Hyrum Smith:

> October 8, 1840, Edward Hunter was baptized by Elder Orson Hyde, then on his way to Palestine, and soon after received a visit from Elder Hyrum Smith, the Prophet's brother. He attended conference at Philadelphia, and subscribed liberally to the building of the Nauvoo House and the Temple. At a subsequent visit of Brother Hyrum Smith, as they were walking along the banks of the Brandywine, the conversation turned upon the subject of the departed; and Brother Hunter was constrained to inquire about his children whom he had lost, particularly a little boy, George Washington by name, an excellent child to whom he was devotedly attached. *'It is pretty strong doctrine,'* said Elder Smith, 'but I believe I will tell it. *Your son will act as an angel to you; not your guardian angel, but an auxiliary angel, to assist you in extreme trials.'* The truth of this was manifested to him about a year and a half later, when, in an hour of deep depression, the little boy appeared to him in vision. Brother Hunter says: 'In appearance he was more perfect than in natural life—the same blue eyes, curly hair, fair complexion, and a most beautiful appearance. I felt disposed to keep him, and offered inducements for him to remain. He then said, *in his own familiar voice:* "George has many friends in heaven."' (Andrew Jenson, *Latter-day Saint Biographical encyclopedia, op. cit.,* Vol. I, pp. 229-230.)

[32]JD 4:136. Dec. 4, 1856.

I saw the figure of a little child standing at the foot of the bed. I looked closely and recognized my little brother Teddy, who had been drowned nearly twenty years before. I seemed to know that he had come from the spirit world, and in my anxiety I sprang from the bed, and, resting one knee upon the floor, I gazed intently at him. *He stepped near me, and I took one little arm in my hand. Although a spirit, he seemed palpable to my touch.* I said:

'I think you are my little brother Teddy; but it is so long since I saw you that I had almost forgotten how you looked.'[33]

While in the spirit world Ella Jensen saw a large group of children:

Finally I reached the end of that long room. I opened a door and went into another room *filled with children. They were all arranged in perfect order, the smallest ones first, then larger ones, according to age and size,* the largest ones in the back rows all around the room. They seemed to be convened in a sort of a Primary or a Sunday School presided over by Aunt Eliza R. Snow. *There were hundreds of small children.*[34]

It appears that she didn't fully understand the meaning of what she saw until later when a conversation with Brother and Sister Alphonzo H. Snow showed that the spirits appeared as children to help her identify little Alphie Snow, who had just died. Brother Alphonzo Snow related,

My wife, Minnie, and I heard of Ella Jensen's death and restoration to life and called at her home to see her. As we entered the room she said: 'Oh! Come here, Alphonzo and Minnie, I have something to tell you. After my return to earth I told my parents of some of the remarkable experiences which I had while in the spirit world. But there was one experience that seemed very strange, and I could not understand it.

'You know your little son, Alphie, has been in my Sunday School class in the First ward. I have always loved him very much. While I was in Aunt Eliza R. Snow's class of children in the spirit world, I recognized many children. But all of them had died excepting one, and this was little Alphie. I could not understand how he should be among them and still be living. When I told this to mother, she said: 'Yes, Ella, little Alphie is dead, too. He died early this morning while you were so very sick. We knew you loved him and that it would be a shock to you, so we did not tell you about his death.'

It was very consoling, indeed, to hear Ella tell of seeing our dear little boy and that he was very happy. She said it was not right

---

[33]Thomas A. Shreeve, *Helpful Visions, op cit.*, p. 60.

[34] LeRoi C. Snow, *Improvement Era, op cit.*, Vol. XXXII, p. 974.

for us to grieve and mourn so much for him and that he would be happier if we would not do so.[35]

Different Spheres and Levels

The spirit world should not be regarded as being one vast populated area. It would seem that it is divided into different communities, and those of various levels of advancement apparently dwell in the area where they are most compatible with those around them. There would seem to be numerous degrees of advancement represented in the various spheres or dwelling areas.

Brigham Young taught,

> We have no time to spend foolishly, for we have just as much on our hands as we can probably do, to keep pace with that portion of our brethren who have gone into the other room.
>
> And when we have passed into the sphere where Joseph is, *there is still another department, and then another, and another, and so on to an eternal progression in exaltation and eternal lives.* That is the exaltation I am looking for.[36]

As President Young understood the matter, an individual will enjoy considerable freedom to choose those with whom he will associate when he reaches the spirit world, saying that "if they associate together, and collect together in clans and in societies as they do here, it is their privilege."[37]

Yet there is definitely an element of classification according to degree of progression and righteousness in the spirit realm. President Heber Q. Hale, who saw and understood this principle while in the spirit world, said

> That the inhabitants of the spirit world are classified according to their lives of purity and their subserviency to the Father's will, was subsequently made apparent.[38]

There is movement and progression from one area to

[35]*Ibid.*, pp. 976-977.

[36]JD 3:375. June 22, 1856. Parley P. Pratt commented, "There are many places and degrees in that world, as in this." (JD 1:9) See also Orson Pratt's teachings concerning progression in the spirit world in "Questions and Answers," *Millennial Star,* I, 257-258.

[37]JD 2:137. Dec. 3, 1854. See Orson Pratt's teaching concerning spirit world "classes and distinctions," in JD 2:370.

[38]Heber Q. Hale, *op cit.*

another in the spirit world. Jedediah M. Grant discovered that this was true during his spirit world visit when

> He asked his wife Caroline where Joseph and Hyrum and Father Smith and others were: she replied, *'they have gone away ahead, to perform and transact business for us.'* The same as when brother Brigham and his brethren left Winter Quarters and came here to search out a home: they came to find a location for their brethren.[39]

Wilford Woodruff, while telling of a visit from beyond the veil which Brigham Young made, told of an understanding given to him during this conversation with the departed leader:

> The thought came to me that Brother Joseph had left the work of watching over this church and kingdom to others, and that *he had gone ahead,* and that he had left this work to men who have lived and labored with us since he left us. This idea manifested itself to me, that *such men advance in the spirit world.*[40]

It would appear that an individual is not allowed to progress to a higher sphere or level in the spirit world until he has perfected himself to the point where he is eligible to dwell there. This is especially true when one is seeking to pass from the spirit prison into paradise. According to Heber Q. Hale, there is much activity among the different spheres as righteous missionaries attempt to aid others in their progress and development:

> *Particularly was it observed that the wicked and unrepentant are confined to a certain district by themselves, the confines of which are as definitely determined and impassable* as the line marking the division of the physical from the spiritual world, a mere film but *impassable until the person himself has changed.* This world of spirit is a temporary abode of all spirits pending the resurrection from the dead and the judgment. *There was much activity within the different spheres* and the appointed ministers of salvation were seen *coming from the higher to the lower spheres* in pursuit of their missionary appointments.[41]

Church of This Dispensation in Spirit World Under Direction of Joseph Smith

It is the understanding of Latter-day Saints that activity in the spirit world will be directed by the Church, with proph-

---

[39]JD 4:136. Dec. 3, 1856.
[40]JD 21:318. Oct. 10, 1880.
[41]Heber Q. Hale, *op cit.*

ets of the Lord in positions of leadership. When one leaves mortality he is to continue his responsibilities in the Church beyond the veil. As Wilford Woodruff taught,

> The same Priesthood exists on the other side of the veil. Every man who is faithful in his quorum here will join his quorum there. When a man dies and his body is laid in the tomb, he does not lose his position. . . . Every Apostle, every Seventy, every Elder, etc., who has died in the faith, as soon as he passes to the other side of the veil, enters into the work of the ministry.[42]

Brigham Young had expressed the teaching with equal clarity, saying that

> When the faithful Elders, holding this priesthood, go into the spirit world they carry with them the same power and priesthood that they held while in the mortal tabernacle.[43]

It appears that priesthood authority is even more necessary in the spirit world than here on earth, for work beyond the veil is not divided between spiritual and temporal objectives as it is here on earth, but is devoted almost exclusively to the furthering of God's great plan of salvation, under direction of priesthood authority.[44] According to President Young, possession of the priesthood will allow a man in the spirit world to labor on a much higher plane than those without this power:

---

[42]JD 22:333-334. Oct. 8, 1881.

[43]JD 3:371. June 22, 1856. The Lord's statement concerning an early martyr to the Church is significant: "David Patten I have taken unto myself; behold, his priesthood no man taketh from him." (D&C 124:130)

[44]Apparently the importance of the Melchizedek Priesthood beyond the veil is so pronounced that the Lord on occasion delays death until individuals have received it or causes them to be ordained before the normal age of ordination for worthy Church members. A case in point is that of Briant Stevens, who died at the age of thirteen. Promptings that he should be ordained to the Melchizedek Priesthood were given to the Elders who had watched by his sick bed, to his father, and to his stake president:

> The next day this Elder was sitting in Fast meeting, when the dream recurred to his mind; and *instantly he felt that Briant should be ordained to the Melchisedcc* [sic] *Priesthood before his death.* The Elder would have gone to the house, but a sudden impression came to him that he need have no anxiety, for this matter was already receiving attention.
>
> On the morning of the 3rd of February, which was Fast-day, *Brother Stevens was prompted to ordain Briant to the Melchisedec Priesthood; but he endeavored to banish the thought from his mind. It constantly recurred to him, each time growing more imperative. He was not alone in this feeling, for several Elders who had watched with Briant felt the same influence at the same time,* although they were not all present. But one of them, who was sitting at the bedside, said:

> Much has been said about the power of the Latter-day Saints. Is it the people called Latter-day Saints that have this power, or is it the Priesthood? It is the Priesthood; and if they live according to that Priesthood, they can commence their work here and gain many victories, and be prepared to receive glory, immortality, and eternal life, that *when they go into the spirit world, their work will far surpass that of any other man or being that has not been blessed with the keys of the Priesthood here.*[45]

According to the testimony of latter-day prophets, the Church is organized in the spirit world according to the dispensations in which men lived on earth, with the prophet who is responsible for each generation standing at the head of the Church among his people. Concerning this organization Joseph Smith said,

> *This then, is the nature of the Priesthood; every man holding the Presidency of his dispensation,* and one man holding the Presidency of them all, even Adam: and Adam receiving his Presidency and authority from the Lord, but cannot receive a fullness until Christ shall present the Kingdom to the Father, which shall be at the end of the last dispensation.[46]

It would appear that the Churches of the various dispensations will not be completely organized in their relationship to one another until the great council at Adam-ondi-Ahman is held

---

'Brother Stevens, I have felt for several hours that I ought to speak to you about ordaining Briant to be an Elder in the Church. I think that you ought to do this at once.'

Brother Stevens admitted that the same feeling had been in his mind; but that he had hesitated, for fear that such a course might seem like giving up a hope of Briant's recovery. But after such admonitions he could no longer neglect the warning, and he sent for the Bishop. The messenger, on his way to the Bishop's place, met President Shurtliff and spoke to him of Briant; and *the President seemed to have entertained the same thought, for he said that he was led to believe that Briant should receive the Melchisedec Priesthood.*

When this holy ordination was conferred upon him, Briant became serene, though he had been in great pain for some time preceding, and he sank at once into an easy slumber.

He woke not in this world. In an hour his breathing ceased and his spirit left the tortured clay to undergo the transition of nature, while the noble life went to another realm to perform its destined mission. (Kennon, *Helpful Visions, op cit.,* pp. 33-34.)

While preaching at the funeral of his son, Joseph, President Heber C. Kimball said,

"Eight years ago he came near dying; I was impressed to ordain him a High Priest. I ordained him, and I do know that that had a saving effect upon the boy and God has had respect to him. He now lives in the spirit. . . ." (JD 10:372, Nov. 29, 1864.)

[45]JD 7:288-289. Oct. 9, 1859.

[46]HC 4:209. Oct. 5, 1840.

in the last days under the direction of Adam (who is Michael and is known as the Ancient of Days). Orson Pratt explained,

> This man, will sit upon his throne, and ten thousand times ten thousand immortal beings—his children—will stand before him, with all their different grades of Priesthood, according to the order which God has appointed and ordained. *Then every quorum of the Priesthood in this Latter-day Saint Church will find its place, and never until then. If we go behind the vail we will not see this perfect organization of the Saints of all generations until that period shall arrive. That will be before Jesus comes in his glory.* Then we will find that there is a place for the First Presidency of this Church; for the Twelve Apostles called in this dispensation; for the twelve disciples that were called among the remnants of Joseph on this land in ancient times; for the Twelve that were called among the ten tribes of Israel in the north country; for the Twelve that were called in Palestine, who administered in the presence of our Savior; *all the various quorums and councils of the Priesthood in every dispensation that has transpired since the days of Adam until the present time will find their places, according to the callings, gifts, blessings, ordinations and keys of Priesthood which the Lord Almighty has conferred upon them in their several generations.* This, then, will be one of the grandest meetings that has ever transpired upon the face of our globe.[47]

Joseph Smith is recognized as the leader for the Church of this dispensation in paradise. Brigham Young said,

> *Joseph Smith holds the keys of this last dispensation, and is now engaged behind the vail in the great work of the last days. . . . He holds the keys of that kingdom for the last dispensation—the keys to rule in the spirit world; and he rules there triumphantly,* for he gained full power and a glorious victory over the power of Satan while he was yet in the flesh, and was a martyr to his religion and to the name of Christ, which gives him a most perfect victory in the spirit world. *He reigns there as supreme a being in his sphere, capacity, and calling, as God does in heaven.* Many will exclaim—'Oh, that is very disagreeable! It is preposterous! We cannot bear the thought!' But it is true.
>
> I will now tell you something that ought to comfort every man and woman on the face of the earth. Joseph Smith, junior, will again be on this earth dictating plans and calling forth his brethren to be baptized for the very characters who wish this was not so, in order to bring them into a kingdom to enjoy, perhaps, the presence of angels or the spirits of good men, if they cannot endure the presence of the Father and the Son; and *he will never cease his operations under the direc-*

[47]JD 17:187. Oct. 11, 1874. The time, place, purpose and scope of the Council at Adam-ondi-Ahman is carefully considered in the author's book, *Prophecy—Key to the Future* (Salt Lake City, Utah: Bookcraft, Inc., 1962), pp. 167-177.

tions of the Son of God, until the last ones of the children of men are saved that can be, from Adam till now.

Should not this thought comfort all people? *They will, by-and-by, be a thousand times more thankful for such a man as Joseph Smith, junior, than it is possible for them to be for any earthly good whatever.* It is his mission to see that all the children of men in this last dispensation are saved, that can be, through the redemption. *You will be thankful, every one of you, that Joseph Smith, junior, was ordained to this great calling before the worlds were.*[48]

The same teaching was echoed by President Wilford Woodruff, who said that

> *The Prophet Joseph Smith held the keys of this dispensation on this side of the vail, and he will hold them throughout the countless ages of eternity.* He went into the spirit world to unlock the prison doors and to preach the Gospel to the millions of spirits who are in darkness.[49]

Parley P. Pratt taught the same principle:

> I bear this testimony this day, that Joseph Smith was and is a Prophet, Seer, and Revelator—an Apostle holding the keys of this last dispensation and of the kingdom of God, under Peter, James, and John. *And not only that he was a Prophet and Apostle of Jesus Christ, and lived and died one, but that he now lives in the spirit world, and holds those same keys to usward and to this whole generation. Also that he will hold those keys to all eternity;* and no power in heaven or on the earth will ever take them from him; for *he will continue holding those keys through all eternity,* and will stand—yes, again in the flesh upon this earth, as the head of the Latter-day Saints under Jesus Christ, and under Peter, James, and John.[50]

References to the work of Joseph Smith in the spirit world are common in the discourses of the Church leaders who knew him intimately and best understood the functions that he was to fulfill. Typical of these comments are the words of Brigham Young, who said,

> The spirit of Joseph, . . . is active in preaching to the spirits in prison and preparing the way to redeem the nations of the earth, those who lived in darkness previous to the introduction of the Gospel by himself in these days.
>
> He has just as much labor on hand as I have; he has just as

[48]JD 7:289. Oct. 9, 1859.
[49]JD 22:333-334. Oct. 8, 1881.
[50]JD 5:195. Sept. 7, 1856.

much to do. *Father Smith and Carlos and Brother Partridge, yes, and every other good saint, are just as busy in the spirit world as you and I are here. They can see us, but we cannot see them unless our eyes were opened. What are they doing there? They are preaching, preaching all the time, and preparing the way for us to hasten our work in building temples here and elsewhere.*[51]

On the same theme President Wilford Woodruff said,

> If the vail could be taken from our eyes and we could see into the spirit world, we would see that Joseph Smith, Brigham Young and John Taylor had gathered together every spirit that ever dwelt in the flesh in this Church since its organization.[52]

Of perhaps greater significance than comments of this type are the reports of those who have seen the prophet Joseph and other early Church leaders in the spirit world or in dreams or visions. When David P. Kimball suffered from pneumonia in November of 1881, he received a number of visitors from beyond the veil, including his father, Heber C. Kimball, who commented on his association with Joseph Smith and Brigham Young:

> Just then my father commenced talking to me, the voice seeming to come from a long distance. *He commenced by telling me of his associations with President Young, the Prophet Joseph, and others in the spirit world,* then enquired about his children, and seemed to regret that his family were so scattered, and said there would be a great reformation in his family inside of two years. He also told me where I should live, also yourself and others, and a great many other things. *I conversed freely with father, and my words were repeated three times by as many different persons, exactly as I spoke them, until they reached him, and then his words to me were handed down in a like manner.*
>
> After all this I gave way to doubt, thinking it might be only a dream, and to convince myself that I was awake, I got up and walked out-doors into open air.[53]

In 1898, when Peter E. Johnson was given his choice of remaining in paradise or returning to mortality, he recorded that "I was informed that I would preach the Gospel to the spirits there, as I had been preaching it to the people here, and that I would do so under the immediate direction of the

[51]JD 3:369-370. June 22, 1856.

[52]N. B. Lundwall (comp.), *The Vision* (Salt Lake City, Utah: Bookcraft Publishing Co.), p. 96. This discourse of President Woodruff was given April 7, 1893.

[53]O. F. Whitney, *Helpful Visions, op cit.*, p. 11.

Prophet Joseph."[54] President Joseph F. Smith reported in his "Vision of the Redemption of the Dead," received October 3, 1918, that

> *The Prophet Joseph Smith, and my father, Hyrum Smith, Brigham Young, John Taylor, Wilford Woodruff, and other choice spirits who were reserved to come forth in the fulness of times to take part in laying the foundations of the great latter-day work,* including the building of the temples and the performance of ordinances therein for the redemption of the dead, were also in the spirit world. I observed that they were also among the noble and great ones who were *chosen in the beginning to be rulers in the Church of God. Even before they were born, they, with many others, received their first lessons in the world of spirits,* and were prepared to come forth in the due time of the Lord to labor in his vineyard for the salvation of the souls of men.[55]

That same year President Smith recorded contact he had experienced with the prophet Joseph on an earlier mission (apparently his mission to the Hawaiian Islands in 1854):

> I dreamed that I was on a journey, and *I was impressed that I ought to hurry—hurry with all my might, for fear I might be too late.* I rushed on my way as fast as I possibly could, and I was only conscious of having just a little bundle, a handkerchief with a small bundle wrapped in it. I did not realize just what it was, when I was hurrying as fast as I could; but finally *I came to a wonderful mansion, if it could be called a mansion. It seemed too large, too great to have been made by hand,* but I thought I knew that was my destination. As I passed towards it, as fast as I could, I saw a notice, 'Bath.' I turned aside quickly and went into the bath and washed myself

[54]Peter E. Johnson, *Relief Society Magazine, op cit.,* Vol. VII, p. 452. The information given to Elder Johnson which accompanied this statement is of interest:

> . . . and that I would do so under the immediate direction of the Prophet Joseph. This remark brought to my mind a question which has been much discussed here, as to whether or not the Prophet Joseph is now a resurrected being. While I did not ask the question, *they read it in my mind,* and immediately said: 'You wish to know whether the Prophet has his body or not?' I replied: 'Yes, I would like to know.' *I was told that the Prophet Joseph Smith has his body, as also his brother Hyrum, and that as soon as I could do more with my body than I could do without it, my body would be resurrected.*

However, the Reorganized Church claims to have disinterred the remains of Joseph and Hyrum Smith in 1928, making photographs of the remains. See *Saints' Herald,* Jan. 18, 1954. Also *Doctrines of Salvation* 1:200-201; *Millennial Star* 90:158.

[55]Joseph F. Smith, *Gospel Doctrine, op cit.,* p. 475. The context of this passage, which is centered in the period preceding Christ's resurrection in the meridian of time, may mean that he was seeing these men as pre-mortal spirits rather than at the time of his vision. It is believed, of course, that many of the Old Testament prophets he saw earlier in his vision are now resurrected beings. See D&C 132:29, 37.

clean. I opened up this little bundle that I had, and there was a *pair of white, clean garments,* a thing I had not seen for a long time, because the people I was with did not think very much of making things exceedingly clean. But my garments were clean, and I put them on. Then I rushed to what appeared to be a great opening, or door. I knocked and the door opened, and the *man who stood there was the Prophet Joseph Smith.* He looked at me a little reprovingly, and the first words he said: 'Joseph, you are late.' Yet I took confidence and said:

'Yes, but I am clean—I am clean!'

He clasped my hand and drew me in, then closed the great door. I felt his hand just as tangible as I ever felt the hand of man. I knew him, and when I entered I saw my father, and Brigham and Heber, and Willard, and other good men that I had known, standing in a row. I looked as if it were across this valley, and it seemed to be filled with a vast multitude of people, but on the stage were all the people that I had known. *My mother was there, and she sat with a child in her lap; and I could name over as many as I remember of their names, who sat there, who seemed to be among the chosen, among the exalted.*

The Prophet said to me, 'Joseph,' then pointing to my mother, he said: 'Bring me that child.'

I went to my mother and picked up the child, and thought it was a fine baby boy. I carried it to the Prophet, and as I handed it to him *I purposely thrust my hands up against his breast. I felt the warmth* —I was alone, on a mat, away up in the mountains of Hawaii—no one was with me. *But in this vision I pressed my hand up against the Prophet, and I saw a smile cross his countenance.* I handed him the child and stepped back. President Young stepped around two steps, my father one step, and they formed a triangle. Then Joseph blessed that baby, and when he finished blessing it they stepped back in line; that is, Brigham and father stepped back in line. Joseph handed me the baby, wanted me to come and take the baby again; and this time I was determined to test whether this was a dream or a reality. I wanted to know what it meant. So I purposely thrust myself up against the Prophet. *I felt the warmth of his stomach. He smiled at me, as if he comprehended my purpose.* He delivered the child to me and I returned it to my mother, laid it on her lap.

When I awoke that morning I was a man, although only a boy. There was not anything in the world that I feared. I could meet any man or woman or child and look them in the face, feeling in my soul that I was a man every whit. That vision, that manifestation and witness that I enjoyed at that time has made me what I am, if I am anything that is good, or clean, or upright before the Lord, if there is anything good in me. That has helped me out in every trial and through every difficulty.

> Now, I suppose that is only a dream? *To me it is a reality. There never could be anything more real to me. I felt the hand of Joseph Smith. I felt the warmth of his stomach, when I put my hand against him. I saw the smile upon his face.* I did my duty as he required me to do it, and when I woke up I felt as if I had been lifted out of a slum, out of a despair, out of the wretched condition that I was in; and naked as I was, or as nearly as I was, I was not afraid of any white man nor of anyone else, and I have not been very much afraid of anybody else since that time. *I know that that was a reality, to show me my duty, to teach me something, and to impress upon me something that I cannot forget.* I hope it never can be banished from my mind.[56]

During his entry into the spirit world in 1920, President Heber Q. Hale was guided by President Joseph F. Smith, who had died two years previously, and was introduced to both Joseph Smith and Brigham Young:

> He then turned and led me to the little group of men from whom he had just separated. Immediately I recognized *Pres. Brigham Young and the Prophet Joseph Smith. I was surprised to find the former a shorter and heavier built man than I had expected to find him. Both they and Pres. Smith were possessed of a calm and holy majesty which was at once kindly and kingly.* Pres. Smith introduced me to the others, who greeted me warmly. We then turned our steps and Pres. Smith took his leave, saying he would see me again.[57]

Paradise Visited by Jesus Christ

The Savior visits paradise to direct the affairs of His Church and people there. His visit there following His crucifixion was summarized by President Joseph F. Smith, who wrote,

> While this vast multitude waited and conversed, rejoicing in the hour of their deliverance from the chains of death, the Son of God appeared, declaring liberty to the captives who had been faithful, and there he preached to them the everlasting gospel, the doc-

---

[56] *Ibid.*, pp. 542-543. This dream was recorded by President Joseph F. Smith April 7, 1918. Of the circumstances in which it was received President Smith wrote,

> I did have a dream one time. To me it was a literal thing; it was a reality.
>
> I was very much oppressed, once, on a mission. I was almost naked and entirely friendless, except the friendship of a poor, benighted, degraded people. I felt as if I was so debased at my condition of poverty, lack of intelligence and knowledge, just a boy, that I hardly dared look a white man in the face.
>
> While in that condition, I dreamed. . .

[57] Heber Q. Hale, *op cit.*

> trine of the resurrection and the redemption of mankind from the fall, and from individual sins on conditions of repentance. . . . Among the righteous there was peace, and the saints rejoiced in their redemption, and bowed the knee and acknowledged the Son of God as their Redeemer and Deliverer from death and the chains of hell. Their countenances shone and the radiance from the presence of the Lord rested upon them and they sang praises unto his holy name. . . . Thus was it made known that our *Redeemer spent his time during his sojourn in the world of spirits, instructing and preparing the faithful spirits* of the prophets who had testified of him in the flesh, *that they might carry the message of redemption unto all the dead* unto whom he could not go personally because of their rebellion and transgression, that they through the ministration of his servants might also hear his words.[58]

The Savior has made numerous appearances to mortals in the last days.[59] Most of these appearances, however, have not been connected with the world of spirits but have been visits to mortals on earth or have been visions of the Master in the celestial kingdom. At least two meetings with the Lord, however, have taken place in the spirit realm. Two days before he died, David Whitmer went beyond the veil and saw Jesus:

> On Monday last (Jan. 23, 1888), at 10 o'clock a.m., after awakening from a short slumber, *he said he had seen beyond the veil and saw Christ on the other side.*[60]

Heber Q. Hale, after describing the temple he saw in the spirit world, told how he also saw the Savior there:

> In the little group of men my eyes rested upon *one more splendorous and holy than all the rest.* While I thus gazed, Pres. Joseph F. Smith parted from the others and came to my side. 'Do you know him?' he inquired. I quickly answered, 'Yes, I know him.' *My eyes beheld my Lord and Savior. 'It is true'* said Pres. Joseph F. Smith, and *oh how my soul thrilled with rapture, unspeakable joy filled my soul.*[61]

Thus it is seen that the Savior is concerned over this work in the spirit world and manifests His presence among the righteous there.

---

[58]Joseph F. Smith, *Gospel Doctrine, op cit.*, pp. 473-474.

[59]A number of these are compiled and discussed in the author's book, *Gifts of the Spirit* (Salt Lake City, Utah: Bookcraft, Inc., 1965), pp. 51-66.

[60]Andrew Jenson, *Latter-day Saint Biographical Encyclopedia, op cit.*, Vol. I, p. 270.

[61]Heber Q. Hale, *op cit.*

Freedom from Cares and Sorrows

Alma, while describing the world of spirits to his son, Corianton, said that

> The righteous are received into a state of happiness, which is called paradise, a state of rest, a state of peace, where they shall rest from all their troubles and from all care, and sorrow.[62]

Some people, in considering this passage, have understood it to mean that men will be left without labors to perform. It would seem that they are mistaken in this interpretation. According to latter-day prophets, they will have a great deal of work to do. They will be aided in their work, however, by being free from physical suffering and needs, from sin, and from mortal cares and sorrows. Brigham Young had much to say on this theme. While preaching at the funeral of Thomas Williams he taught,

> When we contemplate the condition of man here upon the earth, and understand that we are brought forth for the express purpose of preparing ourselves through our faithfulness to inherit eternal life, *we ask ourselves where we are going, what will be our condition, what will be the nature of our pursuits in a state of being in which we shall possess more vigor and a higher degree of intelligence than we possess here? Shall we have labor? Shall we have enjoyment in our labor? Shall we have any object of pursuit,* or shall we sit and sing ourselves away to everlasting bliss? These are questions that arise in the minds of people, and they many times feel anxious to know something about hereafter. What a dark valley and a shadow it is that we call death! To pass from this state of existence as far as the mortal body is concerned, into a state of inanition, [sic] how strange it is! How dark this valley is! How mysterious is this road, and we have got to travel it alone. I would like to say to you, my friends and brethren, if we could see things as they are, and as we shall see and understand them, this dark shadow and valley is so trifling that we shall turn round and look upon it and think, when we have crossed it, *why this is the greatest advantage of my whole existence, for I have passed from a state of sorrow, grief, mourning, woe, misery, pain, anguish and disappointment into a state of existence, where I can enjoy life to the fullest extent as far as that can be done without a body. My spirit is set free, I thirst no more, I want to sleep no more, I hunger no more, I tire no more, I run, I walk, I labor, I go, I come, I do this, I do that, whatever is required of me, nothing like pain or weariness, I am full of life, full of vigor, and I enjoy the presence of my heavenly Father, by the power of his Spirit.*[63]

---

[62]Al. 40:12.

[63]JD 17:142. July 19, 1874.

On another occasion, the funeral of Aurelia Spencer, he said,

> Here, we are continually troubled with ills and ailments of various kinds, and our ears are saluted with the expressions, 'My head aches,' 'My shoulders ache,' 'My back aches,' 'I am hungry, dry, or tired;' but *in the spirit world we are free from all this and enjoy life, glory, and intelligence; and we have the Father to speak to us, Jesus to speak to us, and angels to speak to us, and we shall enjoy the society of the just* and the pure who are in the spirit world until the resurrection.[64]

While speaking of evil spirits in the spirit world, President Young said,

> When you are in the spirit world, *everything there will appear as natural as things now do.* Spirits will be familiar with spirits in the spirit world—*will converse, behold, and exercise every variety of communication* one with another as familiarly and naturally as while here in tabernacles. There, as here, all things will be natural, and you will understand them as you now understand natural things.
>
> You will there see that those spirits we are speaking of are *active: they sleep not.* And you will learn that they are striving with all their might—*labouring and toiling diligently as any individual would to accomplish an act in this world*—to destroy the children of men.[65]

Work Being Performed

The spirit world serves as a place for progression and growth for the righteous. Those who labor diligently there will increase in knowledge, power and happiness. As Brigham Young explained,

> We have more friends behind the vail than on this side, and they will hail us more joyfully than you were ever welcomed by your parents and friends in this world; and you will rejoice more when you meet them than you ever rejoiced to see a friend in this life; and then *we shall go on from step to step, from rejoicing to rejoicing, and from one intelligence and power to another, our happiness becoming more and more exquisite and sensible as we proceed in the words and powers of life.*[66]

A major labor for the righteous in the spirit world is to gain knowledge and understanding of the things of God. Joseph Smith taught that

> Here, then, is eternal life—to know the only wise and true God; and

[64]JD 14:231. Sept. 16, 1871.
[65]JD 7:239. Sept. 1, 1859.
[66]JD 6:349. July 31, 1859.

> *you have got to learn how to be gods yourselves, and to be kings and priests to God, the same as all gods have done before you, namely, by going from one small degree to another, and from a small capacity to a great one; from grace to grace, from exaltation to exaltation, until you attain to the resurrection of the dead,* and are able to dwell in everlasting burnings, and to sit in glory, as do those who sit enthroned in everlasting power.[67]

Later in his sermon, the King Follett Discourse, he added the explanation that

> *Knowledge saves a man; and in the world of spirits no man can be exalted but by knowledge.* So long as a man will not give heed to the commandments, he must abide without salvation. *If a man has knowledge, he can be saved; although, if he has been guilty of great sins, he will be punished for them.* But when he consents to obey the gospel, whether here or in the world of spirits, he is saved.[68]

On this theme President Brigham Young taught that

> If we are striving with all the powers and faculties God has given us to improve upon our talents, to prepare ourselves to dwell in eternal life, and the grave receives our bodies while we are thus engaged, with what disposition will our spirits enter their next state? *They will be still striving to do the things of God, only in a much greater degree—learning, increasing, growing in grace and in the knowledge of the truth.*[69]

While in the spirit world Henry Zollinger observed that "people had their free agency there like we do here and that *gaining knowledge was the only way to progression.*"[70]

A second type of work performed in the spirit world is service as ministering servants to those who have attained a higher degree of perfection in that realm. Such service undoubtedly provides opportunity for growth through association with more advanced beings. In the prophet Joseph's remarks at the demise of James Adams, he said,

> The spirits of just men are made ministering servants to those who are sealed unto life eternal, and it is through them that the sealing power comes down. . . . The spirits of the just are exalted to a greater and more glorious work; hence they are blessed in their departure to the world of spirits.[71]

---

[67]HC 6:306. April 7, 1844.
[68]*Ibid.,* p. 314.
[69]JD 7:333. Oct. 8, 1859.
[70]Henry Zollinger, *op cit.*
[71]HC 6:51, 52. Oct. 9, 1843.

A third labor performed in the spirit world consists in preparations for future events which are to take place upon the earth. Apparently important groundwork must be laid beyond the veil in anticipation of significant events of the last days. As Brigham Young declared,

> They are preaching, preaching all the time and *preparing the way for us to hasten our work in building temples here and elsewhere, and to go back to Jackson County and build the great temple of the Lord.* They are hurrying to get ready by the time that we are ready, and we are all hurrying to get ready by the time our Elder Brother is ready. . . . In the spirit world those who have got the victory *go on to prepare the way for those who live in the flesh,* fulfilling the work of saviors on Mount Zion.[72]

A fourth labor performed by those in paradise is the teaching of the righteous. Ella Jensen saw this work in process in the spirit world when she observed a group "convened in a sort of a Primary or Sunday School presided over by Aunt Eliza R. Snow."[73] Surely, if the Church continues to function in its same pattern of organization beyond the veil, there is a continued need for effective teachers and administrators beyond the veil.

There is evidence that great stress is placed on music in the paradise of spirits and that choirs are formed which perform at numerous important occasions on earth as well as in the spirit world. David P. Kimball, who was near death with pneumonia, heard words of blessing and instruction sung by a choir from the spirit world and identified the spirit of his departed wife by her singing:

> At this point *I heard the most beautiful singing I ever listened to in all my life.* These were the words, repeated three times by a choir: *'God bless Brother David Kimball.'* I at once distinguished among them the voice of my second wife, Julia Merrill, who in life was a good singer. This, of course, astonished me. . . . After all this I gave way to doubt, thinking it might be only a dream, and to convince myself that I was awake, I got up and walked out doors into the open air.
>
> I returned and still the spirit of doubt was upon me. To test it further I asked my wife Julia to sing me a verse of one of her old songs. At that, *the choir, which had continued singing, stopped and she*

---

[72]JD 3: 370, 372. June 22, 1856.

[73]LeRoi C. Snow, *Improvement Era, op cit.,* Vol. XXXII, p. 974.

sang the song through, every word being distinct and beautiful. The name of the song was, 'Does He Ever Think of Me.'

My eyes were now turned toward the south, and there, as in a large parquette, I beheld hundreds, even thousands, of friends and relatives. I was then given the privilege of asking questions and did so. This lasted for some time, after which *the singing commenced again, directly above me.* I now wrapped myself in a pair of blankets and went out-doors, *determined to see the singers, but could see nothing, though I could hear the voices just the same.* I returned to my couch and *the singing, which was all communicative and instructive, continued until the day dawned.*[74]

Choirs from beyond the veil have been heard at the dedication of at least two of the Latter-day Saint temples. Eliza R. Snow wrote that "the singing of heavenly choirs was heard"[75] during the early days of the Kirtland Temple. When the Manti Temple was dedicated another such choir was heard:

On the first day, just as Professor Smyth was concluding the voluntary—a selection from Mendelssohn—*a number of the Saints in the body of the hall and some of the brethren in the west stand heard most heavenly voices singing. It sounded to them as angelic,* and appeared to be behind and above them, and many turned their heads in that direction wondering if there were not another choir in some other part of the building. There was no other choir, however.[76]

A sixth area of labor in paradise is the gathering of genealogical data. President Heber Q. Hale recorded that during his visit to the spirit world,

I met Brother John Adamson, his wife, his son James and daughter Isabelle, all of whom were killed by the band of foul assassins in Carrey, Idaho, in the evening of Oct. 29, 1915. They seemed to divine that I was on my way back to mortality and immediately said, Brother Adamson speaking: 'Tell the children that *we are very happy,* and that they should not mourn our departure, nor worry their minds over the manner by which we were taken. There is a

---

[74]O. F. Whitney, *Helpful Visions, op cit.,* pp. 10-11.

[75]N. B. Lundwall (comp.), *Temples of the Most High* (tenth edition, Salt Lake City, Utah: Bookcraft), p. 24. For a consideration of what type of beings these angels may have been, see *Types of Angels Who Minister on Earth,* Chapter IV.

[76]*Ibid.,* p. 123. Of this same dedication, Franklin D. Richards wrote,

When we dedicated the Temple at Manti, many of the brethren and sisters saw the presence of spiritual beings, discernable only by the inward eye. The Prophets Joseph, Hyrum, Brigham and various other Apostles that have gone were seen and not only this, but the ears of many of the faithful were touched, and they heard the music of the heavenly choir. (*Ibid.,* p. 124)

> purpose in it and *we have a work here to do which requires our collective efforts and which we could not do individually!' I was at once made to know that the work referred to was that of genealogy on which they were working in Scotland and England.*[77]

Harriet Salvina Beal also learned of the great genealogical labors being conducted in the spirit world when she was escorted into paradise by her mother, Clarissa Allen Beal. Harriet journeyed into the spirit realm at the age of sixteen, shortly after the arrival of her family in the valley of the Great Salt Lake in 1852. At this point in the account Harriet is in paradise and her mother has just left the room for a few moments:

> Watching mother down the hall I turned to go back to my chair, but in turning I saw the door across the hall just a short distance from where I was standing, and it was open. Well I just had to see what was in that room, so I crossed very carefully and looked in. All my life I have been of a very inquisitive nature. Many times it has caused me much trouble. But this time I was very pleasantly surprised to see the *Prophet Joseph Smith walking up and down a very long room and he had his hands clasped behind him, his head bowed as though in thought. At long tables on either side of the room and down the center also, many men sat writing as fast as they could and once in awhile the Prophet would stop and speak to one of the men and they would answer then go right on writing as fast as before. Among these men were the Prophet's brother Hyrum,* also other men I had known well. . . .

Her mother returned and Harriet sought information concerning what she had seen:

> 'But Mother,' I said, 'what is the Prophet Joseph and his brother, Hyrum, and all the other men doing in there?' She answered, *'Preparing genealogy so that the work can be done on earth for those who have died without having the privilege of hearing the gospel themselves.'*[78]

---

[77]Heber Q. Hale, *op cit.*

[78]Cora Anna Beal Peterson, *Biography of William Beal, op cit.,* pp. 9-10. Harriet Beal also learned from her mother that spirit beings have more commonplace tasks to perform. Her mother had told her, "I must go to the *kitchen* for awhile and I want you to sit right there in that chair until I return." Harriet asked her *"if she had to work in the kitchen and she said, 'Of course, I take my turn just like the rest.' "* (*Ibid.,* p. 8)

Her allusion to the kitchen raises the unavoidable question of whether spirit beings eat as mortals do. The limited evidence available seems to indicate that they eat, and that resurrected beings do also. For instance, the Lord said, "To him that overcometh will I give to *eat* of the tree of life, which is in the midst of the *paradise* of God." (Rev. 2:7) Abraham fed cakes, meat, butter, and milk to the pre-mortal Lord and His two companions and "they did eat." (Gen. 18:1-8) Lot was visited by "two angels" (presumably spirit beings, for their visit long preceded the resurrection) and "he made them a feast, and did bake unleavened bread, and *they did eat.*" (Gen. 19:1-3)

In other chapters of this book comment is made on other labors performed in the spirit world, including missionary work,[79] checking temple records,[80] watching over mortals as guardian angels,[81] preparing clothing for those about to enter the spirit realm,[82] guiding newcomers in the spirit world,[83] serving as messengers to earth and other spheres,[84] and constructing buildings, etc.[85]

SUMMARY

1. The term "paradise" is used in three senses:
   - A. meaning "heaven," or man's final resting place. This is the sectarian usage and is not common usage among Latter-day Saints;
   - B. meaning the entire world of spirits;
   - C. meaning the habitation of the righteous within the spirit world.

   The third usage is the most common within the Church and is used in this book.

2. Numerous descriptions of paradise show that it contains
   - A. lakes
   - B. forests
   - C. grass
   - D. wilderness trails

References to gardens, fruit trees, and agricultural pursuits in the spirit realm are common in the discourses of early church leaders (see for example, JD 4:136; 14:231). Herbs, seeds, fruit, cattle, beasts, and fowl were created spiritually and given to man for food before the physical creation of the earth and still exist in spiritual form (Moses 2:11-3:7; JD 14:231). That spirit beings should eat is logical. Their spirit bodies are the image and pattern for their physical bodies for, as Jesus said, "Man have I created after the body of my spirit." (Eth. 3:16) As Parley P. Pratt expressed the principle, the spirit body

> Possesses every organ after the pattern and in the likeness or similitude of the outward or fleshly tabernacle it is designed eventually to inhabit. Its organs of thought, speech, sight, hearing, *tasting, smelling,* feeling, etc. all exist in their order as in the physical body; the one being the exact similitude of the other. (*Key to the Science of Theology, op cit.,* p. 56. See also p. 125.)

For comments concerning eating by resurrected beings see pp. 249-250, 355-356.

[79]See pp. 202-208.

[80]See pp. 220-225.

[81]See pp. 136-141.

[82]See p. 80.

[83]See pp. 147-148, 197-199, 4-5.

[84]See pp. 127-128.

[85]See pp. 77, 78.

E. vines
F. flowers
G. bright foliage, including pink, orange, lavender, and gold
H. landscaped parks
I. shrubbery
J. walled compartments
K. a sweet calmness
L. gardens
M. the Tree of Life
N. an unchanging spring climate
O. many buildings constructed in a manner superior to Solomon's temple
P. large buildings built on the plan of the Order of Zion
Q. apartment houses
R. workmanship suited to the merits of one's earth life
S. a temple with golden domes
T. an atmosphere of peace and happiness
U. order and government
V. people organized in various grades
W. no death, darkness, disorder or confusion
X. people living and organized in family capacities
Y. families left incomplete because of the unrighteousness of some family members
Z. self-thinking, self-acting people
AA. everyone performing some task
BB. work similar to Church work on earth
CC. people conversing
DD. people walking
EE. meetings being held
FF. standard dress was loose white robes
GG. clothing being prepared
HH. some people dressed in temple clothing
II. no babies in arms

3. Before coming to earth all spirits have grown to be adults. Mortals who die as children are adult spirits in the spirit world.

4. Spirits are able to change clothing, form, age and size for purposes of recognition by mortals.

5. The spirit world is not a place of physical growth but of spiritual development.

6. There is evidence of communication between the pre-mortal abode and the paradise of post-mortal spirits.

7. Paradise is divided into different spheres or communities. Departed spirits dwell with others of a similar degree of advancement. There is movement and progression from one area to another.

8. Faithful Latter-day Saints who die are to resume their Church responsibility and quorum membership in paradise. Priesthood authority will be of even greater significance in the spirit world than on earth.

9. The Church in paradise is organized by dispensations of time, with the prophets of each period standing at its head. These Church units are to be combined and organized into one at the Council at Adam-ondi-Ahman shortly before the second coming of Christ in glory.

10. Joseph Smith stands at the head of the Church members who lived during the dispensation of the fullness of times. There is some indication that he may have delegated this responsibility to others and progressed to even greater responsibility.

11. Those who have visited in the spirit world have seen Jesus Christ, Joseph Smith, Hyrum Smith, Brigham Young, John Taylor, Wilford Woodruff, Joseph F. Smith and other Church leaders there.

12. The inhabitants of the spirit world enjoy freedom from body pain, hunger, fatigue, sleep, etc. Those in paradise are permitted rest from all their trouble, care and sorrow.

13. Gaining knowledge is the means of progression in paradise.

14. Work performed in the spirit world includes

    A. learning and gaining knowledge
    B. service as ministering spirits to those of a higher level
    C. making preparations for future earth events
    D. teaching others
    E. performance in musical organizations
    F. gathering genealogical data
    G. missionary work
    H. checking temple records
    I. watching over mortals as guardian angels
    J. preparing clothing for anticipated spirit world entrants
    K. guiding newcomers
    L. serving as messengers to earth and to other spheres
    M. constructing buildings
    N. Kitchen labors

    Undoubtedly this list is but a brief representation of the tasks being performed beyond the veil.

CHAPTER IV

SPIRIT BEINGS VISIT THE EARTH

Spirits Observe and Participate in Earth Events

THERE ARE INDICATIONS THAT BEINGS FROM BEYOND THE veil are well aware of happenings on earth and occasionally return to the mortal dimension to participate in them. Many examples of this are found in the early Kirtland era of the Church. During the great pentecostal times in the early months of 1836 when a tremendous outpouring of the spirit was experienced, visitors from beyond the veil were received on numerous occasions. For instance, during the meetings of January 21st and 22nd, Joseph Smith recorded that "the gift of tongues fell upon us in mighty power, *angels mingled their voices with ours, while their presence was in our midst,* and unceasing praises swelled our bosoms for the space of half-an-hour."[1] He told how in an earlier meeting, "Some of them saw the face of the Savior, and *others were ministered unto by holy angels,* and the spirit of prophecy and revelation was poured out. . . ."[2] On March 27th of that year he recorded a similar experience, saying that "many began to speak in tongues and prophesy, others saw glorious visions; and *I beheld the Temple was filled with angels,* which fact I declared to the congregation."[3] On the day of the Kirtland Temple's dedication "angels administered to many, for they were also seen by many."[4] George A. Smith testified that "on the evening after the dedication of the Temple, hundreds of the brethren *received the ministering of angels, saw the light and personages of angels,* and bore testimony of it.[5]

---

[1]HC 2:383. For information concerning the various kinds of angelic beings who minister upon the earth, see a later section of this chapter: *Types of Angels who Minister on Earth.*

[2]HC 2:382.

[3]HC 2:428.

[4]Orson F. Whitney, *Life of Heber C. Kimball, op cit.,* p. 105.

[5]JD 2:215. March 18, 1855.

On April 7, 1893, the day following the offering of the dedicatory prayer for the Salt Lake Temple, President Wilford Woodruff taught that beings in the spirit world had joined in the dedicatory exercises:

> I feel at liberty to reveal to this assembly this morning what has been revealed to me since we were here yesterday morning. If the veil could be taken from our eyes and we could see into the spirit world, *we would see that Joseph Smith, Brigham Young and John Taylor had gathered together every spirit that ever dwelt in the flesh in this Church since its organization. We would also see the faithful apostles and elders of the Nephites who dwelt in the flesh in the days of Jesus Christ. In that assembly we would also see Isaiah and every prophet and apostle that ever prophesied of the great work of God. In the midst of these spirits we would see the Son of God, the Savior, who presides and guides and controls* the preparing of the kingdom of God on the earth and in heaven.
>
> *From that body of spirits, when we shout 'Hosannah to God and the Lamb!' there is a mighty shout goes up of 'Glory to God, in the Highest!' that the God of Israel has permitted his people to finish this Temple* and prepared it for the great work that lies before the Latter-day Saints.
>
> These patriarchs and prophets, who have wished for this day, rejoice in the spirit world that the day has come when the saints of the Most High God have had power to carry out this great mission.
>
> *There is a mighty work before this people. The eyes of the dead are upon us.* This dedication is acceptable in the eyes of the Lord. *The spirits on the other side rejoice far more than we do, because they know more of what lies before in the great work of God in this last dispensation than we do.*
>
> *The Son of God stands in the midst of that body of celestial spirits, and teaches them their duties concerning the day in which we live and the dedication of this temple,* and instructs them what they must do to prepare and qualify themselves to go with him on the earth when he comes to judge every man according to the deeds done in the body.[6]

During his entry into the spirit world, President Heber Q. Hale was shown the manner in which the spirits were permitted to view the mortal world. Although his view was comprehensive, it was revealed that views of the earth were limited and allowed only to those who had specific purpose and need for the vision:

[6]Archibald F. Bennett, *Saviors on Mount Zion, op cit.*, pp. 142-143. This is a copy of the stenographic report of the services. Parley P. Pratt taught that Joseph Smith and the saints were present at the laying of the temple cornerstone in 1853. See JD 1:14.

From a certain point of vantage, I was permitted to view this earth and what was going on here. *There was no limitation to my vision,* and I was astounded at this. . . . *I saw my wife and children at home. I saw Pres. Heber J. Grant* at the head of the Great Church and Kingdom of God and felt the divine power that radiates from God, giving it light and truth and guiding its destiny. *I beheld this nation,* founded as it is on correct principles and designated to endure, and beset by evil and sinister forces that seek to lead men astray and thwart the purposes of God.

I saw towns and cities; the sins and wickedness of men and women. I saw vessels sailing upon the ocean, and scanned the battle-scarred fields of France and Belgium. In a word, I beheld the whole world as if it were a panorama passing before my eyes. Then there came to me the unmistakable impression that *this earth and scenes and persons upon it are open to the vision of the spirits only when special permission is given and when they are assigned to a special service here.* This is particularly true of the righteous who are busily engaged in the service of the Lord who cannot be engaged in two fields of activity at the same time.[7]

The Dead Concerned About Earth Conduct

While righteous spirits are seemingly permitted to view and visit the entire earth only on special occasions, it would appear that the obtaining of knowledge concerning the personal conduct of a specific mortal being is common and, indeed, a task assigned to certain spirits. As Heber C. Kimball observed,

Some may think that the Almighty does not see their doings, but if He does not, *the angels and ministering spirits do. They see you and your works, and I have no doubt but they occasionally communicate your conduct to the Father, or to the Son, or to Joseph, or to Peter, or to some one who holds the keys in connection with them.* Perhaps there are some who do not believe in spirits, but I know that they exist and visit the earth.[8]

Joseph Smith taught that the spirits of the just "are not far from us, and know and understand our thoughts, feelings and motions, and are often pained therewith."[9]

Departed spirits are aware of the conduct of their loved ones still on earth. Merrill Neville, for instance, was so concerned about his family that he called his sister into the spirit world and then sent her back to caution them:

---

[7]Heber Q. Hale, *op cit.*
[8]JD 3:228-229. March 2, 1856.
[9]HC 6:52. Oct. 9, 1843.

> May put her finger on each one of the family present and told them of their failings, which they must endeavor to overcome if they would go to that beautiful home which was being prepared for them. She said that all must go to Sunday School and to meeting; they should attend to their prayers, and pay their tithing. She said impressively to all present: 'Give to the poor; the more you give the more you will have to give.'[10]

Apparently May was able to learn the future concerning her family while beyond the veil because she told her mother, "you are going to live to be a real old lady; you will have better health than you have ever had."[11] Mrs. Neville subsequently received another visitor from the spirit world whose message also demonstrated that departed spirits know of the thoughts and actions of mortals. Her father returned and said,

> 'Eliza, . . . the Lord wanted Merrill and I needed him in my missionary work, but *alas for my children on earth! I can't accomplish the work that I want to accomplish on account of my children on earth!'*
>
> 'Why, father,' she asked, 'your children have never done anything very bad, have they?' He replied, *'They are dying, dying spiritually.* Look, and I'll show you!'

[10]"Manifestation About Building of Temples," *Deseret Evening News,* May 18, 1918. It would appear that not all departed spirits are aware of the conduct of their mortal relatives, and that there must be some assignment of specific responsibility which leaves other spirits free from concern. Some spirits are not assigned to watch over particular individuals; consequently they are not aware of the mortal actions of distant relatives. Yet they show the same casual interest in others as mortals do on earth. For instance, Ella Jensen reported that while in the spirit world she saw her grandfather, H. P. Jensen, who "looked up somewhat surprised to see me and said: 'Why, there is my granddaughter Ella.' " She met others whom she knew, and said that "Some inquired about their friends and relatives on the earth."

Statements by Heber Q. Hale also give indication that spirit beings are not constantly aware of the actions of their mortal loved ones. He told of his mother's surprise at seeing him in the spirit world, which implies that she was not constantly aware of his earth actions or she would have known he was coming:

> As I passed forward, I met my beloved Mother. She greeted me most affectionately and *expressed surprise at seeing me there and reminded me that I had not yet completed my allotted mission on the earth.* She seemed to be going somewhere and *was in a hurry* and accordingly took her leave with saying that she would see me again.

He also told of the requests others made that he carry greetings and counsel back to various mortals, indicating either a casual relationship or inability of the spirit beings to communicate with mortals:

> Quite a distance through various scenes and passing innumerable people, *I travelled before I reached the sphere which I had first entered.* On my way I was greeted by many friends and relatives, *certain of whom sent words of greeting and counsel to their dear ones here, my mother being one of them.*

[11]*Ibid.*

Then she saw that they were not united, but were standing with their backs toward each other. He explained: *Some are complaining about paying their tithing; they say the Church is better off than they are. If they could only see! The tithing will be used for the building of temples. Look!'*

As she looked she saw myriads of people reaching out just as far as her eyes could see, and her father said, 'They couldn't walk through the two or three temples on earth in a century's time, much less do the work which must be done. Now, Eliza, *I put this responsibility on you to see that my family is united and working in harmony with the Church.'*[12]

Henry Zollinger also learned in the spirit world that his deceased mother was concerned about his conduct and knew what the future would hold for his family:

She then warned me to be very careful and keep the faith. Also told me to warn my brothers and sisters to live more closely to the Gospel and not let worldly things lead them astray as that is the way the Nephites of old were led away. Mother informed me that my brother John, who has been somewhat careless in a religious way *would someday take a turn* in regard to him and his family.

Also at the death of my father, *my brother William would have the privilege of being in charge of the records.*[13]

President George Albert Smith told how he lay near death in St. George, Utah, so weak that he could hardly turn over in bed, and recorded that in vision or in spirit his conduct was challenged by his grandfather:

I hurried my steps to reach him, because I recognized him as my grandfather. In mortality he weighed over three hundred pounds, so you may know he was a large man. I remember how happy I was to see him coming. I had been given his name and had always been proud of it.

When grandfather came within a few feet of me, he stopped. His stopping was an invitation for me to stop. Then—and this I would like the boys and girls and young people never to forget—he looked at me very earnestly and said: *'I would like to know what you have done with my name.'*

Everything I had ever done passed before me as though it were a flying picture on a screen—everything I had done. Quickly this vivid retrospect came

---

[12]*Ibid.*

[13]Henry Zollinger, *op cit.*

down to the very time I was standing there. My whole life had passed before me. I smiled and looked at my grandfather and said: 'I have never done anything with your name of which you need be ashamed.'

He stepped forward and took me in his arms, . . .[14]

Not only do departed spirits feel concern for their mortal family, but they are concerned about the condition of the Church upon the earth, to which they devoted their mortal efforts. Two statements by President Wilford Woodruff show the concern of Joseph Smith and Brigham Young, who both returned from the spirit world to counsel and caution him:

I believe the eyes of the heavenly hosts are over this people; I believe they are watching the elders of Israel, the prophets and apostles and men who are called to bear off this kingdom. I believe they watch over us all with great interest.

I will here make a remark concerning my own feelings. *After the death of Joseph Smith I saw and conversed with him many times in my dreams in the night season. On one occasion he and his brother Hyrum met me when on the sea going on a mission to England.* I had Dan Jones with me. He received his mission from Joseph Smith before his death; and *the prophet talked freely to me about the mission I was then going to perform. And he also talked to me with regard to the mission of the Twelve Apostles in the flesh, and he laid before me the work they had to perform; and he also spoke of the reward they would receive after death.* And there were many other things he laid before me in his interview on that occasion. *And when I awoke many of the things he had told me were taken from me, I could not comprehend them.* I have had many interviews with Brother Joseph until the last 15 or 20 years of my life; I have not seen him for that length of time. But during my travels in the southern country last winter *I had many interviews with President Young, and with Heber C. Kimball, and Geo. A. Smith, and Jedediah M. Grant, and many others who are dead.* They attended our conference, they attended our meetings. And on one occasion, I saw Brother Brigham and Brother Heber ride in carriage ahead of the carriage in which I rode when I was on my way to attend conference; and they were dressed in the most priestly robes. When we arrived at our destination I asked Prest. Young if he would preach to us. He said, 'No, I have finished my testimony in the flesh; I shall not talk to this people any more. But (said he) *I have come to see you; I have come to watch over you, and to see what the people are doing. Then (said he) I want you to teach the people—and I want you to follow this counsel yourself—that they must labor and so live as to obtain the Holy Spirit, for without this you cannot*

[14]Preston Nibley, *Sharing the Gospel With Others, op cit.*, pp. 111-112.

build up the kingdom; without the spirit of God you are in danger of walking in the dark, and in danger of failing to accomplish your calling as apostles and and as elders in the church and kingdom of God. And, said he, Brother Joseph taught me this principle.'[15]

Sixteen years later he again related these events, and this time gave greater detail:

> One morning, while we were at Winter Quarters, Brother Brigham Young said to me and the brethren that he had had a visitation the night previous from Joseph Smith. I asked him what he said to him. He replied that *Joseph had told him to tell the people to labor to obtain the Spirit of God; that they needed that to sustain them and to give them power to go through their work in the earth.*
>
> Now I will give you a little of my experience in this line. *Joseph Smith visited me a great deal after his death, and taught me many important principles.* The last time he visited me was while I was in a storm at sea. I was going on my last mission to preside in England. . . . Joseph and Hyrum visited me, and the Prophet laid before me a great many things. *Among other things he told me to get the Spirit of God; that all of us needed it. He also told me what the Twelve Apostles would be called to go through on the earth before the coming of the Son of Man, and what the reward of their labors would be; but all that was taken from me for some reason.* Nevertheless I know it was most glorious, although much would be required at our hands.
>
> Joseph Smith continued visiting myself and others up to a certain time and then it stopped. *The last time I saw him was in heaven. In the night vision I saw him at the door of the temple in heaven.* He came and spoke to me. He said he could not stop to talk with me because he was in a hurry. The next man I met was *Father Smith;* he could not talk with me because he was in a hurry. *I met a half dozen brethren who had held high positions on earth* and none of them could stop and talk with me because they were in a hurry. I was very much astonished. By and by I saw the Prophet again, and I got the privilege to ask him a question. 'Now,' said I, 'I want to know why you are in a hurry. I have been in a hurry all through my life but I expected my hurry would be over when I got into the kingdom of heaven, if I ever did.' Joseph said, *'I will tell you, Brother Woodruff, every dispensation that has had the Priesthood on the earth and has gone into the celestial kingdom, has had a certain amount of work to do to prepare to go to the earth with the Savior when He goes to reign on the earth. Each dispensation has had ample time to do this work. We have not. We are the last dispensation, and so much work has to be done and we need to be in a hurry in order to accomplish it.'* Of course, that was satisfactory with me, but it was new doctrine to me.

---

[15]JD 21:317-318. Oct. 10, 1880.

> *Brigham Young also visited me after his death. On one occasion he and Brother Heber C. Kimball came in a splendid chariot, with fine white horses, and accompanied me to a conference that I was going to attend.* When I got there I asked Brother Brigham if he would take charge of the conference. 'No,' said he, 'I have done my work here. *I have come to see what you are doing and what you are teaching the people.'* And he told me what Joseph Smith had taught him in Winter Quarters, to teach the people to get the Spirit of God. He said, *'I want you to teach the people to get the Spirit of God. You cannot build up a Kingdom of God without that.'*[16]

Man must realize that his conduct is under constant observation by both good and evil spirits from beyond the veil. Heber C. Kimball taught that there were multitudes of spirit beings who were viewing the actions of the Saints:

> I called upon brother Joseph, and we walked down the bank of the river. He there told me what contests he had had with the devil; *he told me that he had contests with the devil, face to face. He also told me how he was handled and afflicted by the devil, and said, he had known circumstances where Elder Rigdon was pulled out of bed three times in one night.* After all this some persons will say to me, that there are no evil spirits. I tell you they are thicker than the 'Mormons' are in this country, but *the Lord has said that there are more for us than there can be against us. 'Who are they,' says one? Righteous men who have been upon the earth. . . .*
>
> That is the God whom I serve, *one who has millions of angels at His command.* Do you suppose that there are any angels here to-day? *I would not wonder if there were ten times more angels here than people. We do not see them, but they are here watching us, and are anxious for our salvation.* Will one out of twenty of those who are here to-day go through the gates into the celestial City?[17]

Brigham Young also asserted that many spirits were observing the conduct of the Saints. While speaking in the bowery in Salt Lake City he said,

> *Can you see spirits in this room? No.* Suppose the Lord should touch your eyes that you might see, could you then see the spirits? Yes, as plainly as you now see bodies, as did the servant of Elijah. If the Lord would permit it, and it was His will that it should be

[16]"Discourse Delivered at the Weber Stake Conference, Ogden, Monday, October 19th, 1896, by Prest. Wilford Woodruff," *The Deseret Weekly,* Vol. 53, No. 21, pp. 642-643, November 7, 1896.

[17]JD 3:229-230. March 2, 1856.

done, *you could see the spirits that have departed from this world, as plainly as you now see bodies with your natural eyes.*[18]

Evil Spirits Return to Earth Indiscriminately; Righteous Spirits Only For a Purpose

Spirits who reside in paradise are carefully organized and controlled through principles of righteousness. They are not free to wander about the earth without an assigned purpose. In contrast, the spirits under Satan's influence are given ample opportunity to haunt the earth and create whatever mischief and evil they choose. Elder Parley P. Pratt wrote that

> Many spirits of the departed, who are unhappy, linger in lonely wretchedness about the earth, and in the air, and especially about their ancient homesteads, and the places rendered dear to them by the memory of the former scenes.[19]

The mischief caused by these evil and undisciplined spirits is well-known in this present age, and reference to it is common in modern periodicals and newspapers. Typical of these reports is the following, which appeared in a Utah newspaper with a UPI byline:

> 'UNSEEN FORCE' EVEN MOVES HIS FURNITURE
>
> Osceola, Indiana (UPI) — Strange things have been happening at the Walter Szlanfucht home here, and his family won't come home until he finds out what is causing them.
>
> Szlanfucht told police Sunday night *an 'unseen force' has been moving furniture, making sounds and throwing pebbles against the side of his house.*

---

[18]JD 3:368. June 22, 1856. The spirits were seen by Elisha's servant, not Elijah's:

> And when the servant of the man of God was risen early, and gone forth, behold, an host compassed the city both with horses and chariots. And his servant said unto him, Alas, my master! how shall we do?
>
> And he answered, Fear not: for *they that be with us are more than they that be with them.*
>
> And Elisha prayed, and said, Lord, I pray thee, open his eyes, that he may see. And *the Lord opened the eyes of the young man; and he saw: and, behold, the mountain was full of horses and chariots of fire round about Elisha.* (2 Ki. 6:15-17)

The same sight was apparently shown to Sylvester Smith in the Kirtland Temple on January 22, 1836. The prophet Joseph recorded that "The heavens were opened unto Elder Sylvester Smith, and he, leaping up, exclaimed: *'The horsemen of Israel and the chariots thereof.'* " (HC 2:383) This may also be the sight seen in vision by Joseph's scribe the day previous, for the prophet recorded that he "saw, in a vision, *the armies of heaven* protecting the Saints in their return to Zion." (HC 2:381)

[19]Parley P. Pratt, *Key to the Science of Theology, op cit.,* p. 117.

> Police Capt. Richard Handley said he went to the home in this community east of South Bend and *saw a picture [fall] off the wall and a heavy ashtray shattered into pieces.*
>
> 'If I had not been a witness to this,' Handley said, 'I certainly would not have believed it could happen.'
>
> Handley said a *30-40 pound chair was lifted off the floor and dropped at his feet.* He said he sat the chair up again and went on to investigate the house, *only to find the chair tipped over again when he returned.* There was no one else in the house, he said.
>
> Szlanfucht said his wife and 9-year-old son will not return to the house until the poltergiests move out. His family is currently living with relatives. But some of his relatives are having similar problems.
>
> David Colbert, Szlanfucht's uncle, has reported similar happenings in the past few weeks at his home a mile away. Colbert said *pictures, vases and plates have been flying around the living room. Stones have been flying from the ground against the side of the house, he said, sometimes breaking windows.* Szlanfucht said he had heard sounds like pebbles hitting the side of his house.
>
> St. Joseph County Deputy Sheriff Joseph Molnar said he found some strange plastic objects outside the Colbert home. He described them as green and just larger than a robin's egg.[20]

This type of activity was also common in Brigham Young's day. He warned that these manifestations were the devil's counterfeits of true revelation:

> Pertaining to the present state of the world, *you know what evil spirits are doing. They are visiting the human family with various manifestations.* I told the people, years and years ago, that the Lord wished them to believe in revelation; and that if they did not believe what he had revealed, *he would let the Devil make them believe in revelation. Do you not think that the Devil is making them believe in revelation? What is called spirit-rapping, spirit-knocking and so forth, is produced by the spirits that the Lord has suffered to communicate to people on the earth, and make them believe in revelation.* There are many who do not believe this; but I believe it, and have from the beginning.
>
> If true principles are revealed from heaven to men, and if there are angels, and there is a possibility of their communicating to the human family, *always look for an opposite power, an evil power, to give manifestations also: look out for the counterfeit.*
>
> There is evil in the world, and there is also good. Was there

[20] *The Herald Journal*, Logan (Cache County) Utah, October 11, 1966.

> ever a counterfeit without a true coin? No. Is there communication from God? Yes. From holy angels? Yes, and we have been proclaiming these facts during nearly thirty years. *Are there any communications from evil spirits? Yes; and the Devil is making the people believe very strongly in revelations from the spirit world. This is called spiritualism, and it is said that thousands of spirits declare that 'Mormonism' is true; but what do that class of spirits know more than mortals? Perhaps a little more in some particulars than is known here, but it is only a little more.* They are subject in the spirit world to the same powers they were subject to here.[21]

In particular it should be observed that righteous spirits will not respond to the summons of spiritualist mediums and ouija board operators. Those who seek manifestations through these sources are placing themselves open to the influence and false guidance of evil spirits only, and are unable to summon the righteous from paradise. As President Charles W. Penrose stated while explaining the necromancy of the witch of Endor whom Saul visited,

> *It is beyond rational belief that such persons could at any period in ancient or modern times, invoke the spirits of departed servants or handmaidens of the Lord. They are not at the beck and call of witches, wizards, diviners or necromancers.* Pitiable indeed would be the condition of spirits in paradise if they were under any such control. They would not be at rest, nor be able to enjoy that liberty from the troubles and labors of earthly life which is essential to their happiness, but be in a condition of bondage, subject to the will and whims of persons who know not God and whose lives and aims are of the earth, earthy.
>
> *Nor is it in accordance with correct doctrine that a prophetess or prophet of the Lord could exercise the power to bring up or bring down the spirits of prophets and saints at will, to hold converse with them on earthly affairs.* That is not one of the functions of a prophet or a prophetess. The idea that such things can be done at the behest of men or women in the flesh ought not to be entertained by any Latter-day Saint.[22]

President Heber Q. Hale observed this principle to be true while in the spirit world:

> *The wicked and unrepentant spirits having still like all the rest, their free agency, and applying themselves to no useful or wholesome undertaking,* seek pleasure about their old haunts and exult to the sin and wretchedness of degenerate humanity. To this extent, they are still the tools

---

[21]JD 7:239-240. Sept. 1, 1859.

[22]Charles W. Penrose, "The Witch of Endor," *Improvement Era,* Vol. I, No. 7, p. 498, May, 1898. See also 1 Sam. 28:4-19; 1 Chron. 10:13; Deut. 18:10-12; etc.

> of Satan. *It is these idle mischievous and deceptive spirits who appear as miserable counterfeits at the spiritualistic scenes, table dancing and ouija board operations. The noble and great do not respond to the call of the mediums and to every curious group of meddlesome inquirers.* They would not do it in mortality, certainly they would not do it in their increased state of knowledge in the work of immortality. *These wicked and unrepentant spirits, as allies of Satan and his host, operate through willing mediums in the flesh. These three forces constitute an unholy trinity* upon the earth and are responsible for all the sin, wickedness, distress and misery among men and nations.[23]

Elder Parley P. Pratt also taught that the spirits of the righteous would hold themselves aloof from mediums and diviners:

> It is, then, a matter of certainty, according to the things revealed to the ancient Prophets, and renewed unto us, that *all the animal magnetic phenomena, all the trances and visions of clairvoyant states, all the phenomena of spiritual knockings, writing mediums, etc., are from impure, unlawful, and unholy sources; and that those holy and chosen vessels which hold the keys of Priesthood in this world, in the spirit world, or in the world of resurrected beings, stand as far aloof* from all these improper channels, or unholy mediums, of spiritual communication, as the heavens are higher than the earth, or as the mysteries of the third heaven, which are unlawful to utter, differ from the jargon of sectarian ignorance and folly, or the directions of foul spirits, abandoned wizards, magic-mongers, jugglers, and fortune-tellers.[24]

Evil Spirits Overcome Mortal Bodies, Prompt Evil Actions and Thoughts

Throughout time evil spirits under the influence of Satan have sought to possess mortal bodies. Jesus, during his mortal ministry, often cast such devils out of mortal bodies.[25] Instances of the influence of evil spirits upon mortals in the last days are also common. In his *Key to The Science of Theology* Elder Parley P. Pratt summarized the effect they have upon their victims:

> The more wicked of these are the kind spoken of in scripture, as *'foul spirits,' 'unclean spirits,'* spirits who afflict persons in the flesh, and *engender various diseases* in the human system. They will sometimes enter human bodies, and will *distract them, throw them into fits,* cast them

[23]Heber Q. Hale, *op cit.*
[24]JD 2:46. April 6, 1853.
[25]See Mk. 1:21-28; Lk. 8:26-39; Mt. 9:32-34; Mk. 9:14-29; Lk. 11:14-36.

> into the water, into the fire, etc. They will *trouble them with dreams, nightmares, hysterics, fever,* etc. They will also *deform them* in body and in features, by convulsions, cramps, contortions, etc., and will *sometimes compel them to utter blasphemies, horrible curses, and even words of other languages.* If permitted, they will *often cause death.* Some of these spirits are *adulterous, and suggest to the mind all manner of lasciviousness, all kinds of evil thoughts and temptations.*[26]

President Brigham Young also warned of their nearness and the influence which they exercise among mankind, saying that they often prompt man to do wrong:

> You may now see people with legions of evil spirits in and around them; *there are men who walk our streets that have more than a hundred devils in them and round about them, prompting them to all manner of evil, and some too that profess to be Latter-day Saints,* and if you were to take the devils out of them and from about them, you *would leave them dead corpses;* for I believe there would be nothing left of them.
>
> I want you to understand these things; and if you should say or think that I know nothing about them, be pleased to find out and inform me. You can see the acts of these evil spirits in every place, *the whole country is full of them, the whole earth is alive with them, and they are continually trying to get into the tabernacles of the human family, and are always on hand to prompt us to depart from the strict line of our duty.*
>
> You know that we sometimes need a prompter; if any one of you was called by the government of the United States to go to Germany, Italy, or any foreign nation, as an Ambassador, if you did not understand the language somebody would have to interpret for you. *Well, these evil spirits are ready to prompt you. Do they prompt us? Yes, and I could put my hands on a dozen of them while I have been on this stand; they are here on the stand.* Could we do without the devils? No, we could not get along without them. *They are here, and they suggest this, that, and the other.*[27]

Discerning Between Righteous and Evil Spirits

A number of keys have been set forth by latter-day prophets to aid man in determining the nature of spirits which he may encounter. These representatives from beyond the veil may take any of several forms, and each type of being must be identified by different characteristics.

The greatest probability of encounter with alien spirits rests in confrontation with mortal bodies which have been

---

[26]Parley P. Pratt, *Key To The Science of Theology, op cit.,* p. 117.

[27]JD 3:369. June 22, 1856.

overcome by evil spirits. Parley P. Pratt offered the following as a means of identifying such individuals:

> A person, on looking another in the eye, who is possessed of an evil spirit, *will feel a shock—a nervous feeling, which will, as it were, make his hair stand on end:* in short, a shock resembling that produced in a nervous sytem by the sight of a serpent.
>
> Some of these foul spirits, when possessing a person, will cause *a disagreeable smell about the person thus possessed* which will be plainly manifest to the senses of those about him, even though the person thus afflicted should be washed and change his clothes every few minutes.
>
> There are, in fact, most awful instances of the spirit of *lust, and of bawdy and abominable words and actions,* inspired and uttered by persons possessed of such spirits, even though the persons were virtuous and modest so long as they possessed their own agency.
>
> *Some of these spirits cause deafness, others dumbness, etc.*
>
> We can suggest no remedy for these multiplied evils, to which poor human nature is subject, except a good life, while we are in possession of our faculties, prayers and fastings of good and holy men, and the ministry of those who have power given them to rebuke evil spirits, and cast out devils, in the name of Jesus Christ.[28]

Concerning spirit manifestations which come from beyond the earth, Elder Pratt set forth other tests based on authority and correct channels of communication:

> The fact of spiritual communication being established, by which the living hear from the dead—being no longer a question of controversy with the well informed, we drop that point, and *call attention to the means of discriminating or judging between the lawful and the unlawful mediums or channels of communication—between the holy and impure, the truths and falsehoods, thus communicated.*
>
> The words of the holy Prophet in our text, while they admit the principle of the living hearing from the dead, *openly rebuke, and sharply reprove, persons for seeking to those who have familiar spirits, and to wizards that peep and mutter,* and remind us that a people should seek unto their God for the living to hear from the dead!
>
> By what means, then, can a people seek unto their God, for such an important blessing as to hear from the dead?

---

[28]Parley P. Pratt, *Key to the Science of Theology, op cit.,* pp. 117-118. An editorial by Joseph Smith in the *Times and Seasons* entitled "Try the Spirits," gives an excellent coverage of the problems involved in determining whether revelations have come from God or Satan. It is reprinted in HC 4:571-581.

And how shall we discriminate between those who seek to Him, and those who seek the same by unlawful means?

In the first place, *no persons can successfully seek to God for this privilege, unless they believe in direct revelation in modern times.*

Secondly, *it is impossible for us to seek Him successfully, and remain in our sins.* A thorough repentance and reformation of life are absolutely necessary, if we would seek to Him.

Thirdly, *Jesus Christ is the only name given under heaven, as a medium through which to approach to God. None, then, can be lawful mediums, who are unbelievers in Jesus Christ, or in modern revelation; or who remain in their sins; or who act in their own name, instead of the name appointed.*

And moreover, *the Lord has appointed a Holy Priesthood on the earth, and in the heavens, and also in the world of spirits;* which Priesthood is after the order or similitude of His Son; and *has committed to this Priesthood the keys of holy and divine revelation, and of correspondence, or communication between angels, spirits, and men,* and between all the holy departments, principalities, and powers of His government in all worlds.[29]

The *Doctrine and Covenants* sets forth another test whereby man may discern the nature of supernatural beings whom he may encounter:

There are two kinds of beings in heaven, namely: Angels, who are resurrected personages, having bodies of flesh and bones.

For instance, Jesus said: *Handle me and see, for a spirit hath not flesh and bones, as ye see me have.*

Secondly: The spirits of just men made perfect, they who are not resurrected, but inherit the same glory.

When a messenger comes saying he has a message from God, offer him your hand and request him to shake hands with you.

If he be an angel he will do so, and you will feel his hand.

If he be the spirit of a just man made perfect he will come in his glory; for that is the only way he can appear—

Ask him to shake hands with you, but *he will not move,* because it is contrary to the order of heaven for a just man to deceive; but *he will still deliver his message.*

If it be the devil as an angel of light, when you ask him to shake hands he will offer you his hand, and you will not feel anything; you may therefore detect him.

---

[29]JD 2:45-46. April 6, 1853.

> These are three grand keys whereby you may know whether any administration is from God.[30]

Important counsel is revealed to the Church by the Lord in which He instructs members how they should proceed if visited by an unidentified spirit being:

> If you behold a spirit manifested that you cannot understand, and you receive not that spirit, *ye shall ask of the Father in the name of Jesus; and if he give not unto you that spirit, then you may know that it is not of God.*
>
> *And it shall be given unto you, power over that spirit; and you shall proclaim against that spirit with a loud voice that it is not of God—*
>
> Not with railing accusation, that ye be not overcome, neither with boasting nor rejoicing, lest you be seized therewith.
>
> He that receiveth of God, let him account it of God; and let him rejoice that he is accounted of God worthy to receive.[31]

Types of Angels Who Minister on Earth

An angel is a servant or assistant. A ministering angel represents his master by visiting or ministering to others in his name. In addition to mortal servants, the powers of good and evil have five types of angels who represent them on the earth.

1. *Pre-mortal Spirits.* There is only one instance where an angel of this type is known to have visited the earth—that was the "angel of the Lord [who] appeared unto Adam, saying: Why dost thou offer sacrifices unto the Lord?"[32] The scriptures are mute concerning the appearance of such beings, other than implying that they have spirit bodies in human form.[33] On the basis of present scripture it cannot be stated whether they are surrounded with glory as are just men made perfect.

2. *Translated Beings.* Certain individuals have been changed so that their lives are extended and they are freed

---

[30]D&C 129:1-9.

[31]D&C 50:31-34.

[32]Moses 5:6-8. There is a certain amount of supposition in this interpretation. The prophet Joseph taught that "there are no angels who minister to this earth but those who do belong or have belonged to it." (D&C 130:5) Since no mortals are known to have died or to have been translated during this period the assumption is made that this was a pre-mortal spirit.

[33]See Eth. 3:15-16.

from bodily growth and suffering. Those who have undergone such a change are known as translated beings and become "ministering angels unto many planets." Concerning the nature of such beings the prophet Joseph Smith said,

> Many have supposed that the doctrine of translation was a doctrine whereby men were taken immediately into the presence of God, and into an eternal fullness, but this is a mistaken idea. *Their place of habitation is that of the terrestrial order, and a place prepared for such characters He held in reserve to be ministering angels unto many planets, and who as yet have not entered into so great a fullness as those who are resurrected from the dead.* . . .
>
> This distinction is made between the doctrine of the actual resurrection and translation: *translation obtains deliverance from the tortures and sufferings of the body, but their existence will prolong as to the labors and toils of the ministry, before they can enter into so great a rest and glory.* . . .
>
> They rest from their labors for a long time, and yet *their work is held in reserve for them, that they are permitted to do the same work, after they receive a resurrection* for their bodies.[34]

A year later the Prophet Joseph taught that

> *Translated beings cannot enter into rest until they have undergone a change equivalent to death. Translated bodies are designed for future missions.*
>
> The angel that appeared to John on the Isle of Patmos was a translated or resurrected body [i.e. personage], Jesus Christ went in body after His resurrection, to minister to resurrected bodies.[35]

Many mortal beings have been translated, including

A. Enoch and his city. (See Gen. 5:24; Heb. 11:5; Moses 7:18-21, 31, 63, 69; D&C 38:4; 45:11-14)

B. Many Saints between the time of Enoch and Noah. (Moses 7:27)

C. The priests and people in the days of Melchizedek. (Inspired Version Gen. 14:30-34)

D. Moses. (Al. 45:18-19; Mt. 17:1-6; HC 3:387)

E. Elijah. (2 Ki. 2:11; Mt. 17:1-6; HC 3:387)

F. Alma the younger? (Al. 45:18-19)

G. Nephi, son of Helaman? (3 Ne. 1:3)

[34] HC 4:210. Oct. 5, 1840.
[35] HC 4:425. Oct. 2, 1841.

If the accepted interpretation of D&C 133:53-55 is correct, then these beings "were with Christ in his resurrection," and are now resurrected rather than translated beings.

Several others were translated and are, apparently, still on the earth in translated form:

H. John the Revelator. (Mt. 16:28; Jn. 21:21-23; D&C 7; 3 Ne. 28:6-8)

I. Three Nephite disciples. (3 Ne. 28:1-23)

J. There may be another group of beings who have been translated, of whom the Lord revealed, "All are under sin, *except those which I have reserved unto myself,* holy men that ye know not of." (D&C 49:8)

Apparently there is no difference distinguishable to the mortal eye between translated beings and mortal bodies. Indeed, it may be that Paul was referring to translated beings when he said that "some have entertained angels unawares."[36]

3. *Righteous Spirits from Paradise—Just Men Made Perfect.* These are the spirits of the righteous who have died and entered paradise. They have worked out or are working out their salvation and exaltation in the righteous portion of the spirit world and will eventually be "made perfect through Jesus the mediator of the new covenant, who wrought out this perfect atonement through the shedding of his own blood."[37] The spirits of just men made perfect are "they who are not resurrected, but inherit the same glory"[38] as all who have or will eventually attain perfection: the celestial kingdom. The prophet Joseph Smith chose to term such beings spirits and reserved the term angel for resurrected beings.[39] He explained

[36]Heb. 13:2.

[37]D&C 76:69. In the strict sense, no man can become perfect until after the judgment (when the Savior stands as his mediator before the Father and allows him to partake of the benefits of the atonement) and the resurrection (which will restore the body necessary for him to experience a fulness of joy). It would thus seem that just men made perfect are not yet perfect but are still laboring to achieve that goal in a situation where their glory is assured upon completion of their preparatory tasks.

[38]D&C 129:3.

[39]Though spirits also fill the function of angels by being servants or assistants and by visiting or ministering to others, there is evidence that spirit beings may refer to themselves as angels (see, for example, pp. 136-141). Most other Church leaders made no such distinction in terminology. Orson Pratt said, for instance, "There are angels who have been to this

the glory which surrounds righteous spirit beings, and implied by his reference to James Adams, who had just died, that a righteous man automatically qualified as a "just man made perfect" by entry into the spirit world:

> The Hebrew Church 'came unto the spirits of just men made perfect, and unto an innumerable company of angels, unto God the Father of all, and to Jesus Christ, the Mediator of the new covenant.' What did they learn by coming of the spirits of just men made perfect? Is it written? No. What they learned has not been and could not have been written. What object was gained by this communication with the spirits of the just? *It was the established order of the kingdom of God: the keys of power and knowledge were with them to communicate to the Saints.* Hence the importance of understanding the distinction between the spirits of the just and angels.
>
> *Spirits can only be revealed in flaming fire or glory. Angels have advanced further, their light and glory being tabernacled; and hence they appear in bodily shape. The spirits of just men are made ministering servants to those who are sealed unto life eternal, and it is through them that the sealing power comes down.*
>
> *Patriarch Adams is now one of the spirits of the just men made perfect; and, if revealed now, must be revealed in fire; and the glory could not be endured.* Jesus showed Himself to His disciples, and they thought it was His spirit, and they were afraid to approach His spirit. *Angels have advanced higher in knowledge and power than spirits.*
>
> Concerning Brother James Adams, . . . *He has had revelations concerning his departure, and has gone to a more important work. When men are prepared, they are better off to go hence. Brother Adams has gone to open up a more effectual door for the dead. The spirits of the just are exalted to a greater and more glorious work; hence they are blessed in their departure to the world of spirits.* Enveloped in flaming fire, they are not far from us, and know and understand our thoughts, feelings, and motions, and are often pained therewith.[40]

These are the spirits for whom the handshake test of Doctrine and Covenants, section 129 applies: They will appear in glory, and they will not deceive mortals by shaking hands with them but will deliver a message.

4. *Evil Spirits from Hell.* Elder Parley P. Pratt described the difference in appearance between these spirits and the righteous spirits which dwell in paradise.

---

world and have never yet received a resurrection, whose spirits have gone hence into celestial paradise." (JD 15:321) The scriptures also use the term *angel* to mean righteous spirits. See Heb. 1:7, 13-14.

[40]HC 6:51-52. Oct. 9, 1843.

Persons who have departed this life, and have not yet been raised from the dead are spirits.

These are two kinds, viz.—good and evil.

These two kinds also include many grades of good and evil.

The good spirits, in the superlative sense of the word, are they who, in this life, partook of the Holy Priesthood, and of the fulness of the gospel.

This class of spirits minister to the heirs of salvation, both in this world and in the world of spirits. They can appear unto men, when permitted; but not having a fleshly tabernacle, they cannot hide their glory. *Hence, an unembodied spirit, if it be a holy personage, will be surrounded with a halo of resplendent glory, or brightness, above the brightness of the sun.*

Whereas, spirits not worthy to be glorified will appear without this brilliant halo, and although they often attempt to pass as angels of light, there is more or less of darkness about them. So it is with Satan and his hosts who have not been embodied.[41]

The same lack of glory will characterize all the hosts of Satan, including those cast down to earth without the privilege of obtaining bodies. Though Satan's angels may attempt to masquerade as angels of light,[42] yet they may still be identified by their effort to deceive when subjected to the handshake test of Doctrine and Covenants, section 129.

Clues to aid in distinguishing evil spirits which have overcome and possessed mortal bodies have been given earlier in this chapter.

5. *Resurrected Beings.* These angels, who have been reunited with their physical bodies of flesh and bones,[43] no longer dwell in the spirit world, and they "do not reside on a planet like this earth; But they reside in the presence of God."[44] These beings are surrounded by glory in accordance with the heavenly kingdom which they are to inherit.[45] This glory is visible to those who observe them. Joseph Smith, as an example, described the angel, Moroni, who was a "messenger sent from the presence of God," as having a visible glow.

---

[41]Parley P. Pratt, *Key To The Science of Theology, op cit.*, p. 116.

[42]2 Cor. 11:14. See Moses 1:12-18.

[43]D&C 129:1-2.

[44]D&C 130:6-7.

[45]D&C 88:28-31.

Not only was his robe exceedingly white, but his whole person was glorious beyond description, and his countenance truly like lightning. The room was exceedingly light, but not so very bright as immediately around his person.[46]

Such beings, when they come to earth as messengers, can be identified by their surrounding glory and by the tangible feel of their body when subjected to the handshake test of Doctrine and Covenants, section 129.

Righteous Spirits Return to Earth For Many Purposes

The return of spirits from paradise to earth is a common event. It appears that spirits usually return to those whom they have known in mortality, and that their return is to fulfill a variety of purposes. President Joseph F. Smith taught that

We are told by the Prophet Joseph Smith, that 'there are no angels who minister to this earth but those who do belong or have belonged to it.' Hence, when messengers are sent to minister to the inhabitants of this earth, *they are not strangers, but from the ranks of our kindred, friends, and fellow-beings and fellow-servants. . . . Our fathers and mothers, brothers, sisters and friends* who have passed away from this earth, having been faithful, and worthy to enjoy these rights and privileges, *may have a mission given them to visit their relatives and friends upon the earth again, bringing from the divine Presence messages of love, of warning, or reproof and instruction, to those* whom they had learned to love in the flesh.[47]

Parley P. Pratt was well aware of the interest spirits beyond the veil hold in their mortal loved ones. While writing of the manner in which such beings often communicate with mortals through dreams, he explained that

When the outward organs of thought and perception are released from their activity, the nerves unstrung, and the whole of mortal humanity lies hushed in quiet slumbers, in order to renew its strength and vigor, it is then that the spiritual organs are at liberty, in a certain degree, to assume their wonted functions, to recall some faint outlines, some confused and half-defined recollections, of that heavenly world, and those endearing scenes of their former estate, from which they have descended in order to obtain and mature a tabernacle of flesh. *Their kindred spirits, their guardian angels then hover about them with the fondest affection, the most anxious solicitude. Spirit com-*

---

[46]JS 2:32. This glory is typical of all resurrected beings. See JS 2:16-20; 3 Ne. 19:25; Lk. 17:24; Acts 7:55-56; D&C 76:19-21; D&C 110:2-4; Rev. 21:23; etc.

[47]Joseph F. Smith, *Gospel Doctrine, op cit.,* pp. 435, 436.

> *munes with spirit, thought meets thought, soul blends with soul in all the raptures of mutual, pure, and eternal love.*
>
> In this situation, the spiritual organs are susceptible of converse with Deity, or of communion with angels, and the spirits of just men made perfect.
>
> In this situation, *we frequently hold communication with our departed father, mother, brother, sister, son or daughter; or with the former husband or wife of our bosom, whose affection for us, being rooted and grounded in the eternal elements, or issuing from under the sanctuary of love's eternal fountain, can never be lessened or diminished by death, distance of space, or length of years.*
>
> We may, perhaps, have had a friend of the other sex, whose pulse beat in unison with our own; whose every thought was big with the aspirations, the hopes of a bright future in union with our own; whose happiness in time or in eternity, would never be fully consummated without that union. Such a one, snatched from time in the very bloom of youth, lives in the other sphere, with the same bright hope, *watching our every footstep, in our meanderings through the rugged path of life, with longing desires for our eternal happiness, and eager for our safe arrival in the same sphere.*
>
> With what tenderness of love, with what solicitude of affection will *they watch over our slumbers, hang about our pillow, and seek to communicate with our spirits, to warn us of dangers or temptation, to comfort and soothe our sorrow, or to ward off the ills which might befall us, or perchance to give us some kind token of remembrance or undying love!*[48]

A careful analysis of numerous accounts of visits to earth by those in paradise reveals that almost all such visits are to fulfill one of seven purposes. The spirits return to

1. give counsel,
2. give comfort,
3. obtain or give information,
4. serve as guardian angels,
5. prepare others for death,
6. call mortals into the spirit world, and
7. escort the dying through the veil of death.

Examples of each of these activities will be considered.

---

[48]Parley P. Pratt, *Key To The Science of Theology, op cit.*, pp. 120-122.

Spirits Return To Give Counsel

Spirits beyond the veil apparently learn the effect that their mortal actions have had upon others when they go into the spirit world and sometimes seek to correct conditions on earth which they may have caused by counseling the loved ones they have left behind. Elder Jacob Hamblin told how a visit of his deceased father-in-law caused his wife to cease ridiculing the Church and to accept baptism:

> My wife's father took great pains to abuse and insult me with his tongue. Without having any conception how my prediction would be fulfilled, I said to him one day, 'You will not have the privilege of abusing me much more.' A few days after he was taken sick, and died.
>
> Soon after the death of her father, my wife asked me, good-naturedly, why I did not pray in the house or with her. I replied, that I felt better to pray by myself than I did before unbelievers. *She said that she was a believer; that her father had appeared to her in a dream, and told her not to oppose me any more as she had done; and that he was in trouble on account of the way he had used me.* Soon after that she was baptized, which was a great comfort to me.[49]

On other occasions spirits may return to counsel their loved ones against unfortunate moves or dangerous situations. Ruth E. Christensen told of the unheeded warning given by her deceased grandfather to her mother the day before her home burned to the ground and she was badly burned:

> In 1924 when I was twelve years old, our home in Teton Basin burned, and my sister and I were trapped in it. We were alone when the tragedy struck, as our mother and father were in Rexburg purchasing necessary winter supplies and my two brothers were away. . . .
>
> Mother and Dad did not know about the fire until the next day. Dad had gone ahead in the car and Mother was to follow on the train. An unusual thing happened to her this day. *On her way to the train, her father, who had been dead for ten years, came to her and said, 'Ellen, stay home and take care of what you have.'*
>
> It seemed very strange to her and yet she didn't want to disappoint Dad, who was waiting for her, so she went on and they stayed that night at Dad's cousin's place. *And all night she could smell smoke.* She asked Mrs. Cherry to get up and look around to see if anything was burning. Finally she dozed off and *she dreamed she saw*

[49]*Jacob Hamblin, op cit.*, p. 13.

two little girls standing by a burning house, with their arms out to her. This happened the night our home was burned.[50]

It appears that spirits also manifest themselves to their mortal companions to counsel them to continue their mortal labors and to assure them of their eventual companionship in the future life. For these purposes Briant S. Stevens returned and visited his youthful companion, Fred J. Bluth, in a dream two nights after his body was buried. Brother Bluth, who attended school with Briant Stevens and was accustomed to walking home with his departed companion at the end of classes each day, recorded the manifestation in this manner:

> I thought that Briant was waiting for me at the gate as usual—only *he was dressed in white raiment, like that in which he lay in the coffin.* When I came near him, he sprang to my side and threw his arms around my neck. He took my hand, and said: 'Come, Fred, with me.' . . .
>
> A large wagon stood before the door. The driver came down from his seat, and we got in and drove to a building like a granary. Briant opened the doors. And then I heard a voice saying:
>
> 'You must fill the wagon with corn.'
>
> Briant and I began to shovel corn into the wagon; but soon he stopped. I asked;
>
> 'Is it enough?'
>
> And he answered:
>
> 'Not yet.'
>
> I worked a little longer, and again I called to him:
>
> 'Is it enough, Briant?'
>
> And once more he replied:
>
> 'Not yet, Fred.'
>
> After a still longer time, during which I worked dilligently, I asked him for the third time:
>
> 'Is it enough?'
>
> And Briant replied:
>
> *'Yes, it is enough. Now you must come with me, Fred.'*

---

[50]Dorothy South Hackworth, *The Master's Touch* (Salt Lake City, Utah: Bookcraft, Inc., 1961), pp. 17, 18.

I climbed into the wagon with him; and then we drove away together. At once I awoke.

Little Fred felt startled by this dream. He related it to Edgar Peterson, when the latter asked:

'Do you know the meaning of your dream?'

'No.'

'Then I will give you the interpretation. *It means that your earthly work is not yet finished and that when it is done, Briant will call for you.*'[51]

Spirits Return To Give Comfort

Just as spirits return to earth to give counsel to loved ones in certain situations, they also come back through the veil to give comfort and assurance to their relatives and friends. Elder Parley P. Pratt, as an example, wrote of the visit he received from his deceased wife as he was held by a mob in a Missouri dungeon in 1839. After months of captivity, he cried to the Lord in fasting and prayer to know if he would ever escape from confinement. The appearance of his wife was the answer he was given:

> After some days of prayer and fasting, and seeking the Lord on the subject, I retired to my bed in my lonely chamber at an early hour, and while the other prisoners and the guard were chatting and beguiling the lonesome hours in the upper apartment of the prison, I lay in silence, seeking and expecting an answer to my prayer, when suddenly I seemed carried away in the spirit, and no longer sensible to outward objects with which I was surrounded. A heaven of peace and calmness pervaded my bosom; *a personage from the world of spirits stood before me with a smile of compassion in every look, and pity mingled with the tenderest love and sympathy in every expression of the countenance. A soft hand seemed placed within my own, and a glowing cheek was laid in tenderness and warmth upon mine. A well-known voice saluted me,* which I readily recognized as that of the wife of my youth, who had for nearly two years been sweetly sleeping where the wicked cease from troubling and the weary are at rest. I was made to realize that she was sent to commune with me, and answer my question.
>
> Knowing this, I said to her in a most earnest and inquiring tone, 'Shall I ever be at liberty again in this life and enjoy the society of my family and the Saints, and preach the Gospel as I have done?' She answered definitely and unhesitatingly, 'YES!'

---

[51]Kennon, *Helpful Visions, op cit.*, pp. 38-39.

> I then recollected that I had agreed to be satisfied with the knowledge of that one fact, but now I wanted more. Said I: 'Can you tell me how, or by what means, or when I shall escape?' She replied, *'That thing is not made known to me yet.'* I instantly felt that I had gone beyond my agreement and my faith in asking this last question, and that I must be contented at present with the answer to the first.
>
> Her gentle spirit then saluted me and withdrew. I came to myself. The doleful noise of the guards, and the wrangling and angry words of the old apostate again grated on my ears, but heaven and hope were in my soul.
>
> Next morning I related the whole circumstance of my vision to my two fellow prisoners, who rejoiced exceedingly. This may seem to some like an idle dream, or a romance of the imagination, but to me it was and always will be a reality, both as it regards what I then experienced and the fulfillment afterwards.[52]

David P. Kimball received comfort and aid from his parents who resided beyond the veil as he wandered and suffered on the Salt River desert in Arizona:

> Another long and dreary day passed, but I could see nothing but wolves and ravens and a barren desert covered with cactus, and had about made up my mind that the promise of two years life, made by my father, was not to be realized. While in this terrible plight, and when I had just about given up all hope, *my father and mother appeared to me and gave me a drink of water and comforted me, telling me I would be found by my friends who were out searching for me, and that I should live two years longer as I had been promised.* When night came I saw another fire a few hundred yards from me and could see my friends around it, but I was so hoarse I could not make them hear. By this time my body was almost lifeless and I could hardly move, but my mind was in a perfect condition and I could realize everything that happened around me.[53]

Similar comfort was given to Merrill Neville the night before his death. His grandfather, who had died previously, appeared to both Merrill and his mother to give them comfort:

> Merrill Neville, son of Eliza Dean Neville, aged 19 years, was lying near death's door; Sister Neville knelt by his bedside in prayer.

[52]Parley P. Pratt, *Autobiography of Parley P. Pratt* (sixth edition; Salt Lake City, Utah: Deseret Book Company, 1966), pp. 238-239. Shortly after this incident Elder Pratt was able to escape from the mobocrats and make his way to Illinois to join the body of the Church.

[53]O. F. Whitney, *Helpful Visions, op cit.*, p. 15. For information concerning his promise of two years more life see p. 141.

As she prayed *she felt her deceased father's presence in the room and was impressed with these words: 'Eliza, Merrill shall live. You know, Eliza, I always had the desire to go on a mission, but I never had the privilege. I want Merrill to take a mission for me now.'* Sister Neville was encouraged, thinking that her son would surely live.

The next day Merrill called his mother to his bedside, and taking her face between his hands he said, 'O, mother, you've been a good mother to me; you've done all you could do for me.'

'Yes, Merrill, I think I have never whipped you in my life. You have been a good boy. You have always done whatever we asked you to do.'

'Both you and father have always been so good to me,' repeated the dying boy.

Taking his mother's hands in his, he said, 'Mother, you won't feel bad if I die, will you?'

Then his mother repeated to him the impression she had received the day before. *'Yes, mother, I shall live; and I'm going on a mission for Grandpa Dean, but the mission's not upon this earth. If I'm permitted to come back, mother, I'll come and tell you all I can.'*

The next morning he said, *'I feel like a new man this morning, mother; Grandpa Dean held my head all night.'* His spirit left his body about 7 o'clock in the evening of the same day.[54]

The indication and comfort that Heber J. Grant would survive a serious operation was given by Lucy Stringham Grant, his deceased first wife, to Augusta Winters Grant, his second wife:

When he was operated on for appendicitis, *his wife Lucy, who as stated, is dead, visited his home and promised his wife Augusta Winters, to whom he was married May 6, 1884, that he should recover.* He felt so impressed himself, and believed that he should live through the ordeal. When, therefore, after the operation the doctors said that blood poison had set in, and he could not live, neither his wife nor himself felt any alarm, but both had a perfect assurance that he should recover and their faith was not in vain.[55]

President Edward J. Wood, first president of the Cardston (Alberta, Canada) temple, recorded an experience which took place in that sacred edifice. A Canadian Elder had been called to fill a mission to South America but had been drowned

---

[54]"Manifestation About Building of Temples," *Deseret Evening News,* May 18, 1918.

[55]Andrew Jenson, *Latter-day Saint Biographical Encyclopedia, op cit.,* Vol. I, p. 151.

when his ship was wrecked two days out of New York City. His parents, who were officiators in the Cardston temple, grieved about his death a great deal. President Wood wrote the following concerning the message of comfort this missionary gave to his father as he spoke to him in the temple:

> It was very difficult for them to be reconciled, but they carried on, however, as officiators in the Temple, praying always that something would happen to alleviate their mental suffering.
>
> One evening, several months after the accident, the father had finished his part in the Temple and very strange to say, he did not prepare to go home as had been his custom; but instead he went upstairs and sat down at a small stand in the Celestial room, which is not far from one of the three sealing rooms. That evening I was officiating at the only one being used. The father wondered why he was sitting there alone, all members and officiators of the company having gone downstairs, and he started to leave the room, when to his great surprise he thought *he heard the voice of his lost son, saying: 'Father, you and mother have been greatly worried over my being shipwrecked but you wouldn't be grieved at all if you knew the missionary work I have been called to do in the spirit world where I am now laboring, which is more important than if I had gone to South America.'* As the father seemed to awaken from the experience, he wondered if it was just his imagination about hearing from his son, and was about to leave the room when again the heavenly feeling came over him and again he thought he heard the voice of his son saying: *'Father, you are in doubt as to my having actually delivered my message to you. To prove to you that you have heard from your missionary son, from the spirit world, Brother Wood will call you into the sealing room where he is officiating to bear your testimony, something he has never done before. He doesn't know you are here. This should be a testimony to you that you have heard from me, so that you and mother will no longer refuse to be reconciled at my passing.'*[56]

---

[56]Edward J. Wood, "A Deceased Missonary Son Speaks To His Father," as reprinted in N. B. Lundwall, *Faith Like the Ancients, op cit.*, p. 183. President Wood continued his account of the experience by telling how he was prompted to call the brother into the sealing room:

> The father wondered: 'How will Brother Wood call me when he thinks I have long since left the Temple?' He went downstairs and hesitated several times about going home, but after several attempts to leave the Temple he went upstairs again, and on reaching the top of the stairs leading to the Celestial room, was met by one of the brethren acting as a proxy, who said to him: 'I am looking for you, Brother ________, Brother Wood wants you to come in the sealing room and speak to the few people there.'
>
> *I shall always remember how I felt when the impression came to me to call for this certain brother. At first I thought to myself, 'He has gone home.' I have never asked any one to speak in the sealing room, and no doubt this good man has gone home several hours ago. And yet the feeling was so strong,* I asked the Brother helping me to see if Brother________

Spirits Return to Obtain or Give Information

Just as spirit beings return from paradise to earth to give counsel and comfort, they also return to both obtain and give information. Elder Thomas A. Shreeve recorded the spirit visitor who appeared to him to obtain an account of his missionary labors in Australia:

> Brother May was at a table in the room, and we were conversing. Across the room, to the right of my head, was an open door, which I could see without lifting my head from the pillow.
>
> While I lay there listening to the words of Brother May, *a personage clothed in a white robe entered the room. He appeared to be a young man, and had a very pleasing countenance.* This personage passed around the bed and stood near the table. Brother May rose and offered the visitant a chair, and then withdrew. The young man seated himself at the table and opened a book. He said,
>
> *'Are you ready to report the Sydney Branch?'*
>
> 'Yes, sir,' I responded.
>
> 'Then proceed.'
>
> I gave him an account of all our doings in Sydney, beginning with our first effort of reorganizing and closing with my last act previous to sailing—*for all these things seemed plain to my mind.* The recital seemed to occupy me several minutes and I continued to speak freely. He wrote in the book rapidly, and never once interrupted me. *I felt that he was taking every word I uttered.* When I stopped, he asked,
>
> 'Have you anything more to say?'
>
> 'No, sir,' I answered.
>
> Then he turned the leaves back, and seemed to read from the beginning. He said:

---

was in the building; if so, please ask him to come here a few minutes and bear his testimony.

When the good brother appeared in the door of the sealing room, he seemed very pale but quite happy. *He came inside and to our great astonishment told us with the finest spirit possible of his experience in receiving the message from his lost missionary son, and of how he wondered whether I would call him into the sealing room when I should know he had gone home.* A very fine spirit was present, and how pleasing it was to all who knew him and his wife who were in the room when he said: 'We will hereafter feel quite reconciled. *It is a wonderful testimony to me and will be to his mother and all members of our family that the Lord certainly moves in a mysterious way to accomplish His purposes.'*

Melvin S. Tagg also makes reference to this instance in *The Life of Edward James Wood,* pp. 110-111, and identifies the missionary as Keith Burt, of Alberta Stake.

'Very well. Now where are you going?'

'To New Zealand.'

He recorded my answer in the book, and then signed his name —I could not see the words of his name, but *I felt that he was writing his own signature.* He closed the book and walked around to the right side of the bed, *shook hands with me, and said:*

'Good-by; *I will be there before you.*'[57]

Anthon H. Lund, president of the Manti temple from 1891 to 1893, recorded an instance of spirits returning from beyond the veil to impart information to their descendant still on earth, which came to his attention during his temple labors:

I remember one day in the temple at Manti, a brother from Mount Pleasant rode down to the temple to take part in the work, and as he passed the cemetery in Ephraim, he looked ahead (it was early in the morning), and *there was a large multitude all dressed in white,* and he wondered how that could be. Why should there be so many up here; it was too early for a funeral, he thought; but he drove up and *several of them stepped out in front of him and they talked to him.* They said, 'Are you going to the temple?' 'Yes,' 'Well, *these that you see here are your relatives and they want you to do work for them.*' 'Yes,' he said, 'but I am going down today to finish my work. I have no more names and I do not know the names of those who you say are related to me.' *'But when you go down to the temple today you will find there are records that give our names.'* He was surprised. He looked until they all disappeared, and drove on. As he came into the temple, Recorder Farnsworth came up to him and said, 'I have just received records from England and they all belong to you.' And there were hundreds of names that had just arrived, and what was told him by these persons that he saw was fulfilled. You can imagine what joy came to his heart, and what a testimony it was to him that the Lord wants this work done.[58]

Spirits Serve as Guardian Angels

There is evidence that some mortal beings are watched over and shielded from danger by spirit world beings functioning as guardian angels. Peter Johnson, as he went into

[57]Thomas A. Shreeve, *Helpful Visions, op cit.,* pp. 59-60. Prior to relating the account of this visitation, Elder Shreeve told of the intense fever and suffering which brought him near to death and apparently enabled him to receive this communication in the form of a dream.

[58]N. B. Lundwall, *Temples of the Most High, op cit.,* p. 124.

the spirit world, was met by a spirit being who said, "You did not know that I was here." Peter replied, "No, but I see you are. Who are you?" The reply: *"I am your guardian angel; I have been following you constantly while on earth."*[59] Henry Zollinger recorded his entry into the spirit realm, saying that "at that moment *my guardian angel,* my mother and my sister Ann were beside me."[60]

The departed sister of Elder Thomas A. Shreeve appeared to him during his missionary labors and told him that she would come to warn him if danger threatened, thus showing that she was functioning as his guardian angel:

> While I lay, wide awake, in my bed I suddenly saw a *hand and arm, clothed in a white sleeve which extended down midway between the elbow and the wrist,* and holding a torch in its hand—thrust out from the side of a dark fireplace which was in the room.
>
> At first there was but a spark of light at the top of the torch, but gradually the flame grew greater and the light stronger, until it filled the whole room; and then from out the darkness behind the arm and torch stepped the figure of a little girl.
>
> I recognized it instantly as that of my young sister Sophia, who had died six years before in England, while I was in Utah. At the time of her death she was eight and a half years old, and had but recently been baptized into the Church. She came toward the bed, and *I saw that she was dressed in beautiful white raiment. From her whole person a pleasing light seemed to emanate. She approached the bed and leaned over it, placing her arms around my neck and kissing me upon the lips.* Then, still with her hands clasped, she leaned back and looked intently into my face, saying at the same time:
>
> *'Tom, don't be afraid! Whenever you are in danger I will come to warn you.'*
>
> *She bent forward and kissed me again; afterward leaning back to take another look at my face. Repeating the same words as before, once more she kissed me;* and then slowly withdrew her arms and moved back from the bed. She approached the arm, which still held the torch, and as she did so I saw that the *light of the torch paled before the greater glory which surrounded her person.* When she neared the fireplace the arm

---

[59]Peter E. Johnson, *Relief Society Magazine, op cit.,* Vol. VII, p. 451. Concerning the identity of guardian angels, Wilford Woodruff expressed his belief that "these men who have died and gone into the spirit world had this mission left with them, that is, a certain portion of them to watch over the Latter-day Saints." (JD 21:318.)

[60]Henry Zollinger, *op cit.*

stretched out around her, and she stepped back into the darkness. She waved her hand three times with a farewell gesture toward me. Soon she was enveloped in the darkness of the fireplace, and the light of the torch grew for a moment brighter, then suddenly it vanished and I found myself leaning upon my elbow in the bed and gazing fixedly at the blank darkness where the glorious presence and the light torch had disappeared. *So real and certain had been the presence of my sister that after she was gone, I still felt the pressure of her warm arms around my neck.*[61]

Apostle Orson F. Whitney recorded the coming of his departed wife and the understanding he had that she was watching over him as his guardian angel:

Early on the morning of April 24, 1918 . . . while I lay on my pillow, half asleep, half awake, *a pair of hands were laid upon my head.* My first thought was that someone was in the house who ought not to be, and that I must lie perfectly still in order to be safe. *But the touch was so soft and gentle that all fear left me, and with my own hands I took hold of those resting upon my head. They were a woman's hands. Presently I saw my wife Zina, who had been dead for eighteen years.* She was hovering over me. I held out my arms to her, and she came into them. It was all so real. *I could not doubt that she was actually there, a guardian angel, watching over her children and me.*[62]

Another function of guardian angels was clearly revealed to Elder John Mickelson Lang, a temple worker in the St. George Temple, in 1928:

One day while baptismal rites were being performed, *I distinctly heard a voice at the east end of the font, very close to the ceiling, calling the names of the dead to witness their own baptism, allowing a moment for each spirit to present itself.* After hearing many names called, I noticed a difference in the pronunciation of some of them. It seemed that the spirit who was calling must have a different list to ours.

I was so impressed at the time that I placed my arm about the shoulders of Bro. W. T. Morris, clerk, who was passing, and called his attention to the sound of the voice, but it was not discernable to him.

This occurrence had taken place in March of 1928, and it continued to prey upon my mind for some months, until one day in

---

[61]Thomas A. Shreeve, *Helpful Visions, op cit.*, pp. 68-69.

[62]Orson F. Whitney, *Through Memory's Halls* (Independence, Mo.: Zion's Printing and Publishing Co., 1930), p. 413. A blessing upon the head of Elder Whitney by Abraham O. Smoot had promised, "If need be, thou shalt commune with the spirits that have gone hence, and they shall visit and revisit thee." (*Ibid.*, p. 413)

Oct. I had gone to an upper room of the Temple, as was my custom, to offer secret prayer, asking for the assistance of God in my work, and to thank Him for showing me that there was a recording angel in His house, to keep a perfect record of that which transpired. I had finished my prayer and was about to leave the room when the question flashed through my mind, 'But where and how does He get these names? Some of them were not pronounced the same as ours.'

God knew my thoughts; I never asked of Him to know. The explanation came to me in these words: *'Every spirit that comes to earth has a guardian angel, whose duty it is to keep a record of the individual's parentage, the conditions under which it was born, its inheritance, environment, thoughts and desires, and when the individual's life is completed, the guardian angel's mission ends. It returns, makes its report and hands in the record it has kept. This record is placed upon the other book, spoken of as The Book of Life.'*

All this gave me to understand that in this other book is preserved the names and perfect dates of every spirit that ever came to earth.

It is also made plain therein, how all things will be proven by two or three witnesses; for instance, in case a child is left on a doorstep, the guardian angel of the child, that of the father and of the mother constitute three witnesses to the child's parentage. There are two witnesses to all things which transpire between any two persons. Also, God can give into the Temples a perfect record of the Lamanites, for instance, or any other people who have no earth record.

God is perfect. His record is perfect. We will be judged from the books.

I bear record that this testimony is true, for I received it from an angel in the house of the Lord.[63]

---

[63]"A Testimony Received by John Mickelson Lang in the St. George Temple in the Year 1928," unpublished manuscript in the possession of Sister Ruth Gregory, Smithfield, Utah.

Others have seen spirit beings being called as vicarious baptisms were performed in their behalf. Witness the account of Elder J. Hatton Carpenter, a former recorder in the Manti Temple, which is recorded in the *Utah Genealogical and Historical Magazine* (Salt Lake City, Utah: The Genealogical Society of Utah), Vol. XI, p. 119, July, 1920. (Certain grammatical corrections have been made in this account from the original.)

> A venerable patriarch, who is now dead, once related to the writer the following: The patriarch, who we will call Brother C., came to the Manti Temple some years ago when President John D. McAllister presided there. It was on a Tuesday when baptisms were being performed. Having none of his own to officiate for, he was invited into the room where this sacred ordinance is performed. As he sat and witnessed the ceremony, he became very much interested, as indeed he might be for he was gazing into the spirit world. *To his view appeared the spirits of those for whom they were officiating in the font by proxy. There the spirits stood awaiting their turn, and, as the Recorder called out the name of a person to be baptized for, the patriarch noticed a pleasant*

Hyrum Smith taught that there were not only guardian angels, but also other angels who minister to mortals in times of extreme difficulty. He told Edward Hunter, concerning the latter's deceased son, George Washington Hunter, that "your son will act as an angel to you; *not your guardian angel, but an auxiliary angel, to assist you in extreme trials.*"[64]

It is not clear whether every man is watched over by a guardian angel and enjoys its guidance and protection throughout the entire length of his mortal span. It is evident that upon occasion more than one being functions to guard and protect mortal beings. As an example, Wilford Woodruff told of the three messengers who protected the early missionaries to England when they were attacked by hordes of evil spirits:

> When Brother Kimball, Brother George A. Smith and myself went to London, we encountered these evil spirits. They sought to destroy us. The first house that was opened to us was filled with devils. They had gathered there for our destruction, so that we should not plant the Gospel in that great city. Brother Kimball went to Manchester on some business, and left Brother George A. Smith and myself there. One night we sat up till 11 o'clock, talking Mormonism, and then we went to bed. We had only just laid down when these spirits rested upon us, and we were in a very fair way of losing our lives. It was as if a strong man had me by the throat, trying to choke me to death. *In the midst of this a spirit told me to pray. I did so, and while praying, the door opened, the room was filled with light and three messengers came in. Who they were I know not. They came and laid their hands upon us, and rebuked those powers, and thereby saved our lives. Not only so, but by the power they held they rebuked the whole army of devils that were in that great city,* and bound them so they had never troubled any elder from that day to this.[65]

---

smile come over the face of the spirit whose name had been called, and he would leave the group of fellow spirits and pass over to the side of the Recorder. There he would watch his own baptism performed by proxy, and then with a joyful countenance would pass away, making room for the next favored personage who was to enjoy the same privilege.

As the eyes of Brother C. were riveted on this beautiful scene, he noticed at last that *some were beginning to turn away with sorrowful countenances.* Then his mind and sight came to things material. He looked around him and saw that the font room was nearly empty, the day's baptisms were at an end, and the Recorder was gathering up his records and stepping down from his desk.

'I often think of this event,' says Brother Carpenter, 'for I so often sit at the font, and call off the names for the ordinances to be performed which means so much to the dead.'

[64]Andrew Jenson, *Latter-day Saint Biographical Encyclopedia, op cit.,* Vol. I, p. 229. For the account of Bishop Hunter's son's later return to earth, see pp. 83-84.

Parley P. Pratt taught that when men turned to wickedness their kindred spirits beyond the veil would abandon them and cease to guard them:

> Those who are habitually given to vice, immorality and abomination; those who walk in the daily indulgence of unlawful lust; those who neither believe in Jesus Christ, nor seek to pray to him, and keep his commandments; those who do not cultivate the pure, refined and holy joys of innocent and heavenly affection, but who would sacrifice every finer feeling at the shrine of lawless pleasure and brutal desires—those persons will not understand and appreciate these views, because *their good angels, their kindred spirits have long since departed, and ceased to attend them, being grieved and disgusted with their conduct.*
>
> *The Spirit of the Lord has also been grieved, and has left them to themselves, to struggle alone amid the dangers and sorrows of life; or to be the associates of demons and impure spirits.* Such persons dream of adultery, gluttony, debauchery, and crimes of every kind. Such persons have the fore-shadowings of a doleful death, and of darkness, and the buffetings of fiends and malicious spirits.[66]

Spirits Prepare Mortal Beings for Death

There is evidence that some mortals are told the time of their death or in some other manner are prepared to pass through the veil of death by spirit beings. Heber C. Kimball, for instance, appeared to his son while the latter had ventured into the spirit world. He there reproved him of his weaknesses and told him that his mortal span would end in two years:

> *My father told me many things, and I received many reproofs for my wrong-doings.* Yet he was loth to have me leave, and seemed to feel very badly when the time came for me to go. He told me I could remain there if I chose to do so, but I pled with him that I might stay with my family long enough to make them comfortable, to repent of my sins, and more fully prepare myself for the change. Had it not been for this, I never should have returned home, except as a corpse. *Father finally told me I could remain two years, and to do all the good I could during that time, after which he would come for me, he mentioned four others that he would come for also, though he did not say it would be at the same time.*[67]

---

[65] "Discourse Delivered at the Weber Stake Conference, Ogden, Monday, October 19th, 1896, by Prest. Wilford Woodruff," *The Deseret Weekly,* Vol. 53, No. 21, p. 642, November 7, 1896. See also JD 3:227-230; 4:2.

[66] Parley P. Pratt, *Key To The Science of Theology, op cit.,* p. 122.

[67] O. F. Whitney, *Helpful Visions, op cit.,* p. 14.

Ella Jensen was given a shorter time to prepare for death. At three o'clock in the morning she suddenly called to those watching over her during her illness and "told them that her Uncle Hans, who was dead, had suddenly appeared in the room, while she was awake, with her eyes open, and told her that *messengers would be there at ten o'clock to conduct her into the spirit world.*"[68]

President Edward J. Wood recorded the coming of Yellow Face, a Kree Indian chief from Eastern Canada, to Cardston, Alberta, Canada in 1910. He told how the chief, along with about twenty families from his tribe, came and asked permission to camp and trap near the Mormon community. His people were treated well and returned to dwell there for three trapping seasons. During the third year of their sojourn there they suddenly summoned Bishop Parker, foreman of the Church ranch upon whose lands they had been allowed to camp, to address their tribal council. He spoke to them on two occasions. The first time his words were treated with disinterest. On his second visit, however, he was prompted to speak concerning the Book of Mormon, which immediately caught their undivided attention. At the conclusion of his sermon, Bishop Parker was told the following story by Chief Yellow Face:

> The year before our company came here first, I was taken very sick, and *was told by some of my Indian friends who had been dead many years, that I would soon be better, but I would get sick again some day, and that when I did again, I would die, but my family should not think I was dead and bury me for I was not to be buried till my body was cold all over.* When I woke up I called my family together and also the council of five chiefs, of which I was a member, for our tribe now lived in Manitoba, and I told them of my dream, and they laughed at me and didn't believe me, but I was afraid. Time went on and one day some time afterward, I was taken very sick, and I at once feared my dream would come true, so I warned my family not to be in a hurry to bury me even if I died, till they were sure I was cold all over. *So I got weaker and weaker till I left my body, and I went away among a lot of Indians that I knew were dead; some I knew and some I didn't, as they had been dead so long, but they were not dead at all, and they told me to die was only to leave the body for your folks to take care of, and I would be where they were, but as for me, I had to go back and use my body again for several years.*

[68]LeRoi C. Snow, *Improvement Era, op cit.*, Vol. XXXII, p. 882.

They said *I was to go among the white people till I found a book that told of the history of these dead Indians who were not dead.* I asked them how I would know the people who had the book, and they gave me five keys by which I would know the people who had the book that would tell my live Indian friends all about who they were and about their dead relatives, as follows:

1st—They will let you camp on their own lands, and trap and hunt.
2nd—They will treat you like one of them in business with them.
3rd—They will invite you in their meetings and ask you to speak.
4th—They will invite you to sit with them at their tables to eat.
5th—They will visit you in your camp and their men will not bother your women nor molest any of you.

When you find this kind of people, have them meet in your council, and tell you what they believe, and they will tell you about this book.

I then woke up and found my wife and my friends had about decided to bury me as I had been dead several days and was cold all over except a small place over my heart, but when I came back to life and told them where I had been and that our Indian relatives were not dead at all, they wondered at me and when I told them I would pick about 20 families and would travel till I found the book, they again wondered, but as they all believed in a God, they would follow me, so in due time, we made up our company and started and made many camps, and traveled many seasons, but it was hard to find a people who answered the five keys till we landed among you, as we find not many people who are true friends of the Indian.[69]

Spirits Call Mortals Into the Spirit World

Spirits sometimes summon mortals into the spirit realm. Just as the Indian friends of Chief Yellow Face called him into the spirit world, Merrill Neville was able to summon his sister, May, beyond the veil. Five hours after his death, he began to call for her:

At midnight his sister, May, who was very ill, said, 'Mother, *Merrill is knocking for me.*' Her mother replied, 'O, May, don't say that.'

---

[69]Edward J. Wood, "A Dream of Yellow Face," as recorded in Lundwall, *Faith Like the Ancients, op cit.*, pp. 186-187. Melvin S. Tagg also treats this experience in *The Life of Edward James Wood,* pp. 86-90.

The next evening at about 7, May said in a whisper, *'Mother, you didn't believe me last night when I told you Merrill was knocking for me. He is knocking again now.'*

'Oh, May,' the heartbroken mother said, 'I didn't disbelieve you but I couldn't bear to think that it was so.' After suffering the agonies of death, May's spirit left her struggling body. Both her father and mother clung to her, working in every way possible to restore the life to the now still form, but it was of no avail. The father lifted the drooping chin and closed the mouth. The distracted mother went from room to room, and finally returning to the scene of death she began praying aloud: 'Oh, Father in heaven, I don't see why I have been called upon to go through such trying scenes as this. I've had all the children I could have, and I've tried to raise them as near right as I knew how. Why have I been called upon to go through this?'

At that Bessie touched her mother on the shoulder, saying, 'Mother, May wants you.' Her mother replied, 'Must I go, too?'

'No, Mother,' the sister assured her, *'May has come back to life and wants to tell you what Merrill has said to her.'*[70]

A summons beyond the veil, however, usually does not involve the return of the individual to mortality. More common is the summons like that given by Ira N. Hinckley, who returned to the mortal dimension on three occasions to summon his son, Apostle Alonzo A. Hinckley, into paradise:

Shortly before Alonzo died he went to Southern California, hoping that a change in climate might help him. While there on one occasion, he was pondering the fact that his health had not permitted him to discharge his duties as an apostle in a way that was satisfactory to him. While in this mood, *his father, Ira N. Hinckley, who had been dead for more than thirty years, appeared to him and told him that he greatly needed his assistance on the other side of the veil, that he had more work than he could possibly do, and really needed him.*

Alonzo explained that there was so much here to do, that his health had retarded him, and he would like to stay and finish it. And so they talked face to face with one another. The experience was repeated the second time, and with the same results. Then his father appeared for the third time, and *told him he would have to have him. That was the final word.*

Soon after Alonzo returned to Salt Lake City, and died, but not until after he had fought a brave and gallant fight for his life, did he pass away in peace to his great reward.[71]

---

[70]"Manifestation About Building of Temples," *Deseret Evening News,* May 18, 1918.
[71]Bryant S. Hinckley, *The Faith of Our Pioneer Fathers, op cit.,* pp. 238-239.

It would appear that the spirits in paradise know in advance whom they are to summon in the future and the order in which they are to come into the world of spirits. For instance, Walter P. Monson, who went into the spirit world for only a few moments, was sent back through the veil by his daughter because it was not yet his turn to leave mortality:

> As I turned my head in the direction I intended to go, I saw my little daughter, Elna, who had died twenty-one years before. *She was more mature than when she passed away, and was most beautiful to my eyes, so full of life, intelligence, and sweetness.* As she came towards me she raised her right hand and said, *'Go back, Papa, I want Richard first. Then Grandma must come, and then Mama is coming, before you.'*
>
> The next thing I knew was my body gasping for breath. I felt my heart action start and was conscious of the coldness leaving my body. All numbness left me and the natural warmth returned. I felt the nurse shaking me and heard her say, 'Mr. Monson, you must not let yourself slip like that again.'[72]

---

[72]Jeremiah Stokes, *Modern Miracles, op cit.,* p. 79. Elder Monson left the following account of the passing of the others of his family in fulfillment of Elna's order:

> For five weeks I remained in the hospital, gaining a little strength each day. I was administered to frequently by Brothers James E. Talmage, George Albert Smith, Patriarch Kirkham and others, and my family exercised all the faith within their power in my behalf. Mrs. Monson visited me every day with my son Richard. She was told by the doctor, C. F. Wilcox, that there was no hope for my recovery, and, of course, her visits were attended with deep emotion.
>
> Many times little Richard, for he was barely six years old, took my hand and pressed it affectionately against his cheek. 'Daddy,' he would say anxiously, 'you're not going to die, are you?' I could not control my emotions, try as I would, but I managed to say, 'No, Dick, it is not my turn.'
>
> *Four weeks after I returned home, my boy, Richard, passed away.* During the last hours of his life he sat up in bed, opened his big blue eyes and looked toward the door with intense interest. *'Come in, Elna,'* he said, *'there's only papa and mama here.'*
>
> I asked him whom he could see and he answered, '*Elna is there. It's funny you can't see her. And there are a whole lot of people with her who want me to come.'*
>
> He called his mother to the bed and put his arms around her neck. *'Can I go with Elna?'* he asked.
>
> 'Yes, my dear,' she answered, 'you have suffered enough.'
>
> 'Then I'll go. And I'll be happy if you will promise not to cry once for me,' he pleaded.
>
> Mrs. Monson gave him the promise he wished and left the room.
>
> 'Daddy,' he said to me, 'come here. I guess mama has gone out to cry.'
>
> He paused a moment, then turned and looked in the direction of the door and listened intently at something he evidently heard.
>
> *'Dear old daddy,'* he went on at length, *'so you promised at the hospital I could go. Now I know why you cried when I said, 'You are not going to die, are you, daddy?'*
>
> Three hours later his eyes closed in eternal sleep.

Indications that individuals are being summoned beyond the veil are often found in conversations which dying persons carry on with visitors which are unseen and unheard by others who are present or by the dying person calling his visitor by name. The death of David P. Kimball, who had entered paradise previously and had been told by his father that "I could remain two years, . . . after which he would come for me; he mentioned four others that he would come for also," was recorded in a letter by his nephew, Charles S. Whitney. The letter, under date of November 22, 1883, said,

> Uncle David died this morning at half-past six, easily, and apparently without a bit of pain. *Shortly before he died, he looked up and called, 'Father, father!' All night long he had called for Uncle Heber.* You remember hearing him tell how grand-pa came to him when he was lost on the desert, and how he pled for two more years and was given that much longer to stay. Last Saturday, the day he was so bad, was just two years from the day he was lost, and *to-day is just two years from the day his father and mother came to him and gave him a drink of water,* and told him that his friends would find him and he should live two years longer. *He knew that he was going to die, and bade Aunt Caroline good-by day before yesterday.*[73]

With the death of most individuals, of course, there is no outward sign that they are being summoned through the veil. In some cases, however, a change in their countenance and a glow which has come over them as if they are in the presence of the glory of another spirit being has provided slight indication of their summons. Such was the case with the passing of David Whitmer:

How he knew that I wept because I had been told by Elna that he was to go first and that my coming back was equivalent to a promise that he might precede me to the great beyond, can only be explained through knowledge given him from Elna herself, for he knew nothing of the circumstance of what I saw and heard while my spirit was separated from my body at the hosptial.

Three weeks after his passing, I visited my mother, Ellen Monson, at Preston, Idaho. Mother had been a sufferer for many years, but her constitution was strong and the doctor had told her that she had every chance of living for ten or fifteen years. She lamented the fact that she was spared, while my boy was taken. She said she had desired to die for twenty-two years. Without realizing what I said, I made her this promise: *'Mother, you haven't twenty-two days to suffer.'*

Nineteen days from that time, mother left us. And six years from the time of mother's death, Mrs. Monson passed away. (Ibid., pp. 79-81)

[73]O. F. Whitney, *Helpful Visions, op cit.,* p. 22. Concerning the death of his brother, Alvin, Joseph Smith recorded that "When he died the angel of the Lord visited him in his last moments." (HC 5:127. Aug. 22, 1842.)

David Whitmer bore his long illness with great patience and fortitude, his faith never for a moment wavering, and when the summons came he sank peacefully to rest, with a smile on his countenance, just as if he was being lulled to sleep by sweet music. Just before the breath left the body, *he opened his eyes, which glistened with the brightness of his early manhood. He than turned them toward heaven, and a wonderful light came over his countenance, which remained several moments,* when the eyes gradually closed and David Whitmer was gone to rest.[74]

Spirits Escort the Dying Through the Veil of Death

It seems that spirit beings not only summon others through the veil, they also serve as messengers to provide them escort into the spirit world. Thus Heber J. Grant, shortly before the death of his son, saw that "his mother, who was dead, came for him, and that she brought with her a messenger, and she told this messenger to take the boy."[75] Perhaps the messengers seen by Phoebe Whittemore Carter Woodruff as her spirit left her body were sent to fulfill the same function. She told how she saw her body lying on the bed, the sisters weeping, her husband and baby, and "while gazing upon this scene, two personages came into the room carrying a coffin and told her they had come for her body." They then gave her the choice of remaining on earth or continuing into the spirit world. When she elected to continue in mortality, "She saw the messengers carry the coffin out at the door."[76]

To escort President George Osmond into the spirit world may have been the reason for the return of John D. Wilkes, of Afton, Wyoming, as was seen by his wife, Luella Child Wilkes. During the years following his death in 1905, Brother Wilkes, or "Johnny" as he was better known, returned to earth on several occasions, according to the account of his niece, Fern R. Morgan:

---

[74]Andrew Jenson, *Latter-day Saint Biographical Encyclopedia, op cit.,* Vol. I, p. 270. This is an extract from David Whitmer's obituary which was published by the non-Mormon weekly newspaper, the *Richmond Democrat,* on February 2, 1888. David Whitmer died Jan. 25, 1888.

[75]Bryant S. Hinckley, *Life of a Great Leader, op cit.,* p. 247.

[76]Wilford Woodruff, *Leaves From My Journal, op cit.,* p. 60. This experience leaves unanswered questions. Why would spirit beings come for her body? Was this a symbolic demonstration that they were prepared to escort her spirit into paradise?

When the Star Valley Stake in Wyoming was organized in August 1892, Elder George Osmond was chosen as the first Stake President.

Aunt Luella and Uncle Johnny worked together on the Sunday School Stake Board and became very close and friendly with Pres. Osmond. After her husband's untimely death he often counselled and helped her with many problems. His spiritual and kindly advice gave her much consolation. . . .

About 1907-1908, President Osmond became critically ill and for days it was feared he would die. He finally recovered and afterward he told my aunt that *on a certain night Johnny had appeared at his bedside. President Osmond asked Johnny, 'Am I to go with you?' Johnny told him that they were 'not ready for him yet—he was to finish his work here, and he would live to see it finished.' He was dressed in white and his voice was as natural as ever, Pres. Osmond said.* The singular thing about this experience was that on that very same night *Johnny had also appeared to my aunt in a dream and told her that 'everything will be alright, do not worry.'*

Aunt Luella also commented on Johnny's voice. *He had always had a beautiful resonant voice and that when he spoke to her this same night he appeared to President Osmond, he sounded so natural.* It gave her great peace of mind as she had had many business worries and the visit of her husband gave her confidence and reassurance that all things would work out alright.

At the age of 77 President Osmond died on the 25th of March, 1913. *The night he died Johnny again appeared to my aunt in a dream. He was walking down the street on which President Osmond lived. She saw him turn in at the gate at his house and go into his home.* The next morning she was notified of President Osmond's death.[77]

SUMMARY

1. There is evidence that spirits are aware of important events in the mortal sphere and that on certain occasions they participate in them. This seems to be true primarily with major Church events.

2. Views of the full scope of earth events are available to certain righteous spirits to whom special permission has been given. The privilege of observing earth, however, is apparently not open to all spirits. Those allowed to view the earth are able to envision the entire globe and to see the actions of nations, cities, and individuals.

[77]Personal records of Fern R. Morgan, in the possession of her daughter, Mrs. Dean (Jaynann) Payne, of Provo, Utah.

3. Spirits in paradise are concerned about the conduct of their loved ones on earth. They are able to discern the thoughts and feelings of mortal beings. There is evidence that they also know the future events which their loved ones will experience. They hold their loved ones responsible for the integrity of their good name.

4. Departed spirits are aware of the degree of progress of the Church upon the earth. Upon occasion they have returned to those in mortality to direct Church activities or to give special guidance to mortal Church leaders.

5. Man's conduct is constantly observed by many spirit beings, both good and evil.

6. Righteous spirits in paradise are controlled in their relationships with earth and are not permitted to return to earth without legitimate reason. Spirits from the realms of Satan, however, are not subject to such controls and often linger about the places they frequented in mortality.

7. Evil spirits often indulge in the mischief and pranks of haunting houses, rattling and moving furniture, etc. At times their actions serve as the devil's counterfeit to divine revelation.

8. Righteous spirits will not respond to mediums, witches, wizards, ouija board operators, clairvoyants, etc. Manifestations obtained through these sources will come from evil spirits which will probably mingle truth with falsehood in order to deceive their listeners.

9. Evil spirits often occupy the bodies of mortal beings, and great numbers of them enter the same mortal body. They cause the human being they have possessed to suffer greatly, and often afflict him with fits, convulsions, nightmares, and tempt him with all manner of evil and lasciviousness.

10. Mortals are often surrounded by dozens or even hundreds of evil spirits which constantly tempt them to perform evil acts.

11. Satan and his hosts are able to afflict man with sickness and death.

12. Certain tests have been proposed for detecting and resisting evil spirits. Mortals possessed by evil spirits may be identified by one or more of the following characteristics:

    A. Lack of bodily control, including fits, temporary disfigurement, loss of speech, etc.

    B. A disagreeable smell about the person thus possessed.

C. A shock experienced by the person who beholds the individual possessed by demoniac spirits.

D. A strong tendency to lustful and bawdy words and actions.

13. Certain tests of authority for the ministration of spirits have been proposed:

A. No person can receive manifestations from righteous spirits unless he believes in modern revelation.

B. It is impossible to seek God or his messengers successfully while one remains in his sins.

C. Christ is the mediator between man and God. Those who seek manifestations from the spirit world but not in His name are unlawful mediums.

D. The priesthood holds the keys to revelation and the ministration of angels. Spirit beings functioning outside of this power are not authorized messengers from God.

14. A handshake test to aid in detecting evil spirits posing as authorized servants of God is set forth in the Doctrine and Covenants:

A. Resurrected beings will answer one's request to shake hands by doing so. They can be felt.

B. The disembodied spirits of just men made perfect will refuse to shake hands so as not to deceive, but will still give their message. They will be seen in light and glory.

C. Evil spirits masquerading as angels of light will attempt to deceive mortals by shaking hands with them when requested to do so. Their hands will not be felt.

15. An angel is a servant or assistant. A ministering angel represents his master by visitng or ministering to others in his name. Five types of angels minister to mortals:

A. Pre-mortal spirits, who have not yet received a mortal body.

B. Translated beings, who have had their mortal life extended and are freed from bodily needs and suffering. These individuals must still be changed into resurrected beings.

C. Righteous spirits from paradise, who have passed through mortality, died, and entered paradise. Apparently all such beings are considered as "just men made perfect." These beings are surrounded by glory.

D. Evil spirits from hell or the spirit prison. These beings are under the influence of Satan to varying degrees, and are not surrounded by glory. They include both the spirits which were cast out of the heavens which have had no opportunity to receive a mortal body and also those who have passed through mortality and death without meriting the privilege of dwelling in paradise.

E. Resurrected beings who have passed through mortality and death and then have had their physical body restored to them. They are surrounded with glory in accordance with the type of resurrected body they inherit.

16. Righteous spirits return to earth to

A. Give counsel,
B. Give comfort,
C. Obtain or give information,
D. Serve as guardian angels,
E. Prepare others for death,
F. Summon mortals into the spirit world,
and to
G. Escort the dying through the veil of death.

CHAPTER V

HELL

Meaning of Terms Hell, Hades, Sheol, Tartarus and Gehenna

NUMEROUS PASSAGES OF SCRIPTURE MAKE REFERENCE TO A hell in which the spirits of the wicked must suffer following their death. The English word hell is a translation of words from other languages which hold the same meaning. These words are

1. *Hades*—This is the Greek term. Most New Testament references to hell are translations of this word.
2. *Sheol*—This is the Hebrew term which is usually translated *hell* in English. In some instances the Authorized Version has sheol translated as *grave* (Gen. 44:29, 31; Job 7:9; Ps. 30:3) or as *pit* (Nu. 16:30, 33; Job 17:16). Joseph Smith used this term in D&C 121:4.

In his explanation of these words the prophet Joseph regarded them as terms which denoted the entire world of spirits, rather than specifically the abode of the wicked. Such usage is similar to the multiple meanings of the term *paradise,* discussed in chapter III. His comment:

> There has been much said about the word hell, and the sectarian world have preached much about it, describing it to be a burning lake of fire and brimstone. *But what is hell? It is another modern term, and is taken from hades.* I'll hunt after hades as Pat did for the woodchuck.
>
> *Hades, the Greek, or Shaole, the Hebrew: these two significations mean a world of spirits. Hades, Shaole, paradise, spirits in prison, are all one: it is a world of spirits.*[1]

Two other terms are used in connection with the doctrine of hell in the Bible. They are

[1]HC 5:425. June 11, 1843.

3. *Tartarus*—This is a classical Greek term used only once in the New Testament. Peter used it in 2 Peter 2:4. Like *Hades,* it is translated *hell* in English.

4. *Gehenna*—A valley which curves around the city of Jerusalem on the southwest was known in Old Testament times as the *Valley of the Son of Hinnom.* In the time of Christ it was also known as *Gehenna.* Before the fall of Judah to Babylonia many children were slain in this valley at Topheth (a "high place," or place of worship) as offerings to the heathen god Molech and it became known as "the valley of slaughter." (2 Ki. 23:10; 2 Chron. 28:3; 33:6; Is. 30:33; Jer. 7:31-34; 19:6, 11-15) The valley was later used as the city garbage dump and fires were kept burning there to destroy the refuse and prevent sickness and disease. In such passages as Mark 9:43-48 and Matthew 5:22, the Savior apparently made use of the ever-burning fires of the dismal place as a comparison to the agony and horror which the wicked would suffer after death.

In this chapter the term *hell* is used in a specific sense meaning the spirit world abode of the wicked, as contrasted with paradise and the spirit prison, rather than in the general sense which refers to the entire spirit world.

Separation of the Righteous From the Wicked in Paradise and Hell

There is extensive evidence that the righteous and the wicked spirits dwell in different areas of the spirit world and that the wicked are not permitted to enter paradise. President Joseph F. Smith, in his Vision of the Redemption of the Dead, observed that the two groups were clearly separated and taught that association with the just in paradise was limited to righteous members of the Church:

> The eyes of my understanding were opened, and the Spirit of the Lord rested upon me, and I saw the hosts of the dead, both small and great. And *there were gathered together in one place an innumerable company of the spirits of the just, who had been faithful in the testimony of Jesus while they lived in mortality, and who had offered sacrifice in the simili-*

tude of the great sacrifice of the Son of God, and had suffered tribulation in their Redeemer's name. All these had departed the mortal life, firm in the hope of a glorious resurrection, through the grace of God the Father and his Only Begotten Son, Jesus Christ. . . . The Son of God appeared, declaring liberty *to the captives who had been faithful,* and there he preached to them the everlasting gospel, the doctrine of the resurrection and the redemption of mankind from the fall, and from individual sins on conditions of repentance. *But unto the wicked he did not go, and among the ungodly and the unrepentant who had defiled themselves while in the flesh, his voice was not raised, neither did the rebellious who rejected the testimonies and the warnings of the ancient prophets behold his presence, nor look upon his face. Where these were, darkness reigned, but among the righteous there was peace, and the saints rejoiced in their redemption.*[2]

Jedediah M. Grant also saw that the wicked were not privileged to dwell with the righteous in the spirit world. As Heber C. Kimball related President Grant's account, he said that "He saw the righteous gathered together in the spirit world, and *there were no wicked spirits among them.*"[3] President Grant's observation corresponded exactly with the teachings on the subject uttered two years earlier by Heber C. Kimball:

Can those persons who pursue a course of carelessness, neglect of duty, and disobedience, when they depart from this life, expect that their spirits will associate with the spirits of the righteous in the spirit world? *I do not expect it, and when you depart from this state of existence, you will find it out for yourselves.*[4]

Others who have visited the world of spirits continually testify that the righteous were separated from the wicked. Often they will describe one group or the other as being separate, which would show that the two groups are not intermingled. Lorenzo Dow Young, for example, was shown the condition of the damned in Hell:

As we went on from this place, my guide said, '*I will now show you the condition of the damned.*' Pointing with his hand, he said, 'Look!'

I looked down a distance which appeared incomprehensible to me. I gazed on a *vast region filled with multitudes of beings.* I could see everything with the most minute distinctness. The multitude of

---

[2]Joseph F. Smith, *Gospel Doctrine, op cit.,* pp. 472-473.

[3]JD 4:136. Dec. 4, 1856. Orson F. Whitney taught that "the spirits of the unjust are separated from the righteous, and are not in a state of rest. Light and darkness divide that realm, each domain having its appropriate population." (Orson F. Whitney, *Life of Heber C. Kimball, op cit.,* p. 291.)

[4]JD 2:150. April 2, 1854.

people I saw were miserable in the extreme. *'These,'* said my guide, *'are they who have rejected the means of salvation, that were placed within their reach,* and have brought upon themselves the condemnation you behold.'

The expression of the countenances of these sufferers was clear and distinct. They indicated extreme remorse, sorrow and dejection. They appeared conscious that none but themselves were to blame for their forlorn condition.

This scene affected me much, and I could not refrain from weeping.[5]

The wretched misery of the spirits in hell can be contrasted with the descriptions of the joy and felicity of the righteous in paradise cited previously. There is no evidence that these two situations are intermingled except as missionaries go from paradise into the spirit prison, and there encounter representatives who have come from hell.

A definite difference between those who dwell in paradise and those who are in hell is that the former are freed from the temptations of Satan. The apostle Paul, speaking of those who are "dead with Christ," taught that "he that is dead is freed from sin."[6] President Brigham Young, in one of his discourses, explained this principle, saying that the righteous Saints who "have brought the flesh into subjection by the power of the Priesthood" will be the ones who will escape from Satan's power:

When the faithful Elders, holding this Priesthood, go into the spirit world they carry with them the same power and Priesthood that they had while in the mortal tabernacle. They have got the victory over the power of the enemy here, consequently when they leave this world they have perfect control over those evil spirits, and *they cannot be buffeted by Satan.* But as long as they live in the flesh no being on this earth, of the posterity of Adam, can be free from the power of the devil.

When this portion of the school is out, the one in which we descend below all things and commence upon this earth to learn the first lessons for an eternal exaltation, if you have been a faithful scholar, and have overcome, *if you have brought the flesh into subjection by the power of the Priesthood, if you have honored the body,* when it crumbles to the earth and your spirit is freed from this home of clay, *has the devil any power over it? Not one particle.*

---

[5]Lorenzo Dow Young, *Fragments of Experience, op cit.,* p. 28. For his contrasting description of the spirit prison see p. 197.

[6]Ro. 6:7-8.

This is an advantage which the faithful will gain; but while they live on earth they are subject to the buffetings of Satan. *Joseph and those who have died in the faith of the Gospel are free from this;* . . . Joseph and the faithful who have died *have gained a victory over the power of the devil,* which you and I have not yet gained. So long as we live in these tabernacles, so long we will be subject to the temptations and power of the devil; *but when we lay them down, if we have been faithful, we have gained the victory so far; but even then we are not so far advanced at once as to be beyond the neighborhood of evil spirits.*[7]

In the same sermon he contrasted the malicious spirit of those who go into hell, and have remained under the influence of Satan:

Those that were wicked designedly, who knowingly lived without the Gospel when it was within their reach, they are given up to the devil, they become tools to the devil and spirits of devils.

Go to the time when the Gospel came to the earth in the days of Joseph, take the wicked that have opposed this people and persecuted them to the death, and *they are sent to hell. Where are they? They are in the spirit world,* and are just as busy as they possibly can be to do everything they can against the Prophet and the Apostles, against Jesus and His Kingdom. *They are just as wicked and malicious in their actions against the cause of truth, as they were while on the earth in their fleshly tabernacles. Joseph, also, goes there, but has the devil power over him? No, because he held the keys and power of the eternal Priesthood here, and got the victory while here in the flesh.*[8]

Brigham Young also taught that

[7]JD 3:371. June 22, 1856.

[8]*Ibid.,* p. 370. There are those who have held that Brigham Young taught that there was to be no separation of the righteous and the wicked. Their misunderstanding seemingly exists because they have not understood President Young's explanation of the fate of the two different groups as quoted above. This explanation was offered by President Young to clarify and amplify his introduction of the spirit world topic:

Where is the spirit world? It is right here. Do the good and evil spirits go together? Yes, they do. Do they both inhabit one kingdom? Yes, they do. (JD 3:369. See also JD 2:137.)

With his clarifying statements cited in the text above as a guide, one can see that he was saying that all departed spirits go into the same spirit world, without asserting that they lived together and constantly associated with one another. It is in this same general sense that the prophet Joseph's assertion, which is also quoted out of context, should be understood. He said, while explaining Luke 23:43, that "The righteous and the wicked will go to the same world of spirits until the resurrection." (HC 5:425) To interpret these two statements as meaning that the righteous are not separated from the wicked within the vast spirit world where they both dwell would be to disregard the heavy weight of contrary evidence.

> If we are faithful to our religion, when we go into the spirit world, the fallen spirits—Lucifer and the third part of the heavenly hosts that came with him, and the spirits of wicked men who have dwelt upon this earth, *the whole of them combined will have no influence over our spirits.* Is not that an advantage? Yes. *All the rest of the children of men are more or less subject to them, and they are subject to them as they were while here in the flesh.*
>
> If we conquer here and overcome in the Gospel, in the spirit world our spirits will be above the power of evil spirits.[9]

Similar comment was made by Heber C. Kimball, who warned that

> If men and women do not qualify themselves and become sanctified and purified in this life, they will go into a world of spirits where *they will have a greater contest with the devils than ever you had with them here.*[10]

On another occasion Brigham Young taught that it was rejection of the gospel and refusal to heed the spirit of revelation that caused men to be banished to hell rather than enjoy the happiness of paradise:

> *When the light of the knowledge of God comes to a man and he rejects it, that is his condemnation.* When I have told all I have been authorized to declare to him in the name of the Lord, if he does not have the visions of eternity, it is all nonsense to him. To know the truth of my testimony he must have the visions and revelations of God for himself. *And when he gets them, and turns aside, becoming a traitor to the cause of righteousness, the wrath of God will beat upon him, and the vengeance of the Almighty will be heavy upon him.* This comes, not because their fathers lived in darkness before them, and the ancestors of their fathers before them; not because the nations have lived and died in ignorance; but because the Lord pours the spirit of revelation upon them, and *they reject it. Then they are prepared for the wrath of God, and they are banished to another part of the spirit world, where the devil has power and control over them.*[11]

The Darkness of Hell

The prophet Alma, while describing the spirit world to his son, spoke of the unrighteous spirits who are not permitted to enjoy the choice association of the righteous in paradise. He

---

[9]JD 7:240. Sept. 1, 1859. See also 14:229.
[10]JD 3:230. March 2, 1856.
[11]JD 2:140-141. Dec. 3, 1854.

told of the fate they would experience while in the spirit hell and described it as "outer darkness."

> And then shall it come to pass, that the spirits of the wicked, yea, who are evil—for behold, they have no part nor portion of the Spirit of the Lord; for behold, they chose evil works rather than good; therefore *the spirit of the devil did enter into them and take possession of their house—and these shall be cast out into outer darkness;* there shall be weeping, and wailing, and gnashing of teeth, and this because of their own iniquity, being led captive by the will of the devil.
>
> Now this is the state of the souls of the wicked, yea, *in darkness, and a state of awful, fearful looking for the fiery indignation of the wrath of God upon them;* thus they remain in this state, as well as the righteous in paradise, *until the time of their resurrection.*[12]

Others have also described hell as a place of darkness. Peter, for example, wrote that "God spared not the angels that sinned, but *cast them down to hell,* and delivered them into *chains of darkness,* to be reserved unto judgment."[13] Jude also made reference to hell as a place of darkness, saying that "the angels which kept not their first estate, but left their own habitation, *he hath reserved in everlasting chains under darkness* unto the judgment of the great day."[14]

Numerous references in the Doctrine and Covenants describe hell as being a place of darkness. On one occasion reference was made to "the devil, and the *dark and benighted dominion* of Sheol."[15] The Lord revealed that the wicked must be cast into *"outer darkness,* where there is weeping, and wailing, and gnashing of teeth."[16] To the wicked who cast out His servants He proclaimed the warning,

> Ye believed not my servants, and when they were sent unto you ye received them not.
>
> Wherefore, they sealed up the testimony and bound up the law, and *ye were delivered over unto darkness.*
>
> *These shall go away into outer darkness,* where there is weeping, and wailing, and gnashing of teeth.[17]

---

[12]Al. 40:13-14.
[13]2 Pet. 2:4.
[14]Jude 6.
[15]D&C 121:4.
[16]D&C 101:91.
[17]D&C 133:71-73.

And on yet another occasion He revealed that the "residue of the wicked have I kept in *chains of darkness* until the judgment of the great day."[18]

But terms such as "darkness," "outer darkness," and "chains of hell" are difficult to understand. Do the evil spirits float around in outer space drifting from place to place? Or are they also "on this earth" with the rest of the spirits in the spirit world? Are they bound and fettered? Is this darkness a state of pitch-black night where one cannot even see his hand before his face?

Hell is not the vastness of outer space, but is a specific location. The Lord revealed that there is a specific "place" prepared for the devil and his angels, "which place is hell."[19]

A careful reading of statements cited in chapter I concerning the location of the spirit world will indicate that hell, like paradise, is also believed to be here on this planet. Concerning the great population of the region, the prophet Joseph Smith once commented that "The sectarian world are going to hell *by hundreds, by thousands and by millions.*"[20]

What is the darkness in which these spirits dwell? It appears that it is a complete absence of the light, guidance, truth, and inspiration of Christ. It is the influence, darkness and wickedness of Satan. Jesus Christ is the "life and light of the world."[21] He "giveth light to every man that cometh into the world . . . that hearkeneth to the voice of the Spirit."[22] The light which emanates from Him comes in such a manner that it "quickeneth your understandings."[23] The light of Christ is truth,[24] and "light and truth forsake that evil one,"[25] the devil. Thus Satan and his followers are left in the darkness of wickedness and sin without the enlightment and influence of the gospel of Christ. Because of the devil's labors and

[18]D&C 38:5.
[19]D&C 29:38.
[20]HC 5:554. Aug. 27, 1843.
[21]D&C 10:70.
[22]D&C 84:45-46.
[23]D&C 88:6-13.
[24]*Ibid.*, see also D&C 93:36.
[25]D&C 93:37. See also Al. 40:13.

temptations, the earth has become so corrupt that the "whole world groaneth under *sin and darkness* even now."[26]

Man, during his mortal life, is subjected to the evil "powers of darkness" which "prevail upon the earth, among the children of men,"[27] unless he accepts the gospel of Christ. To do so is to win release from the darkness and bondage of Satan in this life and from hell after death. As the prophet Alma said concerning the converts of his era,

> They awoke unto God. Behold *they were in the midst of darkness; nevertheless, their souls were illuminated by the light of the everlasting word;* yea, they were encircled about by the bands of death, and the chains of hell, and an everlasting destruction did await them.[28]

It is the Lord's desire that "you may know the truth, that you may *chase darkness from among you.*"[29] Those who knowingly reject the truth of the gospel are doomed to hell at death, for "they *love darkness rather than light,* because their deeds are evil,"[30] and Satan "leadeth them along until he draggeth their souls down to hell."[31] Once in hell, they are in "outer darkness" where they *"have no part nor portion of the Spirit of the Lord,"*[32] and are thus completely without the light of Christ. Without the light of Christ, man becomes completely subjected to Satan in hell. As Jacob taught,

> Our spirits must have become like unto him, and we become devils, angels to a devil, *to be shut out from the presence of God,* and to remain with the father of lies, in misery, like unto himself.[33]

Amulek saw that those thrust down to hell

> Have become subjected to the spirit of the devil, and he doth seal you his; therefore, the *Spirit of the Lord hath withdrawn from you, and hath no place in you,* and the devil hath all power over you.[34]

Is the darkness of hell literal, or is it only a figurative ex-

[26]D&C 84:53, 49; 112:23.
[27]D&C 38:11.
[28]Al. 5:7.
[29]D&C 50:25. See the two preceding verses.
[30]D&C 10:21.
[31]D&C 10:26.
[32]Al. 40:13.
[33]2 Ne. 9:9.
[34]Al. 34:35.

pression meaning the absence of the gospel, truth, and light of Christ? It would appear that it is a literal darkness, for to be without the light of Christ is to be without the source of light, for light, as man knows it, emanates from Him:

> Truth shineth. This is the light of Christ. As also he is in the sun, and the *light of the sun,* and the power thereof by which it was made.
>
> As also he is in the moon, and is the *light of the moon,* and the power thereof by which it was made;
>
> As also the *light of the stars,* and the power thereof by which they were made;
>
> And the earth, also, and the power thereof, even the earth upon which you stand.
>
> *And the light which shineth, which giveth you light, is through him who enlighteneth your eyes,* which is the same light that quickeneth your understandings;
>
> *Which light proceedeth forth from the presence of God to fill the immensity of space—*
>
> *The light which is in all things, which giveth life to all things, which is the law by which all things are governed, even the power of God,* who sitteth upon his throne, who is in the bosom of eternity, who is in the midst of all things.[35]

It is not known however, whether artificial light is used in the realm of Satan, nor whether the spirit beings in his dominion even have need for light.

What are the chains with which Satan binds his subjects? Alma, the Book of Mormon missionary, answered this question. He taught that when men reject the gospel and fail to seek answers to the mysteries of Christ's precepts, they

> Harden their hearts, *to them is given the lesser portion of the word until they know nothing concerning his mysteries; and then they are taken captive by the devil, and led by his will down to destruction. Now this is what is meant by the chains of hell. . . .*
>
> Then is a time that whosoever dieth in his sins, as to a temporal death, shall also die a spiritual death, *yea, he shall die as to things pertaining unto righteousness.*
>
> Then is the time when . . . they shall be *chained down* to an everlasting destruction, according to the power and captivity of Satan, *he having subjected them according to his will.*[36]

---

[35]D&C 88:7-13. This light apparently emanates directly from the Savior's person. John the Revelator, while describing the new, redeemed Jerusalem, said that "the city had no need of the sun, neither of the moon, to shine in it: for *the glory of the Lord did lighten it,* and the Lamb is the light thereof . . . there shall be *no night there.*" (Rev. 21:23, 25)

[36]Al. 12:11, 16-17.

Thus the chains of hell represent the complete subjugation of man's will to the will of Satan. Being dead as to the things of righteousness and without the light and truth of Christ, man is left powerless to resist Satan's demands while suffering in hell.

Pre-Mortal Spirits Who Followed Satan and Deceased Mortal Spirits in Hell Are Together

The scriptures record that shortly after the creation of this earth there was strife in the heavens which resulted in the expulsion of Satan and a third of the heavenly hosts. The Lord revealed to Joseph Smith that Lucifer

> Rebelled against me, saying, Give me thine honor, which is my power; and also *a third part of the hosts of heaven turned he away from me* because of their agency;
>
> And they were thrust down, and *thus came the devil and his angels;*
>
> And, behold, there is a place prepared for them from the beginning, *which place is hell.*[37]

John the Revelator envisioned the fall of Satan from his exalted place in the heavens, and recorded that

> There was war in heaven: Michael and his angels fought against the dragon; and the dragon fought, and his angels,
>
> And prevailed not; *neither was their place found any more in heaven.*
>
> And the great dragon was cast out, that old serpent, called the *Devil, and Satan, which deceiveth the whole world: he was cast out into the earth, and his angels were cast out with him.*[38]

Reference has already been made to the statement of the apostle Peter that "God spared not the angels that sinned, but cast them down to hell."[39] It appears that the pre-mortal spirits who were cast out with Satan mingle in hell with those who have been condemned to that sphere as a result of an unrighteous mortal life. An experience of David P. Kimball in which he was assailed by both types of evil spirits demonstrates that they mingle and combine their efforts to fulfill Satan's bidding. Elder Kimball saw them as he was being driven in a wagon to Wickenburg, Arizona on November 5, 1881. Ac-

[37]D&C 29:36-38. See also D&C 76:25-27; Is. 14:12-15; Lk, 10:18; 2 Ne. 2:17-18; 9:8; Moses 4:1-4; Abra. 3:27-28.

[38]Rev. 12:7-9; see also verse 4.

[39]2 Pet. 2:4.

cording to his account, a severe fever from pneumonia had brought him near death's door the previous day, and a group of eight righteous spirits had come to watch over him:

> We drove on until about 11 a.m., when *a host of evil spirits made their appearance.* They were determined to destroy me, but I had power of mind to pay no attention to them, and let them curse all day without heeding them any more than possible. *Five times they made a rush en masse to come into the wagon, the last one, where I was, but were kept off by my friends (spiritual).* About 2 p.m., I told my boy to stop and we would water our horses. We used for this purpose barrels that we had along with us. After this I walked to the west side of my wagons, and looking to the east, *I saw and heard the evil spirits floating in the air and chanting curses upon Brigham Young. I saw two other groups of the same kind, but did not hear them.* Then I looked to the south and *the whole atmosphere was crowded with fallen spirits, or those who had not obtained bodies. Others who tried to torment me were spirits who had lived upon the earth.* Having seen so many and being complimented by my guard for seeing so well, I became a little timid and asked my spiritual friends if they had any help. The answer was, *'Yes, plenty.'*[40]

Evil Spirits Return to Places of Earthly Sins

It appears that the evil spirits in hell are at liberty to return to the places on earth in which they had committed great sins. There they have great power to afflict mortals who may be in the vicinity. This principle was expressed by Joseph Smith at the time of the great wave of unusual sickness which afflicted the Saints when they first moved into Commerce, Illinois. The Church members had moved into a number of abandoned log houses. According to Oliver B. Huntington, who recorded the Prophet's statement,

> Soon the inmates became sick—sickness increased until Joseph Smith began to be alarmed and saw something very unusual in the new affliction. He looked into the matter as only a Seer and Prophet could look. He saw the trouble and where it came from. Those houses had been dens of iniquity. He instituted means to empty them again by moving the people into tents and doubling up families in better houses. My father's family he took into his own house and tent.
>
> I once heard him *say concerning houses that had been inhabited by wicked people, that before the Saints moved into them they should be thoroughly*

[40]O.F. Whitney, *Helpful Visions, op. cit.*, p. 12.

cleansed, then fumigated with brimstone and whitewash. Afterward there should be a season of prayer in the house, and it should be dedicated unto the Lord for the use they designed for it.

Those old houses had been owned or occupied by wicked, unprincipled men, gamblers, outlaws, licentious robbers, etc., and those that were of the same stamp *had met there for evil practices and criminal purposes and there carried on their orgies. While this was the pastime or work of men and women in bodies, disembodied spirits of the same ilk stood around in highest glee and in various ways manifested to one another their enjoyment of the performance of the vilest of sins.*

When the owners or occupants of the houses were dead, they enjoyed each other's society with their new pals in the spirit state, and when the righteous took possession of their old houses, all combined to kill the new inhabitants, and hence so much sickness—for *all evil spirits whether in the body or out of the body, are opposed to this work and this people, and the spirits in the spirit world have means by which they can affect people on earth, and are as diligent there as here to do good or evil.*[41]

President Brigham Young taught in the same manner concerning the Gadianton Robbers, a ferocious band of murderers and thieves whose exploits are recorded in the Book of Mormon:

Upon one occasion President Brigham Young was in the Tabernacle at St. George and was speaking on the spirit world. He stated that it was not far from us and if the veil could be taken from our eyes there wouldn't be either a man, woman or child who would dare go out of 'this tabernacle *as the spirits of the Gadianton robbers were so thick out there. This is where they lived in these mountains,'* said he.[42]

On another occasion, he stated, "If you could see, you would walk over many parts of North America, . . . would you see

---

[41]O.B. Huntington, "The Prophet On Old Houses," *Young Woman's Journal,* Vol. II, pp. 467-468, July, 1891. Heber C. Kimball related a similar incident in which the children of Joseph Smith were made sick because of the influence of evil spirits who had occupied their home previously:

I will relate one circumstance that took place at Far West, *in a house that Joseph had purchased, which had been formerly occupied as a public house by some wicked people.* A short time after he got into it, one of his children was taken very sick; he laid his hands upon the child, when it got better; as soon as he went out of doors, the child was taken sick again; he again laid his hands upon it, so that it again recovered. This occurred several times, when Joseph inquired of the Lord what it all meant; then he had an open vision, and *saw the devil in person, who contended with Joseph face to face, for some time. He said it was his house, it belonged to him, and Joseph had no right there. Then Joseph rebuked Satan in the name of the Lord, and he departed and touched the child no more.* (Orson F. Whitney, *Life of Heber C. Kimball, op. cit.*, pp. 269-270)

[42]N.B. Lundwall, *Temples of the Most High, op. cit.,* p. 89.

the spirits of the wicked? Yes. Could you see the spirits of devils? Yes, . . ."[43]

Evil Spirits in Hell Attempt to Thwart the Work of God

Though the spirits from hell often lurk and linger aimlessly about their previous earthly scenes of evil doing, it should not be assumed that they are indifferent and disorganized in their efforts against the Church and representatives of God. The Lord warned the Church that "earth and hell" would "combine against you,"[44] and that "hell shall rage against thee,"[45] but repeatedly promised that if they were faithful "the gates of hell shall not prevail against you; yea, and the Lord God will disperse the powers of darkness from before you."[46] He also warned that Satan's followers were organized into a militant fighting force, saying that "the devil shall gather together his armies; even the hosts of hell."[47]

Heber C. Kimball, while on a mission to England, saw the legions and companies of Satan's army. He later described the incident in a Utah conference:

> Where will those go to that reject this Gospel? . . . They will remain where they are, *in hell, where my spirit was for a short time,* when I was in England. Where was my body during that brief period? It was in Preston, on the corner of Wilford street, but my spirit could see and observe those evil spirits as plainly as it ever will after I die. *Legions of disembodied evil spirits came against me, organized in companies that they might have more power,* but they had not power over me to any great extent, because of the power that was in and sustaining me. I had the Priesthood, and the power of it was upon me. *I saw the invisible world of the condemned spirits, those who were opposed to me and to this work, and to the lifting up of the standard of Christ in that country.*[48]

---

[43]JD 3:368. June 22, 1856.

[44]D&C 6:34.

[45]D&C 122:1.

[46]D&C 21:6. See also D&C 17:8; 18:5; 33:13; 98:22; 128:10; Mt. 16:18.

[47]D&C 88:113.

[48]JD 4:2. June 29, 1856. See also JD 3:229; 4:274. Another account of this incident which Elder Kimball left is also informative:

> While thus engaged, I was struck with great force by some invisible power, and fell senseless on the floor. The first thing I recollected was being supported by Elders Hyde and Richards, who were praying for me; Elder Richards having followed Russell up to my room. Elders Hyde and Richards then assisted me to get on the bed, but my agony was so great I could not endure it, and I arose, bowed my knees and prayed. I then arose and sat up on the bed, when a vision was opened to our minds, and *we could distinctly see the evil spirits, who foamed and gnashed their teeth*

On another occasion, President Kimball warned that "the spirits of the wicked, who have died for thousands of years past, are at war with the Saints of God upon the earth."[49]

Brigham Young stated that the apostates who attempted to thwart the progress of the Church while on earth will continue their malicious actions while consigned to hell:

> Go to the time when the Gospel came to the earth in the days of Joseph, *take the wicked that have opposed this people and persecuted them to the death, and they are sent to hell.* Where are they? They are in the spirit world, and *are just as busy as they possibly can be to do everything they can against the Prophet and the Apostles, against Jesus and His kingdom.* They are just as wicked and malicious in their actions against the cause of truth, as they were while on the earth in their fleshly tabernacles.[50]

It should not be assumed that the wicked spirits are without knowledge that they are attempting to thwart the work of God. Though it was shown earlier in the chapter that they have forfeited the privilege of the light of Christ and that they have become dead pertaining to the things of righteousness, they still have knowledge of the Lord and His works. Indeed, it is their personal decision to rebel against the knowledge of God which they possessed that has enabled Satan to encircle and bind them.

Biblical passages give indication that the fallen spirits are aware of the gospel program and know of the priesthood power and authority possessed by Christ and His representatives.

---

at us. We gazed at them about an hour and a half (by Willard's watch). We were not looking towards the window, but towards the wall. Space appeared before us, and *we saw the devils coming in legions, with their leaders, who came within a few feet of us. They came towards us like armies rushing to battle. They appeared to be men of full stature, possessing every form and feature of men in the flesh, who were angry and desperate; and I shall never forget the vindictive malignity depicted on their countenances as they looked me in the eye;* and any attempt to paint the scene which then presented itself, or portray their malice and enmity, would be vain. I perspired exceedingly, my clothes becoming as wet as if I had been taken out of the river. I felt excessive pain, and was in the greatest distress for some time. I cannot even look back on the scene without feelings of horror; yet by it, I learned the power of the adversary, his enmity against the servants of God, and got some understanding of the invisible world. *We distinctly heard those spirits talk and express their wrath and hellish designs against us.* However, the Lord delivered us from them, and blessed us exceedingly that day. (Orson F. Whitney, *Life of Heber C. Kimball, op. cit.*, pp. 144-145.)

[49]JD 3:229. Mar. 2, 1856.

[50]JD 3:370. June 22, 1856.

When Jesus met the two Gadarene demoniacs, for instance, the evil spirits cried out, saying, "What have we to do with thee, Jesus, thou Son of God? art thou come hither to torment us before the time?"[51] When Christ, in the synagogue at Capernaum, rebuked the evil spirits who had possessed a man's body, they protested loudly, saying, "Let us alone; what have we to do with thee, thou Jesus of Nazareth? art thou come to destroy us? I know who thou art; the Holy One of God."[52] But when the seven sons of Sceva, who were without priesthood authority, attempted to cast out an evil spirit, the demon challenged, "Jesus I know, and Paul I know; but who are ye?"[53] and then beat them and chased them from the house in a naked and wounded condition. James, while speaking of the ineffectiveness of faith without works, said "Thou believest that there is one God; thou doest well: the devils also believe, and tremble."[54]

Sins Which Can Lead to Hell

The inhabitants of hell are those who have lived only a telestial law upon the earth, and have knowingly refused to accept and live the principles of Christ's gospel. It should be realized that to merit hell and a telestial resurrection one must know a higher law and be accountable for it, and then rebel or refuse to live it. Knowledge is prerequisite for man to be "accountable and capable of committing sins,"[55] and man must know divine law to be able to break it, for "sin is the transgression of the law."[56]

A number of sins are specifically listed in the scriptures, the knowing commission of which would doom the individual to suffer in hell if he did not repent. These sins include

1. Refusal to accept the gospel and the testimony of Jesus (D&C 76:82, 103-106; Al. 12:10-11)
2. Murder (D&C 42:18-19, 79)

[51] Mt. 8:29.
[52] Lk. 4:34. See also verse 41.
[53] Acts 19:13-16.
[54] Jas. 2:19.
[55] Moro. 8:10.
[56] 1 Jn. 3:4.

3. Adultery (D&C 76:103-106)
4. Whoring and harlotry (D&C 76:103-106; 2 Ne. 9:36; 28:15; Rev. 21:8; Prov. 7:6-27; 5:3-5)
5. Being filthy and abominable (Rev. 21:8; 2 Ne. 9:16; 1 Ne. 15:34-35)
6. Idolatry (Rev. 21:8)
7. Sorcery (D&C 76:103-106; Rev. 21:8)
8. Hypocrisy (Mt. 23:27-28, 33)
9. Loving lies and telling them (D&C 76:103-106; Rev. 21:8; 2 Ne. 9:34)
10. Preaching false doctrine (2 Ne. 28:9-15)
11. Leading others into sin (Al. 36:13-14; Al. 14:6; 1 Ne. 14:3-4; Lk. 12:5)
12. Lying in wait to ensnare others (D&C 10:22-27)
13. Rebellion against God (Al 36:13-14)
14. Forgetting God (Ps. 9:17)
15. Being fearful and unbelieving (Rev. 21:8)
16. Persecuting God's people (D&C 121:23)
17. Pride (2 Ne. 28:9-15)
18. Failure to aid the poor and needy (Mt. 25:31-41; D&C 104:18)
19. Cursing one's fellow man (Mt. 5:22)
20. Failure to repent (Mk. 9:43-48)
21. Believing in infant baptism (Moro. 8:14, 21)
22. Being an unprofitable servant (Mt. 25:30).

Certainly other sins will have the same result as those above which the scriptures have stated specifically. The conscious decision to perform any sin tends to drive out the Spirit of the Lord and open the way for the devil to lead men down to hell. As Nephi prophesied concerning his people,

> They sell themselves for naught; for, for the reward of their pride

> and their foolishness they shall reap destruction; for *because they yield unto the devil and choose works of darkness rather than light, therefore they must go down to hell.*
>
> For the Spirit of the Lord will not always strive with man. And *when the Spirit ceaseth to strive with man then cometh speedy destruction,* and this grieveth my soul.[57]

The Nature of Suffering In Hell

The fate of those who are cast down to hell is exquisite and terrible. They suffer greater agonies than mortals can endure on earth. The Savior, who suffered these things for all men so that those who came unto Him could escape them, described the intense agonies those who do not heed His gospel must endure:

> I command you to repent—repent, lest I smite you by the rod of my mouth, and by my wrath, and by my anger, *and your sufferings be sore —how sore you know not, how exquisite you know not, yea, how hard to bear, you know not.*
>
> For behold, I, God, have suffered these things for all, that they might not suffer if they would repent;
>
> But *if they would not repent they must suffer even as I.*
>
> Which suffering caused myself, even God, the greatest of all, *to tremble because of pain, and to bleed at every pore, and to suffer both body and spirit—and would that I might not drink the bitter cup, and shrink—*
>
> Nevertheless, glory be to the Father, and I partook and finished my preparations unto the children of men.
>
> Wherefore, I command you again to repent, lest I humble you with my almighty power; and that you confess your sins, *lest you suffer these punishments of which I have spoken, of which in the smallest, yea, even in the least degree you have tasted at the time I withdrew my Spirit.*[58]

The prophet Alma described the agonies of the pains of hell which he suffered as he laid in a coma for three days and three nights after being smitten by an angel of God:

> I was racked with eternal torment, for *my soul was harrowed up to the greatest degree and racked with all my sins.*
>
> Yea, *I did remember all my sins and iniquities,* for which I was tormented with the pains of hell; yea, *I saw that I had rebelled against my God, and that I had not kept his holy commandments.*
>
> Yea, and I had murdered many of his children, or rather led them away unto destruction; yea, and in fine so great had been my

[57]2 Ne. 26:10-11.
[58]D&C 19:15-20.

iniquities, that the *very thought of coming into the presence of my God did rack my soul with inexpressible horror.*

Oh, thought I, that I could be banished and become extinct both soul and body, *that I might not be brought to stand in the presence of my God, to be judged of my deeds.*

And now, for three days and for three nights was I racked, *even with the pains of a damned soul.*[59]

Exactly what is the nature of the suffering which the spirits confined to hell must endure? The many clues available may be combined to show that it consists of at least nine factors:

1. *A bright recollection of guilt*—Alma's report that he was "racked with all my sins" and that he "did remember all my sins and iniquities" was an accurate statement of the plight of the damned in hell. In commenting on Alma's account Elder Orson Pratt said,

> The memories of the wicked, after they leave this body, will be so increased that they will have a bright recollection, Alma says, of all their guilt. Here they forget a good many things wherein they have displeased God; but in that condition, even before the resurrection, *they will have a bright recollection of all their guilt, which will kindle in them a flame like that of an unquenchable fire, creating in their bosoms a feeling of torment, pain and misery,* because they have sinned against their own Father and their own God, and rejected His counsels.[60]

On another occasion Orson Pratt explained,

> We might now inquire, what is the cause of this intense suffering and misery? Is it the action of the elements upon the spirit?

---

[59]Al. 36:12-16. Alma's description of the joy he received after being released from the pains of hell is of equal interest:

> And it came to pass that as I was thus *racked with torment, while I was harrowed up by the memory of my many sins,* behold, I remembered also to have heard my father prophesy unto the people concerning the coming of one Jesus Christ, a Son of God, to atone for the sins of the world.
>
> Now, as my mind caught hold upon this thought, I cried within my heart: O Jesus, thou Son of God, *have mercy on me, who am in the gall of bitterness, and am encircled about by the everlasting chains of death.*
>
> And now, behold, when I thought this, *I could remember my pains no more;* yea, I was harrowed up by the memory of my sins no more.
>
> *And oh, what joy, and what marvelous light I did behold; yea, my soul was filled with joy as exceeding as was my pain!*
>
> Yea, I say unto you, my son, that there could be *nothing so exquisite and so bitter as were my pains.* Yea, and again I say unto you, my son, that on the other hand, there can be *nothing so exquisite and sweet as was my joy.* (Al. 36:17-21)

[60]JD 16:365. Jan. 27, 1874.

> Is it the materials of nature, operating from without upon it, that causes this distress, this weeping, wailing, mourning, and lamentation? It may be in some measure; it may help to produce the misery and the wretchedness; but there is something connected with the spirit itself that no doubt produces this weeping, wailing, and mourning. What is this something? *It is memory, and remorse of conscience; a memory of what they have once done, a memory of their disobedience. . . .* Things that may have been erased from your memory for years will be presented before you with all the vividness as if they had just taken place. This will be like a worm upon the conscience; it will prey upon the spirit and produce unhappiness, wretchedness and misery.[61]

When he considered this fate Parley P. Pratt wrote,

> But, oh! the pain, the dark despair, the torments of a guilty conscience, the blackness of darkness, in the lower hell, which the guilty wretches will experience before that happy day of deliverance![62]

2. *Fear of the judgment of God*—Alma recorded that as he suffered the pains of hell, "The very thought of coming into the presence of my God did rack my soul with inexpressible horror!"[63] To his son, Corianton, he stated that "this is the state of the souls of the wicked, yea, in darkness, and *a state of awful, fearful looking for the fiery indignation of the wrath of God upon them.*"[64] The doubt and suspense which the wicked experience in hell takes a heavy toll on them. According to Joseph Smith, "There is no pain so awful as that of suspense. This is the punishment of the wicked; their doubt, anxiety and suspense cause weeping, wailing and gnashing of teeth."[65]

3. *Knowledge that they have failed to achieve their full potential*—Certainly the realization that they have failed to attain the heights of achievement they could have reached is a cause for grief among the spirits cast down to hell. As the prophet Joseph stated,

> The great misery of departed spirits in the world of spirits, where they go after death, is *to know that they come short of the glory that others enjoy, and that they might have enjoyed themselves,* and they are their own accusers.[66]

---

[61]JD 2:239, 240. Oct. 15, 1854.
[62]Parley P. Pratt, *Key to the Science of Theology, op. cit.,* p. 82.
[63]Al. 36:14.
[64]Al. 40:14.
[65]HC 5:340. Apr. 8, 1843.
[66]B.H. Roberts, *Rise and Fall of Nauvoo, op. cit.,* p. 216.

In his King Follett address, Joseph Smith said that

> A man is his own tormentor and his own condemner. Hence the saying, They shall go into the lake that burns with fire and brimstone. The *torment of disappointment in the mind of man is as exquisite as a lake burning with fire and brimstone.* I say, so is the torment of man.[67]

4. *Misery of evil companionship*—Taught Orson Pratt, while discussing the fate of the spirits in hell,

> *There is something that is calculated to render their society disagreeable to themselves, which increases as the degradation of the society is increased.* Then a wicked man entering into the company of such beings has not only a hell within himself—a conscience gnawing like a worm, but *he sees misery and wretchedness; and they cleave one to another in their wickedness,* and in their conversation, and acts, and doings, and intercourse with each other; *all these things are calculated in their nature to produce misery and wretchedness, as well as their own consciences.* It should then be our constant study to escape this order of things.[68]

On another occasion he explained that the wretchedness experienced by these spirits is due in great measure to their loss of capacity to love one another:

> If we should inquire what constitutes the misery of the fallen angels, the answer would be, *they are destitute of love; they have ceased to love God; they have ceased to have pure love one towards another; they have ceased to love that which is good.* Hatred, malice, revenge, and every evil passion have usurped the place of love; and unhappiness, wretchedness, and misery are the results. *Where there is no love, there will be no desire to promote the welfare of others.* Instead of desiring that others may be happy, each desires to make all others miserable like himself; each seeks to gratify that hellish disposition against the Almighty which arises from his extreme hatred of that which is good. *For the want of love the torment of each is complete.* All the wicked who are entirely overcome by these malicious spirits will have the heavenly principle of love wholly eradicated from their minds, and *they will become angels to these infernal fiends, being captivated by them, and compelled to act as they act.* They cannot extricate themselves from their power, nor ward off the fiery darts of their malicious tormentors. Such will be the condition of all beings who entirely withdraw themselves from the love of God.[69]

5. *Inability to progress*—The Lord has revealed that "he

---

[67]HC 6:314. Apr. 7, 1844.

[68]JD 2:241. Oct. 15, 1854.

[69]Orson Pratt, *The Seer,* Vol, I, No. 10, October 1853, p. 156.

that believeth not shall be damned."[70] Surely a degree of the misery of this inability to progress is felt in hell, for there the wicked encounter "the night of darkness *wherein there can be no labor performed.*"[71]

6. *Inability to fulfill lustful desires*—Those who are cast down to hell, though they are without a body, are still plagued with lustful desires which they did not conquer in mortality. As Melvin J. Ballard taught,

> Do not let any of us imagine that we can go down to the grave not having overcome the corruptions of the flesh and then lose in the grave all our sins and evil tendencies. They will be with us. They will be with the spirit when separated from the body.[72]

Because they have no body to fulfill their lustful desires, these spirits often seek to seize mortal bodies or attempt to view evil deeds by returning to mortal places of iniquity. As Parley P. Pratt stated it, "Some of these spirits are adulterous, and suggest to the mind all manner of lasciviousness, all kinds of evil thoughts and temptations."[73]

Earlier in the chapter, reference has been made to several other aspects of hell which the wicked will encounter and which would seemingly be a source of misery for them. Though the references will not be reconsidered, the items should be recalled in this context. They include:

7. *Loss of agency and enslavement to the will of Satan.*
8. *Loss of the light and truth of Christ.*
9. *Spiritual death, or death pertaining to the things of righteousness.*

Spirit World Hell Ends With Second Resurrection

The punishment of the wicked in hell is a long and agonizing process, and will continue until they have made full payment for their mortal crimes. As Joseph Smith put it, they "shall welter for ages in torment, even until they shall have paid the uttermost farthing."[74]

---

[70]D&C 68:9.
[71]Al. 34:33.
[72]N.B. Lundwall, *The Vision, op. cit.,* p. 46.
[73]Parley P. Pratt, *Key to the Science of Theology, op. cit.,* p. 117.
[74]HC 6:315. Apr. 7, 1844.

Yet the hell in the spirit world will not continue forever. It is the message of the scriptures that hell will continue beyond the coming of Christ in glory and his millennial reign until the time of the second resurrection. Then even the spirits who have sinned grievous sins while in mortality will have suffered for their sins sufficiently in hell,[75] and will come forth in a resurrected form, be judged, and will be consigned to a degree of glory. President Brigham Young explained this principle when he taught,

> Jesus will bring forth, by his own redemption, every son and daughter of Adam, except the sons of perdition, who will be cast into hell. *Others will suffer the wrath of God—will suffer all the Lord can demand at their hands, or justice can require of them; and when they have suffered the wrath of God till the utmost farthing is paid, they will be brought out of prison.* Is this dangerous doctrine to preach? Some consider it dangerous; but *it is true that every person who does not sin away the day of grace, and become an angel to the Devil will be brought forth to inherit a kingdom of glory.*[76]

What passages give indication that the spirit hell is only a temporary abode? John the Revelator, for instance, while commenting on his vision of the second resurrection, said that "death and *hell* delivered up the dead which were in them: and they were judged every man according to their works."[77] The Book of Mormon prophet Jacob also testified that the spirits would be called out of hell, saying,

> This death of which I have spoken, which is the spiritual death, *shall deliver up its dead; which spiritual death is hell;* wherefore, death and hell must deliver up their dead, and *hell must deliver up its captive spirits,* and the grave must deliver up its captive bodies, and the bodies and the spirits of men will be restored one to the other; and it is by the power of the resurrection of the Holy One of Israel.[78]

According to the vision of the degrees of glory which the Lord bestowed upon Joseph Smith and Sidney Rigdon,

> These are they who are thrust down to hell.
> These are they who shall *not be redeemed from the devil until the*

[75]With the exception of the sons of perdition, who have committed unpardonable sins. Their fate will be discussed in chapter IX.

[76]JD 8:154. Aug. 26, 1860.

[77]Rev. 20:13.

[78]2 Ne. 9:12.

> *last resurrection,* until the Lord, even Christ the Lamb, shall have finished his work. . . .
>
> These are they who suffer the vengeance of eternal fire.
>
> These are they who *are cast down to hell and suffer the wrath of Almighty God, until the fulness of times,* when Christ shall have subdued all enemies under his feet, and shall have perfected his work.[79]

Alma taught that the wicked would remain "in darkness, and a state of awful, fearful looking for the fiery indignation of the wrath of God upon them . . . *until the time of their resurrection.*"[80] It would seem that the knowledge of the temporary nature of the spirit world hell is what prompted King David, of Old Testament times, to exclaim, to the Lord, "Thou wilt not leave my soul in hell."[81]

Yet if the spirit world hell is only a temporary situation, why do the scriptures speak of it as "*endless* torment," and say the inhabitants suffer "*eternal* damnation" and endure "*eternal* fire"? Explanation of the proper interpretation of these passages was revealed by the Lord, as follows:

> *I am Alpha and Omega, Christ the Lord;* yea, even I am he, the beginning and the end, the Redeemer of the world.
>
> I, having accomplished and finished the will of him whose I am, even the Father, concerning me—having done this that I might subdue all things unto myself—
>
> *Retaining all power, even to the destroying of Satan and his works at the end of the world, and the last great day of judgment,* which I shall pass upon the inhabitants thereof, judging every man according to his works and the deeds which he hath done.
>
> And surely every man must repent or suffer, for I, God, am endless.
>
> Wherefore, I revoke not the judgments which I shall pass, *but woes shall go forth, weeping, wailing and gnashing of teeth,* yea, to those who are found on my left hand.
>
> Nevertheless, *it is not written that there shall be no end to this torment, but it is written endless torment.*
>
> *Again, it is written eternal damnation;* wherefore it is more express than other scriptures, that it might work upon the hearts of the children of men, altogether for my name's glory.
>
> Wherefore, I will explain unto you this mystery, for it is meet unto you to know even as mine apostles.

---

[79]D&C 76:84-85, 105-106.

[80]Al. 40:14.

[81]Ps. 16:10. See Acts 2:27.

> I speak unto you that are chosen in this thing, even as one, that you may enter into my rest.
>
> For, behold, the mystery of godliness, how great is it! For, behold, *I am endless, and the punishment which is given from my hand is endless punishment, for Endless is my name, Wherefore—*
>
> *Eternal punishment is God's punishment.*
> *Endless punishment is God's punishment.*[82]

Thus the hell of the spirit world is regarded as being a temporary abode for the wicked spirits. For most of them, the agony and misery of their hellish punishment will cease at the time of the second resurrection, when they shall come forth and inherit the telestial kingdom.

Lest confusion arise at this point, brief reference should be made to a certain group of the inhabitants of hell. These individuals, who have committed sin for which there is no forgiveness, will not come forth in the telestial resurrection. Though the spirit world hell will come to an end, these spirits must stand before God in judgment and then be cast out to dwell with Satan and his angels for all eternity in a second state of hell. These spirits, known as the sons of perdition, are "the only ones who shall not be redeemed in the due time of the Lord, after the sufferings of his wrath."[83] Their fate, together with the nature of the unpardonable sin they have committed, will be considered in chapter IX.

SUMMARY

1. The term *hell* is a translation of the Hebrew *sheol* and the Greek *hades* and *tartarus.* In the general sense these terms all have reference to the entire world of spirits, as does the term *paradise.* In the specific sense, as they are used in this chapter, they refer to the abode of the wicked in the spirit world. References to the fire and brimstone of hell may be metaphors related to *Gehenna,* a rubbish heap where fires continually burned outside of Jerusalem.

2. Hell is often described as a place of darkness. This darkness is, apparently, literal, for the inhabitants of hell are shown to be without the light of Christ and the Spirit of the Lord.

[82]D&C 19:1-12.
[83]D&C 76:38.

3. Hell is a vast region filled with multitudes of beings. According to statements by Latter-day Saint leaders, it is with the remainder of the spirit world on or near this planet.

4. The chains of hell represent the complete subjugation of man's will to the will of Satan. Man is thus encircled and bound when he hardens his heart and chooses to reject righteousness.

5. The spirits without bodies who were cast out of heaven with Lucifer mingle in hell with those who were evil while upon earth. They combine their talents in molesting righteous men upon earth.

6. Evil spirits from hell return to the places of their earthly sins. They have especially great power to afflict mortals with sickness and temptation in these places.

7. There is a definite separation between the righteous and the wicked. Though they are all in the spirit world, they live in separate areas and have no association with one another, except as missionaries and ministering spirits come from paradise and hell into the spirit prison.

8. The devil has no control over the righteous spirits in paradise, but has complete dominion over the spirits in hell.

9. Acceptance of the gospel and adherence to its principles qualifies one for residence in paradise. Rejection of the gospel and of God's authorized servants condemns one to hell, as does the committing of evil deeds while in mortality.

10. Evil spirits from hell are organized in companies, legions and armies. They attempt to thwart the work of God upon earth and in the spirit realm.

11. Evil spirits from hell have knowledge of priesthood power and authority. They render obedience to the higher power of priesthood commands, though they are committed to a course in opposition to divine power and will.

12. The inhabitants of hell are primarily those who have abided only telestial law while on earth. Numerous sins are listed in the scriptures as bringing those who knowingly commit them the punishment of hell.

13. Nine causes of suffering are set forth as the reasons for the "weeping, wailing, and gnashing of teeth" which is suffered by its inhabitants. There are

    A. A bright recollection of guilt,
    B. Fear of the judgment of God,
    C. Knowledge that they have failed to achieve their full potential,

D. Misery of evil companionship,
E. Inability to progress,
F. Inability to fulfill lustful desires,
G. Loss of agency and enslavement to the will of Satan,
H. Loss of the light and truth of Christ, and
I. Spiritual death, or death pertaining to the things of righteousness.

14. The spirit world hell will end at the second resurrection, when most of the spirits will have paid the "uttermost farthing" and will receive a telestial resurrection.

15. Though the spirit world hell will end, there is still to be another hell or special place reserved for the devil, his angels, and the ex-mortal sons of perdition, to which they will be consigned forever following the final judgment.

CHAPTER VI

THE GREAT MISSIONARY LABOR IN THE SPIRIT PRISON

Every Man Must Have Opportunity To Accept the Gospel Plan

THE GOSPEL OF JESUS CHRIST IS A PROGRAM WHEREBY MAN can achieve and fulfill his ultimate destiny. It is "Christ's way to perfection."[1] It is a path of principles, ordinances, and covenants[2] which man can walk to attain his exaltation. Basic to the gospel plan is the role of Jesus Christ, who died on the cross to assume the debt of sin and death owed by all mankind, and thus won the power to draw all men unto himself and the privilege of supervising them as they travel the path to life eternal.[3] Under His direction a program of growth and progression has been outlined which is available for every man to accept or reject as he may choose. In His wisdom and infinite justice, He has seen fit that every being who has come to earth should have an opportunity to understand and choose whether to accept or reject His gospel plan. Indeed, He has proclaimed that the "gospel of the kingdom shall be preached in all the world,"[4] unto "every nation, and kindred, and tongue, and people."[5]

He has not forced His plan upon mortals, however. Neither has He allowed His gospel program to function upon the earth when conditions were not proper for it to serve man properly. There have been many places and many eras in which men walked the earth without knowledge that such a pathway to perfection even existed. In the theology of the sectarian world, such unfortunate men are condemned and

[1]See Jn. 14:6 and Mt. 5:48.
[2]See 3 Ne. 27:19-21.
[3]See 3 Ne. 27:9-18.
[4]Mt. 24:14.
[5]Rev. 14:6.

subjected for all eternity to the sufferings of an awful hell. Yet, in the justice of God, those who died without an understanding of the gospel are also entitled to hear and make their choice whether to accept or reject Christ's plan and live in accordance with it.

Since the majority of mankind has passed through mortality without hearing the gospel of Christ, the Lord has seen fit to institute a great missionary program in the world of spirits beyond the grave, and to allow men to prove their fidelity to the gospel plan by their actions there. Thus all men can stand before Him in the day of judgment and can be examined by the same standard of righteousness. This was the program the apostle Peter foresaw when he said that men

> Shall give account to him that is ready to judge the quick and the dead.
>
> *For this cause was the gospel preached also to them that are dead, that they might be judged according to men in the flesh, but live according to God in the spirit.*[6]

True Latter-day Saints recognize that theirs is the responsibility of preaching the gospel both to mortal beings and in the next life. This is regarded as a solemn, God-inspired duty. As Brigham Young once said,

> Our Father in heaven, Jesus, our elder brother and the Savior of the world, and the whole heavens, *are calling upon this people to prepare to save the nations of the earth, also the millions who have slept without the Gospel.*[7]

It is not the belief of Latter-day Saints, however, that all mankind will accept Christ's way to perfection and pursue it till they achieve their ultimate goal. To the contrary, they recognize that the majority will choose to reject the gospel of Christ,[8] and that but a relatively small group will reach the ultimate development of the gospel of Christ:

> Except ye abide my law ye cannot attain to this glory.

---

[6] 1 Pet. 4:5-6. See Eph. 4:8-9.

[7] JD 18:77. Aug. 31, 1875.

[8] See D&C 45:38-39. It is understood that in the time of judgment "every knee shall bow" (Mos. 27:31), yet this does not imply they will accept and live gospel principles. Note that many who will bow the knee to Christ will inherit only the lowest, or telestial, kingdom. (D&C 76:109-110). See also 2 Ne. 28:32.

> For strait is the gate, and narrow the way that leadeth unto the exaltation and continuation of the lives, and *few there be that find it. . . .*[9]

The Doctrine of Vicarious Work For The Dead

The doctrine of vicarious work for the dead is one of the most profound truths of the gospel of Jesus Christ. It is a teaching which was known in New Testament times, was lost to sectarian Christianity during the dark centuries of apostasy from divine truth, and was restored in the last days. In its basic form, the doctrine consists of five principles:

1. *To receive the benefits of Christ's atoning sacrifice, man must*
   - A. *Partake of gospel ordinances,*
   - B. *Seek righteousness by forsaking sin, and*
   - C. *Serve God by doing His will.*

Christ said much more concerning each of these provisions of His gospel plan than can be recorded here. His teaching can be summarized, though, by recalling certain key passages. Concerning ordinances, for instance, He proclaimed that "Except a man be born of water and of the Spirit, he cannot enter into the kingdom of God."[10] Pertaining to the seeking of righteousness He admonished His followers to "Be ye therefore perfect, even as your Father which is in heaven is perfect"[11] and "Seek ye first the kingdom of God, and his righteousness."[12] Of serving God He taught that "Not everyone that saith unto me, Lord, Lord, shall enter into the kingdom of heaven; but he that doeth the will of my Father which is in heaven."[13] He warned that those who would benefit from His atonement must enter "at the strait gate"[14] by fulfilling these three prerequisites, and that to those who sought His kingdom by any other method He would "profess unto them, I never knew you: depart from me, ye that work iniquity."[15]

---

[9]D&C 132:21-22.

[10]Jn. 3:5.

[11]Mt. 5:48.

[12]Mt. 6:33.

[13]Mt. 7:21.

[14]Mt. 7:13-14.

[15]Mt. 7:23. The doctrine of the first principles of the gospel is too extensive to be considered in greater detail here. For more extensive coverage of these principles the reader is invited to consult such basic texts as James E. Talmage, *Articles of Faith,* pp. 96-170, and LeGrand Richards, *A Marvelous Work and a Wonder,* pp. 84-113. Both works are readily available at L.D.S. bookstores.

2. *The ordinances of the gospel must be performed on the earth. The living who understand the gospel and have opportunity to do so must receive these ordinances themselves. Otherwise the ordinances may be performed vicariously for the dead.* Latter-day Saints understand that the following ordinances must be performed by and for them while on earth:[16]

A. *Baptism* (by immersion; for the remission of sins)[17]

B. *Confirmation* (acceptance into the Church; includes the bestowal of the gift of the Holy Ghost)[18]

C. *Melchizedek Priesthood Ordination* (bestowal of authorization to act in the name of Christ; available only to males)[19]

D. *Washings and Anointings* (cleansing ordinances and preparation for priesthood and governmental rule in the celestial kingdom)[20]

E. *Temple Endowment* (ordinance which teaches basic information necessary to enter the most advanced of the heavenly kingdoms)[21]

---

[16]The final four must be performed in Latter-day Saint temples by living members. All must be performed in the temple when done vicariously for the dead.

[17]See Ro. 6:1-5; Mk. 1:4-5; etc.

[18]See Acts 8:14-17; 1 Tim. 4:14; etc.

[19]See Mt. 10:1; Mk. 3:14; Jn. 15:16; etc.

[20]See Jn. 13:4-15; 1 Sam. 10:1; 1 Sam. 16:13; etc.

[21]See D&C 105:10-12; D&C 110:8-10; etc. President Brigham Young defined the temple endowment in this manner:

> Your *endowment* is, to receive all those ordinances in the House of the Lord, which are necessary for you, after you have departed this life, to enable you to walk back to the presence of the Father, passing the angels who stand as sentinels, being enabled to give them the key words, the signs and tokens, pertaining to the Holy Priesthood, and gain your eternal exaltation in spite of earth and hell. (JD 2:31. April 6, 1853. See also D&C 132:18-19.

In his book, *The House of The Lord* (Salt Lake City, Utah: Bookcraft, Inc., 1962), pp. 99-101, Elder James E. Talmage explained the temple endowment as follows:

> The *temple endowment,* as administered in modern temples, comprises instruction relating to the significance and sequence of past dispensations, and the importance of the present as the greatest and grandest era in human history. This course of instruction includes a recital of the most prominent events of the creative period, the condition of our first parents in the Garden of Eden, their disobedience and consequent expulsion from that blissful abode, their condition in the lone and dreary world when doomed to live by labor and sweat, the plan of redemption by which the great transgression may be atoned, the restoration of the gospel with all its ancient powers and privileges, the absolute and indispensable condition of personal

F. *Eternal Marriage* (marriage which continues the family unit beyond death and allows the continued procreation of children for certain worthy beings when they are resurrected)[22]

F. *Sealing of Families* (the eternal binding of children to parents to make the family units complete. This is unnecessary for a child born to parents who were already joined in eternal marriage at the time of the child's birth)[23]

Since these ordinances can be performed only on earth and cannot be performed in the spirit world, the Lord has provided a program whereby mortals may stand as proxies for those who are dead, receiving these ordinances "for and in behalf of" their departed loved ones. Vicarious ordinances were performed for the dead in New Testament times. The Apostle Paul, while teaching about the resurrection, queried, "Else what shall they do which are baptized for the dead, if the dead rise not at all? why are they then baptized for the dead?"[24]

3. *The gospel will be taught to all in the spirit prison who have not had opportunity to hear it. They will have their agency to*

---

purity and devotion to the right in present life, and a strict compliance with gospel requirements.

As will be shown, the temples erected by the Latter-day Saints provide for the giving of these instructions in separate rooms, each devoted to a particular part of the course; and by this provision it is possible to have several classes under instruction at one time.

The ordinances of the endowment embody certain obligations on the part of the individual, such as covenant and promise to observe the law of strict virtue and chastity, to be charitable, benevolent, tolerant and pure; to devote both talent and material means to the spread of truth and the uplifting of the race; to maintain devotion to the cause of truth; and to seek in every way to contribute to the great preparation that the earth may be made ready to receive her King—the Lord Jesus Christ. With the taking of each covenant and the assuming of each obligation a promised blessing is pronounced, contingent upon the faithful observance of the conditions.

No jot, iota, or tittle of the temple rites is otherwise than uplifting and sanctifying. In every detail the endowment ceremony contributes to covenants of morality of life, consecration of person to high ideals, devotion to truth, patriotism to nation, and allegiance to God. The blessings of the House of the Lord are restricted to no privileged class; every member of the Church may have admission to the temple with the right to participate in the ordinances thereof, if he comes duly accredited as of worthy life and conduct.

[22]See D&C 131:1-4; 132:15-20.

[23]See D&C 132:4-7.

[24]1 Cor. 15:29.

accept or reject it, as they choose. If they accept the gospel and the vicarious ordinances performed in their behalf on earth, they are permitted to leave the spirit prison and dwell in paradise. If necessary, they are punished for their earthly sins while in the spirit prison.

Concerning the agency of spirits who first hear the gospel in the spirit world, Elder Orson Pratt wrote,

> When these holy and sacred institutions are made known to the spirits in prison by holy messengers holding the Priesthood, *they will be left to their own agency, either to receive or reject these glad tidings,* and will be judged according to men in the flesh who have the privilege of hearing the same things.[25]

Of their release from the confines of the spirit prison President Joseph F. Smith, in his Vision of the Redemption of the Dead, said,

> Thus was the gospel preached to the dead. And the chosen messengers went forth to *declare the acceptable day of the Lord, and proclaim liberty to the captives who were bound; even unto all who would repent of their sins and receive the gospel.* Thus was the gospel preached to those who had died in their sins, without a knowledge of the truth, or in transgression, having rejected the prophets. These were *taught faith in God, repentance from sin, vicarious baptism for the remission of sins, the gift of the Holy Ghost by the laying on of hands, and all other principles of the gospel that were necessary* for them to know in order to qualify themselves that they might be judged according to men in the flesh, but live according to God in the spirit. . . .
>
> I beheld that the faithful elders of this dispensation, when they depart from mortal life, continue their labors in the preaching of the gospel of repentance and redemption, through the sacrifice of the Only Begotten Son of God, among those who are in darkness and under the bondage of sin in the great world of the spirits of the dead. *The dead who repent will be redeemed, through obedience to the ordinances of the house of God, and after they have paid the penalty of their transgressions,*

---

[25]Orson Pratt, "Celestial Marriage," *The Seer,* Vol. I, No. 9, pp. 141-142, September, 1853. President Heber Q. Hale, in commenting on the agency of the beings in the spirit world, told how they accepted the gospel principles there and the manner in which they became recipients of the vicarious ordinances performed on earth:

> *Vicarious work done here does not become automatically effective there.*
>
> The recipient must first believe, repent and accept baptism and confirmation, *then certain consummating ordinances are performed, effectualizing these saving principles in the lives of these regenerated beings,* and so the great work is going on; they doing a work there which we cannot do here, and we doing a work here which they cannot do there, both necessary, each the complement of the other, thus bringing about the salvation of all of God's children who will be saved.

and are washed clean, shall receive a reward according to their works for they are heirs of salvation.[26]

4. *Man is obliged to aid his deceased ancestors by performing genealogy and temple work for them while he is on earth, and by preaching the gospel to them when he passes into the spirit world. He cannot achieve his perfection until all his forefathers have had their opportunity to accept the gospel.*

The prophet Joseph Smith taught,

> Hence the responsibility, *the awful responsibility, that rests upon us in relation to our dead, for all the spirits who have not obeyed the Gospel in the flesh must either obey it in the spirit or be damned.* Solemn thought!—dreadful thought! . . .
>
> *The greatest responsibility in this world that God has laid upon us is to seek after our dead.* The apostle says, 'They without us cannot be made perfect'; for it is necessary that the sealing power should be in our hands to seal our children and our dead for the fulness of the dispensation of times—a dispensation to meet the promises made by Jesus Christ before the foundation of the world for the salvation of man.
>
> Now, I will speak of them, I will meet Paul half way. I say to you, Paul, you cannot be perfect without us. *It is necessary that those who are going before and those who come after us should have salvation in common with us; and thus hath God made it obligatory upon man.*[27]

His statement was a commentary on Hebrews 11:40, which concludes Paul's exposition on the suffering and death of the early Saints by asserting that God has "provided some better thing for us, that *they without us should not be made perfect.*[28]

5. *The major objective of missionary work and vicarious work for the dead is to bind the righteous of all eras into an unbroken chain of family relationships, under the patriarchal order of the priesthood. The righteous who are thus united are to dwell in this family relationship following the resurrection.*

President Brigham Young explained this teaching as follows:

> The fathers cannot be made perfect without us; we cannot be made perfect without the fathers. *There must be this chain in the holy Priest-*

[26]Joseph F. Smith, *Gospel Doctrine, op cit.*, pp. 474, 476.
[27]HC 6:312-313. April 7, 1844.
[28]Heb. 11:40. See D&C 128:18.

> *hood; it must be welded together from the latest generation that lives on the earth back to Father Adam,* to bring back all that can be saved and placed where they can receive salvation and a glory in some kingdom. This Priesthood has to do it; this Priesthood is for this purpose.[29]

Elder Parley P. Pratt amplified this doctrine when he explained that

> The celestial order is designed not only to give eternal life, but also *to establish an eternal order of family government,* founded upon the most pure and holy principles of union and affection. . . . They will then be organized each over his department of the government according to their birthright and office, in their families, generations and nations. *Each one will obey and be obeyed according to the connection which he sustains as a member of the great celestial family.*[30]

In the great chain of family relationships which is to exist in the celestial kingdom, special provisions will be made in instances where families are incomplete. A generation of a family may be omitted if none of that era of mortality merit exaltation, and the links of the chain will be sealed to exclude them. In some cases, where children have died and merit exaltation but are left without family connection because of the unrighteousness of their family, the power of adoption will come into effect, as explained by President Brigham Young:

> But what of the ungodly parents of the tabernacles of these children, will they have the privilege of going there? No, where God and Christ are they cannot come. Perhaps some of them may have had an offer of the Gospel and rejected it, then what will become of the children? They swarm in the Courts of Heaven; there are myriads and myriads of them there already, and more are going continually. What are you going to do with them? Perhaps I might say *somebody will have the privilege of saying to our young sisters who have died in the faith, 'I design so many of these children for you, and so many for you, and they are given you by the law of adoption, and they are yours just as much as*

[29]JD 13:280. Oct. 30, 1870. Concerning the linking of righteous family relationships beyond the veil Heber Q. Hale recorded,

> One of the grandest and most sacred things of heaven is family relationship. *The establishment of a complete chain without any broken links brings a fullness of joy.* Links wholly bad will be stopped out and other new links put in or two adjoining links welded together. Men and women through the world are moved upon by their dead ancestors to gather genealogies. These are the links for the chains. The ordinances for baptism, endowments and sealings performed in the Temples of God by the living for the dead are the welding of links.

[30]Lynn A. McKinley, *Life Eternal* (by the Author, 1950), pp. 173-174.

though you had borne them on the earth, and your seed shall continue through them for ever and ever.' It may be thought by some that when young persons die they will be cut short of the privileges and blessings God designs for His children; but this is not so. *The faithful will never miss a blessing through being cut off while here.*[31]

The Spirit Prison

Like the words "paradise" and "hell," the term "spirit prison" conveys different meanings when used by various people and in a variety of contexts. These meanings must be understood in order to fully comprehend the numerous statements made concerning the afterlife by Church Authorities. Three interpretations of the term "spirit prison" should be considered:

1. *The entire spirit world, including paradise and hell.* In this sense the term is synonymous with "spirit world." I Peter 3:18-20, when coupled with President Joseph F. Smith's "Vision of the Redemption of the Dead," appears to be used in this sense.

2. *All of the spirit world except paradise.* Some explanations concerning hell include the spirits in prison in the general category of the "wicked." When the term is used in this manner there sometimes is no differentiation made between those who have rejected the gospel and lived lives of great wickedness and those who have never heard the gospel.

3. *An area separate from both paradise and hell.* The accounts of those who have visited and/or seen in vision the spirit world imply that the primary use of the term "spirit prison" should be to distinguish a large group of spirit beings who are not in paradise but who are not under the complete subjugation of Satan. This is the usage employed in this chapter. Whether their abode lies within the "geographical boundaries" of hell or in an outside area cannot as yet be clearly documented. But apparently there is a large group of individuals, not yet committed to either Christ or Satan, who by choice or assignment are living with one another apart from the spirits of the condemned in hell. As was shown in Chapter III, the inhabitants of the spirit world dwell in numerous "spheres" or

[31]JD 14:230. Sept. 16, 1871.

"departments," and progress from one level to another as they advance in their eternal preparation. The spirit prison appears to be a level or series of "spheres" for inhabitants more advanced than the level of hell but not as yet prepared for the higher blessings and associations of paradise.

There is no scriptural passage which clearly defines whether hell and the spirit prison are the same or separate areas. There is no doctrinal position which has been adopted by the Church on this question. No authority of the Church has set forth any revelation which he has received which specifically defines whether hell and the spirit prison are the same or different areas. The matter has been treated only with expressions of opinion, which have been numerous. These expressions, based on extremely limited evidence, have been varied, but the concensus has seemingly held that hell and the spirit prison are the same area and the words are synonymous. Several past and current commentators have followed this line and have set forth their views, based upon this assumption. With this usage, the terms hell, prison, spirit prison, bondage, darkness, etc. have become so intertwined and confused that it is difficult to be completely sure of the correct meaning of any documentation found on this subject.

The author has long felt that the only way the question can be resolved is through the obtaining of new evidence, for the rehashing of formerly expressed opinions has led only to continuing confusion and uncertainty on this point for many individuals. Thus he has turned to eye-witness accounts for information previously unconsidered by other commentators. In the many dozens of testimonies which he has examined of those who have seen beyond the veil, he has sought particularly for the answer to this problem. Many individuals have been shown the gospel being preached beyond the veil, and numerous such accounts are cited throughout this and previous chapters of the book. The author has noted that not once, in any of the many eye-witness accounts considered, was there the slightest indication that the spirits committed to Satan in hell were dwelling among those who had not yet heard the gospel and were residents in the spirit prison. To the contrary, there seems to be impressive evidence that those in the spirit prison to whom the gospel is being taught are dwelling in special cities and areas, apart from Satan's spirit realm. Based on this evidence, he is led to conclude that the spirit prison and hell are separate places, and each is inhabited by a different category of individuals.

The following simple chart differentiates between those who are understood to inhabit each area:

Spirit Prison	*Hell*
1. Inhabitants have neither accepted nor rejected the gospel. Their eternal fate is still undecided.	1. Inhabitants have rejected the gospel.
2. Inhabitants still have agency as in mortality. They may be enticed by both good and evil.	2. Inhabitants are subjected to Satan, and compelled to obey his will.
3. Inhabitants can still "live according to God in the spirit."	3. Inhabitants are committed to a course of gospel rejection and rebellion.
4. Inhabitants have the light of Christ. They may be prompted as in mortality.	4. Inhabitants are without the light of Christ.
5. Inhabitants are living in a state of expectancy, awaiting the preaching of the gospel and the performance of vicarious ordinances.	5. Inhabitants are living in a state of extreme sorrow, with continual "weeping, wailing, and gnashing of teeth." They are fearful of the coming judgment.
6. Inhabitants are visited by missionaries, as related in numerous accounts.	6. No evidence that inhabitants are visited by missionaries. They are separated from the righteous by a "great gulf."
7. Inhabitants may dwell in pleasant circumstances with honorable neighbors of their choosing, as in mortality.	7. Inhabitants are associated with the wicked only.
8. Inhabitants are engaged in constructive activity, primarily related to gospel study.	8. Inhabitants are engaged in evil deeds and mischief calculated to hinder the work of God.

9. Inhabitants may return to the mortal sphere only for a legitimate purpose, as directed by Priesthood authority.	9. Inhabitants are allowed by Satan to return to places of mortal wickedness and to wander upon the earth promiscuously.
10. Inhabitants may leave the spirit prison before the resurrection if they accept the gospel and the vicarious ordinances performed for them.	10. Inhabitants must dwell in the spirit hell until the second resurrection. Sons of perdition among them will remain "filthy still" and will go to post-resurrection hell.
11. Inhabitants can still merit celestial or terrestrial glory.	11. Inhabitants can only merit the telestial glory or the kingdom of no glory.
12. Inhabitants may still be cast down to hell if they reject the gospel.	12. Inhabitants have no further alternative available. They are committed to hell.

Thus the status, opportunities, and possibilities of the inhabitants of the spirit prison are completely different from the status and course of action available to those who are under the complete dominion of Lucifer in hell. Those in the spirit prison are not classified as inhabitants of hell, as defined in the third definition, but are considered separately in God's divine plan of salvation.

In the author's view, the acknowledgement that hell and the spirit prison are separate areas and inhabited by different types of beings resolves a number of problems left unsolved by the opposing theory. Numerous scriptural conflicts are also solved. For instance, if the inhabitants of the spirit prison and hell are different and separate, there no longer exists the glaring conflicts between passages which assert the continued agency of the imprisoned spirits, as contrasted with passages which hold that those in hell are bound with the chains of darkness and are subjected to the will of Satan (for the devil's plan has been from the beginning to deprive man of his agency). If the spirit prison and hell are separate, then the conflict vanishes which arises from contrasting teachings that men may go from the prison into paradise when they accept the gospel but those in hell must remain until the second resurrection. If the inhabitants of the spirit prison are separate from the populace of hell, then the conflict ceases between the apparent necessity for man to have the Spirit and light of Christ to know the truthfulness of the missionary message being taught in the prison and the passages which indicate that those in hell have no part nor portion of the spirit of the Lord. If inhabitants of the spirit prison and hell are separate, then there remains no conflict between passages which depict some inhabitants of the prison attaining the terrestrial resurrection and references asserting that those in hell will gain no more than the telestial realm. If inhabitants of the spirit prison differ from those in hell, no problem arises from passages showing the inhabitants of the prison coming forth in the first resurrection, while those in hell must await the second resurrection. If missionaries labor in the spirit prison but are not laboring in hell, they are not, then, having to preach in the repugnant darkness of the of the latter realm, which would undoubtedly prove most distressing.

If men of integrity who have not yet heard the gospel but who will gladly accept it when it is preached to them are in the spirit prison rather than hell, then they are not continually subjected to the foul associations of the wicked and unjust, which would be a gross injustice. If the spirit prison and hell are distinct from one another, there is no reason for alarm in noting that the many individuals who have seen the gospel being preached in the spirit world have given no intimation of the darkness of hell nor of the devil or his angels being present in the scenes they viewed. And if the spirit prison and hell are separate areas, no confusion arises from the reports of such men as Lorenzo Dow Young, who saw that the prison and hell are distinct and apart, or James LeSueur, who saw the inhabitants of the spirit prison gathered into special cities where their time was devoted to gospel study.

Scriptural passages make a distinction between hell and the spirit prison, and show that the fate of those in hell is sealed until the second resurrection, while the avenue of repentance, gospel acceptance, and advancement is still available to those in the spirit prison. "The Vision," for instance, speaks of the group who "died without law . . . who received not the testimony of Jesus in the flesh, but afterwards received it" as being they "who are *the spirits of men kept in prison, whom the Son visited, and preached the gospel unto them,* that they might be judged according to men in the flesh" and gain "terrestrial" glory.[32] They are contrasted in the revelation with a less worthy group "who are thrust down to hell" and *"shall not be redeemed from the devil* until the last resurrection," because of their rejection of "the testimony of Jesus" and will be rewarded with only "telestial" glory.[33] It appears that the group in the spirit prison were still entitled to an opportunity for repentance, while those in hell had rejected the opportunity.

In the Pearl of Great Price, the Lord again differentiated between the inhabitants of hell and those of the spirit prison. He spoke of the wickedness of the parents prior to Enoch's day, and said that *"Satan shall be their father, and misery shall be their doom;* and the whole heavens shall weep over them."[34] This fate was hell. Then he spoke of those who lived over five centuries later, at the time of the flood, and said,

> These which thine eyes are upon shall perish in the floods; and behold, I will shut them up; *a prison have I prepared for them.*
>
> And that which I have chosen hath plead before my face. Wherefore, *he suffereth for their sins; inasmuch as they will repent* in the day that my Chosen shall return unto me. . . .[35]

Thus again the Lord differentiated between the inhabitants of hell and of the spirit prison, and again showed that those in the spirit prison were to have a later opportunity to repent while those in hell had forfeited that privilege and had become angels to the devil until at least the time of the second resurrection.

A careful reading of the parable of the rich man and Lazarus also indicates that hell and the spirit prison are not the same place. While it is beyond dispute that missionaries from paradise are able to enter the spirit prison, the Savior's

[32]D&C 76:71-74.

[33]D&C 76:81-84.

[34]Moses 7:36-37.

[35]Moses 7:38-39. See 1 Pet. 3:18-20; 4:6. Some commentators have failed to note the chronological difference between the days of Enoch and the time of the flood and have assumed that the passage spoke of only one group. But the groups are separate, divided by over five hundred years.

words make it clear that entry from paradise (depicted in the parable as Abraham's bosom) into hell is impossible, just as movement from hell to paradise is not allowed. If hell were not separate from the spirit prison, the Lord would be saying that no missionaries from paradise could enter the spirit prison:

> And it came to pass, that the beggar died, and was *carried by the angels* into Abraham's bosom: the rich man also died, and was buried;
>
> And *in hell he lift up his eyes, being in torments,* and seeth Abraham afar off, and Lazarus in his bosom.
>
> And he cried and said, Father Abraham, have mercy on me, and send Lazarus, that he may dip the tip of his finger in water, and cool my tongue; for I am tormented in this flame.
>
> But Abraham said, Son, remember that thou in thy lifetime receivedst thy good things, and likewise Lazarus evil things: but now he is comforted, and thou art tormented.
>
> And beside all this, *between us and you there is a great gulf fixed: so that they which would pass from hence to you cannot; neither can they pass to us, that would come from thence.*[36]

That Christ sent missionaries from paradise to the spirit prison following His crucifixion, as is pointed out by various interpreters of the passage, is accepted without question. Yet if hell is separate from the spirit prison, the gulf mentioned in this parable is not that which He bridged. Does the gulf still remain? To the author's knowledge, no scripture, vision of the spirit world nor authority of the Church teaches that spirits from hell have access to paradise, nor that spirits from paradise are preaching to Satan and his angels and ex-mortal followers in hell. To the contrary, all evidence indicates that the gulf still exists. The prophet Lehi, in 2 Nephi 1:13, calls the gulf "the *eternal gulf* of misery and woe." An angel speaking to the prophet Nephi (1 Nephi 12:16-18) says that "a great and terrible gulf divideth them." In Helaman 3:29

[36]Lk. 16:22-26. The occasionally expressed explanation that Christ bridged the gulf following His crucifixion is based entirely on the assumption that the spirit prison is synonymous with hell. If that assumption is not valid, then the "bridging the gulf" theory is likewise invalid. If the spirit prison and hell are separate, then Christ bridged no gulf between paradise and hell when He instructed the missionaries in paradise, a third area, and the gulf between paradise and hell still remains. Christ taught with clarity and emphasis that a gulf and complete separation between paradise and hell existed. It is difficult to believe that He would completely reverse his teaching less than two months after he pronounced it, when He was crucified and went into the spirit realm.

reference is again made to the *"everlasting gulf* of misery which is prepared to engulf the wicked." It is not the spirits in hell, under Satan's complete dominion, who are receiving the missionaries. It is the uncommitted spirits in the spirit prison. That they are being visited in this manner is indication that they are separate from the area of hell—in the spirit prison.

The Prophet Joseph Smith indicated his understanding that the spirit prison was distinct and separate from hell when he said,

> I do not believe the . . . doctrine of sending honest men and noble-minded men to hell, along with the murderer and the adulterer. . . . I will send men to preach to them in prison and save them if I can.[37]

Orson Pratt also understood that the spirit prison and hell were separate areas, and drew a strong line of demarcation between the two:

> I have mentioned those who inherit the glory of the stars. Who are they? They are not the heathen, for they come up higher—into the terrestrial glory. Who are they, then, who are permitted only to inherit a glory typified by the stars? They are the general world of mankind, *those who have heard the Gospel of the Son of God but have not obeyed it.* They are to be punished. How long? Until Jesus has reigned here on the earth a thousand years. . . . Where will their spirits be all that time? Not in any glory; they cannot inherit a glory until their punishment is past. *They are not permitted to enter into prison.* A great many people, and perhaps some of the Latter-day Saints, have supposed that these characters will go into prison. *I do not know of any revelation anywhere intimating that any one of this class of persons will ever be put in prison. Where do they go? To another place altogether different from a prison. A prison is designed for those who never heard the Gospel here in the flesh, but yet have committed a few sins without the knowledge of the revealed law, and who have to be beaten with few stripes in prison.* But those persons who hear the Gospel, as the nations of the present dispensation are doing, can not go to prison, it is not their place. *They fall below a prison, into outer darkness or hell, where there will be weeping and wailing and gnashing of teeth. There they have to remain with the devil and his angels in torment and misery until the final end, then they come forth.*[38]

Those who have seen the spirit prison report that it is a

[37]HC 6:365. May 12, 1844.
[38]JD 15:322. Jan. 19, 1873.

place for those who have neither accepted nor rejected the gospel. The divine plan is taught to the inhabitants there, and they may pass into paradise upon accepting it and upon accepting the vicarious ordinances performed for them upon the earth.[39] Similarly, it appears that they pass into hell if they choose to reject the gospel message. The spirit prison, then, is a temporary abode—a place of learning, evaluating and testing—prior to receiving a higher or lower plane of existence. The nature of this area of the spirit world was emphasized by his angelic guide to Lorenzo Dow Young as he was shown the spirit prison:

> Almost instantly [we] were in another world. *It was of such magnitude that I formed no conception of its size.* It was filled with innumerable hosts of beings, who seemed mixed up promiscuously, as they are in this world. Their surroundings and manner indicated that *they were in a state of expectation, and awaiting some event of considerable moment to them.*[40]

An important demonstration of the nature and activity of the spirit prison was given to Elder James W. LeSueur in the summer of 1900. Four years previously, Elder LeSueur had received the promise from a prophet in the Church that "at the touch of thy Guardian Angel, thy spiritual vision shall be quickened and thou shalt look beyond this world of flesh into a world of spirits and commune with thy dead for their redemption."[41] In response to his continual pleading with the Lord that he be able to see his recently slain brother, he received the following manifestation:

> In a few weeks after my return home my father and I made a trip to the mountains to the sheep camps, the first made since Frank's death. *I felt that Frank's spirit was there visiting the camps with us.* I wanted to see him, wanted to talk to him, wanted to know what he was doing on the other side.
>
> My father and I made our bed under the pines and my father retired early, while I went out into the thick grove nearby and knelt in supplication to the Lord for the privilege of seeing Frank and

---

[39]See Is. 24:22; 42:6-7; 61:1; Job 33:27-30; *Doctrines of Salvation* II:135, 160.

[40]Lorenzo Dow Young, *Fragments of Experience, op cit.,* p. 28. Contrast this scene with the view he was given of hell. See pp. 155-156.

[41]James W. LeSueur, "A Peep Into the Spirit World," unpublished manuscript in the possession of Mrs. Ruth Gregory, Smithfield, Utah. Elder LeSueur was a counselor in the Arizona Temple Presidency.

knowing what he was doing. I had full faith that my prayer would be answered. Returning to the bed to retire, no sooner did I lie down upon it than *my spirit left my body.* I could see my own and my father's bodies lying upon the bed. *By the side of my spirit stood a personage I knew to be my Guardian Angel.* In a voice of sweetness, he said to me, 'Come go with me.' Instantly we began passing through space with a speed of lightning and in what seemed but a few moments, *we came into a large and beautiful city, far superior to any I had seen. The buildings were not highly ornamented. They stood in simple grandeur. The streets were wide and paved and perfectly clean. They were bordered with trees and flowers, whose beauty could not be told in words. Most of the houses were white and gray, and marble seemed to be the predominant building material. This grand city was one of the cities in which the spirits of those who had died without an acceptance of the Gospel of Christ, were being prepared for its acceptance by missionary service of those who had given faithful allegiance to the Lord, while living in mortality. . . .*

In the midst of this stood a marble structure of four stories, covering nearly an entire block. As we came before it the angel said, 'We will go in here.' Immediately a door opened and a beautiful young lady, whose face was radiant with joy, welcomed us. In answer to the query in my mind, the angel said, 'This young lady is a relative of yours, assisting as a missionary among the spirits of your kindred, who died without a knowledge of the Gospel. While living in mortality she was killed, and *all those you see in this room are your relatives assembled to hear the Gospel taught.'*

I looked over *the large, well lighted, well arranged auditorium.* I was pleased with its *beauty and simplicity. The speakers' pulpit was in the center of the hall, fully twenty feet lower than where I stood. The seats were arranged in a circle beginning on a level with the speaker's floor, and rising, each tier higher than the other, so that the speaker could see everyone present and they did not seem to be very far away from him. I estimated an audience of ten to twelve thousand* seated all in a state of expectancy, as though they were waiting for something with a keen anticipation. Presently, as I was looking into the faces of the interesting audience, I heard a person begin speaking to them. He told of the great atonement made by the Savior, of the life and labors of the Lord, Jesus Christ, and His teachings. [The speaker] plead with them to accept of Him as their Redeemer, to repent of their sins and obey the Gospel. If they would do so, ordinances which they should have attended to in mortality, would be performed for them vicariously . . . upon the earth by relatives and friends living in mortality.

As he finished his discourse, he looked up at me and I saw it was my brother, Frank, who had been killed. His face fairly shown with a radiance of happiness. How my spirit thrilled with rapture! He was supremely happy in this service he was giving. *By Frank's side stood a beautiful young lady attired in robes, whiter than the driven snow. She was of medium height with dark hair, a full round face, large brown eyes, and she too was happy beyond language to* express. 'Who is she?' was the thought that came into my mind. *'She is to be Frank's wife,'* said the attending angel. Frank was nineteen years of age when he died and was unmarried.

Frank gave me a smile and sign of parting, I looked at the audience and saw how pleased they were at the service and the Angel said, 'We will now pass into other rooms.' *The next large hall contained thousands of people arranged in classes, some with teachers, some studying alone and they were deeply interested in the lessons and books they were considering. We then went into another large hall where there were other thousands. These seemed to be of a much lower order of intelligence.* They were quarreling and jangling. There was a veritable hub-bub of confusion. I was informed that *all in both of these rooms were relatives who were being prepared to be brought to a state where they would eventually be ready to hear and accept the Gospel of the Lord, Jesus Christ. Those in the last room lived upon the earth during the dark ages and at the period of great wickedness and ignorance. It would take ages to redeem them.*

'We will now return to your tabernacle of flesh,' said the Guardian Angel. With the speed of light we traveled and in what seemed but a few minutes, we stood by the shepherd's camp in the mountains. There were the sheep all huddled together in repose, there the stately pines and at our feet, the bed. I took a good look at my own body and at my father. The Angel smiled and nodded and in the twinkling of an eye my spirit returned to my tabernacle of flesh. I called my father from his slumbers and told him of my wonderful experience.[42]

---

[42]James W. LeSueur, *op cit.* Elder LeSueur included the following substantiating evidence with his account of entry into the spirit prison:

'What, a dream' did I hear you say. No, you are mistaken. My spirit actually left my body, just as surely as Lazarus's spirit left his and later was called back by Jesus. The young lady who greeted us at the door was a cousin of mine, Margaret Odekirk. While living in mortality she was thrown off a horse, her feet caught in the stirrup, her body drug along the ground as the frightened horse ran for a quarter of a mile. When the horse stopped, she was dead.

I did not know of this at the time of my experience, but when I told it to my mother and described the young lady to her, she recognized in the description this cousin.

The young lady who was to be Frank's wife was a mystery until a Mrs. Kempe came to see us from a neighboring town and told us that her daughter who had died said on her death-bed that she wanted to be sealed in marriage for eternity to Frank LeSueur, that he had appeared to her from the Spirit World and asked that this be done. My brother and this young lady had kept company at college. Mrs. Kempe brought with her the young lady's photo and I recognized at once, the young lady whose spirit stood by Frank as he delivered the Gospel discourses. This was attended to, for my brother-in-law stood proxy for Frank and my sister for Jennie Kempe and they were sealed together as husband and wife, the living for the dead, for all eternity.

It may have been the same building or one similar in nature in the spirit prison which was shown to Elder James W. Ure, who, while baptizing in the Salt Lake Temple font on March 16, 1897,

> *Saw a large building,* apparently on the north side of the font. *The door of the building was open and he observed a great crowd of people inside. They seemed to be anxiously waiting for an opportunity to come out. A man in white apparel stood on guard at the door, and another was inside who seemed to be calling the names* of certain ones to come out at the very time the Recorder at the font called the same names. As they came out of the building they stood and witnessed the baptism and confirmation administered in their behalf, and then walked away, giving evidence of feeling great joy.[43]

President Rudger Clawson, while telling in a general conference of the labors of a faithful temple worker, told of a

> The Bible tells us (Matthew 22nd Chap. 23 to 30th verses) there is neither marrying nor giving in marriage in heaven. Marriage like baptism is an earthly ordinance (1 Corinthians 15 chap. 29th verse) and must be attended to here. It must be done by God's appointed agents too or it will not be binding, someone like Peter who has authority to bind on earth and it shall be bound in heaven, to seal on earth and it shall be sealed in Heaven. (Matthew 16 chap. 19 verse).
>
> That one can stand proxy for another is a Gospel doctrine, for did not Jesus stand proxy for us all, the just for the unjust. We too can stand proxy for others and become Saviors upon Mount Zion. The prophecy of Malachi (4th Chap. 5 & 6 verses) has been fulfilled and the hearts of the children are turning to their fathers (who are dead) to do a work for them, and the spirits of the fathers (who are dead) are seeking for this work to be done, lest the earth be smitten with a curse and the great majority of mankind not having the privilege of salvation.
>
> Besides the evidence given above, I have the words of the prophet written down and recorded four years before that I would have the experience of looking beyond this world of flesh into a world of spirits, and I know of a surety that my spirit left my body and visited the Spirit World. It was a grand experience and I thank God for it.
>
> (Signed: James W. LeSueur)

Elder Melvin J. Ballard related a manifestation he received which supports the concept of mates being chosen by those who have died:

> I lost a son six years of age, and *I saw him a man in the spirit world after his death, and I saw how he had exercised his own freedom of choice and would obtain of his own will and volition a companionship, and in due time to him, and all those who are worthy of it, shall come all of the blessings and sealing privileges of the house of the Lord.* Do not worry over it. They are safe; they are all right.
>
> Now, then, what of your daughters who have died and have not been sealed to some man? Unless it is made known to you, let their case rest. *They will make known to you the agreements and contracts they have mutually entered into. The sealing power shall be forever and ever with this Church, and provisions will be made for them. We cannot run faster than the Lord has provided the way.* Their blessings and privileges will come to them in due time. In the meantime, they are safe.
>
> (Bryant S. Hinckley, *Sermons and Missionary Services of Melvin Joseph Ballard,* Salt Lake City, Utah: Deseret Book Co., 1949), p. 260.)

---

[43]*A Book of Remembrance, op cit.,* p. 90.

vision that a worker had received concerning the status of couples in the spirit prison who have not been sealed for eternity:

> He further said: 'Upon one occasion I saw in vision my father and mother who were not members of the Church, who had not received the gospel in life, and I discovered that *they were living separate and apart in the spirit world,* and when I asked them how it was that they were so, my father said, '*This is an enforced separation,* and you are the only individual who can bring us together. You can do this work. Will you do it?' —meaning that he should go into the House of the Lord and there officiate for his parents who were dead, and by the ordinance of sealing bring them together and unite them in the family relation beyond the veil.'[44]

According to Brigham Young, in addition to receiving missionaries from paradise, spirit beings in the spirit prison are also visited and molested to a limited extent by evil ambassadors from hell. However, they do not suffer from the influence of Satan to the degree that the wicked in hell are afflicted. President Brigham Young explained,

> *The spirits of people that have lived upon the earth according to the best light they had, who were as honest and sincere as men and women could be, if they lived on the earth without the privilege of the Gospel and the Priesthood and the keys thereof are still under the power and control of evil spirits, to a certain extent.* No matter where they lived on the face of the earth, all men and women that have died without the keys and power of the Priesthood, though they might have been honest and sincere and have done everything they could, are under the influence of the devil, more or less. *Are they as much so as others? No, no. Take those that were wicked designedly, who knowingly lived without the Gospel when it was within their reach, they are given up to the devil, they become tools to the devil and spirits of devils.*[45]

Spirits in the spirit prison maintain their agency and are free to accept or reject the gospel message when it is preached to them. In contrast, as was seen in the preceding chapter, the spirits in hell are under the complete control of Satan during their sojourn there, and are compelled to do his bidding.

Just as missionaries from paradise labor among the spirits

---

[44]Archibald F. Bennett, *Saviors on Mount Zion, op cit.*, p. 207.
[45]JD 3:370. June 22, 1856.

in prison, evil ambassadors from hell come among those spirits also, and try to influence them to reject the gospel message. As President Brigham Young put it,

> Those who have died without the Gospel are continually afflicted by those evil spirits, who say to them—'Do not go to hear that man Joseph Smith preach, or David Patten, or any of their associates, for they are deceivers.[46]

Undoubtedly the missionaries who come from paradise to the spirit prison will find a degree of joy as they win converts to Christ, yet there will be a difference in levels of association which may prove disagreeable to them as they come into the spirit prison. As Orson Pratt observed,

> Suppose you were a righteous spirit, and you . . . were sent out, on a mission to the abodes of darkness, or to those who are not as righteous as yourselves, *though you might have peace of conscience and happiness dwelling within your own bosoms in reflecting upon your past conduct, yet the society with which you are compelled to mingle* for a short period, in order to impart knowledge and wisdom and such information as is calculated to benefit them, *is, in a measure, disagreeable; you are compelled, for a season, to mingle with those who are inferior to yourself in their capacities.* When you go and associate with them *there is something disagreeable in the nature of this association;* you feel to pity them in their ignorance, in their condition and circumstances; their conversation is not agreeable to you as that of your own associates in the presence of God.[47]

Missionary Labors in the Spirit Prison

The major effort of the spirits in paradise is directed to missionary labors among the spirits in the spirit prison. The nature of the missionary program beyond the veil was revealed to President Joseph F. Smith, in his "Vision of the Redemption of the Dead":

> My eyes were opened, and my understanding quickened, and I perceived that *the Lord went not in person among the wicked and the disobedient who had rejected the truth, to teach them; but behold, from among the righteous he organized his forces and appointed messengers, clothed with power and authority,* and commissioned them to go forth and carry the light of the gospel to them that were in darkness, even to all the spirits of men. And thus was the gospel preached to the dead.[48]

---

[46] *Ibid.,* p. 371.

[47] JD 2:241. Oct. 15, 1854.

[48] Joseph F. Smith, *Gospel Doctrine, op cit.,* p. 474. It is not clear whether the missionary work in the spirit prison *began* with the Savior's visit following His crucifixion or whether the

It appears that this missionary program has continued in the spirit prison since the death of Christ and that it is organized in a manner similar to present day missionary work upon the earth. Evidence of this is found in the report of Henry Zollinger, who met his two brothers-in-law in the spirit world and saw one of them laboring as a mission president:

> We then had the privilege of visiting my brothers-in-law who had died. William, who had been on a mission in Australia . . . told me *he was presiding over a large mission and was very happy in his labors* and to tell his parents and his people not to mourn about him as he was losing nothing but doing much good. We next went to see his older brother, John. I found him discussing the gospel to a large congregation, bearing a strong testimony to them. When he got through he told me *he was very happy in his labors and had no regrets that he was there* and told his people not to mourn.[49]

While in the spirit world, Heber Q. Hale saw that the missionary work, in addition to the preaching function, also extended to the gathering of genealogical data to facilitate the vicarious work for the dead upon the earth:

> All worthy men and women were *appointed to special and regular service under a well organized plan of action, directed principally toward preaching the Gospel to the unconverted, teaching those who seek knowledge, and establishing family relationships and gathering genealogies* for the use and benefit of mortal survivors of their respective families, that the work of baptism and the sealing ordinances may be vicariously performed for the departed in the temples of God upon the earth.[50]

It appears that in a similar manner to the way a man's talent and experience are utilized by the Church on earth, an effort is also made in the spirit world to place him in positions where he can be most effective. President Hale saw, for instance, General Richard W. Young, a past commander of the Utah National Guard and a veteran of the Spanish-American War and the Philippine Insurrection, preaching to a vast host of soldiers who had died during the First World War:

---

work had already been in process. A vision shown to the prophet Enoch may be an indication that much missionary work had already taken place. He was shown the resurrection of the Saints following Christ's crucifixion and then saw that "as many of the *spirits as were in prison came forth,* and stood on the right hand of God; and the *remainder* were reserved in chains of darkness until the judgment of the great day." (Moses 7:55-57)

[49]Henry Zollinger, *op cit.*

[50]Heber Q. Hale, *op cit.*

I presently beheld *a mighty multitude of men*, the largest I had ever seen gathered in one place, who *I immediately recognized as soldiers; the millions who had been slaughtered and rushed so savagely into the world of spirit during the great World War.* Among them moved calmly and majestically a great general in supreme command. As I drew nearer I received the kindly smile and generous welcome of the great and loving man, General Richard W. Young. *Then came the positive conviction to my soul, that of all men, living or dead, there is not one who is so perfectly fitted for the great mission unto which he has been called.* He commands immediately the attention and respect of all the soldiers. *He is at once a great General and High Priest of God. No earthly field of labor to which he could have been assigned can compare with it* in importance and extent. I passed from this scene to return later when I found *General Young had this vast army completely organized with officers over successive divisions* and all were seated, and he was preaching the Gospel in great earnestness to them.[51]

A manifestation given to Luella Child Wilkes Blacker indicates that her departed husband and son, John and DeLloyd Wilkes, may have taken their places in this or a similar organization:

During World War II her son died. She became ill with the 'flu' shortly before his death. One night her husband and younger son appeared to her. She said her husband came to her bedside and touched her on the shoulder and seemed to have awakened her. He bent over close to her and asked 'How are you, my dear?' She said to him, 'Oh, Johnny, have you come for me now?' He answered and said, 'No, not yet, *we are so very busy, there is so much to do. I will come for you my dear when your work is finished.'*

Then she saw him move away and *he was leading what seemed to be a large column of people—like soldiers.* As she watched them march away along came her younger deceased son, *as a full grown man, altho he had died at the age of 10. He was also leading a column of people.* She hadn't recognized DeLloyd at first, until he smiled and said 'Mother.' Then they all disappeared.

She told me this was all so vivid and real that as she laid in bed next morning, and all that day, she kept putting her hand on her shoulder where Johnny had touched her in the night. The sound of his voice was as natural as life and kept ringing in her ears all day.[52]

---

[51] *Ibid.*

[52] Personal records of Fern R. Morgan, in the possession of her daughter, Mrs. Dean (Jaynann) Payne, of Provo, Utah.

There are indications that not all missionary work beyond the veil is a general program of preaching to the unredeemed. One's obligation will still be to seek out his own kindred dead and bring to them the gospel message.[53] There is evidence that family organizations function beyond the veil and that some who die begin immediately to carry the gospel to their own progenitors. Merrill Neville, for instance, called his sister into the spirit world and then sent her back with the word that he was living with his grandparents there. "He said that so many of grandpa's people had been killed in the war that *his grandfather needed Merrill to help him with his missionary work among his kindred dead.*"[54] Wilford Woodruff learned by revelation that his son, Brigham, who drowned in northern Utah, had been called to labor for his relatives beyond the veil:

> About this time, one of his choicest and most spiritual-minded sons, Brigham Y. Woodruff was drowned in Bear River, in Cache Valley. President Woodruff, having attached considerable importance to the future of this noble son, was very much grieved because of his death. Although he never murmured at the providences of the Almighty, he inquired of the Lord to know why it should be thus. *The Lord revealed to him that as he was doing such an extensive work in the Temples for the dead, his son Brigham was needed in the spirit world to preach the gospel and labor among those relatives there.*[55]

[53]This will be a continuation of the present Church program of genealogical research. *The Handbook for Genealogy and Temple Work* (1956 edition, published by the Genealogical Society of The Church of Jesus Christ of Latter-day Saints, p. 68) states:

> The following paragraph is a quotation from the Prophet Joseph Smith: 'But how are they to become saviors on Mount Zion? By building their temples, erecting their baptismal fonts, and going forth and receiving all the ordinances, baptisms, confirmations, washings, anointings, ordinations and sealing powers upon their heads in behalf of all *their progenitors* who are dead, and redeem them that they may come forth in the first resurrection. . . .'
>
> *It will be noted that the Saints are commanded to seek out 'their progenitors.' In other quotations from the Prophet relating to genealogical and temple work, he repeatedly refers to 'our dead' and 'our progenitors.' In every instance the possessive pronoun is used.*
>
> In order that members of the Church may fulfil the commandments already referred to, *all genealogical research must tend toward establishing connected pedigrees and family groups which will link every generation with succeeding and preceding generations.* If this precaution is not taken, there is no assurance that the data obtained in research will pertain to 'our kindred dead.' *All of the ordinances required in temple work cannot be performed in behalf of the dead, unless the family groups are connected.* Every parent of necessity is also a child in another family group, and conversely, most children will appear as parents in another family group. The connections thus referred to are required if all of the sealings are to be properly administered in the House of the Lord.

[54]"Manifestation About Building of Temples," *Deseret Evening News,* May 18, 1918.

[55]Andrew Jenson, *Latter-day Saint Biographical Encyclopedia, op cit.,* Vol. I, p. 24. President Woodruff later commented,

Apostle Merriner W. Merrill was also shown that his son had passed through the veil of death in order to labor with his kindred dead:

> On one occasion soon after the death of his son, as he was returning to his home, he sat in his carriage so deeply lost in thought about his son that he was quite oblivious to things about him. He suddenly came into a state of awareness when his horse stopped in the road. As he looked up, his son stood in the road beside him. His son spoke to him and said, 'Father, you are mourning my departure unduly! You are over concerned about my family (his son left a large family of small children) and their welfare. *I have much work to do* and your grieving gives me much concern. *I am in a position to render effective service to my family. You should take comfort, for you know there is much work to be done here and it was necessary for me to be called. You know that the Lord doeth all things well.' So saying, the son departed.*[56]

Others are called into the spirit world as missionaries because

---

> We cannot always comprehend the ways and means of Providence, . . . I now feel calm and composed and reconciled in this bereavement. *I have done and am doing a great deal of work for the dead. It may be necessary that one of my family be in the spirit world to labor among those for whom we are officiating in the Temple of the Lord.* (Matthias F. Cowley, *Wilford Woodruff, op cit.,* p. 499.) See also his reference to this event in *Millennial Star,* 58:742.

[56]Bryant S. Hinckley, *The Faith of our Pioneer Fathers, op cit.,* pp. 182-183. Elder Joseph F. Merrill, a member of the Quorum of the Twelve, described this visit of the deceased son to his father, Marriner W. Merrill, while speaking at a funeral on December 28, 1937:

> My father once asked that question when his oldest son was taken away. The oldest son had the responsibility, in a measure, of looking after father's interests in his home town, taking care of business and economic affairs. But the son was called home, leaving a family of small children of his own. Father grieved. He had never grieved so much in his life. It was difficult. How could his son be needed as much on the other side as he was needed at home in Montana? And father related that one evening as he sat thinking of this matter, he looked up, and there the son stood beside him in spirit form, and speaking to him said, 'Father, do not grieve. You want to know why it is so? You know you are doing work for the dead here. You have gathered your genealogy, gotten all possible you could secure from the records, and you can be here doing temple work for those dead. *Those dead are not yet converted, and I am engaged in the spirit world preaching the gospel as it was promised me in a patriarchal blessing that I could do. I am very busy. My time is given to that work. You and I are saving our family. You are doing the temple work and I am laboring among them.'* My father never grieved again, but praised the Lord for this kindness in making it possible for our kindred dead to enjoy the blessings of eternal salvation, because if they accepted, the gates of the Celestial Kingdom would be opened to them.
>
> We may not be privileged to know just all the conditions which surround our loved ones who have passed on before us, but we do have the assurance that they are near us . . . and their influence for good is felt by us in our daily struggle here. There are many who do not have the opportunity to know very much about the other world and it is difficult for them to understand why it is not possible for them to have that knowledge. They have not fulfilled the conditions necessary to see. We live in a great universe of law and order. (From a transcript of the funeral services.)

of the language skills they possess. Elder Glen Wood, son of President Edward J. Wood of the Canadian Temple, was seemingly summoned through the veil because of his knowledge of the Samoan language:

> June, 1933, was a sad month for President Wood. His firstborn son, Glen, Bishop of the Glenwood Ward, was taken to the hospital with 'blood poisoning.' 'He seemed to know from the first that he would not recover,' wrote the father. *He told his father of a dream he had in which he was in a sealing room of the temple and a 'messenger' came and said he could not be healed. He also told his father of his uncle and others who were dead who had come to visit him, and that he had been called to preach to Samoans in the Spirit World.* (He had fulfilled a mission in Samoa.) He began speaking in Samoan to his father and said he was going on a 'malanga fou,' a new journey; whereupon he told his brothers, who were at his bedside, not to delay him, for he had to go. *'Near the end,'* wrote President Wood, *'he began speaking in Samoan to Saints in the Spirit World, then died.'*[57]

In the fall of 1915 Sister Lerona A. Wilson received a spiritual manifestation in which she learned, among other things, of a relative's being called into the spirit world because of her ability as an interpreter:

> When my life seemed to be hanging in the balance, and I was suffering pain and distress, lying upon my bed at midday, I was praying most fervently for deliverance, with all the faith I could exercise. *My room suddenly became lighted brightly with a soft, white light, then a number of my deceased relatives came into my room. My father came first, then my mother, my sister and her son's wife and two doctors, who were among our ancestors for whom we had done ordinance work in the temple.* All stood around my bed, and father addressed me, saying: 'You seem to be in distress.'
>
> I answered that I was, and did not know how I could endure it much longer.
>
> Father was dressed in a uniform such as he wore as an officer of the Nauvoo Legion, in the early history of the Church. Many still remember Major Monroe, when he lived in Ogden and took part in the Echo Canyon campaign and in Indian troubles.
>
> Continuing he said: *'I have come to talk to you about doing the temple work for our dead ancestors.'*
>
> At that point I caught the eye of my nephew's wife, whose death was the most recent, and who left four very young boys, one

[57]Melvin S. Tagg, *The Life of Edward James Wood, op cit.*, p. 108.

an infant, and to whose death I could hardly become reconciled; and I said to her: 'O, Lydia, how are your little boys?'

She replied: 'They are all right, they are with their father.'

I asked again: 'But why did you leave them?'

Father answered for her: *'We required her for an interpreter. We could not get along without her.'*

I asked: 'What calling is greater for a mother than to care for her infant children?'

Father replied: 'Others can take good care of her children, but *there are few people who are qualified for the work she is doing. She had prepared herself.'* (I knew that to be true.)[58]

The labors for the dead in the spirit world are extensive and varied. Yet all the work moves forward in accordance with the will of God in fulfillment of His divine plan of salvation.

Death Does Not Change One's Attitude Concerning the Gospel

The great Book of Mormon missionary, Amulek, forcefully warned those to whom he ministered that death would not alter one's attitude toward the gospel. He saw, too, that deathbed repentance is an impossibility:

> Ye cannot say, when ye are brought to that awful crisis, that I will repent, that I will return to my God. Nay, ye cannot say this; for *that same spirit which doth possess your bodies at the time that ye go out of this life, that same spirit will have power to possess your body in that eternal world.*[59]

The teaching that the departed spirits will carry with them the same devotion or antagonism to the things of righteousness is basic to one's understanding of the Gospel plan. There will be no change in attitude as one walks through the veil. The righteous will find themselves among like spirits in paradise; the wicked will find themselves subjected to the will of Satan as they were influenced by him on earth. Brigham Young asserted,

---

[58]Lerona A. Wilson, "My Testimony Concerning Temple Work," *Relief Society Magazine,* Vol. III, No. 2, p. 82, February, 1916.

[59]Al. 34:34.

> Suppose, then, that a man is evil in his heart—wholly given up to wickedness, and in that condition dies, *his spirit will enter the spirit world intent upon evil.*[60]

Apostle Melvin J. Ballard strongly warned that man will awake beyond the grave with the same weaknesses and problems as he possessed while on earth:

> A man may receive the priesthood and all its privileges and blessings, but until he learns to overcome the flesh, his temper, his tongue, his disposition to indulge in the things God has forbidden, he cannot come into the Celestial Kingdom of God—he must overcome either in this life or in the life to come. But this life is the time in which men are to repent. *Do not let any of us imagine that we can go down to the grave not having overcome the corruptions of the flesh and then lose in the grave all our sins and evil tendencies.* They will be with us. They will be with the spirit when separated from the body, . . . *Some folks get the notion that the problems of life will at once clear up and they will know that this is the Gospel of Christ when they die.* I have heard people say they believe when they die they will see Peter and that he will clear it all up. I said, 'You never will see Peter until you accept the Gospel of the Lord Jesus Christ, at the hands of the elders of the Church, living or dead. . . .'
>
> *So, men won't know any more when they are dead than when they are living, only they will have passed through the change called death. They will not understand the truths of the Gospel only by the same process as they understand and comprehend them here.*[61]

Because death does not change one's attitude, it appears that many of the dead in the spirit prison will still refuse to accept the gospel and the vicarious ordinances when they have the opportunity. This was discovered by Henry Zollinger who together with his mother in the spirit world visited many for whom his father had performed the vicarious ordinances, and found that "some still remained dormant."[62] As Melvin J. Ballard stated,

> When you die and go to the spirit world you will labor for years, trying to convert individuals who will be taking their own course. *Some of them will repent; some of them will listen. Another group will be rebellious, following their own will and notion,* and that group will get smaller and smaller until every knee shall humbly bow and every tongue confess.[63]

[60]JD 7:333. Oct. 8, 1859.

[61]N. B. Lundwall, *The Vision, op cit.*, pp. 46, 47-48.

[62]Henry Zollinger, *op cit.*

[63]N. B. Lundwall, *The Vision, op cit.*, p. 48.

Many Forfeit Opportunity to Accept Gospel and Perform Exalting Ordinances While on Earth Through Procrastination

Amulek described the fate of the unrighteous who refuse to repent during mortality and said that this life was the time to prepare to meet God. Apparently those who reject the gospel message and procrastinate their repentance are subjected to the spirit of the devil after death, and he clings to them, making their subjection their "final state" while in the spirit world:

> For behold, *this life is the time for men to prepare to meet God;* yea, behold the day of this life is the day for men to perform their labors.
>
> And now, as I said unto you before, as ye have had so many witnesses, therefore, I beseech of you that ye do not procrastinate the day of your repentance until the end; for after this day of life, which is given us to prepare for eternity, behold, *if we do not improve our time while in this life, then cometh the night of darkness wherein there can be no labor performed.* . . .
>
> For behold, if ye have procrastinated the day of your repentance even until death, behold, *ye have become subjected to the spirit of the devil, and he doth seal you his; therefore the Spirit of the Lord hath withdrawn from you, and hath no place in you, and the devil hath all power over you; and this is the final state of the wicked.*[64]

The question is frequently asked whether man has more than one opportunity to accept the gospel. Will those who refuse to accept the gospel message on earth have the privilege of hearing it preached again in the spirit world and accepting it there? There is no scriptural indication that they will have such an opportunity; they are guaranteed no second chance. According to President Joseph Fielding Smith, if some individuals do hear the gospel for the second time and accept it in the spirit world, after having procrastinated and having failed to accept it while in the flesh, they will have already forfeited exaltation. They can attain only the second, or terrestrial kingdom following the resurrection:

> *The justice of the Lord is manifest in the right he grants to all men to hear the plan of salvation and receive it.* Some have that privilege in this life; if they obey the gospel, well and good; *if they reject it, then in the spirit world the same opportunities with the same fulness do not come to them.*

---

[64]Al. 34:32-33, 35.

If they die without that opportunity in this life, it will reach them in the world of spirits. The gospel will there be declared to them, and if they are willing to accept, it is counted unto them just the same as if they had embraced it in mortality. In this way justice is meted out to every man; all are placed on an equality before the bar of God.

Those who have the opportunity here, those unto whom the message of salvation is declared, who are taught and who have this truth presented to them in this life—yet who deny it and refuse to receive it—shall not have a place in the kingdom of God. They will not be with those who died without that knowledge and who yet accepted it in the spirit world. . . .

There are too many people in this world, who have heard the message of the gospel, who think they can continue on to the end of this mortal life, living as they please, and then accept the gospel after death and friends will perform the ordinances that they neglect to perform for themselves, and eventually they will receive blessings in the kingdom of God. *This is an error.*

It is the duty of men in this life to repent. *Every man who hears the gospel message is under obligation to receive it. If he fails, then in the spirit world he will be called upon to receive it, but he will be denied the fulness* that will come to those who in their faithfulness have been just and true, whether it be in this life or in the spirit world.[65]

Elder Bruce R. McConkie, of the First Council of Seventy, teaches the same belief:

There is no such thing as a second chance to gain salvation by accepting the gospel in the spirit world after neglecting, failing, or refusing to accept it in this life. It is true that there may be a second chance to hear and accept the gospel, but those who have thus procrastinated their acceptance of the saving truths will not gain salvation in the celestial kingdom of God.

Salvation for the dead is the system by means of which those who *'die without a knowledge of the gospel'* (D&C 128:5) may gain such knowledge in the spirit world and then, following the vicarious performance of the necessary ordinances, become heirs of salvation on the same basis as though the gospel truths had been obeyed in mortality. *Salvation for the dead is limited expressly to those who do not have opportunity in this life to accept the gospel but who would have taken the opportunity had it come to them. . . .*
There is no promise in any revelation that those who have opportunity in this life to accept the gospel, and who do not do it, will have another chance in the

[65]Bruce R. McConkie (comp.), *Doctrines of Salvation—Sermons and Writings of Joseph Fielding Smith* (Salt Lake City, Utah: Bookcraft, 1955), Vol. II, pp. 182-183.

> *spirit world to gain salvation.* On the contrary, there is the express stipulation that men cannot be saved without accepting the gospel in this life, if they are given opportunity to accept it. . . .
>
> Those who have opportunity to accept the gospel in this life and who do not do it, but who then (by some miracle of conversion) do accept it when they hear it in the spirit world will go not to the celestial, but to the terrestrial kingdom.[66]

The statements of Presidents Smith and McConkie are based, in part, on the revelation of the three degrees of glory given to Joseph Smith in 1832. A major difference between those who attain the celestial kingdom and those who are restricted to the terrestrial kingdom is that among the latter "are they who *are not valiant* in the testimony of Jesus."[67] Those who are so lacking in faith and love of the Lord that they procrastinate their acceptance of the gospel till beyond the grave are certainly not sufficiently valiant in the cause of Christ to merit exaltation. The revelation states this with clarity when it says, while describing those who will inherit the terrestrial kingdom:

> Behold, these are they who died without law;
>
> And also they who are *the spirits of men kept in prison,* whom the Son visited, and preached the gospel unto them, that they might be judged according to men in the flesh;
>
> *Who received not the testimony of Jesus in the flesh, but afterwards received it.*
>
> These are they who are honorable men of the earth, who were *blinded by the craftiness of men.*
>
> These are they who receive of his glory, but not of his fulness.[68]

Others, though they have accepted the gospel on earth, procrastinate the performance of the temple ordinances and forfeit their right to the eternal blessings and privileges which are derived from them. A visitor from beyond the veil, who appeared to Sister Eliza Neville in January 1917, made it abundantly clear that one must do the work himself and not leave it to be performed vicariously after his death. She came just before the death of Sister Neville's daughter, as the

---

[66]Bruce R. McConkie, *Mormon Doctrine—A Compendium of the Gospel* (Salt Lake City, Utah: Bookcraft, Inc., 1958), pp. 617, 618.

[67]D&C 76:79.

[68]D&C 76:72-76.

mother was watching by her dying daughter's bedside in the hospital:

While in the hospital with her daughter, Sister Neville prepared to rest, on one occasion, in a reclining position, while also making it possible to watch her daughter's every move from across the room. Suddenly she was overcome by a sensation that was entirely new to her and she saw her husband's grandmother standing at the foot of the bed, *who looked exactly as Sister Neville remembered her in life, her body being bent from age and much stooping.* She seemed in a great hurry. Sister Neville exclaimed, 'Why, there's Grandmother Stiff! Whatever does she want?' At that the grandmother walked up to the side of the bed, stood perfectly straight, *her face shone and her hands were as white as pearl,* and as she spoke, she kept rubbing them together. *'Tell them to hurry; tell them to hurry; they have got the work to do; they have got the work to do—none can do the work for those who have had the privilege of doing it for themselves here—it's got to be done on this earth—it can't be done hereafter.'* She was silent a moment and Sister Neville said: 'Whatever does she mean?'

Finally the grandmother replied, *'William and Elizabeth have never had their children sealed to them. There must be a perfect link back to father Adam and if they neglect their work there will be a missing link.'* She seemed in such a hurry, Sister Neville said: 'Do they have to hurry and worry on the other side like this?'

Grandmother said: 'Look!' As Sister Neville looked she *saw masses of people and it appeared that Grandmother Stiff had something to do for them, which accounted for her being in such a hurry.* Striking the palm of her hand with the forefinger of the other, she said, *'Now I put this work on to you for you to see that this duty is done.'* Then she disappeared.[69]

President Joseph Fielding Smith sets forth the same teaching, asserting that those who have the opportunity to perform these ordinances but procrastinate and fail to do so forfeit the blessings. However, those who do not have the privilege of coming to the temple may enjoy these blessings through vicarious work in their behalf after their death:

The Lord did not offer to those who had *every* opportunity while in this mortal existence the privilege of *another* chance in the world of spirits.

The endowment and sealing work for the dead is for those who died without having had the opportunity to hear and receive the gospel; also, for

[69]"Manifestation About Building of Temples," *Deseret Evening News,* May 18, 1918.

> *those who were faithful members of the Church who lived in foreign lands or where, during their life time, they did not have the privilege to go to a temple, yet they were converted and were true members of the Church.* The work for the dead is not intended for those who had every opportunity to receive it, who had it taught to them, and who then refused to receive it, or had not interest enough to attend to these ordinances when they were living.[70]

In this area it is difficult to judge who has had sufficient opportunity to accept the gospel and to perform the necessary ordinances and who has been without such a privilege. Man is fortunate that he does not have to judge in this matter. The Lord will judge, and He has revealed that

> All who have died without a knowledge of this Gospel, who would have received it if they had been permitted to tarry, shall be heirs of the celestial kingdom of God; also all that shall die henceforth without a knowledge of it, who would have received it with all their hearts, shall be heirs of that kingdom, *for I, the Lord, will judge all men according to their works, according to the desire of their hearts.*[71]

Spirits in Prison Seek That Temple Work Be Done for Them

It appears that there are many who go into the spirit prison, hear the gospel there, and then find themselves compelled to wait for long periods of time until mortal beings perform the necessary ordinances vicariously for them upon the earth. Such a delay would undoubtedly prove extremely distressing to them. Brigham Young described what they must feel during the dedication of the St. George Temple when he said,

> What do you suppose the fathers would say if they could speak from the dead? Would they not say; '*We have lain here thousands of years in this prison house, bound and fettered in the association of the filthy and corrupt.*' If they had the power the very thunders of heaven would resound in our ears.[72]

According to the evidence at hand, those who have accepted the gospel in the spirit world and are awaiting the performance of the vicarious ordinances are sometimes able

---

[70]Bruce R. McConkie, *Doctrines of Salvation, op cit.*, Vol. II, p. 184.

[71]HC 2:380. Jan. 21, 1836.

[72]Matthias F. Cowley, *Wilford Woodruff, op cit.*, p. 494.

to communicate their needs to mortal beings and thus hasten the progress in their behalf. This was made evident to President Heber Q. Hale while he was in the spirit world, and he reported that "men and women through[out] the world *are moved upon by their dead ancestors to gather genealogies.*"[73]

Not only do spirit beings move mortals to seek genealogical data, but they are aware of the data which is available and who will have it in their possession. Henry Zollinger, for instance, was told by his mother while he was in the spirit world that "My father would receive another large record of our dead kindred." He also recorded that while he was in the spirit world another "guide told me Thomas Stirland would get a record for his dead relations."[74] Reference has already been made to the Manti Temple worker who was met on the way to the temple by a group of his kindred dead who told him, "When you go down to the temple today you will find there are records that give our names."[75]

Just as spirits seek that genealogical research be conducted they also call upon mortals to perform the necessary vicarious ordinances in the temples in their behalf. A vision given to Martin Harris was indication to him that his father sought that his temple work be done. According to Edward Stevenson, who was influential in causing Brother Harris to return to fellowship with the Saints in Utah, the manifestation was what caused Martin to be rebaptized himself and to be baptized vicariously for his loved ones:

> Martin, soon after his arrival in Salt Lake City, came to my house and said the Spirit of the Lord had made it manifest to him, not only for himself personally, but also that *he should be baptized for his dead, for he had seen his father at the foot of a ladder, striving to get up to him, and he went down to him taking him by the hand and helped him up.*[76]

Henry Zollinger told of the requests he received from two individuals in the spirit world that he perform their vicarious ordinances for them when he returned to mortality:

---

[73]Heber Q. Hale, *op cit.*

[74]Henry Zollinger, *op cit.*

[75]N. B. Lundwall, *Temples of the Most High, op cit.*, p. 124. For the full account of this visitation see p. 136 of this book.

[76]Andrew Jenson, *Latter-day Saint Biographical Encyclopedia, op cit.*, Vol. I, p. 274.

As we were coming back I saw a man who had been a Campbellite Minister down in Texas when I was upon my mission there three years ago. He was a great friend to us and has opened his house many times for us to preach in. He had died while I was still in the mission field. *He asked me if I could do the work in the Temple that was necessary for his salvation.* I told him I would and he seemed pleased. I then met a man whom I had never seen before. His wife had come into the Church and was baptized after he had died. She spoke to me while I was on my mission in regard to having the work done for him in the Temple, but as she had already spoken to other Elders about it to be done [I had ignored her request]. I told him I would see to it.[77]

Another instance of spirit beings requesting that their temple work be performed is found in the return from the dead of the parents of Lerona A. Wilson in the fall of 1915:

Father asked me if I would go to the temple and take up the ordinance work for our kindred dead.

I said: 'How can I leave my work (in my school of dressmaking), and my family?'

My mother spoke this time: 'I had to leave my family just when I was needed the most. You can remain with your family. You will only need to spend a part of your time in the temple.'

Then my sister said: 'I had to leave my family, too, when I was so much needed, and Lydia had to leave her little ones.'

These remarks made my excuse seem very weak. *Father wanted me to promise him that I would do this work, and I gave him my promise that I would.*

'Now remember,' he said, 'it will require much faith. Do you think you can have faith enough?'

'Father, I will do all in my power,' I replied, for while under that exalting influence, it seemed an easy matter to have faith.

Father then drew his sword and flashed it above my head. His tone changed from that of a gentle father, to the loud, stern voice of a commanding officer as he said:

'If you do not, I will mow you down like stubble, and move you out of the way and raise up some one who will.'

Sensing more fully the difficulties of the task I had taken upon myself, I wanted to know how I could obtain means to carry on the work.

---

[77]Henry Zollinger, *op cit.*

Father said: 'Call upon your brethren, they will help you.'

'Why do you not go to them?' I enquired.

He answered: *'I have tried and tried, but I cannot make an impression upon them.'*

'Then how is it that I can hear you?' was my next question.

'Read Section 89 of the Doctrine and Covenants, and you will understand.' (That section contains the Word of Wisdom.)

Father then quoted from the scriptures giving chapter and verse, and *taught me the law of baptism in greater force and beauty than I had ever heard it, and explained that this ordinance cannot be administered in the spirit world. The dead who have died without baptism must have the ordinance performed for them by the living.*

He alluded to our kindred, saying they were a fine people, and they had received the gospel. They were most anxious to be advancing. They need to move on with other spirits who are in like condition and give place to the large numbers who are now crowding into that world.[78]

There is evidence that spirits in the spirit prison who have accepted the gospel are aware of situations where they might be bypassed when temple ordinances are performed and are able to manifest their desires to receive the blessings these ordinances bring. President Edward J. Wood of the Canadian Temple received just such a manifestation:

During yet another of the Northwestern States Mission caravan visits to the temple on July 23, 1931, Mrs. Newlun from Portland, a convert to the Church, was in a sealing room to be sealed to her dead husband and to have their dead children sealed to them. Friends were to act as proxy for the husband and children. As President Wood was ready to seal the children to the parents, he said he felt impressed to ask if the information on the sealing sheet was complete. After being assured that the record was right, he again began the ceremony. He said he again felt impressed to ask if she had other children whose names should be on the sheet. She said she had other living adult children who were not members of the Church and hence their names should not be included. The third time the President started the ceremony, whereupon he stopped and said, 'I heard a voice quite distinctly saying *"I am her child."*' He again asked the mother if she had another child that was not on the sheet. She answered, with tears running down her face, *'Yes, I had another daughter who died when 12 days old and she was overlooked in preparing the information.'* When the group learned how the

[78]Lerona A. Wilson, *Relief Society Magazine, op cit.*, Vol. III, p. 83.

> President knew of the other child, 'All in the room shed tears of joy to know of the apparent nearness of our kindred dead.'[79]

Others have also been prompted that sealing records were incorrect. For instance, from the Salt Lake Temple,

> On October 26, 1896, in the sealing room, while assisting in the ordinance of sealing children to their parents, Sister Amanda H. Wilcox *saw the dead father of those children standing by the altar, and he intimated to her that he and his wife, the mother of the children, had not yet been sealed.* Sister Wilcox then informed President Winder, who was officiating, and the ceremony was deferred until inquiry was made, when it was found that what the spirit man had told her was correct. The sealing of the mother to this man was then duly attended to, and the children were afterward sealed to their parents.[80]

And the same type of experience has occurred in connection with the Manti Temple:

> Last January a lady, whom we will call Mrs. D., was in Manti, having come from the Southern States. She was one who had made many sacrifices for her religion. She was unable herself to go to the Temple that day, but I called to take her names, at her request, to be officiated for. Having occasion later on in the week to call upon her and bring some other temple records she wanted, I heard from [her] the following remarkable instance concerning one of the names on the list she had handed to me the previous Tuesday. I will say that the names she had were of her near relatives, which she had gathered from memory and family sources. We are all aware that the family records of the Southern States are very meager when it comes to vital records being kept by town officials.
>
> Mrs. D. was accustomed to arise, she told me, about 6:20 a.m. as she had certain work to perform. A few mornings before, she had awakened as usual, but a feeling of drowsiness came over her, which she could not shake off, and she went to sleep again. When in that state *her dead mother appeared to her, smiled upon her, and said*

---

[79]Melvin S. Tagg, *The Life of Edward James Wood, op cit.,* pp. 118-119. The same biography yields another experience of a similar nature:

> A very similar incident to the above was also related by Edward J. Wood. He told of a widow who came to have two living children sealed to her and her dead husband. The two children, ages nine and twelve, were standing just inside the sealing room door to witness the sealing of the parents, when a peculiar light appeared over the two children and President Wood said, *'I saw another child standing with the two.'* He asked the mother about a third child, and found there had been such, but by neglect, the information was not recorded. 'As I told her how I knew,' said President Wood, 'the child disappeared from the other two.' (*Ibid.,* p. 119)

[80]*A Book of Remembrance—A Lesson Book for First Year Junior Genealogical Classes* (Salt Lake City, Utah: The Genealogical Society of Utah, 1936), p. 78.

words of encouragement for the work she was performing in the Temple at so much sacrifice to her earthly comforts. She placed before her eyes a temple blank upon which she had written some names, in a fine, clear hand-writing, for she was a well educated and refined lady. The mother called her attention to the name of Sarah, which Mrs. D. had omitted and said she was her father's aunt, a young woman who had been unmarried, yet had reached maturity, and she felt grieved that she had been left out when all her brothers and sisters had been included.

Mrs. D. told me that she had a slight remembrance when a small child of hearing her father speak of an Aunt Sarah, but it passed from her mind in later years. Mrs. D.'s mother was well loved by her father's people, and had been given the privilege of visiting her daughter, Mrs. D., to bring to her this information which she could not have obtained in any other way, for her father was dead. This was a great testimony to Mrs. D. of the worth of the work she was doing for her dead, and how it was appreciated.[81]

Perhaps the best-known instance of the seeking of the spirits in prison for the performance of their temple ordinances is the coming of the signers of the Declaration of Independence to President Wilford Woodruff in the St. George temple in early March of 1877. Six months later he described the coming of these beings to him in an address delivered in the tabernacle:

I feel to say little else to the Latter-day Saints wherever and whenever I have the opportunity of speaking to them, than to call upon them to build these Temples now under way, to hurry them up to completion. *The dead will be after you, they will seek after you as they have after us in St. George. They called upon us, knowing that we held the keys and power to redeem them.*

I will here say before closing, that two weeks before I left St. George, *the spirits of the dead gathered around me, wanting to know why we did not redeem them.* Said they, '*You have had the use of the Endowment House for a number of years, and yet nothing has been done for us. We laid the foundation of the government you now enjoy, and we never apostatized from it, but we remained true to it and were faithful to God.' These were the signers of the Declaration of Independence,* and they waited on me for two days and two nights. I thought it very singular, that notwithstanding so much work had been done, and yet nothing had been done for them. The thought never entered my heart, from the fact, I suppose, that heretofore our minds were reaching after our more immediate friends and relatives. I straightway went into the baptismal font

[81]*The Forefather Quest—A Lesson Book for Third Year Junior Genealogical Classes* (Salt Lake City, Utah: The Genealogical Society of Utah, 1936), pp. 27-28.

> and *called upon brother McCallister to baptize me for the signers of the Declaration of Independence, and fifty other eminent men, making one hundred in all, including John Wesley, Columbus, and others; I then baptized him for every President of the United States, except three;* and when their cause is just, somebody will do the work for them.[82]

According to President Brigham Young, the communication of information concerning temple work from spirit beings to mortals is to become commonplace in the time when Zion, the New Jerusalem, will have been constructed. He said that at that day

> Some of those who are not in mortality will come along and say, 'Here are a thousand names I wish you to attend to in this temple, and when you have got through with them I will give you another thousand;' and the Elders of Israel and their wives will go forth to officiate for their forefathers, the men for the men and the women for the women.[83]

Spirits in Prison Know When Vicarious Work Is Performed for Them

That the spirits in prison are aware of the vicarious temple work performed on earth in their behalf was asserted by Brigham Young. He said,

> A man is ordained and receives his washings, anointings, and endowments for the male portion of his and his wife's progenitors, and his wife for the female portion.

---

[82]JD 19:229. Sept. 16, 1877. See also his conference address of April 10, 1898. In his personal journal for Aug. 21, 1877, President Woodruff recorded,

> I, Wilford Woodruff, went to the Temple of the Lord this morning and was baptized for 100 persons who were dead including the signers of the Declaration of Independence except John Hancock and William Floyd. I was baptized for the following named: (names follow)
>
> Bro. McAllister . . . was baptized by me for all the Presidents of the United States that were not on my list, *except Buchanan, Van Buren and Grant.* It was a very interesting day. I felt thankful that we had the privilege and the power to administer for the worthy dead, especially for the signers of the Declaration of Independence, that inasmuch as they had laid the foundation of our government that we could do as much for them as they had done for us. (Copied from the original Journal of Wilford Woodruff in the Church Historian's Office; as recorded in Archibald F. Bennett, *Saviors on Mount Zion, op cit.,* pp. 153-154.
>
> In his footnotes Brother Bennett indicates that:
>
> —John Hancock had already been baptized, 29 May 1877; and endowed, 30 May 1877, by Levi Ward Hancock, his 3rd cousin.
>
> —President Ulysses S. Grant was then living, and did not die until 1885, hence the omission of his name.)

[83]Brigham Young, "Preaching To Spirits In Prison," *The Contributor,* Vol. X, No. 9, p. 322, July, 1889.

> *Then in the spirit world they will say, 'Do you not see somebody at work for you? The Lord remembers you and has revealed to His servants on the earth, what to do for you.'*[84]

President Joseph F. Smith taught in a similar manner. As he admonished the Saints to perform the ordinances for the dead, he described the effects of such labors by saying,

> Do the work necessary for their release from the prison-house. Through our efforts in their behalf their chains of bondage will fall from them, and the darkness surrounding them will clear away, that light may shine upon them and *they shall hear in the spirit world of the work that has been done for them by their children here, and will rejoice with you in your performance of these duties.*[85]

While in the spirit world President Heber Q. Hale discovered that

> The authorized representatives and families in the spirit world *have access to our Temple records and are kept fully advised* of the work done therein.[86]

He also reported that in order to emphasize the importance of the ordinances performed vicariously upon the earth and to make the spirit world recipients more aware of the obligations they are assuming,

> Ordinances are performed in the spirit world effectualizing in the individual recipients the same principles of the Gospel vicariously performed here.[87]

There is evidence that some spirit beings know of performance of the vicarious ordinances in their behalf on earth, for they have attended and witnessed these ordinances in the Latter-day Saint temples. For instance, Elder Horatio Pickett, a temple worker in the St. George temple, received the following vision on March 19, 1914:

> One day while at the font confirming, when a large list of women were being baptized for, the thought again came into my mind: *Do those people for whom this work is being done, know that it is being done for them, and, if they do, do they appreciate it?* While this thought was running through my mind I happened to turn my eyes toward the south-east corner of the font room and there I *saw a large group of*

[84] JD 3:372. June 22, 1856.
[85] Joseph F. Smith, *Gospel Doctrine, op cit.*, pp. 469-470.
[86] Heber Q. Hale, *op cit.*
[87] *Ibid.*

women. The whole south-east part of the room was filled; they seemed to be standing a foot or more above the floor and were all intently watching the baptizing that was being done; and as the recorder called a name, one of them—*a rather tall, very slim woman, apparently about 35 years of age,* gave a sudden start and looked at the recorder. Then her eyes turned to the couple in the water, closely watching the baptism; then her eyes followed the sister that was being baptized as she came up out of the water and was confirmed, and when the ordinance was completed *the happy, joyous expression that spread over her countenance was lovely to behold.*

The next one called seemed to be a *younger woman, a little below the average height.* She was of a nervous, emotional nature, could not keep still, seemed as though she wanted to jump into the water herself, and when the ordinance was finished *she seemed to be overflowing with joy, turning from one to another of her companions as though she was telling them how happy she was.*

The third was a large muscular-looking woman, not fleshy but bony, masculine build, very high forehead and intelligent countenance, *hair streaked with gray* and combed like elderly ladies used to wear their hair when I was a lad. She seemed to be of a more quiet, stoical nature than the others; no outward demonstration of what her feelings may have been, but there was a look in her eyes that seemed to say that she appreciated what was being done fully as much as the others did, and when the ceremony was finished she nodded her head slightly and moved her lips as though she might have said, 'Amen.'

Just as the work for her was finished there was a noise in President Cannon's office as though a book or something might have fallen to the floor which caused me to turn my eyes in that direction, and though I turned back instantly, the vision had faded and gone and with it also had gone all doubt and queries that may have been in my mind on the subject. *I was satisfied, and am still satisfied that our friends behind the veil know and realize what is being done for them and are anxiously waiting for their time to come.*

I do not think it would be possible for any person to look into the faces of those women as I did and see the earnestness with which they were watching the proceedings, and the joy and happiness that shone in their faces as their names were called and the work done for them, and not feel as I do. *This was not a night vision nor a dream but was about three o'clock on a bright, sunny afternoon while I was standing at the font assisting in the ordinances thereof.*[88]

---

[88]N. B. Lundwall, *The Vision, op cit.,* pp. 142-143. Elder Picket prefaced his account by recording the desire of his heart which the manifestation satisfied:

"While working here in the St. George Temple, I often thought of the great expense and the time and labor necessary to support the Temple, and to perform the

Elder F. T. Pomeroy and his companions experienced a similar manifestation as they participated in the vicarious sealing of his ancient relative, Richimir II, on November 2, 1927:

When the ceremony commenced my head was bowed in prayer. Suddenly I received the impression that something extraordinary was happening. I looked up and to my surprise and joy, I visualized standing just inside the door and gazing directly at me *the dim form and smiling countenance of a personage. He was tall and brawny. He had piercing eyes, and heavy eyebrows, and rather high cheeck bones. The lower part of his face was covered by a gray beard which hung well down upon his breast. I was impressed that he was the personage for whom the ceremony was being performed.* I was nearly overcome, but said nothing about it at the time. After the ceremony Brother Weston asked me for information concerning Richimir II, and I gave him such information as I had.

I thought over and treasured the visitation, as one given to me, and intended to say nothing about it. The next morning Brother Weston came to me and said: 'Brother Pomeroy, I expect you are wondering why I was so anxious to obtain information concerning the man for whom I stood as proxy yesterday. I wanted to write about him in my diary, for *they were present and witnessed the ceremony, for I felt their presence.'* 'I am glad to hear you say that,' I replied, 'as I also know they were there, *for I visualized his countenance and will know him when I meet him on the other side.'* Sister Hayne testified to the same thing and President LeSueur also testified he was impressed with their presence while the ceremony was in progress.[89]

Elder Joseph H. Smith, a laborer in the Salt Lake Temple, recorded the following instance of attendance by spirit beings while their temple ordinances were performed:

Brother Joseph Warburton and his daughter were doing sealings in the Salt Lake Temple on December 1, 1898. After having completed their labors in the sealing room, they walked up to President John R. Winder and expressed their appreciation for his having performed these sealings for them.

After they had gone into the next room the daughter turned to

---

necessary ordinances therein for the salvation of the dead, and the question often arose in my mind: *Do they (the dead) know what is being done for them and do they appreciate the sacrifice that is being made by their brethren and sisters in the Temples for their benefit.*

I often asked the Lord to give me sufficient of His Spirit that I might have a better understanding of the Temple work than I had.

[89]F. T. Pomeroy, "A Genealogical Development and Testimony." *The Genealogical and Historical Magazine,* Mesa, Arizona, Vol. XII, No. 3, July, 1935, pp. 29-30. This experience is of great interest to genealogists, for Richimir II lived 1600 years ago.

> her father and asked, 'Did you see those three couples in the sealing room with us?'
>
> His answer was, 'No, I did not.'
>
> She then said: *'There were three couples in the room. They were dressed in temple clothing, and the room was illuminated by a supernatural light. As we knelt at the altar, and the names were called of the people for whom we were being sealed, each couple in turn knelt by our side. As the ordinance was performed they showed by the expression on their faces how pleased they were. When we walked up to thank President Winder, they came up also, and after we had completed our expression of thanks to him they disappeared.'*
>
> Brother Warburton asked her if she could describe the people she saw. She replied she could do it very well, and she described each couple in turn. Her father then said, 'The first couple are my great-grandparents; the second couple my grandparents; and the third couple are my great uncle and aunt.' He had known them all in life, and from his daughter's description recognized them as the very persons for whom the sealings had been performed that day.[90]

And President Edward J. Wood of the Canadian Temple recorded the following testimony of one of his co-workers:

> A few years after the opening of our temple for ordinance work, one of the temple workers, President Duce, who had spent several years in active temple work in the Logan temple and was now with us in the Alberta temple, was sitting in the sealing room. He stated that *he saw the main corridor to the sealing room filled with people looking into the sealing room and taking note as sealing ordinances were administered for one person after another, in the relationship of wives to husbands or children to parents.*
>
> He said that he saw plainly *as each person's work was done he or she would shake hands with the people still waiting in the corridor and would apparently go away.* When the work in the sealing room was finished, he still saw very many waiting in the corridor. They were apparently very much disappointed in knowing that the work was finished for the day and no work was done for them.
>
> This leads us to believe that there are a good many people in the Spirit World who know just what is being done in the Temple, and that when the work is not done for them, they are greatly disappointed.[91]

It appears that other spirits are able to convey their gratitude to the mortals who perform the necessary genealogical

[90]*A Book of Remembrance, op cit.,* pp. 77-78.
[91]*Ibid.,* pp. 80-81.

and ordinance work for them. J. Hatten Carpenter, a temple recorder in the Manti temple, received such a manifestation:

> On the 15th of April, 1908, I went to the Temple with my wife, and on that day we were sealed for some ten couples of my Carpenter kindred. Among them was a certain Warncombe Carpenter and his wife, Eleanor Taylor. During the ceremony a most peculiar feeling came over me, one I had never experienced before—*a sensation of warmth in my chest which extended upwards which brought tears to my eyes and I melted through the intensity of its effects.* This feeling I did not experience when being sealed for the other nine couples. *I realized that Warncombe and his wife were permitted to show their gratitude to us for the work performed for them and gave us a taste of the joys of heaven, for I had never tasted such exquisite joy before,* but have since on seven or eight occasions. As we went home my wife and I talked over this experience and she had experienced the same feeling as I.[92]

In the majority of instances, of course, mortals receive no indication concerning the status of the dead for whom they labor. Yet they may later learn of the gratitude of the spirits they release from bondage. As the prophet Joseph Smith put it,

> In the resurrection those who had been worked for would fall at the feet of those who had done their work, kiss their feet, embrace their knees and manifest the most exquisite gratitude. We do not comprehend what a blessing to them these ordinances are.[93]

SUMMARY

1. The gospel of Jesus Christ can be defined as "Christ's way to perfection." It is a path of principles, ordinances and covenants which a man can walk to attain his exaltation.
2. Those who had no mortal opportunity to hear the gospel are sent to the spirit prison. There they will have the gospel preached to them. Though they are not subject to Lucifer's commands, they are still influenced by the temptations and promptings of evil spirits, just as they are influenced by the preaching and example of missionaries from paradise.
3. In the wisdom and justice of God, all men are to have the opportunity to hear and accept the gospel of Christ either in this life or in the spirit prison. Thus all men can be judged by the same standard.

---

[92]N. B. Lundwall, *Temples of the Most High, op cit.*, p. 122. Elder Carpenter's account was recorded May 10, 1940.

[93]N. B. Lundwall, *The Vision, op cit.*, p. 141.

4. Latter-day Saints recognize that it is their responsibility to preach the gospel unto every man, although relatively few will accept it.

5. The doctrine of vicarious work for the dead includes the following principles:

   A. To receive the benefits of Christ's atoning sacrifice, man must receive gospel ordinances, seek righteousness by forsaking sin, and serve God by doing His will.

   B. The saving ordinances of the gospel, seven in number, must be performed on earth. Mortals are to seek their performance for themselves and to perform them vicariously for the dead.

   C. The gospel will be taught in the spirit prison to those who were without opportunity to hear it during their mortal life. They will have their agency to either accept it or reject it.

   D. Man is required to labor in behalf of his dead both here on earth and in the spirit world. He cannot attain his own exaltation until the work is done.

   E. The major objective of man's labors for others is for him to establish an unbroken chain of righteous family relationships back to Adam in the patriarchal order of the priesthood.

6. The Savior, following His crucifixion, went into paradise. There He organized the righteous spirits into an effective missionary force and sent them to labor among the spirits in prison.

7. It appears that the missionary effort in the spirit prison is organized in a form similar to the missionary labor on earth, with mission presidents, various congregations, etc.

8. Missionary work in the spirit world includes preaching to nonmembers, teaching the converted, and gathering of genealogical data to aid in the completion of the vicarious ordinances on earth.

9. It appears an effort is made in the spirit world to assign tasks which are appropriate to a man's capacities.

10. Certain facts are known concerning spirit beings and the life they lead:

    A. Those laboring in the spirit world are apparently very busy.

    B. Spirits, when they return to the mortal sphere, are able to stand in the air above the ground.

C. Spirits apparently maintain the same characteristics of build, height, weight, hair style, beards, mannerisms, etc., as they had in mortality.

11. Though many in paradise are apparently assigned to preach the gospel in the spirit prison according to mission areas, others are laboring with and have been called specifically to teach their own kindred dead.

12. Death does not change one's attitude concerning the gospel. Spirit beings will continue to seek out, ignore, or reject the Church and its teachings as they did while on earth.

13. There is evidence that those who fail to perform the necessary ordinances for themselves while on earth forfeit their right to these ordinances when they die. The performing of these ordinances vicariously after their death for those who procrastinated their opportunity will not benefit them. Such labors only benefit those who did not know the gospel or who were actually without opportunity to enter the temples while on earth.

15. Those who hear the gospel for the first time in the spirit prison and accept it are candidates for the celestial kingdom. Those who hear and accept it there after first having refused to do so on earth are believed to be limited to the terrestrial kingdom.

16. The Lord will judge men according to their works and their desires. Those who would have received the gospel on earth had they known of it will still be able to gain the celestial kingdom.

17. The righteous spirits in prison seek that the necessary ordinances be performed for them on the earth. At times they are able to communicate their needs to mortals and to move them to gather genealogies and perform temple work.

18. Spirit beings are aware of the location of their records on earth.

19. The spirits in prison know when the vicarious work is done for them. Certain righteous spirits have access to the temple records on earth. There is evidence that certain ordinances are performed in the spirit world which effectualize an individual's acceptance of the vicarious work performed on earth. Some spirits have been permitted to return to earth and witness the ordinances performed vicariously in their behalf.

CHAPTER VII

THE RESURRECTION

THE DOCTRINE OF THE RESURRECTION IS ONE OF THE MOST glorious teachings of the scriptures. Embodied within this teaching is the hope for eternal life which has given strength and courage to countless millions down through the ages. Christian martyrs have gladly given their lives because of their faith in the afterlife, parents have rejoiced at the promise of being able to once again encounter a lost child in the hereafter, and twisted and sinful lives have been straightened because of a desire for a more glorious future existence. Faith and hope in a glorious resurrection is a bulwark of strength against sin and adversity. With just such faith the suffering Job was able to testify,

> I know that my redeemer liveth, and that he shall stand at the latter day upon the earth:
>
> And *though after my skin worms destroy this body, yet in my flesh shall I see God:*
>
> Whom I shall see for myself, and mine eyes shall behold, and not another; though my reins be consumed within me.[1]

This same faith brought forth the witness of Jacob, who had struggled with his family to arrive in the promised land of America, that "I know . . . that our flesh must waste away and die; nevertheless, *in our bodies we shall see God.*"[2]

Some teachings concerning the resurrection are abundantly and clearly stated in the scriptures, others are based on the teachings of latter-day prophets. Those areas of understanding which are from the scriptures will be considered first.

All Men Will Resurrect

Prominent in the scriptures is the teaching that all men, both the just and the unjust, will resurrect. This was Paul's

---

[1]Job 19:25-27.
[2]2 Ne. 9:4.

teaching when he defended himself before Tertullus and Felix and said that "there shall be a resurrection of the dead, both of the just and unjust."[3] He also taught that as in Adam all die, even so in Christ shall *all be made alive.*"[4]

Jacob taught that all men shall put on incorruptible bodies:

> O how great the plan of our God! . . . *the spirit and the body is restored to itself again, and all men become incorruptible, and immortal, and they are living souls,* having a perfect knowledge like unto us in the flesh, save it be that our knowledge shall be perfect.[5]

The Savior Himself taught that all who are in the grave shall come forth:

> Marvel not at this: for the hour is coming, in the which *all that are in the graves shall hear his voice,*
>
> *And shall come forth;* they that have done good, unto the resurrection of life; and they that have done evil, unto the resurrection of damnation.[6]

Like the Book of Mormon and the New Testament, the Doctrine and Covenants also indicates that every man shall be resurrected. It speaks of a final resurrection, just before the end of the earth, when all men who are still in their graves will come forth:

> Before the earth shall pass away, Michael, mine archangel, shall sound his trump, and *then shall all the dead awake, for their graves shall be opened, and they shall come forth—yea, even all.*
>
> And the righteous shall be gathered on my right hand unto eternal life; and the wicked on my left hand will I be ashamed to own before the Father.[7]

Resurrection Is a Reunion of Spirit and Body

The scriptures clearly teach that the resurrection is the reuniting of the spirit with the body. The Lord revealed through Joseph Smith that

> Through the redemption which is made for you is brought to pass the resurrection from the dead.

[3]Acts 24:15.
[4]1 Cor. 15:22.
[5]2 Ne. 9:13.
[6]Jn. 5:28-29.
[7]D&C 29:26-27.

> *And the spirit and the body are the soul of man.*
> *And the resurrection from the dead is the redemption of the soul.*[8]

Alma taught the same doctrine to his son, Corianton:

> I say unto thee, my son, that the plan of restoration is requisite with the justice of God; for it is requisite that all things should be restored to their proper order. Behold, *it is requisite and just, according to the power and resurrection of Christ, that the soul of man should be restored to its body, and that every part of the body should be restored to itself.*[9]

Many people of other faiths today follow the doctrines which were propounded by Greek philosophers, as well as the Gnostics and Docetists (heretical movements from Christianity in the first centuries A.D.), which held that all material is evil and therefore that Christ, being perfect and good, could have only a spiritual body as a resurrected personage. But His own testimony following His resurrection contradicts such a belief:

> Behold my hands and my feet, that it is I myself: handle me, and see; for *a spirit hath not flesh and bones, as ye see me have.*[10]

And this is reinforced by the Doctrine and Covenants:

> When the Savior shall appear we shall see him as he is. We shall see that he is a man like ourselves.[11]

And by Paul:

> For our conversation is in heaven; from whence also we look for the Saviour, the Lord Jesus Christ:
> *Who shall change our vile body, that it may be fashioned like unto his glorious body,* according to the working whereby he is able even to subdue all things unto himself.[12]

According to the apostle Paul, the spirit of Jesus shall never again be separated from His body, for "Christ being raised from the dead *dieth no more;* death hath no more dominion over him."[13]

---

[8]D&C 88:14-16. While this passage clearly asserts that, in the Lord's terminology, the spirit and the body together form the soul of man, it should be noted that most prophets speaking before this revelation have not used the term *soul* in that sense. Examples of this term being used in reference only to the spirit of man are 1 Ki. 17:21; 2 Ki. 4:27; Mt. 10:28; 1 Thess. 5:23; 1 Ne. 14:3; 15:31; Al. 39:17; 40:11, 15, 18, 21, 23; D&C 63:4; etc. The term is also used on occasion in the scriptures to signify the body only, and not the spirit. See Heb. 4:12; D&C 33:1; etc.

[9]Al. 41:2.

[10]Lk. 24:39.

[11]D&C 130:1. See 1 Jn. 3:2.

[12]Phil. 3:20-21.

[13]Ro. 6:9.

Just as Christ's spirit and body are inseparably connected, all resurrected beings have had their spirit and flesh joined for eternity. This was the Master's teaching when He taught concerning resurrected beings,

> *Neither can they die any more:* for they are equal unto the angels; and are the children of God, being the children of the resurrection.[14]

Resurrected Bodies Conform to Heavenly Kingdoms

According to that which the Lord has revealed, the type of body men will inherit in their resurrection will be determined by the glory which quickens (resurrects) their bodies and will suit them to fully enjoy the kingdom they have merited:

> They who are of a celestial spirit *shall receive the same body which was a natural body; even ye shall receive your bodies, and your glory shall be that glory by which your bodies are quickened.*
>
> Ye who are quickened by a portion of the celestial glory shall then receive of the same, even a fulness.
>
> And they who are *quickened by a portion of the terrestrial glory shall then receive of the same,* even a fulness.
>
> And also they who are *quickened by a portion of the telestial glory shall then receive of the same,* even a fulness.[15]

The apostle Paul set this doctrine forth with clarity, and taught that various types of resurrected bodies would vary in their glory as the light of the sun, moon, and the stars differs in brightness:

> But some man will say, How are the dead raised up? and with what body do they come? . . .
>
> *All flesh is not the same flesh: but there is one kind of flesh of men, another flesh of beasts, another of fishes, and another of birds.*
>
> *There are also celestial bodies, and bodies terrestrial:* but the glory of the celestial is one, and the glory of the terrestrial is another.
>
> *There is one glory of the sun, and another glory of the moon, and another glory of the stars:* for one star differeth from another star in glory.
>
> *So also is the resurrection of the dead.* It is sown in corruption; it is raised in incorruption.[16]

In the seventy-sixth section of the Doctrine and Covenants the

---

[14]Lk. 20:36. See also D&C 63:49.
[15]D&C 88:28-31.
[16]1 Cor. 15:35, 39-42.

Lord tells of the resurrected bodies of those who inherit the celestial kingdom:

> *These are they whose bodies are celestial, whose glory is that of the sun, even the glory of God,* the highest of all, whose glory the sun of the firmament is written of as being typical.[17]

He speaks also of those who will inherit the terrestrial kingdom:

> These are they who receive of the presence of the Son, but not of the fulness of the Father.
>
> Wherefore, *they are bodies terrestrial, and not bodies celestial, and differ in glory as the moon differs from the sun.*[18]

Elder Orson Pratt summed up this teaching by stating that resurrected beings "will have intelligence in proportion to that exalted condition of their spirits and bodies."[19]

Atonement of Christ Makes Resurrection Possible

A basic doctrine of the gospel of Jesus Christ is that the Lord died in order to bring about the resurrection of the dead. The prophet Lehi taught this principle to his son Jacob in this fashion:

> Wherefore, how great the importance to make these things known unto the inhabitants of the earth, that they may know that there is no flesh that can dwell in the presence of God, save it be through the merits, and mercy, and grace of the *Holy Messiah, who layeth down his life according to the flesh, and taketh it again by the power of the Spirit, that he may bring to pass the resurrection of the dead,* being the first that should rise.[20]

And then Jacob explained the same doctrine:

> He cometh into the world that he may save all men if they will hearken unto his voice; for behold, he suffereth the pains of all men, yea, the pains of every living creature, both men, women, and children, who belong to the family of Adam.
>
> And *he suffereth this that the resurrection might pass upon all men,* that all might stand before him at the great and judgment day.[21]

---

[17]D&C 76:70.

[18]D&C 76:77-78.

[19]JD 18:319. Dec. 3, 1876. For a definition of the intelligence to which he had reference, see D&C 93:36.

[20]2 Ne. 2:8.

[21]2 Ne. 9:21-22.

This was also the teaching of Abinadi:

> But there is a resurrection, therefore the grave hath no victory, and *the sting of death is swallowed up in Christ.*[22]

And Samuel the Lamanite also taught that Christ's death was what made the resurrection possible:

> For behold, *he surely must die that salvation may come; yea, it behooveth him and becometh expedient that he dieth, to bring to pass the resurrection of the dead,* that thereby men may be brought into the presence of the Lord.
>
> Yea, behold, *this death bringeth to pass the resurrection, and redeemeth all mankind* from the first death—that spiritual death; for all mankind, by the fall of Adam being cut off from the presence of the Lord, are considered as dead, both as to things temporal and to things spiritual.[23]

Christ Was First to Resurrect; Others Came Out of the Grave at That Time

Though millions had passed into the world of spirits before the meridian of time, they were compelled to await the death and resurrection of the Messiah before being privileged to rise from the grave. According to the apostle Paul, Christ was the first to resurrect:

> But now is Christ risen from the dead, and *become the first-fruits of them that slept. . . .*
>
> For as in Adam all die, even so in Christ shall all be made alive.
>
> But every man in his own order: *Christ the firstfruits; afterward they that are Christ's at his coming.*[24]

Long before Jesus came forth from the grave, the prophet Lehi had foretold that He would be "the first that should rise."[25]

According to both the Bible and the Book of Mormon, others came out of the tomb immediately after Christ's resurrection. Apparently in Jerusalem

> The graves were opened; and many bodies of the saints which slept arose,

---

[22]Mos. 16:8.

[23]Hel. 14:15-16.

[24]1 Cor. 15:20, 22-23. See also Enoch's vision of the resurrection of the saints and also of a portion of the spirits in prison which was to take place at this time: Moses 7:55-57.

[25]2 Ne. 2:8.

> And *came out of the graves after his resurrection,* and went into the holy city, and appeared unto many.[26]

This was also the case on the American continent, for the Savior, during His ministry in Zarahemla, said,

> I commanded my servant Samuel, the Lamanite, that he should testify unto this people, that *at the day that the Father should glorify his name in me that there were many saints who should arise from the dead, and should appear unto many, and should minister unto them.* And he said unto them: Was it not so?
>
> And his disciples answered him and said: Yea, Lord, Samuel did prophesy according to thy words, and *they were all fulfilled.*
>
> And Jesus said unto them: How be it that ye have not written this thing, *that many saints did arise and appear unto many and did minister unto them?*[27]

First and Second Resurrections, or the Resurrections of the Just and the Unjust

The prophets have spoken of two different resurrections: a coming forth of the righteous and the resurrection of the wicked. Daniel looked beyond his time to the last days and saw that "Many of them that sleep in the dust of the earth shall awake, *some to everlasting life,* and *some to shame and everlasting contempt.*"[28] The message of the prophet Abinadi was that "this mortal shall put on immortality . . . if they be good, to the *resurrection of endless life and happiness;* and if they be evil, to the *resurrection of endless damnation.*"[29]

The Lord, who in the meridian of time told of the coming forth of the good "unto the resurrection of life," and the evil "unto the resurrection of damnation,"[30] has revealed in the last days that these resurrections will take place at differing times. A revelation basic to the understanding of the resurrection is Doctrine and Covenants section eighty-eight. This revelation depicts four angelic trumps which will summon four different groups from their graves. The first two trumps (which together comprise the first resurrection, or the resurrec-

[26]Mt. 27:52-53.
[27]3 Ne. 23:9-11. See also Hel. 14:14-26.
[28]Dan. 12:2.
[29]Mos. 16:10-11.
[30]Jn 5:29. See D&C 76:17.

tion of the just) are to precede Christ's coming in glory, and apparently continue the resurrection process throughout the Messiah's millennial reign on the earth. The last two trumps (which together depict the second resurrection, or resurrection of the unjust) announce those who are to come out of their graves after the Savior's thousand-year reign upon the earth and just before the earth comes to the end of its mortal state.

First Trump.

> And he shall sound his trump both long and loud, and all nations shall hear it.
>
> And there shall be silence in heaven for the space of half an hour; and immediately after shall the curtain of heaven be unfolded, as a scroll is unfolded after it is rolled up, and the face of the Lord shall be unveiled;
>
> And the saints that are upon the earth, who are alive, shall be quickened and be caught up to meet him.
>
> And they who have slept in their graves shall come forth, for their graves shall be opened; and they also shall be caught up to meet him in the midst of the pillar of heaven—
>
> They are Christ's, the first fruits, they who shall descend with him first, and they who are on the earth and in their graves, who are first caught up to meet him; and all this by the voice of the sounding of the trump of the angel of God.

Second Trump.

> And after this another angel shall sound, which is the second trump; and then cometh the redemption of those who are Christ's at his coming; who have received their part in that prison which is prepared for them, that they might receive the gospel, and be judged according to men in the flesh.

Third Trump.

> And again, another trump shall sound, which is the third trump; and then come the spirits of men who are to be judged, and are found under condemnation;
>
> And these are the rest of the dead; and they live not again until the thousand years are ended, neither again, until the end of the earth.

Fourth Trump.

> And another trump shall sound, which is the fourth trump, saying: There are found among those who are to remain until that great and last day, even the end, who shall remain filthy still.[31]

---

[31]D&C 88:94-102. Concerning the literal nature of these and other trumps Elder Orson Pratt said,

The first resurrection[32] apparently will include the resurrection of those who will inherit the celestial and terrestrial kingdoms. Says the Doctrine and Covenants in enumerating the characteristics of celestial beings: "These are they who shall have part in the first resurrection. These are they who shall come forth in the resurrection of the just."[33]

Those who have thus come forth in the first resurrection will live on the earth and reign with Christ a thousand years:

> And I saw thrones, and they sat upon them, and judgment was given unto them: and I saw the souls of them that were beheaded for the witness of Jesus, and for the word of God, and which had not worshipped the beast, neither his image, neither had received his mark upon their foreheads, or in their hands; and *they lived and reigned with Christ a thousand years.*
>
> *But the rest of the dead lived not again until the thousand years were finished. This is the first resurrection.*
>
> Blessed and holy is he that hath part in the first resurrection: on such the second death hath no power, but *they shall be priests of God and of Christ, and shall reign with him a thousand years.*[34]

Mortals living during the millennial era who grow old and die will be changed into resurrected beings in the twinkling of an eye:

> The time will come, when the seven angels having the seven last trumps *will sound their trumps literally, and the sound thereof will be heard among the nations,* just preparatory to the coming of the Son of Man. (JD 18:227. Aug. 26, 1876).

[32]There is difficulty in the terminology which is used in discussing the times of the resurrections. Abinadi speaks of a "first" resurrection, and applies his terminology to the time of Christ's resurrection in the meridian of time. (Mos. 15:20-27) Alma uses the same terminology and says that this resurrection will include those from Adam to Christ. (Al. 40:16-20)

But it appears that the prevalent usage of the terms "first" and "second" resurrections in the Church today refer to the resurrections of the just and the unjust in the period which is yet future. Typical of this usage is the following statement by President Joseph Fielding Smith:

> While there was a general resurrection of the righteous at the time Christ arose from the dead, it is customary for us to speak of the resurrection of the righteous at the Second Coming of Christ as the first resurrection. It is the first to us, for we have little thought or concern over that which is past. The Lord has promised that at the time of his Second Advent the graves will be opened, and the just shall come forth to reign with him on the earth for a thousand years. (*Doctrines of Salvation, op cit.*, Vol. II, p. 295.)

[33]D&C 76:64-65. The time of resurrection for those who inherit the terrestrial kingdom is less clear. Only D&C 88:99, when considered in connection with D&C 76:72-74, gives any chronological indication for this resurrection, seemingly showing that this group comes forth in the first resurrection about the time of Christ's coming in glory.

[34]Rev. 20:4-6.

> And he that liveth when the Lord shall come, and hath kept the faith, blessed is he; nevertheless, it is appointed to him to die at the age of man.
>
> Wherefore, children shall grow up until they become old; old men shall die; but *they shall not sleep in the dust, but they shall be changed in the twinkling of an eye.*
>
> Wherefore, for this cause preached the apostles unto the world the resurrection of the dead.[35]

Those mortals who are still living on the earth at the time of the end of the millennium and the end of the earth will also be changed into the resurrected state in the twinkling of an eye:

> For Satan shall be bound, and when he is loosed again he shall only reign for a little season, and then cometh the end of the earth.
>
> And *he that liveth in righteousness shall be changed in the twinkling of an eye,* and the earth shall pass away so as by fire.[36]

The second resurrection will take place at the end of the millennium and will be for those who will inherit the telestial kingdom and those who will be Sons of Perdition. Speaking of the heirs to the telestial kingdom the Doctrine and Covenants says:

> These are they who *shall not be redeemed from the devil until the last resurrection,* until the Lord, even Christ, the Lamb, shall have finished his work.[37]

The Earth to Be Resurrected

The Lord has revealed that the earth itself is to be quickened:

> And again, verily I say unto you, the earth abideth the law of a celestial kingdom, for it filleth the measure of its creation, and transgresseth not the law—
>
> Wherefore, it shall be sanctified; yea, *notwithstanding it shall die, it shall be quickened again, and shall abide the power by which it is quickened,* and the righteous shall inherit it.[38]

Some scriptures indicate that the earth may be a living entity and thus capable of both death and resurrection. The

---

[35]D&C 63:50-52. See D&C 101:30-31; 1 Cor. 15:51-53.

[36]D&C 43:31-32.

[37]D&C 76:85.

[38]D&C 88:25-26. For further information concerning the earth in its final, sanctified state, see Chapter XI.

Prophet Enoch, for example, stated that he heard the earth speak and mourn:

> And it came to pass that Enoch looked upon the earth; and he heard a voice from the bowels thereof, saying: *Wo, wo is me, the mother of men; I am pained, I am weary, because of the wickedness of my children.* When shall I rest, and be cleansed from the filthiness which is gone forth out of me? *When will my Creator sanctify me, that I may rest, and righteousness for a season abide upon my face?*
>
> And when *Enoch heard the earth mourn,* he wept, and cried unto the Lord, saying: O Lord, wilt thou not have compassion upon the earth?[39]

The same prophet was able to command the earth and have it obey. He "spake the word of the Lord, and the earth trembled, and *the mountains fled, even according to his command.*"[40] In like manner a Book of Mormon prophet was able to command a mountain to move and it moved in obedience to his command, "For the brother of Jared said unto the mountain Zerin, *Remove—and it was removed.* And if he had not had faith *it would not have moved.*"[41] At the rebellion of Korah, Moses proclaimed that the earth would swallow the treacherous ones as a sign that he was their true leader, "And the earth opened her mouth, and swallowed them up, and their houses, and all the men that appertained unto Korah, and all their goods."[42] The Savior himself spoke of the earth as responding to the command of authority made with mighty faith, saying "If ye have faith as a grain of mustard seed, ye shall say unto this mountain, Remove hence to yonder place; and it shall remove."[43]

Not only is the earth regarded as being capable of feeling and response to command, but some Latter-day Saint theologians believe that it is going through certain gospel processes to prepare it for its quickening and final state. The flood in Noah's day is regarded as its baptism by water.[44] The cleansing of the earth by fire at the coming of the Savior in glory

---

[39]Moses 7:48-49.
[40]Moses 7:13.
[41]Eth. 12:30.
[42]Num. 16:32.
[43]Mt. 17:20.
[44]See JD 1:274; 1:331; 16:313-314; 21:323-324.

is considered to be its baptism by fire.[45] The dissolution of the earth will be its death,[46] and its re-creation in celestialized form is understood to be its resurrection.

Concerning the resurrection of the earth, Brigham Young said that "We are of the earth, earthy, and not only will the portion of mother earth which composes these bodies get a resurrection, *but the earth itself*. . . . The earth is organized for a glorious resurrection."[47] Orson Pratt's teaching concerning the resurrection of the earth was that

> It will crumble, or in other words, the elements will be separated asunder, and the world will pass away from his presence. What next? Another great change to be wrought. *The same elements, constituting the earth, and the atmosphere will be brought together again, in such a manner and way, that the new earth will look like unto a sea of glass,* and those who are worthy of the celestial glory will inhabit it forever.[48]

In another discourse, while describing the final events of the last days, Elder Pratt taught that

> After the holy city and the New Jerusalem are taken up to heaven, the earth will flee away from before the presence of him who sits upon the throne. The earth itself is to pass through a similar change to that which we have to pass through. As our bodies return again to mother dust, forming constituent portions thereof, and no place is found for them as organized bodies; so it will be with this earth. *Not only will the elements melt with fervent heat, but the great globe itself will pass away. It will cease to exist as an organized world.* It will cease to

---

[45]See JD 1:331.

[46]Concerning the death of the earth, Orson Pratt explained,

The second chapter of Genesis, (new translation) informs us that the spirits of fowls were created in heaven, the spirits of fish and cattle, and all things that dwell upon the earth, had their pre-existence. *They were created in heaven, the spiritual part of them; not their flesh and bones.* We are also told in this inspired translation, that these living trees which we behold—for God has given life unto all things—*had their spiritual existence in heaven before their temporal existence;* every herb and every tree, before it was planted out on the earth, that is, the spiritual part of it, the life of it, that which, in other words, animates that which gives power to the vegetable to bring forth fruit after its likeness—the spiritual part existed in heaven. It was a spiritual creation first. *We are also told that the earth was organized in a spiritual form, that is, that portion that gives life to the earth.* We read about the earth's dying, and that it shall be quickened again. *What is it that will make the earth die? It will be the withdrawing of the spiritual portion from it, that which gives it life—that which animates it, and causes it to bring forth fruit; that which quickens the earth is the Spirit of God.* (JD 24:200-201. Nov. 12, 1879. See also JD 1:282, 291-294)

[47]JD 1:274. Aug. 14, 1853.

[48]JD 21:205. Nov. 12, 1879.

exist as one of the worlds that are capable of being inhabited. *Fire devours all things, converting the earth into its original elements; it passes away into space.*

But not one particle of the elements which compose the earth will be destroyed or annihilated. They will all exist and be brought together again by a greater organizing power than is known to man. *The earth must be resurrected again, as well as our bodies; its elements will be re-united, and they will be brought together by the power of God's word. He will then so organize these elements now constituted upon this earth, that there will be no curse attached to any of its compound thus made.* Now death is connected with them, but then everything will be organized in the most perfect order, just the same as it was when the Lord first formed it.[49]

The Lord has revealed that not only are man, earth and heaven to be resurrected, but that the resurrection will also extend to the lower creations upon the earth. According to His word, all the animal life must also be raised from the dead:

And the end shall come, and the heaven and the earth shall be consumed and pass away, and there shall be a new heaven and a new earth.

For all old things shall pass away, and all things shall become new, *even the heaven and the earth, and all the fulness thereof, both men and beasts, the fowls of the air, and the fishes of the sea;*

And not one hair, neither mote, shall be lost, for it is the workmanship of mine hand.[50]

Manner of Coming Forth From the Grave

The Lord has revealed the process by which men will come forth from the grave. To Joseph Smith He gave just such a vision. Said the Prophet,

Would you think it strange if I relate what I have seen in vision in relation to this interesting theme? Those who have died in Jesus Christ may expect to enter into all that fruition of joy when they come forth, which they possessed or anticipated here.

So plain was the vision, that *I actually saw men, before they had ascended from the tomb, as though they were getting up slowly. They took each other by the hand and said to each other, 'My father, my son, my mother, my daughter, my brother, my sister.'* And when *the voice calls for the dead to arise,* suppose I am laid by the side of my father, what would be the

[49]JD 18:346-347. Feb. 25, 1877.
[50]D&C 29:23-25.

first joy of my heart? To meet my father, my mother, my brother, my sister; and when they are by my side, I embrace them and they me.[51]

The teaching that a voice will call men forth from the grave is also found in the scriptures in the words of Jesus:

> *The dead shall hear the voice of the Son of God:* and they that hear shall live. . . .
>
> Marvel not at this: for the hour is coming, in the which all that are in the graves *shall hear his voice,*
>
> And shall come forth.[52]

It appears, however, that the voice will not be a loud, overall call heard by all simultaneously, nor that it will always be the actual voice of Christ that will be heard. Seemingly in this process, as in many other ordinances, the authority and responsibility will be delegated to others. President Brigham Young taught that the resurrection of those who have lived in the last days would come to pass under the direction of Joseph Smith. He said,

> If we ask who will stand at the head of the resurrection in this last dispensation, the answer is—Joseph Smith, Junior, the Prophet of God. He is the man who will be resurrected and receive the keys of the resurrection, and he will seal this authority upon others, and they will hunt up their friends and resurrect them when they shall have been officiated for, and bring them up. And we will have revelations to know our forefathers clear back to Father Adam and Mother Eve, and we will enter into the temples of God and officiate for them. Then man will be sealed to man until the chain is made perfect back to Adam, so that there will be a perfect chain of priesthood from Adam to the winding-up scene.[53]

On another occasion Brigham Young said that *"some person holding the keys of the resurrection, having previously passed through that ordeal, will be delegated to resurrect our bodies,* and our spirits will be there and prepared to enter into their bodies."[54]

---

[51]HC 5:361-362. Apr. 16, 1843.

[52]Jn. 5:25, 28-29.

[53]JD 15:138-139. Aug. 24, 1872. In another discourse he said,

> But is Joseph glorified? No, he is preaching to the spirits in prison. *He will get his resurrection the first of any one in this kingdom,* for he was the first that God made choice of to bring forth the work of the last days. (JD 3:371. June 22, 1856)

[54]JD 9:139. July 28, 1861.

Elder Erastus Snow, an early apostle, also taught that resurrected beings, to whom had been delegated authority, would call others from the grave. It was his teaching, also, that Joseph Smith would be the first of this dispensation to be resurrected:

> The next mission will be to come and prepare the way in Zion, and in her Stakes, and in the temples of our God for turning the key of the resurrection of the dead, to bring forth those that are asleep, and to exalt them among the Gods. And *who will be first and foremost? Why, he whom God has chosen and placed first and foremost to hold the keys of this last dispensation.* How long will it be? It is not given to me to say the month, the day, or the hour; but it is given unto me to say that that time is nigh at hand. The time is drawing near (much nearer than scarcely any of us can now comprehend) when Joseph will be clothed upon with immortality, when his brother Hyrum will be clothed upon with immortality, when the martyrs will be raised from the dead, together with their faithful brethren who have performed a good mission in the spirit world—*they, too, will be called to assist in the work of the glorious resurrection.* The Lord Jesus, who was the first fruits of the dead, the first fruit of them that sleep, and who holds the keys of the resurrection, will bring to pass the resurrection of the Prophet Joseph and his brethren, and *will set them to work in bringing about the resurrection of their brethren* as He has set them to work in all the other branches of the labor from the beginning.[55]

[55]JD 25:33-34. Feb. 2, 1884. Erastus Snow was among those who believed that Joseph and many of the Saints would be resurrected long before the actual time of Christ's final coming in glory. He went on to say:

> And the Lord Jesus will appear and show Himself unto His servants in His temple in holy places, to counsel and instruct and direct. He will appear in the glory of His Father, in His resurrected body, among those who can endure His presence and glory. *And all this I expect long before He will waste away and destroy the wicked from off the face of the earth.* True, we have, in our limited understandings, perhaps imagined, many of us, that this glorious resurrection was to come upon us, and upon the whole world suddenly, like the rising of the sun. *But you must remember the sun does not rise the same hour and the same moment upon all the earth. It is twenty-four hours in rising and twenty-four hours in setting. So with the resurrection. There is a day appointed for the resurrection of the righteous.* And it is sealed upon the heads of many that if they are faithful and true, they shall come forth 'in the morning of the first resurrection;' but *the morning lasts from the first hour of the day until mid-day, and the day lasts till night.*

Others shared his line of reasoning or belief. Orson Pratt said, while discussing the possibility that Joseph would lead the Saints back to Missouri,

> I do not know but he will yet. *God's arm is not shortened that he cannot raise him up even from the tomb.* We are living in the dispensation of the fullness of times, the dispensation of the resurrection, and *there may be some who will wake from their tombs for certain purposes and to bring to pass certain transactions* on the earth decreed by the Great Jehovah; and *if the Lord sees proper to bring forth that man just before the winding up scene to lead forth the army of Israel, he will do so.* And if he feels disposed to send him forth

It is not clear whether the process of one resurrected being calling another from the grave applies to the second resurrection or not, but the limited evidence at hand indicates that it does not. Wilford Woodruff told of an angelic visitation in which he was shown that resurrection and described it in these words:

> He showed me what is termed the second resurrection. Vast fields of graves were before me, and *the Spirit of God rested upon the earth like a shower of gentle rain, and when that fell upon the graves they were opened, and an immense host of human beings came forth.* They were just as diversified in their dress as we are here, or as they were laid down.[56]

---

as a spiritual personage to lead the camp of Israel to the land of their inheritance, all right. (JD 15:363. Mar. 9, 1873)

Heber C. Kimball, in his prophecy to Amanda H. Wilcox, prophesied that "the Prophet Joseph and others will make their appearance and those who have remained faithful will be selected to return to Jackson County, Missouri, and take part in the upbuilding of that beautiful city, the New Jerusalem." ("Prophecy of Heber C. Kimball," Church Section, p. 3, *The Deseret News,* May 23, 1931.)

A statement which Elder Kimball made in 1861 clearly indicates that he believed the Prophet Joseph would make this return as a resurrected being:

> You will be blessed, and you will see the day when *Presidents Young, Kimball, and Wells, and the Twelve Apostles will be in Jackson County, Missouri, laying out your inheritances. In the flesh? Of course.* We should look well without being in the flesh! We shall be there in the flesh, and all our enemies cannot prevent it. *Brother Wells, you may write that. You will be there, and Willard will be there, and also Jedediah, and Joseph and Hyrum Smith, and David, and Parley;* and the day will be when I will see those men in the general assembly of the Church of the First-Born, in the great council of God in Jerusalem, too. (JD 9:27. Apr. 7, 1861.)

These statements give meaning to the blessing pronounced upon Joseph Smith by his father, the patriarch of the Church:

> Thou shalt hold the keys of this ministry, even the presidency of this Church, both in time and in eternity, and thou shall stand on Mount Zion when the tribes of Jacob come shouting from the north, and with thy brethren, the Sons of Ephraim, crown them in the name of Jesus Christ. (N.B. Lundwall, *Faith Like the Ancients, op cit.,* p. 8)

Peter E. Johnson, who went into the spirit world in 1898, was given information concerning the present status of Joseph Smith. He had been given the option to either remain in the spirit world or return to earth. His record of this portion of his conversation is as follows:

> After some little conversation this question was repeated, with the same answer. Then I asked: 'If I remain, what will I be asked to do?' I was informed that I would preach the Gospel to the spirits there, as I had been preaching it to the people here, and that *I would do so under the immediate direction of the Prophet Joseph.* This remark brought to my mind a question which has been much discussed here, as to whether or not the Prophet Joseph is now a resurrected being. While I did not ask the question, *they read it in my mind,* and immediately said: 'You wish to know whether the Prophet has his body or not?' I replied: 'Yes, I would like to know.' *I was told that the Prophet Joseph Smith has his body, as also his brother Hyrum, and that as soon as I could do more with my body than I could do without it, my body would be resurrected.* (Peter E. Johnson, *The Relief Society Magazine, op. cit.,* Vol. VII, pp. 451-452.)

It is important to note that man will be resurrected at the exact spot his body has been buried.[57] Those who desire to be in the company of their loved ones upon resurrection morn should seek to be interred close to them when they die. The Prophet Joseph Smith remarked, on one occasion, that the Saints would do well to be buried in America, the land of Zion, and close to one another. His comments were made as he read in a letter of the death of Lorenzo Dow Barnes, who died in England four months earlier:

> I would esteem it one of the greatest blessings, if I am to be afflicted in this world to have my lot cast where I can find brothers and friends all around me. But this is not the thing I referred to: *it is to have the privilege of having our dead buried on the land where God has appointed to gather His Saints together, and where there will be none but Saints, where they may have the privilege of laying their bodies where the Son of Man will make His appearance,* and where they may hear the sound of the trump that shall call them forth to behold Him, *that in the morn of the resurrection they may come forth in a body, and come up out of their graves and strike hands immediately in eternal glory and felicity, rather than be scattered thousands of miles apart. . . .*
>
> I believe those who have buried their friends here, their condition is enviable. Look at Jacob and Joseph in Egypt, how they required their friends to bury them in the tomb of their fathers. See the expense which attended the embalming and the going up of the great company to the burial. . . .

[56]Wilford Woodruff, "Obtaining the Spirit of God," *Millennial Star,* Vol. 67, No. 39, p. 612. This discourse was delivered Oct. 19, 1896. It is interesting to note that apparently not only the bodies but the clothing of the dead come forth in the resurrection. Earlier in the vision he saw those who came forth in the first resurrection all dressed in white robes:

> While I was upon my knees praying, my room was filled with light. I looked up and a messenger stood by my side. I arose, and this personage told me he had come to instruct me. He presented before me a panorama. *He told me he wanted me to see with my eyes and understand with my mind what was coming to pass in the earth before the coming of the Son of Man.* He commenced with what the revelations say about the sun being turned to darkness, the moon to blood, and the stars falling from heaven. These things were all presented to me one after another, as they will be, I suppose, when they are manifest before the coming of the Son of Man.
>
> Then he showed me the resurrection of the dead—what is termed the first and second resurrection. In the first resurrection I saw no graves, nor anyone raised from the grave. *I saw legions of celestial beings, men and women who had received the gospel, all clothed in white robes.* In the form they were presented to me, they had already been raised from the grave.

[57]The information given to Peter Johnson as he entered the spirit world is significant in this context: "I was informed with emphasis that my first duty would be to watch the body until after it had been disposed of, as *that was necessary knowledge for me to have in the resurrection.*" (Peter E. Johnson, *Relief Society Magazine, op cit.,* Vol. VII, p. 452.)

I have said, Father, I desire to die here among the Saints. But if this is not Thy will, and I go hence and die, *wilt thou find some kind friend to bring my body back, and gather my friends who have fallen in foreign lands, and bring them up hither, that we may all lie together.*

I will tell you what I want. If tomorrow I shall be called to lie in yonder tomb, in the morning of the resurrection let me strike hands with my father, and cry, 'My father,' and he will say, 'My son, my son,' as soon as the rock rends and before we come out of our graves.

And may we contemplate these things so? Yes, *if we learn how to live and how to die. When we lie down we contemplate how we may rise in the morning; and it is pleasing for friends to lie down together, locked in the arms of love, to sleep and wake in each other's embrace and renew their conversation.*[58]

Resurrected Body Will Be Restored to Perfect State

The scriptures clearly teach the doctrine that the body will be restored to the spirit in perfect condition and that lost limbs, etc. will be restored to the body.

In a debate with the antichrist Zeezrom, the great missionary, Amulek, stated:

> *The spirit and the body shall be reunited again in its perfect form; both limb and joint shall be restored to its proper frame,* even as we now are at this time; and we shall be brought to stand before God, knowing even as we know now, and have a bright recollection of all our guilt.
>
> Now, *this restoration shall come to all,* both old and young, both bond and free, both male and female, both the wicked and the righteous; and even *there shall not so much as a hair of their heads be lost; but every thing shall be restored to its perfect frame, as it is now, or in the body,* and shall be brought and be arraigned before the bar of Christ the Son, and God the Father, and the Holy Spirit, which is one Eternal God, to be judged according to their works, whether they be good or whether they be evil.[59]

The prophet Alma taught this doctrine to his son Corianton:

> The soul shall be restored to the body, and the body to the soul; yea, and *every limb and joint shall be restored to its body; yea, even a hair of the head shall not be lost; but all things shall be restored to their proper and perfect frame.*[60]

[58]HC 5:361. Apr. 16, 1843.
[59]Al. 11:43-44.
[60]Al. 40:23.

And again,

> I say unto thee, my son, that the plan of restoration is requisite with the justice of God; for *it is requisite that all things should be restored to their proper order.* Behold, it is requisite and just, according to the power and resurrection of Christ, that the *soul of man should be restored to its body, and that every part of the body should be restored to itself.*[61]

According to Amulek, a resurrected being is incapable of dying and is "free from corruption":

> Now, behold, I have spoken unto you concerning the death of the mortal body, and also concerning the resurrection of the mortal body. I say unto you that this mortal body is raised to *an immortal body,* that is from death, even from the first death unto life, that *they can die no more; their spirits uniting with their bodies, never to be divided; thus the whole becoming spiritual and immortal, that they can no more see corruption.*[62]

Although resurrected bodies will have tangible flesh and bones, their bodies will be spiritual in their nature. The Lord has revealed that the righteous beings who inherit the earth "also shall rise again, a spiritual body."[63] The apostle Paul taught the same doctrine:

> And so it is written, The first man Adam was made a living soul; the *last Adam was made a quickening spirit.*
>
> Howbeit that was not first which is spiritual, but that which is natural; and *afterward that which is spiritual.*
>
> The first man is of the earth, earthy: the second man is the Lord from heaven.
>
> As is the earthy, such are they also that are earthy: and as is the heavenly, such are they also that are heavenly.
>
> And as we have borne the image of the earthy, we shall also bear the image of the heavenly.
>
> Now this I say, brethren, that *flesh and blood cannot inherit the kingdom of God, neither doth corruption inherit incorruption.*[64]

It appears that though a resurrected body will have flesh and bones[65] it will be without blood, which seems to be the portion of man which makes him mortal.[66] Instead, a finer substance

[61] Al. 41:2.
[62] Al. 11:45.
[63] D&C 88:27.
[64] 1 Cor. 15:45-50.
[65] See again Lk. 24:39; D&C 130:1,22.
[66] Lev. 17:11.

of spiritual matter[67] will flow in his veins. The Prophet Joseph Smith taught that "God Almighty Himself dwells in eternal fire; *flesh and blood cannot go there, for all corruption is devoured by the fire.* 'Our God is a consuming fire.' When our flesh is quickened by the Spirit, *there will be no blood in this tabernacle.*"[68] Thus a resurrected body is a spiritual body for it will be without blood. There is no contradiction between this teaching and Paul's statement above that "flesh and blood cannot inherit the kingdom of God."

The process of sanctification[69] prepares an individual for celestial glory. As the Lord revealed,

> Whoso is faithful unto the obtaining these two priesthoods of which I have spoken, and the magnifying their calling, *are sanctified by the Spirit unto the renewing of their bodies.*[70]

---

[67]Latter-day Saints regard spirit as a matter which is of a finer nature than any of the coarse elements presently known to man. The Doctrine and Covenants states that

> There is no such thing as immaterial matter. All spirit is matter, but it is more fine or pure, and can only be discerned by purer eyes;
>
> We cannot see it; but when our bodies are purified we shall see that it is all matter. (D&C 131:7-8. See also HC 4:575; 5:393; 3:387; 6:308-309.)

[68]HC 6:366. May 12, 1844.

[69]In explaining this process President Brigham Young said,

> I will put my own definition to the term sanctification, and say *it consists in overcoming every sin and bringing all into subjection to the law of Christ. God has placed in us a pure spirit; when this reigns predominant, without let or hindrance, and triumphs over the flesh* and rules and governs and controls as the Lord controls the heavens and the earth, this I call the blessing of sanctification. (JD 10:173. May 24, 1863)

[70]D&C 84:33. See also 89:18-21; Prov. 3:5-8. The understanding that the process of sanctification leads to actual physical change in mortal beings is not new. Elder Orson Pratt, in commenting on this passage, taught,

> He will suddenly come to his Temple, and he will purify the sons of Moses and of Aaron, until they shall be prepared to offer in that Temple an offering that shall be acceptable in the sight of the Lord. In doing this, he will purify not only the minds of the Priesthood in that Temple, but he will purify their bodies until they shall be quickened, renewed and strengthened, and they will be partially changed, not to immortality, but changed in part that they can be filled with the power of God, and they can stand in the presence of Jesus, and behold his face in the midst of that Temple. (JD 15:365-366. Mar. 9, 1873.)

Dr. Sidney B. Sperry, a modern theologian in the Church, writes that

> Whosoever are faithful in obtaining these two Priesthoods and the magnifying their callings are sanctified or made holy by the Spirit unto the renewing of their bodies (vs. 33). As worthy and active holders of the power and authority of God, their very bodies are changed, uplifted, and spiritualized. They become literally a new breed of men, the 'sons of Moses and of Aaron and the seed of Abraham, and the church and kingdom, and the elect of God.' (Sidney B. Sperry, *Doctrine and Covenants Compendium* (Salt Lake City, Utah: Bookcraft, Inc., 1960), p. 395.)

Indeed, the Lord has shown that through the sanctification process the Spirit works a change in man that alters him by filling him with light and making him clean:

> My Spirit is truth; truth abideth and hath no end; and if it be in you it shall abound.
>
> And if your eye be single to my glory, *your whole bodies shall be filled with light, and there shall be no darkness in you; and that body which is filled with light comprehendeth all things.*
>
> *Therefore, sanctify yourselves that your minds become single to God,* and the days will come that you shall see him; . . . Prepare yourselves, and *sanctify yourselves; yea, purify your hearts; and cleanse your hands and your feet before me, that I may make you clean;*
>
> That I may testify unto your Father, and your God, and my God, that you are clean from the blood of this wicked generation.[71]

It appears from the scriptures that resurrected beings can pass through walls and other solid objects.[72]

Those who have been married for eternity and who gain the highest degree of exaltation will have the power of procreation, or a "continuation of the seeds forever and ever."[73]

The scriptures clearly show that resurrected beings eat as mortals do. The Savior, for instance, had reference to a time when the apostles would be resurrected when He told them, "I appoint unto you a kingdom, . . . that *ye may eat and drink at my table in my kingdom,* and sit on thrones judging the twelve tribes of Israel."[74] The resurrected Savior ate fish and honeycomb before His disciples.[75] The Lord probably joined his disciples in the meal he cooked for them on the shores of the Sea of Galilee[76] and when he sat at meat and broke bread with others at Emmaus.[77] While speaking of heavenly beings

---

[71]D&C 88:66-68, 74-75. This process apparently must be completed before man can rise from the grave. As Elder Melvin J. Ballard put it, "No man or woman will come forth in the resurrection until they have completed their work, until they have overcome, until they have done as much as they can do." (N.B. Lundwall, *The Vision, op. cit.*, p. 47)

[72]See JS 2:43-45; John 20:19.

[73]D&C 132:19. See 131:1-4. However, assertions that those who inherit the lesser kingdoms will become sexless and be neither men nor women are so absurd as to be unworthy of examination here. Certainly there is no foundation for such a belief in the scriptures, nor has any such indication been given by the myriads of witnesses who have come from beyond the veil or seen in vision the life to come.

[74]Lk. 22:29-30. See also Mt. 26:29; Mt. 8:11.

[75]Lk. 24:41-43. Brigham Young said, "In the resurrection there will be a reunion of the spirits and bodies, and *they will walk, talk, eat, drink, and enjoy.* (JD 8:225. Oct. 21, 1860)

[76]See Jn. 21:9-15.

[77]See Lk. 24:30.

John the Revelator revealed that "The Lamb which is in the midst of the throne shall *feed* them, and shall lead them unto living *fountains of waters.*"[78] The Lord himself revealed that "the hour cometh that *I will drink of the fruit of the vine* with you on the earth, and with Moroni, . . . Elias, . . . John, . . . Elijah, . . . Joseph, . . . Jacob, . . . Isaac, . . . Abraham, . . . Michael, . . . and also with Peter, James, and John."[79]

According to that which the Lord has revealed, resurrected beings will take with them the knowledge which they have gained in mortality:

> *Whatever principle of intelligence we attain unto in this life, it will rise with us in the resurrection.*
>
> And if a person gains more knowledge and intelligence in this life through his diligence and obedience than another, he will have so much the advantage in the world to come.[80]

Men Will Come Forth as Laid in the Grave, Then Have Deformities Corrected

It is understood that one's physical size, shape, and age will not change while the body is in the tomb, and that the body will come forth just as it was laid down. Joseph Smith commented, "I will merely say that all men will come from the grave *as they lie down, whether old or young;* there will not be 'added unto their stature one cubit,' neither taken from it; all will be raised by the power of God, *having spirit in their bodies, and not blood.*"[81]

However, it is understood that any limbs that may have been lost will be restored as man comes forth in the resurrection.[82] This is made possible because the resurrection process is a re-creation of man's body from the elements of which it was composed originally. As President Brigham Young said,

[78]Rev. 7:17.

[79]D&C 27:5-12. See also 101:101; Rev. 2:17; 21:6; D&C 38:17-18; Is. 25:6-9; 66:17-22; 33:14-17; Lk. 14:15. See also references which seem to indicate that spirit beings eat just as resurrected beings do, on pp. 102-103.

[80]D&C 130:18-19.

[81]HC 4:555. Mar. 20, 1842.

[82]See again Al. 11:43-44; 40:23; 41:2.

> Man's body may be buried in the ocean, it may be eaten by wild beasts, or it may be burned to ashes, they may be scattered to the four winds, *yet the particles of which it is composed will not be incorporated into any form of vegetable or animal life, to become a component part of their structure*. . . . At the sound of the trumpet of God *every particle of our physical structures necessary to make our tabernacles perfect will be assembled*, to be rejoined with the spirit, every man in his order. Not one particle will be lost.[83]

President Young set forth the same teaching in another discourse, saying that

> When the angel who holds the keys of the resurrection shall sound his trumpet, then the peculiar fundamental particles that organized our bodies here, if we do honour to them, *though they be deposited in the depths of the sea, and though one particle is in the north, another in the south, another in the east, and another in the west, will be brought together again in the twinkling of an eye*, and our spirits will take possession of them.[84]

It would appear that following the resurrection there will be a period of adjustment in which defects, deformities, scars, etc. will be removed. As President Joseph F. Smith explained,

> What a glorious thought it is . . . that those from whom we have to part here, we will meet again and see as they are. We will meet the same identical being that we associated with here in the flesh—not some other soul, some other being, or the same being in some other form, but the same identity and the same form and likeness, the same person we knew and were associated with in our mortal existence, *even to the wounds in the flesh. Not that a person will always be marred by scars, wounds, deformities, defects, or infirmities, for these will be removed in their course*, in the proper time, according to the merciful providence of God. *Deformity will be removed; defects will be eliminated, and men and women shall attain to that perfection* of their spirits, to the perfection that God designed in the beginning.[85]

---

[83]Daniel H. Ludlow, *Latter-day Prophets Speak*, (Salt Lake City, Utah: Bookcraft, 1951), p. 42.

[84]JD 8:28. Mar. 25, 1860.

[85]Daniel H. Ludlow, *Latter-day Prophets Speak*, *op. cit.*, pp. 43-44. It is not clear, however, whether this correction takes place over a period of time or simultaneous with the resurrection. President Smith also said,

> *Our tabernacles will be brought forth as they are laid down, although there will be a restoration effected;* every organ, every limb that has been maimed, every deformity caused by accident or in any other way, will be restored and put right. Every limb and joint shall be restored to its proper frame. (JD 24:81-82. Feb. 2, 1883)

The only known case revealed in which man can learn concerning the rectifying of deformities following the resurrection is that of the Lord Jesus Christ. He still had the scars

Status of Children Following the Resurrection

Two statements pertaining to the status of little children following the resurrection were made by Joseph Smith. On March 20, 1842, he said,

> Children will be enthroned in the presence of God and the Lamb *with bodies of the same stature that they had on earth,* having been redeemed by the blood of the Lamb; they will there enjoy the fullness of that light, glory and intelligence, which is prepared in the celestial kingdom.[86]

Two years later, in his funeral sermon for King Follett, the prophet Joseph Smith repeated his teaching:

> A question may be asked—'Will mothers have their children in eternity?' Yes! Yes! Mothers, you shall have your children; for they shall have eternal life, for their debt is paid. There is no damnation awaiting them for they are in the spirit. But *as the child dies, so shall it rise from the dead, and be for ever living in the learning of God. It will never grow*[87]; *it will still be the child, in the same precise form*[88] *as it appeared before it died out of its mother's arms,* but possessing all the intelligence of a God. Children dwell in the mansions of glory and exercise power, but appear in the same form as when on earth. *Eternity is full of thrones, upon which dwell thousands of children, reigning on thrones of glory, with not one cubit added to their stature.*[89]

Apparently there was a degree of misunderstanding or misinterpretation in connection with these two statements by the Prophet. Witnesses have testified that during the two months between the delivery of the King Follett sermon and his martyrdom, Joseph Smith corrected the impression that

---

from the wounds after he came forth from the tomb. These scars were shown to Thomas (Jn. 20:24-28) and to the Nephites (3 Ne. 11:14-15). These scars still remain, it would seem, for they are to be shown to the Jews on the Mt. of Olives during the Battle of Armageddon (D&C 45:48-52; Zech. 13:6). What cannot be asserted with certainty is whether the delay in His case, where such scars serve an obvious purpose, is typical of all resurrected beings.

[86]HC 4:555-556. March 20, 1842.

[87]Here Elder B.H. Roberts, who compiled the history, has inserted the words [in the grave].

[88]Here Elder B.H. Roberts, who compiled the history, has inserted the words [when it rises].

[89]HC 6:316. Apr. 7, 1844. In a sermon on May 12, 1844, the Prophet Joseph said,

> In order for you to receive your children to yourselves you must have a promise—some ordinance; some blessing, in order to ascend above principalities, or else it may be an angel. *They must rise just as they died;* we can there hail our lovely infants with the same glory—the same loveliness in the celestial glory, where they all enjoy alike. *They differ in stature, in size,* the same glorious spirit gives them the likeness of glory and bloom; the old man with his silvery hairs will glory in bloom and glory. (HC 6:366.)

those who die as children retain their same stature following the resurrection and taught that they would grow to maturity after coming forth from the grave. It was not until the administration of President Wilford Woodruff, fifty-two years later, that a concerted effort was made to clarify the matter. According to his statement published in the Improvement Era in 1918, Elder Joseph F. Smith was the one instrumental in asserting this clarification during the era that he served the Church as an apostle and as a counselor in the First Presidency:

> Joseph Smith taught the doctrine that the infant child that was laid away in death would come up in the resurrection as a child; and pointing to the mother[90] of a lifeless child, he said to her: *'You will have the joy, the pleasure, and satisfaction of nurturing this child, after its resurrection, until it reaches the full stature of its spirit. There is restitution, there is growth, there is development, after the resurrection from death.* I love this truth. It speaks volumes of happiness, of joy and gratitude to my soul. Thank the Lord he has revealed these principles to us.'
>
> In *1854,* I met with my aunt, the wife of my uncle, Don Carlos Smith, who was the mother of that little girl that Joseph Smith, the Prophet, was speaking about when *he told the mother that she should have the joy, the pleasure, and the satisfaction of rearing that child, after the resurrection, until it reached the full stature of its spirit; and that it would be a far greater joy than she could possibly have in mortality, because she would be free from the sorrow and fear and disabilities of mortal life, and she would know more than she could know in this life.* I met that widow, the mother of that child, and she told me this circumstance and bore testimony to me that this was what the Prophet Joseph Smith said when he was speaking at the funeral of her little daughter.
>
> One day I was conversing with a brother-in-law of mine, *Lorin Walker,* who married my oldest sister. In the course of the conversation he happened to mention that *he was present at the funeral of my cousin Sophronia, and that he heard the Prophet Joseph Smith declare the very words that Aunt Agnes had told me.*
>
> I said to him, 'Lorin, what did the Prophet say?' and he repeated, as nearly as he could remember, what the Prophet Joseph said in relation to little children. *The body remains undeveloped in the grave, but the spirit returns to God who gave it. Afterwards, in the resurrection,*

[90]From the context which follows it appears that this mother was Agnes Coolbrith Smith, who married Joseph Smith's younger brother, Don Carlos Smith, on July 30, 1835. (HC 4:393). The deceased child was Sophronia C. Smith, (HC 4:399). The father (Don Carlos) died three years before Joseph made the statement to his widow, on Aug. 7, 1841. (HC 4:393).

the spirit and body will be reunited; the body will develop and grow to the full stature of the spirit; and the resurrected soul will go on to perfection. So I had the statement of two witnesses who heard this doctrine announced by the Prophet Joseph Smith, the source of intelligence.

Eventually I was in conversation with *Sister M. Isabella Horne.* She began to relate to me the circumstance of her being present at the funeral that I refer to, when Joseph spoke of the death of little children, their resurrection, as little children, and of the glory, and honor, and joy, and *happiness the mother would have in rearing her little children in the resurrection to the full stature of their spirits.* 'Well,' she said, 'I heard Joseph say that. I was at that funeral.' Sister Isabella Horne told me this.

Then I said to her: 'Why haven't you spoken about it before? How is it you have kept it to yourself all these long years? Why haven't you let the Church know something about this declaration of the Prophet?'

She replied: 'I did not know whether it was my duty to do so, or whether it would be proper or not.'

I said: 'Who else was there?'

'My husband was there.'

'Does he remember it?'

'Yes, he remembers it.'

'Well, will you and Brother Horne give me an affidavit in writing, stating the fact, and let it be sworn to?'

She said, 'With the greatest of pleasure.'

So *I have the testimony in affidavit form of Brother and Sister Horne, in addition to the testimony of my aunt, and the testimony of my brother-in-law, in relation to the Prophet Joseph's remarks at that funeral.*

Just a little while later, to my joy and satisfaction, *the first man I ever heard mention it in public was Franklin D. Richards; and when he spoke of it, I felt in my soul: the truth has come out.* The truth will prevail. It is mighty, and it will live; for there is no power that can destroy it. *Presidents Woodruff and Cannon approved of the doctrine and after that I preached it.*[91]

---

[91]Joseph F. Smith, *Gospel Doctrine, op cit.,* pp. 455-457. The statement with which President Smith followed his account is significant in this context:

> *It is a good thing for us not to attempt to advance new doctrine,* or new and advanced thought in relation to principles and doctrines pertaining to, or presumed to pertain to, the gospel of Jesus Christ, *without weighing it carefully, with the experience of years, before we attempt to make a doctrinal test and to advance it to the people of the Lord.* There is so much simple truth, necessary to be understood, that has been revealed to us in the gospel that it is extreme folly in us to attempt to go beyond the truth that has been

According to Elder B. H. Roberts, the Horne affidavits

Were delivered in the presence of President Angus M. Cannon, of the Salt Lake Stake of Zion, and Elder Arthur Winter, at the residence of Brother Horne, in Salt Lake City, on November 19, 1896, and were reported stenographically by Arthur Winter, the Church official reporter.

Sister M. Isabella Horne said:

'In conversation with the Prophet Joseph Smith once in Nauvoo, the subject of children in the resurrection was broached. *I believe it was in Sister Lenora Cannon Taylor's house.* She had just lost one of her children, and I had also lost one previously. The Prophet wanted to comfort us, and he told us that we should receive those children in the morning of the resurrection just as we laid them down, in purity and innocence, and *we should nourish and care for them as their mothers.* He said that children would be raised in the resurrection just as they were laid down, and that they would obtain all the intelligence necessary to occupy thrones, principalities and powers. *The idea that I got from what he said was that the children would grow and develop in the Millennium, and that the mothers would have the pleasure of training and caring for them, which they had been deprived of in this life.*

This was some time after the King Follett funeral, at which I was present.'

Brother Joseph Horne said:

'I heard the Prophet Joseph Smith say that mothers should receive their children just as they laid them down, and that they would have the privilege of doing for them what they could not do here, the Prophet remarked: "How would you know them if you did not receive them as you laid them down?" *I also got the idea that children would grow and develop after the resurrection, and that the mothers would care for them and train them.'*

We hereby certify that the foregoing is a full, true and correct account of the statements made by Joseph and M. Isabella Horne on the subject mentioned.

Angus M. Cannon
Arthur Winter

We have read the foregoing, and certify that it is correct.

Joseph Horne
M. Isabella Horne[92]

---

revealed, until we have mastered and can comprehend the truth that we have. There is a great deal within our reach that we have not yet mastered.

[92]Note HC 4:556-557.

Elder B. H. Roberts also made note of the testimony of President Wilford Woodruff (who with three others had recorded the King Follett discourse), that Joseph had clarified the matter some time during the two months between the discourse and his martyrdom.

> The writer of this note distinctly remembers to have heard the late President Wilford Woodruff, who reported the above sermon [i.e. of March 20, 1842], say, that *the Prophet corrected the impression that had been made by his King Follett sermon,* that children and infants would remain fixed in the stature of their infancy and childhood in and after the resurrection. President Woodruff very emphatically said on the occasion of the subject being agitated about 1888-9, that *the Prophet taught subsequently to his King Follett sermon that children while resurrected to the stature at which they died would develop to the full stature of men and women after the resurrection:* and that the contrary impression created by the report of the Prophet's King Follett sermon was due to a misunderstanding of his remarks and erroneous reporting.[93]

President Woodruff was apparently unwilling to label the teaching as official doctrine of the Church, though he obviously believed it. As Matthias F. Cowley wrote as he prepared a biography of Wilford Woodruff from the president's private journal, on September 3, 1884,

> He visited Provo where he attended the funeral of Margarette T. Smoot. On that occasion *he gave it as his opinion* that children would grow and develop after the resurrection and obtain all the blessings of adult persons.[94]

It was not until the ministry of President Joseph F. Smith that the teaching took on the stature of doctrine. As B. H. Roberts reported in the conclusion of his explanatory note cited above,

> In the Improvement Era for June, 1904, President Joseph F. Smith in an editorial on the Resurrection said:
>
> 'The body will come forth as it is laid to rest, for there is no growth or development in the grave. As it is laid down, so will it arise, *and changes to perfection will come by the law of restitution.* But the spirit will continue to expand and develop, and *the body, after the resurrection will develop to the full stature of men.'*
>
> This may be accepted as the doctrine of the Church in respect to the resurrection of children and their future development to the full stature of men and women; and it is alike conformable to that which will be regarded as both reasonable and desirable.[95]

SUMMARY

1. The hope of a glorious resurrection is an important bulwark of strength against sin and adversity.
2. All who have passed through mortality will resurrect, though they be just or unjust.
3. Resurrection is a re-entry of the spirit into a body which has been re-created from the same elements of which it consisted in mortality.
4. The resurrected Christ had a tangible body of flesh and bones. The bodies of all other resurrected beings will also be tangible physiques.
5. Resurrected beings cannot die again. They can never undergo the separation of the spirit from the body, which is the death process.
6. The bodies men will inherit will be celestial, terrestrial, telestial, or bodies of no glory. The light and glory that will characterize their bodies will be representative of the kingdom which they will inherit as a result of their pre-mortal, mortal, and spirit world lives.
7. The atonement of Christ made the resurrection possible. "The sting of death is swallowed up in Christ."
8. Christ was the first to resurrect. At the time of His resurrection many others were also resurrected, both in Palestine and in the Americas. This resurrection is termed a preliminary resurrection and is not to be confused with the "first" resurrection which is still future.
9. There is to be a "first" and a "second" resurrection in the last days. The first resurrection is to precede and accompany the coming of Christ in His glory. The second resurrection is to take place a thousand years later, at the end of Christ's millennial reign.
10. Those to inherit the celestial and terrestrial kingdoms are to come forth in the first resurrection, or resurrection of the just. Those who have suffered in hell and who will inherit the telestial kingdom or a kingdom of no glory will come forth in the second resurrection, or resurrection of the unjust.
11. Those who come forth in the first resurrection will dwell on earth with Christ during His millennial reign. Mortal beings

[93]Note HC 4:556.
[94]Matthias F. Cowley, *Wilford Woodruff, op. cit.*, p. 553.
[95]Note HC 4:557.

who die during this thousand year period will not go into the spirit world but will be changed instantaneously to a resurrected state.

12. The earth is to die and then shall be quickened again in a celestial resurrection. There is scriptural evidence that the earth is a living entity. Animals and all other living things will also be perpetuated eternally in resurrected form.

13. While the general times of the resurrections are to be announced by angelic trumps, it appears that people of this dispensation will actually be called from the grave by the voice of the Lord or His authorized representatives acting under the direction of Joseph Smith. In his vision of the second resurrection, President Wilford Woodruff saw that the unrighteous were summoned from the tomb by "the Spirit of God," which "rested upon the earth like a shower of gentle rain."

14. It appears that those who come forth in the first resurrection will be wearing robes of white. Those of the second resurrection will be dressed in a diversified manner. Bodies will come forth from the grave in the same location where they were buried.

15. The bodies of resurrected beings will be in perfect form, and all things shall be restored to their proper and perfect frame. Resurrected beings are free from corruption and bodily deterioration.

16. Blood is the substance which makes man mortal. Blood will be replaced by a finer substance of spirit which will allow resurrected beings to live for eternity. Because of this substance it is said that resurrected bodies are spiritual bodies, though they are still tangible physiques of flesh and bones.

17. Sanctification is the process which prepares man for the resurrected state. As he purges out the darkness of wickedness and worldliness he is filled with the Spirit and light which renews his body and prepares it for celestial glory. From resurrected beings emanates glory in direct proportion to their degree of sanctification.

18. Resurrected beings have the ability to pass through solid objects. Those who gain exaltation in the celestial resurrection will retain the power of procreation. Resurrected beings are free from hunger, thirst, and other bodily needs. The limited evidence available however, indicates that they can eat, etc., but that the things they will need to provide their physical necessities will be readily accessible.

19. Bodies will not change their size, shape, or age in the resurrection. Limbs that have been lost during mortality, however,

will be restored in the resurrection process. It appears that other defects or infirmities will be removed sometime following the resurrection to allow every individual (at least in the celestial resurrection) to live through eternity in a physically perfect condition.

20. The same elements which make up man's mortal body will comprise his resurrected body. Particles from the remains of mortal bodies will not become component parts of any form of vegetable or animal life between death and the resurrection.

21. It is the current teaching of the prophets that children who have died will be resurrected in their child's body in the first resurrection. Their parents will have the privilege of raising them to adult stature during the millennium.

It must be observed that there is much which is yet to be revealed pertaining to the doctrine of the resurrection. Less concerning the actual resurrection process has been shown to man than concerning the spirit world. Far fewer of the statements cited herein on this theme stem from knowledge revealed in the scriptures or from visions or manifestations. This situation requires a greater degree of the spirit of discernment to be manifested on the part of the reader.

CHAPTER VIII

THE FINAL JUDGMENT

The Great Day of Judgment

THE PRE-MORTAL, MORTAL AND SPIRIT WORLD ACTIVITIES OF every man will reach their culmination as they are reviewed and examined in the great and final judgment. That great examination and evaluation serves as the line of demarcation between man's preparation for and his reception of eternal responsibility and inheritance. All of his labors and efforts for countless millenniums have served as a preparation for this great event.

Though each man's personal time before the judgment bar of Christ may be brief, the combined period of judgment for all men must of necessity be a lengthy period. If each man were allotted only ten minutes, just imagine the many years it would take to consider the case of every individual! As Orson Pratt commented,

> We may look for a general reckoning with all the inhabitants of this earth, both the righteous and the wicked. How long this day, called the day of judgment, will be, is not revealed. *It may be vastly longer than what many suppose.*[1]

Although no revelation explicitly states the length of the day of final judgment, clues revealed in various scriptural passages amply demonstrate that it will extend over a thousand-year period or more. In references to the day[2] of judgment, therefore, men would do well to remember Peter's reminder that they "be not ignorant of this one thing, that *one day is with the Lord as a thousand years, and a thousand years as one day.*"[3]

The scriptures give evidence that the final judgment will

---

[1]JD 17:182. Oct. 11, 1874.

[2]The judgment time is often referred to specifically as a "day." See for instance, Acts 17:31; Moses 7:57; D&C 19:3; Jn. 12:48; D&C 41:12; etc.

[3]2Pet. 3:8.

begin immediately after Christ's coming in glory and will continue during His millennial reign and past the second resurrection until the earth passes away and all men are sent to the kingdoms of glory to which they have been assigned. Confusion should not be allowed to arise concerning the nature of the final judgment as its time is discussed. The term *final* judgment refers to the examination men will receive following their resurrection. Though Christ at His coming will judge the mortals on the earth,[4] such judgment is not considered as final, for those slain in that day will still come forth in the resurrection to again give account for their works.

It appears that those who come forth in the first resurrection at the beginning of the millennium will undergo their time of final judgment soon after coming forth from the grave, rather than waiting till the end of the millennium. This is shown in a number of passages which indicate the results of the judgment process but which have chronological reference to the beginning of the millennial era. For example, John the Revelator wrote,

> And I saw *thrones, and they sat upon them, and judgment was given unto them:* and I saw the souls of them that were beheaded for the witness of Jesus, and for the word of God, and which had not worshipped the beast, neither his image, neither had received his mark upon their foreheads, or in their hands; and *they lived and reigned with Christ a thousand years.*
>
> But the rest of the dead lived not again until the thousand years were finished. *This is the first resurrection.*
>
> Blessed and holy is he that hath part in the first resurrection: on such the second death hath no power, but *they shall be priests of God and of Christ, and shall reign with him a thousand years.*[5]

The revealed words of the Savior contain His promise that

> In mine own due time will I come upon the time *in judgment, and my people shall be redeemed and shall reign with me on earth.*
>
> For the great Millennium, of which I have spoken by the mouth of my servants, shall come.[6]

---

[4]See D&C 29:9-11; 101:24-25; JS 2:37; Is. 24:5-6, etc.

[5]Rev. 20:4-6. Ruling and reigning on thrones is characteristic of man's final state, following his day of judgment. See D&C 121:29, 32; 132:19, 49.

[6]D&C 43:29-30. The Lord's people who will be judged and redeemed during the millennium will be resurrected beings (see D&C 88:16) who will have been perfected (see D&C 45:46), which cannot happen without the forgiveness and mediating functions of Christ which will be given to man in the judgment process.

Again, the Master, during the last days of His mortal life, described functions concerning His coming in glory at the beginning of the millennium which indicate that that will be the time of judgment for the righteous who come forth in the first resurrection:

> *When the Son of man shall come in his glory, and all the holy angels with him, then shall he sit upon the throne of his glory:*
>
> And before him shall be gathered all nations: and he shall separate them one from another, as a shepherd divideth his sheep from the goats:
>
> And he shall set the sheep on his right hand, but the goats on the left.
>
> *Then shall the King say unto them on his right hand, Come, ye blessed of my Father, inherit the kingdom prepared for you from the foundation of the world.*[7]

The apostle Paul wrote that the Lord

> May *stablish your hearts unblameable* in holiness before God, even our Father, *at the coming of our Lord Jesus Christ with all his saints.*[8]

And finally, the Lord has revealed that those who are to assist Him in the judging of the righteous house of Israel will come at His coming in glory to judge those who have kept the commandments "and none else":

> It hath gone forth in a firm decree, by the will of the Father, that *mine apostles, the Twelve which were with me in my ministry at Jerusalem, shall stand at my right hand at the day of my coming* in a pillar of fire, being clothed with robes of righteousness, with crowns upon their heads, in glory even as I am, *to judge the whole house of Israel, even as many as have loved me and kept my commandments, and none else.*
>
> For a trump shall sound both long and loud, even as upon Mount Sinai, and all the earth shall quake, and *they shall come forth —yea, even the dead which died in me, to receive a crown of righteousness, and to be clothed upon, even as I am,* to be with me, that we may be one.[9]

Other passages show that the judgment process will either continue or be resumed at the end of the millennium,

---

[7]Mt. 25:31-34. Later in the chapter it will be seen that the final judgment is, in part, the process of assigning men to their abodes in the kingdom of heaven.

[8]1 Thess. 3:13. To become blameless can only be accomplished by partaking of the forgiveness and atonement of Christ, which is again a characteristic of the judgment process when, as Christ says, "I will own them, and *they shall be mine in that day when I shall come to make up my jewels.*" (D&C 101:3)

[9]D&C 29:12-13.

following the second resurrection. The judgment at this time will be concerned with the wicked who come forth in the resurrection of the unjust. The Lord revealed that "the residue of the wicked have I kept in chains of darkness *until the judgment of the great day, which shall come at the end of the earth.*"[10] And while revealing the nature of the trumps which will govern the events of the last days the Lord revealed that

> Another trump shall sound, which is the third trump; and then come *the spirits of men who are to be judged, and are found under condemnation;*
>
> And these are the rest of the dead; and they live not again until the thousand years are ended, neither again, *until the end of the earth.*[11]

Thus it is seen that the day of judgment will encompass and even extend beyond the entire millennial era. Man may expect his personal day of final judgment to follow closely after his resurrection day. Those who come forth in the first resurrection will be judged early in the millennium, while those who are held back till the second resurrection will face their Maker at the end of the earth's mortal existence. Man determines his day of judgment while in mortality, just as he chooses his spirit world kingdom and his degree of resurrected glory. As the Lord revealed,

> Behold, mine eyes see and know all their works, and I have in reserve *a swift judgment in the season thereof,* for them all;
>
> *For there is a time appointed for every man, according as his works shall be.*[12]

All to Be Judged

The great final judgment will be universal; no man will escape it. As Paul wrote to the Corinthian saints,

> *We must all appear before the judgment seat of Christ;* that every one may receive the things done in his body, according to that he hath done, whether it be good or bad.[13]

To the Saints in Rome he wrote,

---

[10]D&C 38:5.
[11]D&C 88:100-101.
[12]D&C 121:24-25.
[13]2 Cor. 5:10.

> *We shall all stand before the judgment seat of Christ.*
>
> For it is written, As I live, saith the Lord, every knee shall bow to me, and *every tongue shall confess to God.*[14]

Mormon wrote to his readers in the last days, with the witness that

> Ye must all stand before the judgment seat of Christ, yea, *every soul who belongs to the whole human family of Adam;* and ye must stand to be judged of your works, whether they be good or evil.[15]

Not only will every man stand judgment, but every hidden act will be examined in the great judgment day. "For God shall bring every work into judgment, with every secret thing, whether it be good, or whether it be evil."[16]

Christ the Judge

The process of judgment is centered in Jesus Christ. Of this the psalmist wrote,

> Our God shall come, and shall not keep silence: a fire shall devour before him, and it shall be very tempestuous round about him.
>
> *He shall call to the heavens from above, and to the earth, that he may judge his people.*
>
> Gather my saints together unto me; those that have made a covenant with me by sacrifice.
>
> And the heavens shall declare his righteousness: *for God is judge himself.*[17]

Though it will be seen that much of the responsibility for judgment will be delegated, this passage seems to indicate that the Savior will bless the righteous with the privilege of meeting Him personally as they receive their eternal rewards. That Jesus is the God of whom the passage speaks is made clear by His statement to a group of critical Jews:

> *The Father judgeth no man, but hath committed all judgment unto the Son:*
>
> That all men should honour the Son, even as they honour the Father.[18]

---

[14]Ro. 14:10-11.
[15]Mor. 3:20.
[16]Eccl. 12:14.
[17]Ps. 50:3-6.
[18]Jn. 5:22-23.

The responsibility for judging the earth is an actual transfer of authority from God the Father to Jesus Christ,

> For as the Father hath life in himself; so hath he given to the Son to have life in himself;
>
> *And hath given him authority to execute judgment* also, because he is the Son of man.[19]

For this reason Paul wrote that Jesus "commanded us to preach unto the people, and to testify that *it is he which was ordained of God to be the Judge* of quick and dead."[20]

Others to Serve as Judges under Christ

On one occasion apostle Orson Pratt, while considering the manner of judgment, commented,

> *It seems to me that unless there were a great number engaged in judging the dead, it would require a very long period of time;* for, for one being to personally investigate all the idle thoughts and words of the children of men from the days of Adam down until that time, it would require a great many millions of years, and therefore *I come to another conclusion, namely, that God has his agents, and that through those agents the dead will be judged.*[21]

His comment was not merely his own logic, for the Lord has revealed that others are to help Him in the judgment process. To His apostles in Palestine He said,

> I appoint unto you a kingdom, as my Father hath appointed unto me;
>
> That ye may eat and drink at my table in my kingdom, and *sit on thrones judging the twelve tribes of Israel.*[22]

According to the prophet Mormon, while the Twelve from Jerusalem are to judge the entire House of Israel, the Twelve disciples Jesus chose in America will judge the Nephites and Lamanites after being judged by the Jerusalem Twelve:

> I write unto all the ends of the earth; yea, unto you, twelve tribes of Israel, *who shall be judged according to your works by the twelve whom Jesus chose to be his disciples in the land of Jerusalem.*
>
> And I write also unto the *remnant of this people, who shall also be judged by the twelve whom Jesus chose in this land;* and they shall be

---

[19]Jn. 5:26-27.

[20]Acts 10:42.

[21]JD 17:182. Oct. 11, 1874.

[22]Lk. 22:29-30. See also D&C 29:12.

judged by the other twelve whom Jesus chose in the land of Jerusalem.[23]

It would seem that in the judgment, as in mortal life, the spirit world, and the resurrection, responsibility will be delegated by dispensations and by generations within the dispensations. Again, Joseph Smith, as head of the dispensation of the fulness of times, will be responsible for the judging of all who have lived during the last days. As Parley P. Pratt taught,

> I bear this testimony this day, that Joseph Smith was and is a Prophet, Seer, and Revelator—*an Apostle holding the keys of this last dispensation and of the kingdom of God, under Peter, James, and John.* And not only that he was a Prophet and Apostle of Jesus Christ, and lived and died one, but that he now lives in the spirit world, and holds those same keys to usward and to this whole generation. Also that he will hold those keys to all eternity; and no power in heaven or on the earth will ever take them from him; for he will continue holding those keys through all eternity, and will stand—yes, again in the flesh upon this earth, as the head of the Latter-day Saints under Jesus Christ, and under Peter, James, and John. *He will hold the keys to judge the generation to whom he was sent, and will judge my brethren that preside over me; and will judge me, together with the Apostles ordained by the word of the Lord through him and under his administration.*
>
> *When this is done, those Apostles will judge this generation and the Latter-day Saints;* and they will judge them with that judgment which Jesus Christ will give unto them; and they will have the same spirit and the same mind as Jesus Christ, and their judgment will be his judgment, for they will be one. . . .
>
> *I expect, by the power of the resurrection and the quickening power of the celestial glory, that my memory will be perfected, and that I will be able to remember all the acts, duties, and doings of my own life.* I will also remember, most correctly and perfectly, every act of benevolence that has ever been done to me in the name of the Lord and because of my calling; and I will remember, most perfectly, every neglect and slighting by those to whom I have been sent.
>
> I will be able to say to a just person, 'Well done, good and faithful servant; for you did do good so-and-so to me or my brethren: therefore, enter into the joy of your Lord.' I will also be able to say to others, 'Depart from me; for I was an-hungered, and ye did not feed me; I was naked, and ye clothed me not; I was sick, or in prison, or in a strait, and ye helped me not; I had a mission to perform, and ye took no interest in it.'

[23]Mor. 3:18-19.

> *So it will be with brother Joseph, or brother Brigham, or any of the Apostles or Elders that hold a portion of the keys of the Priesthood to this generation;* if they hold them faithfully. They will be able to remember and understand all their own doings and all the acts of this generation to whom they are sent; and they will judge them in the name of Jesus Christ. *We will be judged by brother Joseph; and he will be judged by Peter, James, and John, and their associates. Brother Brigham, who now presides over us, will hold the keys under brother Joseph; and he and his brethren, who hold the keys with him, or under his direction, will judge the people;* for they will hold those keys to all eternity, worlds without end. By those keys they will have to judge this generation; and Peter, James, and John, will hold the keys to preside over, and judge, and direct brother Joseph to all eternity; and Jesus Christ will hold the keys over them and over us, under his Father, to whom be all the glory. *This is my testimony; and in obedience to these keys, if God will open my way and spare my life, I will continue to act.*[24]

It appears that to judge is a portion of the heritage of many righteous members of Christ's Church and not just a task required of the apostles. Christ has revealed that

> I, the Lord, have made my church in these last days like unto a judge sitting on a hill, or in a high place, *to judge the nations.*
>
> For it shall come to pass that the *inhabitants of Zion shall judge all things pertaining to Zion.*[25]

The prophet Daniel also looked into the last days and saw that "judgment was given to the saints of the most High; and the time came that the saints possessed the kingdom."[26] And Paul wrote to the Corinthian saints,

> Do ye not know that the *saints shall judge the world?* . . .
>
> Know ye not that *we shall judge angels?* how much more things that pertain to this life?[27]

Thus it is seen that to act as judge is a portion of the blessing and responsibility of those who are to become "priests and kings"[28] in the celestial kingdom. While part of this responsibility may be to participate in the final judgment process, the calling to act as a judge will also involve continuous responsibility as a presiding and governing authority in the

---

[24]JD 5:195-196. Sept. 7, 1856.
[25]D&C 64:37-38.
[26]Dan. 7:22.
[27]1 Cor. 6:2-3.
[28]D&C 76:56.

same sense as did the biblical judges[29] and the judges who governed in the Book of Mormon times[30] and like the Bishops of today. This manner of judging was defined in a revelation from the Lord:

> Whoso standeth in this mission is appointed to be a judge in Israel, like as it was in ancient days, *to divide the lands of the heritage of God unto his children;*
>
> And to *judge his people by the testimony of the just, and by the assistance of his counselors,* according to the laws of the kingdom which are given by the prophets of God.
>
> For verily I say unto you, my law shall be kept on this land.
>
> *Let no man think he is ruler; but let God rule him that judgeth, according to the counsel of his own will,* or, in other words, him that counseleth or sitteth upon the judgment seat.[31]

Purposes of Final Judgment

The final judgment process will accomplish at least eight purposes or objectives which are necessary in the great plan of salvation God has prepared. Each phase of the process is vital to man in his future relationship with God. These objectives are:

1. *Cause man to see that his own actions determined his fate.* "The Lord knoweth all things from the beginning."[32] "The Lord knoweth all things which are to come"[33] and "knoweth all the times which are appointed unto man."[34] He "needed not that any should testify of man: for he knew what was in man."[35] He knows man's abilities, his strengths and weaknesses, and has the divine foreknowledge to know man's ultimate fate before the individual ever comes into mortality. The judgment is not designed for God's benefit, for He already knows its outcome. On the contrary, the judgment is intended to benefit the man under examination.

Man will not be able to claim that God's foreknowledge controlled his actions and predestined him to his fate. Though

[29]Such as Deborah, Gideon, Jephthah, Samson, etc. See the book of Judges.

[30]Such as Alma, Nephihah, Pahoram, Helaman, Nephi, etc. See the books of Alma and Helaman.

[31]D&C 58:17-20.

[32]1 Ne. 9:6.

[33]W. of Morm. 7.

[34]Al. 40:10.

[35]Jn. 2:25.

God may have tested him and challenged him, He has left him his agency to "choose liberty and eternal life . . . or to choose captivity and death,"[36] and He has proclaimed that

> Every man may act in doctrine and principle pertaining to futurity, according to the moral agency which I have given unto him, that every man may be accountable for his own sins in the day of judgment.[37]

At his day of judgment no man will be able to assert that he was denied his agency. He will be compelled to admit that he chose the mortal actions which will govern his eternal fate.

2. *Cause man to review his mortal life.* As man stands before the judgment bar of God he will review his entire mortal probation and will have a perfect knowledge of all his deeds, both good and evil. The process by which this will be accomplished may be the same as that experienced by President George Albert Smith when he was challenged by his grandfather in the spirit world. As he recorded it,

> *Everything I had ever done passed before me as though it were a flying picture on a screen*—everything I had done. Quickly this vivid retrospect came down to the very time I was standing there. My whole life had passed before me.[38]

It would seem that the recollection of his past which President Smith described was the same experience as was prophesied by the prophet Jacob:

> We shall have *a perfect knowledge of all our guilt, and our uncleanness, and our nakedness;* and the righteous shall have *a perfect knowledge of their enjoyment, and their righteousness,* being clothed with purity, yea, even with the robe of righteousness.
>
> And it shall come to pass that when all men shall have passed from this first death unto life, insomuch as they have become immortal, *they must appear before the judgment seat of the Holy One of Israel; and then cometh the judgment, and then must they be judged according to the holy judgment of God.*[39]

As will be seen later in the chapter, the evidence from various records and books, as well as confrontation by witnesses in some cases, will be included in this life review process.

---

[36]2 Ne. 2:27.
[37]D&C 101:78.
[38]George Albert Smith, *Sharing the Gospel With Others, op. cit.,* p. 112.
[39]2 Ne. 9:14-15.

Thus the final judgment will cause all men to review all the deeds of their lives so that they will be able to fully understand the reason for the reward they earn.

3. *Cause man to acknowledge the justice of God's judgment.* A third responsibility man must fulfill at the final judgment is to acknowledge that the Lord's determination of justice upon him is just and true. As Alma taught,

> We must come forth and stand before him in his glory, and in his power, and in his might, majesty, and dominion, and *acknowledge to our everlasting shame that all his judgments are just; that he is just in all his works, and that he is merciful* unto the children of men, and that he has all power to save every man that believeth on his name and bringeth forth fruit meet for repentance.[40]

Every man may be compelled to exclaim the message that John the Revelator heard from the altar of God: "Even so, Lord God Almighty, true and righteous are thy judgments."[41]

4. *Cause man to acknowledge that Jesus is the Christ.* Although many will come before Christ at judgment day who have refused to accept the gospel and order their lives according to His program, every man will be compelled to acknowledge His divinity and that He is their supreme king and lawgiver. The voice of the Lord has proclaimed that "These all shall bow the knee, and every tongue shall confess to him who sits upon the throne forever and ever."[42] The prophet Alma taught that

> *Every knee shall bow, and every tongue confess before him.* Yea, even at the last day, when *all men shall stand to be judged of him, then shall they confess that he is God;* then shall they confess, who live without God in the world, that the judgment of an everlasting punishment is just upon them; and they shall quake, and tremble, and shrink beneath the glance of his all-searching eye.[43]

According to the timetable of last days events set forth in Doctrine and Covenants section 88, the command to bow before God will be sounded by angelic trump. It will be heard and responded to by all men, whether they be in heaven, on earth, or whether their bodies are still in the grave:

---

[40]Al. 12:15.
[41]Rev. 16:7. See also Rev. 19:2; Ro. 2:2; D&C 127:3.
[42]D&C 76:110.
[43]Mos. 27:31.

> And another trump shall sound, which is the fifth trump, which is the fifth angel who committeth the everlasting gospel—flying through the midst of heaven, unto all nations, kindreds, tongues, and people;
>
> And this shall be the sound of his trump, saying to all people, both in heaven and in earth, and that are under the earth—*for every ear shall hear it, and every knee shall bow, and every tongue shall confess, while they hear the sound of the trump,* saying: Fear God, and give glory to him who sitteth upon the throne, forever and ever; for the hour of his judgment is come.[44]

The four purposes of the judgment listed above are all to be fulfilled by the person under examination and judgment. The following four purposes will be accomplished by the Lord or His representatives.

5. *Grant forgiveness for sins.* God has revealed that "no unclean thing can enter into his kingdom"[45] and that "ye cannot be saved in your sins."[46] However, "All have sinned, and come short of the glory of God."[47] Unless there was a way in which man could repent and be forgiven of his sins, no man would be able to enter into the celestial kingdom. Through His atonement, Christ is able either to allow man to suffer for his sins or to excuse him from suffering through the process of forgiveness. This decision must be made by the Lord or His servants based on a person's attitude, works, degree of repentance and willingness to confess his sins at the day of judgment. As the apostle John testified,

> The blood of Jesus Christ . . . cleanseth us from all sin.
>
> If we say that we have no sin, we deceive ourselves, and the truth is not in us.
>
> *If we confess our sins, he is faithful and just to forgive us our sins, and to cleanse us from all unrighteousness.*[48]

This forgiveness and release from responsibility for sins because of repentance is that to which Amulek referred when he said that "the righteous shall sit down in his kingdom, to go

---

[44]D&C 88:103-104. The angel who sounds the trump will apparently be Moroni, who committed to Joseph Smith the gospel found in the Book of Mormon. (See Rev. 14:6-7; JS 2:34; D&C 20:6-9; 27:5.)

[45]3 Ne. 27:19.

[46]Al. 11:37. See also Al. 7:21; Mos. 2:37.

[47]Ro. 3:23. See Ro. 3:10-12.

[48]1 Jn. 1:7-9.

no more out; but *their garments should be made white through the blood of the Lamb.*"[49]

In the great plan of salvation, the time when man is to receive a remission of sins is in mortality, through baptism.[50] Those who do so are commanded to strive to "always retain a remission of your sins."[51] If they do this they will find the Lord's promise fulfilled at judgment day that "their sins and iniquities will I remember no more."[52] Others, however, may not have had their sins remitted in mortality but have bettered their situation before God in the spirit world and will be granted forgiveness at the time of final judgment.

6. *Make intercession to God in behalf of man.* Christ is "the mediator of the new testament."[53] In His responsibility as an intermediary between man and God the Father, "he maketh intercession for the saints according to the will of God."[54] Christ is managing the affairs of earth in behalf of His Father and is preparing to "deliver up the kingdom, and present it unto the Father, spotless."[55] The Father has committed all judgment into the hands of Christ and will accept His witness concerning the worthiness of those who come into the kingdom. Man receives Christ's witness of approval before the Father by striving to keep the Lord's commandments and seeking to be a recipient of His atoning sacrifice. As John wrote,

> If any man sin, we have an advocate with the Father, Jesus Christ the righteous:
>
> And he is the propitiation for our sins: and not for ours only, but also for the sins of the whole world.
>
> And hereby we do know that we know him, if we keep his commandments.[56]

A portion of the judgment process, then, is that Christ will advocate man's cause before the Father and certify of the

[49]Al. 34:36.
[50]Mk. 1:4; Lk. 3:3; Acts 2:38.
[51]Mos. 4:12.
[52]Heb. 10:17. See also Ezek. 18:22; 33:16.
[53]Heb. 9:15.
[54]Ro. 8:27. See also 8:34.
[55]D&C 76:107.
[56]1 Jn. 2:1-3.

correctness of the judgment, witnessing that all men have merited the reward they received.

7. *Restore man to good or evil.* A seventh function of the judgment is to restore men to a reward or life which is compatible to their mortal works and desires. Alma explained this principal by saying,

> *The plan of restoration is requisite with the justice of God; for it is requisite that all things should be restored to their proper order.* Behold, it is requisite and just, according to the power and resurrection of Christ, that the soul of man should be restored to its body, and that every part of the body should be restored to itself.
>
> And it is requisite with the justice of God *that men should be judged according to their works; and if their works were good in this life, and the desires of their hearts were good, that they should also, at the last day, be restored unto that which is good.*
>
> *And if their works are evil they shall be restored unto them for evil.* Therefore, all things shall be restored to their proper order, every thing to its natural frame—mortality raised to immortality, corruption to incorruption—raised to endless happiness to inherit the kingdom of God, or to endless misery to inherit the kingdom of the devil, the one on one hand, the other on the other—
>
> *The one raised to happiness according to his desires of happiness, or good according to his desires of good; and the other to evil according to his desires of evil;* for as he has desired to do evil all the day long even so shall he have his reward of evil when the night cometh.
>
> And so it is on the other hand. *If he hath repented of his sins, and desired righteousness until the end of his days, even so he shall be rewarded unto righteousness.*[57]

Alma continued by explaining that in the judgment a man will be restored to the same level of life that characterized his life in mortality:

> *Is the meaning of the word restoration to take a thing of a natural state and place it in an unnatural state, or to place it in a state opposite to its nature?*
>
> O, my son, *this is not the case; but the meaning of the word restoration is to bring back again evil for evil,* or carnal for carnal, or devilish for devilish—*good for that which is good;* righteous for that which is righteous; just for that which is just; merciful for that which is merciful.
>
> Therefore, my son, see that you are merciful unto your brethren; deal justly, judge righteously, and do good continually; and if ye do all these things then shall ye receive your reward; yea, ye shall have mercy restored unto you again; ye shall have justice restored

[57] Al. 41:2-6.

unto you again; ye shall have a righteous judgment restored unto you again; and ye shall have good rewarded unto you again.

For that which ye do send out shall return unto you again, and be restored; therefore, the word restoration more fully condemneth the sinner, and justifieth him not at all.[58]

Thus man's final reward is regarded as being a continuation of his mortal course, and the judgment serves to restore the conditions he truly sought and created in mortality.

8. *Assign man to the place of his final inheritance.* The final judgment will serve as the time when man will be assigned to his personal inheritance in one of the many mansions of the Father.[59] As the Savior explained in the parable of the talents, there must come a time when the Lord will say to the faithful,

> Well done, good and faithful servant; thou hast been faithful over a few things, I will make thee ruler over many things: enter thou into the joy of thy lord.[60]

And to the wicked He will command, "Depart from me, ye that work iniquity."[61]

It should be noted that man will already be resurrected at the day of judgment and will be aware of which kingdom of glory he is to inherit. Yet it would appear that judgment day will be the time of further summation and delineation of man's status and reward. Man's celestial inheritance, however, cannot be occupied until the earth is reformed as a celestial sphere following Christ's reign, the second resurrection, and the completion of the judgment.

Christ's Law the Norm for Judgment

Before every man comes to the judgment bar of God he will have had the opportunity, either on earth or in the spirit world, to hear the law of Jesus Christ. As President Joseph Fielding Smith expressed this principle:

In the justice of the Father, he is going to give to every man the priv-

[58]Al. 41:12-15.
[59]Jn. 14:2.
[60]Mt. 25:23.
[61]Mt. 7:23.

> *ilege of hearing the gospel. Not one soul shall be overlooked or forgotten.* This being true, what about the countless thousands who have died and never heard of Christ, never had an opportunity of repentance and remission of their sins, never met an elder of the Church holding the authority? Some of our good Christian neighbors will tell you they are lost forever, that they cannot believe in the grave, for there is no hope beyond.
>
> Would that be fair? Would it be just? No! *The Lord is going to give to every man the opportunity to hear and to receive eternal life, or a place in his kingdom.* We are very fortunate because we have had that privilege here and have passed from death unto life.
>
> The Lord has so arranged his plan of redemption that *all who have died without this opportunity shall be given it in the spirit world.* There the elders of the Church who have died are proclaiming the gospel to the dead. . . . The Lord has made it known that his mercy extends to the uttermost bounds and that *every soul is entitled to hear the gospel plan, either in this life or in the spirit world. All who hear and believe, repenting and receiving the gospel in its fulness, whether living or dead, are heirs of salvation in the celestial kingdom of God.*[62]

The law and commandments which are embodied in the teachings of Christ will provide the standard of conduct by which all men will be judged. According to the apostle, Paul, judgment day is "the day when God shall judge the secrets of men by Jesus Christ *according to my gospel.*"[63] He taught that "by the law is the knowledge of sin"[64] and that "as many as have sinned in the law shall be judged by the law."[65]

King Benjamin knew that the commandments of Christ will stand as the judgment norm at the last day. He taught his people,

> I have spoken the words which the Lord God hath commanded me. And thus saith the Lord: *They shall stand as a bright testimony against this people, at the judgment day; whereof they shall be judged, every man according to his works,* whether they be good, or whether they be evil.[66]

During His mortal ministry the Christ taught concerning those who chose not to believe in His words, saying that He

[62]Bruce R. McConkie, *Doctrines of Salvation, op cit.,* Vol. II, pp. 132, 133. See also D&C 1:2, 4, 11; 42:58; 43:20-28; 68:8; 84:75; 88:104; 90:8-11; 133:9-10.

[63]Ro. 2:16.

[64]Ro. 3:20.

[65]Ro. 2:12.

[66]Mos. 3:23-24.

would not personally judge such an individual, but that His word would still serve as the judgment norm:

> If any man hear my words, and believe not, *I judge him not:* for I came not to judge the world, but to save the world.
>
> He that rejecteth me, and receiveth not my words, hath one that judgeth him: *the word that I have spoken, the same shall judge him in the last day.*[67]

In the last days the Master has again revealed that His commandments as they are found in the scriptures will be the judgment criteria:

> These words are given unto you, and they are pure before me; wherefore, beware how you hold them, for *they are to be answered upon your souls in the day of judgment.*[68]

Not only will the scriptures serve as the basis for judgment, but there is an obligation for study and self-preparation which accompanies the word of God. Latter-day Saints, who enjoy greater opportunity for knowledge of the word of God than does the world at large, are also under greater obligation to live according to God's revealed word. As Jesus taught,

> *That servant, which knew his lord's will, and prepared not himself, neither did according to his will, shall be beaten with many stripes.*
>
> But he that knew not, and did commit things worthy of stripes, shall be beaten with few stripes. *For unto whomsoever much is given, of him shall be much required.*[69]

He saw fit to reveal the same principle with even greater clarity in the latter days:

> *Of him unto whom much is given much is required; and he who sins against the greater light shall receive the greater condemnation.*
>
> Ye call upon my name for revelations, and I give them unto you; and *inasmuch as ye keep not my sayings, which I give unto you, ye become transgressors;* and justice and judgment are the penalty which is affixed unto my law.[70]

Man to Judge Himself

Man himself will bear the testimony at the final judgment

---

[67]Jn. 12:47-48.
[68]D&C 41:12.
[69]Lk. 12:47-48.
[70]D&C 82:3-4.

day which will either exalt or condemn himself. As Paul taught, "Every one of us shall *give account of himself* to God."[71] The message of the Master to the Pharisees was that

> Every idle word that men shall speak, *they shall give account thereof* in the day of judgment.
>
> *For by thy words thou shalt be justified, and by thy words thou shalt be condemned.*[72]

President John Taylor explained the justice of this method of judgment as he said,

> Man sleeps for a time in the grave, and by-and-by he rises again from the dead and goes to judgment; and then the secret thoughts of all men are revealed before Him with whom we have to do; *we cannot hide them; it would be in vain for a man to say then: I did not do so-and-so; the command would be: Unravel and read the record which he has made of himself, and let it testify in relation to these things, and all could gaze upon it.* If a man has acted fraudulently against his neighbor—has committed murder, or adultery, or anything else, and wants to cover it up, that record will stare him in the face. *He tells the story himself, and bears witness against himself.* It is written that Jesus will judge not after the sight of the eye, or after the hearing of the ear, but with righteousness shall He judge the poor, and reprove with equity the meek of the earth. It is not because somebody has seen things, or heard anything by which a man will be judged and condemned, but *it is because that record that is written by the man himself in the tablets of his own mind—that record that cannot lie—will in that day be unfolded before God and angels, and those who shall sit as judges.*[73]

It is because of the self-judgment which man will render that Jesus said, "I can of mine own self do nothing: *as I hear, I judge:* and my judgment is just."[74] This self-judgment will deal especially with the stewardships man has been called to fill during mortality. The Lord revealed, for example, the following concerning the stewardship of the leaders of the Church:

> I, the Lord, have appointed them, and ordained them to be stewards over the revelations and commandments which I have given unto them, and which I shall hereafter give unto them;
>
> And *an account of this stewardship will I require of them in the day of judgment.*[75]

---

[71]Ro. 14:12.
[72]Mt. 12:36-37.
[73]JD 11:78-79. Feb. 5, 1865.
[74]Jn. 5:30.
[75]D&C 70:3-4.

How equitable this method of judgment is! For every man will testify concerning his deeds knowing the degree of understanding of good and evil which he had when the deeds were committed. Each man will know if his mortal misdeeds were intentional or accidental—deliberate sin or happenstance, and will testify accordingly. He will judge himself according to the knowledge or judgment he had and used during mortality. For this reason Paul warned,

> Therefore thou art inexcusable, O man, whosoever thou art that judgest: for *wherein thou judgest another, thou condemnest thyself; for thou that judgest doest the same things.*
>
> But we are sure that the judgment of God is according to truth against them which commit such things.
>
> And thinkest thou this, O man, that judgest them which do such things, and doest the same, that thou shalt escape the judgment of God?[76]

Man's judgment will cover every aspect of his life: his thoughts, words, actions and works, his sins of both commission and omission. As Alma warned,

> *Our words will condemn us, yea, all our works will condemn us; we shall not be found spotless; and our thoughts will also condemn us;* and in this awful state we shall not dare to look up to our God; and we would fain be glad if we could command the rocks and the mountains to fall upon us to hide us from his presence.[77]

Witnesses and Books Also Used in Judgment

It appears that in addition to the personal account each man must give in the day of judgment, men will also be confronted by witnesses and the history kept in the earthly and heavenly records. Moroni, for instance, warned the readers of the Book of Mormon that he would confront them at the judgment bar of God:

> I exhort you to remember these things; for the time speedily cometh that ye shall know that I lie not, *for ye shall see me at the bar of God; and the Lord God will say unto you: Did I not declare my words unto you, which were written by this man,* like as one crying from the dead, yea, even as one speaking out of the dust?[78]

---

[76]Ro. 2:1-3. See also Mt. 7:1-5.

[77]Al. 12:14. See Al. 41:3-6.

[78]Moro. 10:27. Joseph Smith left the same type of warning, saying that "When I am called by the trump of the arch-angel and weighed in the balance, *you will all know me then.*" (HC 6:317)

Indeed, angels will act as witnesses, proclaiming the thoughts, intents, and secret acts of all men at the day of judgment:

> Then shall the first angel again sound his trump in the ears of all living, and *reveal the secret acts of men, and the mighty works of God* in the first thousand years.
>
> And then shall the second angel sound his trump, and *reveal the secret acts of men, and the thoughts and intents of their hearts, and the mighty works of God* in the second thousand years—
>
> And so on, until the seventh angel shall sound his trump.[79]

The testimony of heavenly and earthly records will also be considered at that great and final judgment day. John the Revelator saw that *"the dead were judged out of those things which were written in the books, according to their works."*[80] Seven types of books are mentioned in the scriptures as playing a role in the judgment process. They are:

1. *The scriptures*—as seen above, they contain the criteria for judgment. Jesus revealed that

> I command all men, both in the east and in the west, and in the north, and in the south, and in the islands of the sea, that *they shall write the words which I speak unto them; for out of the books which shall be written I will judge the world,* every man according to their works, according to that which is written.[81]

2. *Church minutes and statistical records*—These records will show membership in the Church, the ordinances fulfilled by each member, their degree of activity and attendance, their financial contributions, and the Church assignments and callings they have fulfilled. Those records are to be maintained locally by

> A recorder appointed in each ward of the city, who is well qualified for taking accurate minutes; and let him be very particular and precise in taking the whole proceedings, certifying in his record that he saw with his eyes, and heard with his ears, giving the date and names, and so forth, and the history of the whole transaction.[82]

"A regular list of all the names of the whole church"[83] is to

---

[79]D&C 88:108-110.
[80]Rev. 20:12.
[81]2 Ne. 29:11.
[82]D&C 128:3.
[83]D&C 20:82.

be kept. Those who leave the Church or are excommunicated are to have their names "blotted out of the general church record."[84]

3. *Book of the Law of God*—In the general history and records of the Church there are indications of the valor or lack of diligence of various Church members, together with comment as to their degree of consecration, their faith, their works, their genealogies, etc. These materials are also to be considered in the great judgment day. A letter from Joseph Smith to W. W. Phelps in 1832, which later was included in the Doctrine and Covenants, sets forth the pattern for this record:

> It is the duty of the Lord's clerk, whom he has appointed, to *keep a history, and a general church record of all things that transpire in Zion, and of all those who consecrate properties,* and receive inheritances legally from the bishop;
>
> *And also their manner of life, their faith, and works, and also of the apostates who apostatize after receiving their inheritances.*
>
> It is contrary to the will and commandment of God that those who receive not their inheritance by consecration, agreeable to his law, which he has given, that he may tithe his people, to prepare them against the day of vengeance and burning, *should have their names enrolled with the people of God.*
>
> *Neither is their genealogy to be kept, or to be had where it may be found* on any of the records or history of the church.
>
> Their names shall not be found, neither the names of the fathers, nor the names of the children written in the *book of the law of God,* saith the Lord of Hosts.[85]

Joseph Smith, on several occasions, wrote that he had recorded the names and deeds of faithful Saints in this book.[86] Similar accounts were also kept in other dispensations. The Savior, for instance, commanded the Nephite twelve to

> *Write the works of this people,* which shall be, even as hath been written, of that which hath been.
>
> For behold, *out of the books which have been written, and which shall be written, shall this people be judged,* for by them shall their works be known unto men.[87]

4. *Miscellaneous records and histories*—Various secular rec-

[84]D&C 20:83. See also Ps. 69:28.
[85]D&C 85:1-5.
[86]See HC 5:124-127; 4:518.
[87]3 Ne. 27:24-25.

ords such as court records, school records, histories, personal journals, etc., will also contain commentary on man's deeds during mortality and if necessary and pertinent, may be scrutinized during judgment as all the evidence is considered. Such records may be included in the books seen in vision by John the Revelator, when he saw the judgment day and recorded that "The books were opened . . . and the dead were judged out of those things which were written in the books, according to their works."[88]

5. *Books of Remembrance*—A true book of remembrance is a personal accounting of one's deeds and thoughts, preserved, as Malachi put it, "For them that feared the Lord, and that thought upon his name."[89] It would appear that all who truly seek the Lord and His kingdom are directed by inspiration to keep such a personal record. Moses recorded that from the earliest days of this earth, "A book of remembrance was kept, in the which was recorded, in the language of Adam, for *it was given unto as many as called upon God to write by the spirit of inspiration.*"[90] And Enoch said that "a book of remembrance we have written among us, *according to the pattern given us by the finger of God.*"[91]

Failure to have one's name and vital information recorded in a valid book of remembrance is a serious offense in the sight of the Lord, for He said,

> *All they who are not found written in the book of remembrance shall find none inheritance* in that day, but they shall be cut asunder, and their portion shall be appointed them among unbelievers, where are wailing and gnashing of teeth.[92]

6. *Records of family and family relationships*—Man must be able to properly establish his rightful place in the patriarchal order by having an acceptable record of his ancestors and descendants. This practice had its beginning with Adam, who "spake, as he was moved upon by the Holy Ghost, and *a genealogy was kept of the children of God.*"[93] Failure to have an ade-

[88]Rev. 20:12. See also D&C 128:6-7.
[89]Mal. 3:16. See also 3 Ne. 24:16.
[90]Moses 6:5.
[91]Moses 6:46.
[92]D&C 85:9.
[93]Moses 6:8.

quate genealogical record may have serious consequences, as it did with the unfortunate children of some of the priests in Ezra's day:

> These sought their register among those that were reckoned by genealogy, but they were not found: therefore were they, as polluted, put from the priesthood.[94]

Of this type of record, kept individually and compiled collectively by the Church, the prophet Joseph Smith proposed,

> Let us, therefore, as a church and a people, and as Latter-day Saints, offer unto the Lord an offering in righteousness: and *let us present in his holy temple, when it is finished, a book containing the records of our dead,* which shall be worthy of all acceptation.[95]

Each of the six types of records enumerated to this point are temporal records. They will be written by mortals on perishable materials which may eventually decay or return to dust. They will not be lost to God, however, for *"all things are written by the Father;* therefore out of the books which shall be written shall the world be judged."[96] As the prophet Joseph wrote, "As are the records on the earth in relation to your dead, which are truly made out, so also are the records in heaven."[97] But at another time he warned that "whatsoever you record on earth shall be recorded in heaven, and *whatsoever you do not record on earth shall not be recorded in heaven."*[98]

There is a seventh type of record which will influence man in the great day of final judgment. This record is not a mortal record, but is an important record maintained in heaven. It is

7. *The Lamb's Book of Life*—This is the most important of the judgment records and is the record which receives most frequent mention in the scriptures. It appears that this is "the book of the names of the sanctified, even them of the celestial world."[99] "These are they whose names are written in heaven,"[100] who have joined "the general assembly and church

[94]Ezra 2:62. See also D&C 85:11-12.
[95]D&C 128:24.
[96]3 Ne. 27:26.
[97]D&C 128:14.
[98]D&C 128:8.
[99]D&C 88:2.
[100]D&C 76:68. See also Lk. 10:20; D&C 128:6.

of the firstborn," [101] and who will enter into God's holy city.[102] They are they who have labored in the gospel[103] and have overcome all things, for the Savior revealed that

> *He that overcometh,* the same shall be clothed in white raiment; and *I will not blot out his name out of the book of life,* but I will confess his name before my Father, and before his angels.[104]

This heavenly record will aid in the selection of those who are to come forth in the first resurrection.[105] This book of life represents the binding force of the gospel ordinances,[106] for the Lord has revealed,

> Then shall it be written in the Lamb's book of Life, . . . it shall be done unto them in all things whatsoever my servant hath put upon them, in time, and through all eternity; and shall be of full force when they are out of the world.[107]

Joseph Smith taught that

> Until we have perfect love we are liable to fall and *when we have a testimony that our names are sealed in the Lamb's book of life we have perfect love* and then it is impossible for false Christs to deceive us.[108]

Those who worship falsely, however, will never be entered into the Lamb's book of life,[109] and the Lord has declared that "Whosoever hath sinned against me, him will I blot out of my book."[110]

Mercy Cannot Rob Justice

Since all men have succumbed to sin it is only through the mercy and atonement of Jesus Christ that they can be redeemed. He is able to make intercession to the Father for those who have believed in Him and thereby gain their admission to celestial glory. This cannot be done for the unrepentant and rebellious, however, for the law of opposition demands

---

[101]Heb. 12:23.

[102]Rev. 21:24-27.

[103]Phil. 4:3.

[104]Rev. 3:5.

[105]See Dan. 12:1-2.

[106]See D&C 128:8.

[107]D&C 132:19.

[108]Joseph Fielding Smith (comp.), *Teachings of the Prophet Joseph Smith* (Salt Lake City, Utah: The Deseret News Press, 1938), p. 9. (See also JD 6:297, Aug. 15, 1852.)

[109]Rev. 13:8; 17:8.

[110]Ex. 32:33.

both rewards and punishments. This principle was explained by the prophet Lehi:

> Wherefore, redemption cometh in and through the Holy Messiah; for he is full of grace and truth.
>
> Behold, he offereth himself a sacrifice for sin, to answer the ends of the law, unto all those who have a broken heart and a contrite spirit; and unto none else can the ends of the law be answered.
>
> Wherefore, how great the importance to make these things known unto the inhabitants of the earth, that they may know that there is *no flesh that can dwell in the presence of God, save it be through the merits, and mercy, and grace of the Holy Messiah,* who layeth down his life according to the flesh, and taketh it again by the power of the Spirit, that he may bring to pass the resurrection of the dead, being the first that should rise.
>
> Wherefore, he is the first-fruits unto God, inasmuch as *he shall make intercession for all the children of men; and they that believe in him shall be saved.*
>
> *And because of the intercession for all, all men come unto God; wherefore, they stand in the presence of him to be judged of him* according to the truth and holiness which is in him. Wherefore, the ends of the law which the Holy One hath given, unto the inflicting of the punishment which is affixed, which *punishment that is affixed is in opposition to that of the happiness which is affixed, to answer the ends of the atonement—*
>
> *For it must needs be, that there is an opposition in all things.* If not so, my first-born in the wilderness, righteousness could not be brought to pass, neither wickedness, neither holiness nor misery, neither good nor bad.[111]

According to King Benjamin, rebellion against God causes man to shrink from His presence and thereby forfeit his opportunity to partake of Christ's mercy:

> After ye have known and have been taught all these things, *if ye should transgress and go contrary to that which has been spoken, that ye do withdraw yourselves from the Spirit of the Lord,* that it may have no place in you to guide you in wisdom's paths that ye may be blessed, prospered, and preserved—
>
> I say unto you, that the man that doeth this, *the same cometh out in open rebellion against God;* therefore he listeth to obey the evil spirit, and *becometh an enemy to all righteousness; therefore, the Lord has no place in him,* for he dwelleth not in unholy temples.
>
> Therefore if that man repenteth not, and remaineth and dieth an enemy to God, *the demands of divine justice do awaken his immortal soul to a lively sense of his own guilt, which doth cause him to shrink from*

[111]2 Ne. 2:6-11.

> *the presence of the Lord*, and doth fill his breast with guilt, and pain, and anguish, which is like an unquenchable fire, whose flame ascendeth up forever and ever.
>
> And now I say unto you, that *mercy hath no claim on that man; therefore his final doom is to endure a never-ending torment.*[112]

The prophet Alma gave an even fuller explanation of the relationship of mercy to justice. He taught that Christ's atonement appeased the demands of justice so that Christ could extend mercy to those who repent, but that the demands of justice and punishment would claim all who were unrepentant:

> According to justice, the plan of redemption could not be brought about, only on conditions of repentance of men in this probationary state, yea, this preparatory state; for except it were for these conditions, *mercy could not take effect except it should destroy the work of justice. Now the work of justice could not be destroyed; if so, God would cease to be God.*
>
> And thus we see that *all mankind were fallen, and they were in the grasp of justice;* yea, the justice of God, which consigned them forever to be cut off from his presence.
>
> And now, the plan of mercy could not be brought about except an atonement should be made; *therefore God himself atoneth for the sins of the world, to bring about the plan of mercy, to appease the demands of justice, that God might be a perfect, just God, and a merciful God also.*
>
> Now, repentance could not come unto men except there were a punishment, which also was eternal as the life of the soul should be, affixed opposite to the plan of happiness, which was as eternal also as the life of the soul, . . .
>
> But there is a law given, and a punishment affixed, and a *repentance granted; which repentance mercy claimeth; otherwise, justice claimeth the creature and executeth the law, and the law inflicteth the punishment;* if not so, the works of justice would be destroyed, and God would cease to be God.
>
> But God ceaseth not to be God, and *mercy claimeth the penitent, and mercy cometh because of the atonement;* and the atonement bringeth to pass the resurrection of the dead; and the resurrection of the dead bringeth back men into the presence of God; and thus they are restored into his presence, to be judged according to their works, according to the law and justice.
>
> *For behold, justice exerciseth all his demands, and also mercy claimeth all which is her own; and thus, none but the truly penitent are saved.*
>
> *What, do ye suppose that mercy can rob justice? I say unto you, Nay; not one whit. If so, God would cease to be God.*

---

[112] Mos. 2:36-39.

And thus God bringeth about his great and eternal purposes, which were prepared from the foundation of the world.[113]

SUMMARY

1. The great day of final judgment will extend from the beginning of Christ's millennial reign for over a thousand years, past the second resurrection to the end of the earth in its temporal state. It is not known if it will be going on intermittently or continually during this time.

2. Each man's personal day of judgment will follow immediately after his resurrection. Thus those resurrected in the first resurrection at the beginning of the millennium will be judged early in that thousand-year period, while those resurrected in the second resurrection will not be judged until the millennial era is over.

3. The final judgment should not be confused with previous judgments upon mortals such as is expected when Christ comes in glory. The final judgment represents the last time man will stand before the bar of God for evaluation purposes in connection with this earth in its mortal state.

4. Every man is to face final judgment.

5. The Father has committed all judgment unto His Son, Jesus Christ. Others, however, will serve as judges under the Savior's direction. It appears that the judging process will be organized by dispensations and by generations within each dispensation. Joseph Smith will preside over the judging process for the current dispensation.

6. The twelve apostles from Palestine will judge the whole house of Israel. The Nephite Twelve will be judged by them and then will judge the Nephites and Lamanites. Judgment responsibilities will be given to many of the Saints.

7. The final judgment will fulfill at least eight purposes. The first four will be performed by the person under judgment. The remainder are to be performed by Christ or His representatives:

   A. Man is to see that his own actions determined his fate,
   B. Man is to review his mortal life,
   C. Man is to acknowledge the justice of God's judgment,
   D. Man is to acknowledge that Jesus is the Christ,
   E. Christ is to grant forgiveness for sins,
   F. Christ is to make intercession to God in behalf of man,
   G. Christ is to restore man to good or evil, and
   H. Christ is to assign man to the place of his final inheritance.

[113]Al. 42:13-16, 22-26.

8. The final judgment is basically for man's benefit rather than God's. From the beginning God has had foreknowledge of man's ultimate judgment.
9. The gospel of Jesus Christ is to form the basis for judgment. By the final judgment day, every man will have had opportunity to either accept or reject it and can be judged by the same standard. Those who enjoyed greater knowledge will be obligated to perform on a higher level.
10. Man is to serve as his own defender and prosecutor. He will have perfect recall of all his thoughts, motives, deeds, and actions, and will judge himself with the same knowledge by which he judged himself and others during mortality.
11. Witnesses will testify against some individuals in the day of judgment.
12. Six types of records which are kept on earth will be used as evidence in the judgment process. Some of these records may have been duplicated in heaven to insure their availability at the judgment day.
    A. the scriptures,
    B. Church minutes and statistical records,
    C. the Book of the Law of God,
    D. miscellaneous records and histories,
    E. books of remembrance, and
    F. records of family and family relationship.
13. The Lamb's Book of Life is a record kept in heaven of those who will inherit the celestial kingdom.
14. Mercy cannot rob justice. The atonement of Christ allows Him to extend mercy and forgiveness to those who will repent. Lack of repentance and rebellion against God subject man to the full demands of justice and punishment. God's mercy is no longer available to them.

CHAPTER IX

THE SONS OF PERDITION— THEIR SIN AND THEIR FATE

The Resurrection and Kingdom of No Glory

It has been seen in chapter VII that all men shall come out of the grave and have their body and spirit reunited in the resurrection process. "In Christ shall all be made alive,"[1] and no one who obtained a body in mortality will fail to be reunited to it in the resurrection. The vast majority of men will inherit bodies filled with the glory of the celestial, terrestrial, or telestial kingdoms. The Lord has revealed, however, that some men will be resurrected who will be so lacking in righteousness that they cannot abide the law of those kingdoms and must be sent elsewhere:

> He who cannot abide the law of a telestial kingdom cannot abide a telestial glory; therefore he is not meet for a kingdom of glory. Therefore *he must abide a kingdom which is not a kingdom of glory.*[2]

Such individuals have willingly forfeited the blessings of the kingdoms of glory and will be compelled to return to the type of life they lived in hell before the resurrection:

> They who remain *shall also be quickened; nevertheless, they shall return again to their own place,* to enjoy that which they are willing to receive, because they were not willing to enjoy that which they might have received.[3]

Alma taught that those who inherit the kingdom of no glory are subject there to the domination of Satan. The only benefit they will have received from Christ's atonement will be their resurrected bodies, which cannot be slain or separated from their spirits:

[1] 1 Cor. 15:22.
[2] D&C 88:24.
[3] D&C 88:32.

Then is the time when their torments shall be as a lake of fire and brimstone, whose flame ascendeth up forever and ever; and then is the time that *they shall be chained down to an everlasting destruction, according to the power and captivity of Satan,* he having subjected them according to his will.

Then, I say unto you, *they shall be as though there had been no redemption made; for they cannot be redeemed according to God's justice; and they cannot die, seeing there is no more corruption.*[4]

Inhabitants of Kingdom of No Glory Are Sons of Perdition

Who are the individuals who suffer this tragic fate, and how is it that they come to merit it? The great vision which the Lord revealed to Joseph Smith and Sidney Rigdon in 1832 provided the answers. It showed how Lucifer fell from heaven and became known as "perdition" (meaning "lost"), and that he subjected others to his will, making them "sons of perdition":

> This we saw also, and bear record, that an angel of God who was in authority in the presence of God, who rebelled against the Only Begotten Son whom the Father loved and who was in the bosom of the Father, was thrust down from the presence of God and the Son,
>
> *And was called Perdition, for the heavens wept over him—he was Lucifer,* a son of the morning.
>
> And we beheld, and lo, he is fallen! is fallen, even a son of the morning!
>
> And while we were yet in the Spirit, the Lord commanded us that we should write the vision; for we beheld Satan, that old serpent, even the devil, who rebelled against God, and sought to take the kingdom of our God and his Christ—
>
> Wherefore, *he maketh war with the saints of God, and encompasseth them round about.*
>
> And we saw a vision of the sufferings of those with whom he made war and overcame, for thus came the voice of the Lord unto us:
>
> Thus saith the Lord concerning all those who know my power, and have been made partakers thereof, and *suffered themselves through the power of the devil to be overcome, and to deny the truth and defy my power—*
>
> *They are they who are the sons of perdition, of whom I say that it had been better for them never to have been born;*

---

[4]Al. 12:17-18.

> *For they are vessels of wrath, doomed to suffer the wrath of God, with the devil and his angels in eternity;*
>
> Concerning whom I have said there is no forgiveness in this world nor in the world to come—[5]

As Christ prayed to His Father He showed that all others would inherit some degree of glory but that the sons of perdition would be lost:

> While I was with them in the world, I kept them in thy name: those that thou gavest me I have kept, and *none of them is lost, but the son of perdition.*[6]

The Unpardonable Sin — Sin Against the Holy Ghost

What sin is more serious than all the rest—that plunges man below the level of liars, sorcerers, adulterers, and whoremongers who will suffer in hell but eventually be resurrected to the telestial glory? What is the sin which is unpardonable? Joseph Smith made reference to this sin in his King Follett discourse when he said,

> God hath made a provision that every spirit in the eternal world can be ferreted out and saved *unless he has committed that unpardonable sin which cannot be remitted to him either in this world or the world of spirits.* God has wrought out a salvation for all men, unless they have committed a certain sin; and every man who has a friend in the eternal world can save him, *unless he has committed the unpardonable sin.* And so you can see how far you can be a savior.
>
> *A man cannot commit the unpardonable sin after the dissolution of the body.*[7]

The unpardonable sin is known as blasphemy against the Holy Ghost. Statements from latter-day prophets give a clear understanding of this sin. Joseph Smith defined the unpardonable sin when he said,

> All sins shall be forgiven, except the sin against the Holy Ghost; for Jesus will save all except the sons of perdition. What must a man do to commit the unpardonable sin? He must receive the Holy Ghost, have the heavens opened unto him, and *know God, and then sin against him.* After a man has sinned against the Holy Ghost, there is no repentance for him. *He has got to say that the sun does not shine*

[5]D&C 76:25-34.
[6]Jn. 17:12.
[7]HC 6:313-314. Apr. 7, 1844.

> *while he sees it; he has got to deny Jesus Christ when the heavens have been opened unto him, and to deny the plan of salvation with his eyes open to the truth of it;* and from that time he begins to be an enemy. This is the case with many apostates of The Church of Jesus Christ of Latter-day Saints.
>
> When a man *begins to be an enemy to this work, he hunts me, he seeks to kill me, and never ceases to thirst for my blood. He gets the spirit of the devil—the same spirit that they had who crucified the Lord of Life—the same spirit that sins against the Holy Ghost.* You cannot save such persons; you cannot bring them to repentance; *they make open war, like the devil,* and awful is the consequence.
>
> I advise all of you to be careful what you do, or you may by-and-by find out that you have been deceived. Stay yourselves; do not give way; don't make any hasty moves, you may be saved. If a spirit of bitterness is in you, don't be in haste. You may say, that man is a sinner. Well, if he repents, he shall be forgiven. Be cautious: await. When you find a spirit that wants bloodshed,—murder, the same is not of God, but is of the devil. Out of the abundance of the heart of man the mouth speaketh.
>
> The best men bring forth the best works. The man who tells you words of life is the man who can save you. *I warn you against all evil characters who sin against the Holy Ghost; for there is no redemption for them in this world nor in the world to come.*[8]

President Brigham Young echoed the same definition when he said,

> Who will not be saved? *Those who have received the truth,* or had the privilege of receiving it, *and then rejected it. . . .* You may pray for your persecutors—for those who hate you, and revile you, and speak all manner of evil of you, if they do it ignorantly; *but if they do it understandingly, justice must take its course in regard to them; and except they repent, they will become sons of perdition.* This is my testimony.[9]

Orson Pratt explained the unpardonable sin when he taught,

> We are what the Lord calls Latter-day Saints—we have received light and knowledge to that degree from the heavens that will, if obeyed, exalt us to these high privileges of which I have been speaking. On the other hand, if not obeyed, *that very light and knowledge are sufficient to sink us below all things. Hence we stand on dangerous ground in some respects, and we have need to fear lest we sin against this light and have not the privilege of even the telestial world.* He that rejects this covenant (let me quote the word of the Lord given in these last

---

[8]*Ibid.,* pp. 314-315. See HC 6:304.

[9]JD 8:35-36. Apr. 6, 1860.

days)—*'He that rejecteth this covenant and altogether turns therefrom, shall not have forgiveness of sins in this world nor in the world to come.'* Do you hear it, Latter-day Saints? If you do, then strive with all your hearts to be faithful. Strive to abide in the covenant that you have received. *There is no halfway business with us—we have got to remain faithful to this covenant, for if we turn away from it we can not even claim the glory that the world will have when the last resurrection shall come, but our doom is fixed—we have to dwell with the devil and his angels to all eternity.* Why? Because they once had light and knowledge, dwelt in the presence of God, and knew about the glories of His kingdom. *But they rebelled, and kept not the law that was given to them—they sinned against light and knowledge and were thrust down in chains of darkness, there to remain until the judgment of the great day. If we do not wish to be placed in their society for all eternity we must abide in the covenant that we have made.*[10]

From these statements it can be seen that the unpardonable sin cannot be committed by all men, but only by those who belong to the Church and have received guidance through the Holy Ghost. As Joseph Smith taught,

> No man can commit the unpardonable sin after the dissolution of the body, *nor in this life, until he receives the Holy Ghost;* but they must do it in this world.[11]

Because of the seriousness of this great sin, it is well to examine the scriptures that explain (1) who is eligible and capable of committing it, (2) the exact nature of the sin, and (3) the revealed fate of those who commit it.

Those Capable of Committing Unpardonable Sin

A comprehensive list of requirements which perpetrators of the sin must have fulfilled before committing it may be drawn from the scriptures as follows:

1. *They have received Christ's new and everlasting covenant. (D&C 132:27)* The new and everlasting covenant is the fulness of the gospel of Jesus Christ.[12] To receive the gospel means to have exercised faith and repentance and to have been baptized and commanded to receive the Holy Ghost by those in authority through the ordinance of confirmation.[13] In this

---

[10]JD 15:323. Jan. 19, 1873.
[11]HC 6:314. Apr. 7, 1844.
[12]See D&C 39:11; 66:2; 133:57.
[13]3 Ne. 27:19-21.

age, only those who have been baptized as members of The Church of Jesus Christ of Latter-day Saints are capable of committing the unpardonable sin of blasphemy against the Holy Ghost.

2. *They know Christ's power and have been made partakers thereof.* (*D&C 76:31*)

3. *They have tasted the powers of the world to come.* (*Heb. 6:5*) To fulfill these requirements the individual must hold the priesthood or have had its power manifested in his behalf (such as being healed by priesthood administration). Either to use the priesthood or to have its power manifested in one's behalf implies a substantial degree of righteousness, for "the rights of the priesthood are inseparably connected with the powers of heaven, and . . . the powers of heaven cannot be controlled nor handled only upon the principles of righteousness."[14]

4. *They have received the Holy Spirit.* (*D&C 76:35*)

5. *They have been enlightened.* (*Heb. 6:4*)

6. *They have tasted of the heavenly gift.* (*Heb. 6:4*)

7. *They have been made partakers of the Holy Ghost.* (*Heb. 6:4*) The act of confirmation into the Church is not sufficient to meet these requirements, for that is only the command for an individual to seek the promptings of the Holy Ghost. It appears that there are many who have grown to adulthood as members of the Church and yet have never knowingly received guidance from the Holy Spirit. They have never kept the commandment to "receive the Holy Ghost" and never tasted His promptings and guidance. They have never received revelation. Although their failure to heed this commandment has seriously retarded their religious growth, it has also made them ineligible to commit the sin of blasphemy against the Holy Ghost.

Herein lies the crux of the question of whether a person can commit the unpardonable sin, or commit blasphemy

[14]D&C 121:36. To be a recipient of priesthood power also requires righteousness and/or forgiveness. See, for instance, James 5:14-15; D&C 42:44.

against the Holy Ghost: he can only do so if he has knowingly received guidance and testimony from that Being and therefore understands the divine communication process.

8. *They have a revealed testimony that Jesus is the Christ, the Son of God.* (*D&C 76:43*) Before a person can commit the unpardonable sin he must know through inspiration or revelation that Jesus is truly the Christ. The apostle Paul wrote that "no man can say that Jesus is the Lord, but by the Holy Ghost."[15] Joseph Smith taught that this passage should be translated "no man can *know* that Jesus is the Lord, but by the Holy Ghost."[16] This knowledge of Christ's divinity may come as an overwhelming baptism of fire as it did with Lorenzo Snow,[17] or it may come as a witness that an authorized individual is a true spokesman of God and therefore that his witness of the Savior is true, as was granted to Amasa M. Lyman.[18] A common way by which a testimony of the Savior's divinity is received is to hear, while under the influence of the Holy Ghost, another individual bear testimony of His divine sonship by that same power, for "when a man

---

[15]1 Cor. 12:3.

[16]HC 4:603. Apr. 28, 1842.

[17]Shortly after his baptism and confirmation in June, 1836, Lorenzo Snow grew very concerned because he had not yet received any manifestation from the Holy Ghost. He determined to go to a secluded spot and pour out his desire to God. The following is his account of what ensued:

> I had no sooner opened my lips in an effort to pray than I heard a sound just above my head like the rushing of silken robes; and immediately *the Spirit of God descended upon me, completely enveloping my whole person, filling me from the crown of my head to the soles of my feet, and oh, the joyful happiness I felt!* No language can describe the almost instantaneous transition from a dense cloud of spiritual darkness into a refulgence of light and knowledge, as it was at that time imparted to my understanding. *I received a perfect knowledge that God lives, that Jesus Christ is the Son of God, and of the restoration of the Holy Priesthood, and the fulness of the gospel. It was a complete baptism—a tangible immersion in the heavenly principle or element, the Holy Ghost;* and even more physical in its effects upon every part of my system than the immersion by water. (Andrew Jenson, *Latter-day Saint Biographical Encyclopedia, op. cit.,* Vol. I, p. 27.)

[18]Amasa M. Lyman first met Joseph Smith at the age of nineteen, at which time the Spirit bore to him the following witness:

> This . . . afforded me an opportunity to see the man of God. Of the impressions produced I will here say, although there was nothing strange or different from other men in his personal appearance, yet, when he grasped my hand in that cordial way (known to those who have met him in the honest simplicity of truth), I felt as one of old in the presence of the Lord; my strength seemed to be gone, so that it required an effort on my part to stand on my feet; but in all this there was no fear, but the serenity and peace of heaven pervaded my soul, and *the still small voice of the spirit whispered its living testimony in the depths of my soul, where it has ever remained, that he was the Man of God.* (*Ibid.,* p. 97)

speaketh by the power of the Holy Ghost *the power of the Holy Ghost carrieth it unto the hearts of the children of men.*"[19]

Such a testimony and sure knowledge, revealed through the Holy Spirit, is even more binding upon a man than a personal visitation from the Savior. Jesus himself warned that

> All manner of sin and blasphemy shall be forgiven unto men: but the *blasphemy against the Holy Ghost shall not be forgiven unto men.*
>
> *And whosoever speaketh a word against the Son of Man, it shall be forgiven him: but whosoever speaketh against the Holy Ghost, it shall not be forgiven him,* neither in this world, neither in the world to come.[20]

A revealed testimony of the divinity of Jesus Christ is common among members of the Church who have gained the companionship of the Holy Ghost. Those who have received such a testimony are capable of committing the unpardonable sin.

9. *They have tasted of the good word of God.* (*Heb. 6:5*) This requirement implies a knowledge of gospel principles and doctrines, presumably from both personal study and from the "Spirit of truth," who "will guide you into all truth."[21]

These, then, are the things man must accomplish before he can even be capable of committing the sin of blasphemy against the Holy Ghost. He must hold membership in the Church and have a knowledge of the gospel. But more important, he must be acquainted with the promptings of the Holy Ghost and must have received guidance and a revealed testimony of the divinity of Christ.

The Nature of Unpardonable Sin

After gaining all the above advantages and growth in the gospel, man must reject all of these blessings and rebel against them to commit blasphemy against the Holy Ghost. Again, the scriptures give a detailed analysis of the exact nature of this unpardonable sin. To become a son of perdition,

1. *They deny the truth.* (*D&C 76:31*) They must reject the gospel and their testimony, though they have known of

[19] 2 Ne. 33:1.
[20] Mt. 12:31-32.
[21] Jn. 16:13.

its truthfulness. Their denial must be an outright rejection of righteousness. As Joseph Smith said of an individual making such a denial, "He has got to say that the sun does not shine while he sees it, . . . and to deny the plan of salvation with his eyes open to the truth of it."[22]

2. *They deny the Holy Spirit after having received it.* (*D&C 76:35*)

3. *They speak against the Holy Ghost.* (*Mt. 12:31-32*)

4. *They withdraw themselves from the Spirit of the Lord.* (*Mos. 2:36*) They reject that Holy Being, speak irreverently of the guidance He gives to man, and impiously deny that such a Being has ever manifested Himself unto them. They must reject Him as their guide and revelator.

5. *They deny the Only Begotten Son of the Father.* (*D&C 76: 35,43*)

6. *They put Christ to an open shame.* (*D&C 76:35*) Just as they reject and revile the Holy Ghost, they must also disclaim the divine nature of Jesus Christ. They ridicule and profane His holy name and attempt to bring shame and dishonor upon Him.

7. *They assent unto Christ's death.* (*D&C* 132:27)

8. *They crucify Christ unto themselves.* (*D&C 76:35; Heb. 6:6*) Those who commit the unpardonable sin come out in rebellion against Christ and desire to thwart His Church. In their rebellion they become so wretched that in effect they rejoice in the Savior's suffering and crucifixion and affirm that they would put Him to death if He lived in their day. As Joseph Smith commented,

> This generation is as corrupt as the generation of the Jews that crucified Christ; and if He were here to-day, and should preach the same doctrine He did then, they would put Him to death.[23]

9. *They defy Christ's power.* (*D&C 76:31*)

10. *They come out in open rebellion against God.*[24] (*Mos. 2:37*)

---

[22]HC 6:314. Apr. 7, 1844.

[23]HC 6:58. Oct. 15, 1843.

[24]Concerning such rebellion Joseph Smith admonished,

11. *They turn from and break the oath and covenant of the priesthood.* (*D&C 84:41*) Those who commit the unpardonable sin come out in full rebellion against the power of Christ as it is manifested on the earth. They oppose priesthood authority and actively fight against the Church. They seek the downfall of its leaders and attempt to bring misery to all who are following the paths of truth and righteousness. It is this spirit of opposition and rebellion that removes a disgruntled member of the Church into the category of apostasy and into the fate of the sons of perdition.

12. *They suffer themselves through the power of the devil to be overcome.* (*D&C 76:31*)

13. *They become an enemy to all righteousness.* (*Mos. 2:37*) Those guilty of this sin "listeth to obey the evil spirit,"[25] and "remaineth and dieth an enemy to God."[26] They have come to love Lucifer and hate Christ, for as the Savior warned,

> No man can serve two masters: for either he will hate the one, and love the other; or else he will hold to the one, and despise the other. Ye cannot serve God and mammon.[27]

14. *They commit murder in that they shed innocent blood.* (*D&C 132:27*) For murder to be classed as a portion of the unpardonable sin against the Holy Ghost, it must be committed by one who has been "sealed by the Holy Spirit of promise" after he has received the new and everlasting covenant.[28] President

---

O ye Twelve! and all Saints! profit by this important Key—that in all your trials, troubles, temptations, afflictions, bonds, imprisonments and death, *see to it, that you do not betray heaven: that you do not betray Jesus Christ; that you do not betray the brethren; that you do not betray the revelations of God,* whether in the Bible, Book of Mormon, or Doctrine and Covenants, or any other that ever was or ever will be given and revealed unto man in this world or that which is to come. *Yea, in all your kicking and flounderings, see to it that you do not this thing, lest innocent blood be found upon your skirts, and you go down to hell. All other sins are not to be compared to sinning against the Holy Ghost, and proving a traitor to the brethren.*

I will give you one of the Keys of the mysteries of the Kingdom. It is an eternal principle, that has existed with God from all eternity: *That man who rises up to condemn others, finding fault with the Church, saying that they are out of the way, while he himself is righteous, then know assuredly, that that man is in the high road to apostasy; and if he does not repent, will apostatize, as God lives.* (HC 3:385. July 2, 1839)

[25]Mos. 2:37.

[26]Mos. 2:38.

[27]Mt. 6:24.

[28]D&C 132:26-27.

Joseph Fielding Smith explained and carefully documented the teaching that

> *The new and everlasting covenant is the sum total of all gospel covenants and obligations. . . . It is everything—the fulness of the gospel.* So marriage properly performed, baptism, ordination to the priesthood, everything else—*every contract, every obligation, every performance that pertains to the gospel of Jesus Christ, which is sealed by the Holy Spirit of promise* according to his law here given, *is a part of the new and everlasting covenant.*[29]

An explanation of the sin of murder and its position as a portion of the unpardonable sin was given by the prophet Joseph Smith to William Clayton:

> *Your life is hid with Christ in God, and so are many others. Nothing but the unpardonable sin can prevent you from inheriting eternal life for you are sealed up by the power of the Priesthood unto eternal life,* having taken the step necessary for that purpose.
>
> Except a man and his wife enter into an everlasting covenant and be married for eternity, while in this probation, by the power and authority of the Holy Priesthood, they will cease to increase when they die; that is, they will not have any children after the resurrection. But *those who are married by the power and authority of the priesthood in this life, and continue without committing the sin against the Holy Ghost,* will continue to increase and have children in the celestial glory. *The unpardonable sin is to shed innocent blood, or be accessory thereto.* All other sins will be visited with judgment in the flesh, and the spirit being delivered to the buffetings of Satan until the day of the Lord Jesus.[30]

Thus a member of the Church who has met the qualifications enumerated above to be a son of perdition will be condemned to live forever without forgiveness. Yet it would appear that murderers who do not meet these qualifications do not become sons of perdition. They are cast down to hell until the second resurrection when they will have paid the uttermost farthing; then they receive forgiveness and are permitted to enter into the telestial kingdom. Joseph Smith taught

> That the doctrine of eternal judgment was perfectly understood by the Apostles, is evident from several passages of Scripture. Peter

---

[29]Bruce R. McConkie, *Doctrines of Salvation, op cit.,* Vol. I, pp. 156, 158. See the complete discussion, pp. 152-160.

[30]HC 5:391-392. May 16, 1843. See also D&C 42:18,79.

> preached repentance and baptism for the remission of sins to the Jews who had been led to acts of violence and blood by their leaders; *but to the rulers he said, 'I would that through ignorance ye did it, as did also those ye ruled.'* 'Repent, therefore, and be converted, that your sins may be blotted out, when the times of refreshing (redemption) shall come from the presence of the Lord, for He shall send Jesus Christ, who before was preached unto you.' &c. The time of redemption here had reference to the time when Christ should come; then, and not till then, would their sins be blotted out. Why? *Because they were murderers, and no murderer hath eternal life. Even David must wait for those times of refreshing, before he can come forth and his sins be blotted out.* For Peter, speaking of him says, 'David hath not yet ascended into heaven, for his sepulchre is with us to this day.' His remains were then in the tomb. Now, we read that many bodies of the Saints arose at Christ's resurrection, probably all the Saints, but it seems that David did not. Why? Because he had been a murderer. If the ministers of religion had a proper understanding of the doctrine of eternal judgment, they would not be found attending the man who forfeited his life to the injured laws of his country, by shedding innocent blood; for *such characters cannot be forgiven, until they have paid the last farthing. The prayers of all the ministers in the world can never close the gates of hell against a murderer.*[31]

Yet as David knew that he would not be left in the influence of Satan for all eternity,[32] murderers (apparently not sons of perdition, because they have not sinned against the greater light of the gospel) are linked with the other inhabitants of the telestial kingdom following the final judgment, "For without are *dogs,* and *sorcerers,* and *whoremongers,* and *murderers* and *idolaters,* and whosoever loveth and *maketh a lie.*"[33]

The above fourteen elements, drawn from the scriptures, together comprise the unpardonable sin, or blasphemy against

---

[31]HC 4:359. May 16, 1841. It would appear that eventual forgiveness can be obtained by murderers who partially know the gospel but have not progressed sufficiently to become sons of perdition. Knowledge that the Holy Ghost has been denied seems to be the factor which separates the two degrees of sin. Alma contrasted the two situations when he said,

> For behold, *if ye deny the Holy Ghost when it once has had place in you, and ye know that ye deny it, behold, this is a sin which is unpardonable;* yea, and *whosoever murdereth against the light and knowledge of God, it is not easy for him to obtain forgiveness;* yea, I say unto you, my son, that it is not easy for him to obtain a forgiveness. (Al. 39:6)

[32]See Ps. 16:8-11, Acts 2:27.

[33]Rev. 22:15. See also D&C 76:103-106. Consideration of teachings concerning blood atonement and capital punishment are beyond the scope of this study and are not considered in this context. See Bruce R. McConkie, *Doctrines of Salvation, op cit.,* Vol. I, pp. 133-138; Joseph F. Smith, Jr., *Blood Atonement and The Origin of Plural Marriage* (Salt Lake City, Utah: The Deseret News Press, n.d.); JD 4:219-220.

the Holy Ghost. To commit one of them causes man to become entangled in Satan's web, and before long he may be led farther and farther down until he is guilty of all of them and is beyond the powers of redemption and forgiveness.

Fate of the Sons of Perdition

Much information concerning the final state of the sons of perdition is found in the scriptures. Care must be taken, however, not to confuse passages dealing with their eternal plight following the final judgment with passages telling of their intermediate condition in hell before the second resurrection. Passages linked chronologically with the final judgment so that the specific condemnation follows that event provide this differentiation.

Nephi, when he received the interpretation of his father's vision of the tree, the rod of iron, and the river, was given an understanding of the final state of the wicked. He wrote of the wicked who would be cast out of the realms governed by God following the final judgment into a place of filthiness:

> They said unto me: What meaneth the *river of water* which our father saw?
>
> And I said unto them that *the water which my father saw was filthiness;* and so much was his mind swallowed up in other things that he beheld not the filthiness of the water.
>
> *And I said unto them that it was an awful gulf, which separated* the wicked from the tree of life, and also from the saints of God.
>
> And I said unto them that *it was a representation of that awful hell, which the angel said unto me was prepared for the wicked.*
>
> And I said unto them that our father also saw that the *justice of God did also divide the wicked from the righteous;* and the brightness thereof was like unto the brightness of a flaming fire, which ascendeth up unto God forever and ever, and hath no end.
>
> And they said unto me: Doth this thing mean the torment of the body in the days of probation, or doth it mean the final state of the soul after the death of the temporal body, or doth it speak of the things which are temporal?
>
> And it came to pass that I said unto them that *it was a representation of things both temporal and spiritual; for the day should come that they must be judged of their works,* yea, even the works which were done by the temporal body in their days of probation.
>
> Wherefore, if they should die in their wickedness *they must be cast off also, as to the things which are spiritual, which are pertaining to*

> *righteousness;* wherefore, they must be brought to stand before God, to be judged of their works; and *if their works have been filthiness they must needs be filthy; and if they be filthy it must needs be that they cannot dwell in the kingdom of God;* if so the kingdom of God must be filthy also.
>
> But behold, I say unto you, the kingdom of God is not filthy, and there cannot any unclean thing enter into the kingdom of God; wherefore *there must needs be a place of filthiness prepared for that which is filthy.*
>
> *And there is a place prepared, yea, even that awful hell of which I have spoken, and the devil is the foundation of it; wherefore the final state of the souls of men is to dwell in the kingdom of God, or to be cast out because of that justice of which I have spoken.*
>
> *Wherefore, the wicked are rejected from the righteous,* and also from that tree of life, whose fruit is most precious and most desirable above all other fruits. . .[34]

Jacob, brother to the prophet Nephi, also knew of the final fate of the sons of perdition. He too, referred to their continuing filthiness as he wrote,

> It shall come to pass that *when all men shall have passed from this first death unto life, insomuch as they have become immortal, they must appear before the judgment-seat of the Holy One of Israel;* and then cometh the judgment, and then must they be judged according to the holy judgment of God.
>
> And assuredly, as the Lord liveth, for the Lord God hath spoken it, and it is his eternal word, which cannot pass away, that they who are righteous shall be righteous still, and *they who are filthy shall be filthy still; wherefore, they who are filthy are the devil and his angels; and they shall go away into everlasting fire; prepared for them; and their torment is as a lake of fire and brimstone, whose flame ascendeth up forever and ever and has no end.*[35]

The prophet Alma, while preaching to the people of Gideon, taught the same doctrine:

> He doth not dwell in unholy temples; *neither can filthiness or anything which is unclean be received into the kingdom of God;* therefore I say unto you the time shall come, yea, and *it shall be at the last day, that he who is filthy shall remain in his filthiness.*[36]

The angel whose trump is to announce the second resurrection will proclaim their continuing filthiness also, saying,

---

[34] 1 Ne. 15:26-36.
[35] 2 Ne. 9:15-16.
[36] Al. 7:21.

"There are found among those who are to remain until that great and last day, even the end, *who shall remain filthy still.*"[37]

The sons of perdition are those who have died the second death—a death pertaining to righteousness. Alma defined this terrible death when he said,

> God gave unto them commandments, after having made known unto them the plan of redemption, that they should not do evil, the penalty thereof being a *second death, which was an everlasting death as to things pertaining unto righteousness; for on such the plan of redemption could have no power, for the works of justice could not be destroyed,* according to the supreme goodness of God.[38]

This death will be similar to the first spiritual death which Adam experienced when he was cast from the garden of Eden, for the Lord has revealed,

> I, the Lord God, caused that he should be cast out from the Garden of Eden, from my presence, because of his transgression, wherein he became *spiritually dead, which is the first death, even that same death which is the last death, which is spiritual, which shall be pronounced upon the wicked when I shall say: Depart, ye cursed.*[39]

The prophet Jacob referred to this second death as a lake of fire and brimstone in his great discourse:

> O my brethren, hearken unto my word; arouse the faculties of your soul; shake yourselves that ye may awake from the slumber of death; and loose yourselves from the pains of hell that ye may not become *angels to the devil, to be cast into that lake of fire and brimstone which is the second death.*[40]

John the Revelator alluded to the same fate when he wrote that, following the second resurrection, "Death and hell were cast into the lake of fire. This is the second death."[41]

---

[37]D&C 88:102.

[38]Al. 12:32. See also 12:16-18; 13:30; 2 Ne. 2:28-29.

[39]D&C 29:41. Concerning the second death President Brigham Young warned,

> It is for us to choose whether we will be sons and daughters, joint heirs with Jesus Christ, or whether we accept an inferior glory; or whether we sin against the Holy Ghost, which cannot be pardoned or forgiven in this world, nor in the world to come; the penalty of which is to suffer the second death. What is that we call death, compared to the agonies of the second death? *If people could see it, as Joseph and Sidney saw it, they would pray that the vision be closed up; for they could not endure the sight. Neither could they endure the sight of the Father and the Son in their glory, for it would consume them.* (JD 18:217. Aug. 15, 1876)

[40]Jac. 3:11.

[41]Rev. 20:14. See also 21:8.

Other scriptural passages give additional clues to the fate of the sons of perdition. In "The Vision" given unto Joseph Smith and Sidney Rigdon, the Lord revealed,

> *They are they who are the sons of perdition, of whom I say that it had been better for them never to have been born;*
>
> For they are vessels of wrath, *doomed to suffer the wrath of God, with the devil and his angels in eternity;*
>
> Concerning whom I have said there is *no forgiveness in this world nor in the world to come*—. . .
>
> These are they who shall *go away into the lake of fire and brimstone, with the devil and his angels*—
>
> And the *only ones on whom the second death shall have any power;*
>
> Yea, verily, the *only ones who shall not be redeemed in the due time of the Lord,* after the sufferings of his wrath. . . .
>
> And this is the gospel, the glad tidings, which the voice out of the heavens bore record unto us—
>
> That he came into the world, even Jesus, . . .
>
> Who glorifies the Father, and *saves all the works of his hands, except those sons of perdition* who deny the Son after the Father has revealed him.
>
> Wherefore, he saves all except them—*they shall go away into everlasting punishment, which is endless punishment, which is eternal punishment, to reign with the devil and his angels in eternity, where their worm dieth not, and the fire is not quenched, which is their torment*—[42]

An important commentary on the last verse of this passage, as well as D&C 19:6-12, was written by the prophet Joseph Smith and his companions to W. W. Phelps on June 25, 1833. Apparently some had begun to teach that the time would eventually come when Satan and the sons of perdition would be released from their fate and would be redeemed by the Lord. This erroneous teaching was rebuked in the letter as follows,

> Say to the brothers Hulet and to all others, that *the Lord never authorized them to say that the devil, his angels or the sons of perdition, should ever be restored;* for their state of destiny was not revealed to man, is not revealed, nor ever shall be revealed, save to those who are made partakers thereof: consequently those who teach this doctrine, have not received it of the Spirit of the Lord. *Truly Brother Oliver declared it to be the doctrine of devils. We therefore command that this doctrine be taught no more in Zion. We sanction the decision of the Bishop and his council, in relation to this doctrine being a bar to communion.*[43]

---

[42]D&C 76:32-34, 36-38, 40-41, 43-44.

[43]HC 1:366.

And another clue concerning their fate: Alma revealed that in the resurrection they would be raised "to endless misery to inherit the kingdom of the devil."[44] Yet Satan will some day have to surrender his dominion to another who will gain ascendency over him. Cain, who also became known as "Perdition," was promised by God that he would rule over Lucifer:[45]

> If thou doest not well, sin lieth at the door, and Satan desireth to have thee: and except thou shalt hearken unto my commandments, I will deliver thee up, and it shall be unto thee according to his desire. And *thou shalt rule over him;*
>
> *For from this time forth thou shalt be the father of his lies; thou shalt be called Perdition; for thou wast also before the world.*[46]

Thus, though the picture is far from clear, certain clues can be combined to give somewhat of a description concerning the ultimate fate of the sons of perdition who have lived in mortality. These clues may be summarized as follows:

1. They are resurrected with bodies which can no more die, but which are able to abide only a kingdom of no glory. (D&C 88:24,32; Al. 12:17-18)
2. They return to their own place, to enjoy only that which they were willing to receive. (D&C 88:32)
3. They are vessels of wrath, doomed to suffer the wrath of God with the devil and his angels. (D&C 76:33, 44; 2 Ne. 9:16)
4. They are lost to God. (Jn. 17:12; D&C 76:43)
5. They remain filthy, and dwell in a kingdom of filthiness. (1 Ne. 15:33; 2 Ne. 9:16; Al. 7:21; D&C 88:102)
6. They are completely separated and rejected from the righteous. (1 Ne. 15:28,30,33-34,36)
7. They again dwell in an awful hell. (1 Ne. 15:29,35; Al. 13:30; 2 Ne. 2:29)

---

[44]Al. 41:4.

[45]It would appear that his possession of a physical body will be one factor which would give Cain ascendancy over Satan. Joseph Smith taught that "All beings who have bodies have power over those who have not." (Franklin D. Richards and James A. Little, *A Compendium of the Doctrines of the Gospel,* 1925 edition, Salt Lake City, Utah: Geo. Q. Cannon & Sons Co. Printers, p. 271.)

[46]Moses 5:23-24.

8. They die the second death—a spiritual death pertaining to the things of righteousness. (1 Ne. 15:33; Al. 12:32; D&C 29:41; 76:37)
9. They go away into everlasting fire. (2 Ne. 9:16; D&C 76:36; 43:33)
10. Their torment is as a lake of fire and brimstone, whose flame ascendeth up forever. (2 Ne. 9:16; Al. 12:17; Jac. 3:11; Rev. 20:14; 21:8)
11. They are subjugated to the will of Satan, according to his power and captivity. (Al. 12:17; 2 Ne. 2:29; Jac. 3:11)
12. They cannot be redeemed by God's justice and are as though there had been no redemption made. (Al. 12:18, 32; D&C 76:38)
13. God will curse them and command them to depart. (D&C 29:41)
14. They have no forgiveness in this world or the world to come. (D&C 76:34; Mt. 12:31)
15. Their punishment is everlasting, endless, and eternal. (D&C 76:44)
16. Their worm dieth not, and the fire is not quenched, which is their torment. (D&C 76:44)
17. They suffer endless misery. (Al. 41:4)
18. They cannot enter Christ's glory. (D&C 132:27)
19. They are damned. (D&C 132:27)

From these clues man can derive a small degree of understanding concerning the final state of the sons of perdition. But this knowledge is limited, as God intends, for he has revealed that

> *The end thereof, neither the place thereof, nor their torment, no man knows;*
>
> Neither was it revealed, neither is, neither will be revealed unto man, except to them who are made partakers thereof;
>
> Nevertheless, I, the Lord, show it by vision unto many, but straightway shut it up again;

> *Wherefore, the end, the width, the height, the depth, and the misery thereof, they understand not,* neither any man except those who are ordained unto this condemnation.[47]

The Lord has revealed that

> The earth shall pass away so as by fire.
>
> And the wicked shall go away into unquenchable fire, and *their end no man knoweth on earth, nor ever shall know, until they come before me in judgment.*[48]

Will there be many who will die the second death and become sons of perdition? Joseph Smith, as he gave his definition of blasphemy against the Holy Ghost and stated who would be guilty of the great unpardonable sin, said that *"This is the case with many apostates of The Church of Jesus Christ of Latter-day Saints."*[49]

SUMMARY

1. All men will resurrect. The sons of perdition who have lived in mortality will have their bodies inseparably reunited to their spirits. These bodies will be bodies of no glory, suited only to dwell in a kingdom without glory. The capabilities of these bodies are not revealed, though the scriptural warning that "their worm dieth not" may be an indication that they undergo physical as well as spiritual suffering.
2. The unpardonable sin is blasphemy against the Holy Ghost. It may be defined as *a knowing rejection of the Holy Ghost and the truth He has revealed, coupled with rebellion against the Church of Christ and its doctrines and members, which can only be committed by members of the Church who have experienced spiritual manifestations and have been given a revealed testimony of eternal truths.*
3. The shedding of innocent blood by a member of the Church who has fully entered into the new and everlasting covenant condemns him to the fate of a son of perdition. Those who commit murder without having experienced the benefits of the guidance of the Holy Ghost may possibly receive forgiveness and admittance to the telestial kingdom after paying the uttermost farthing in hell until the second resurrection.

---

[47]D&C 76:45-48. The view of his eventual fate was shown to the apostate, Alphaeus Cutler, who organized "The True Church of Latter-day Saints." See his reference to this experience on pp. 60-61.

[48]D&C 43:32-33.

[49]HC 6:314. April 7, 1844.

4. The unpardonable sin cannot be committed when mortality is over and can only be committed by one who has received the Holy Ghost.

5. Comprehensive lists containing the scriptural information concerning those capable of committing unpardonable sin, the nature of unpardonable sin, and the fate of the sons of perdition were given and should be reviewed.

6. Cain will gain ascendancy over Satan and will eventually rule over him.

7. The condition of the sons of perdition following the second resurrection and the final judgment is permanent and eternal. The teaching that they will someday be redeemed and forgiven is erroneous.

8. The final status of the sons of perdition has not been fully revealed. The Lord has seen fit to withhold the full description of their dwelling place from all except those who will inherit it.

CHAPTER X

THE THREE DEGREES OF GLORY

Worlds Without Number Created by God

THERE ARE MANY KINGDOMS IN WHICH MEN WILL DWELL following their resurrection. To these the Savior made reference when He told Peter, *"In my Father's house are many mansions:* if it were not so, I would have told you."[1] The apostle Paul explained that these kingdoms varied in glory, saying that "There is one glory of the sun, and another glory of the moon, and another glory of the stars: for one star differeth from another star in glory."[2] And then modestly (for he apparently referred to himself) he wrote that "I knew a man in Christ above fourteen years ago, (Whether in the body, I cannot tell; or whether out of the body, I cannot tell: God knoweth;) *such an one caught up to the third heaven."*[3]

A monumental revelation given to Moses showed that there are many earths, and that worlds beyond man's power to enumerate and comprehend have "passed away" and become the final resting places for their inhabitants. In this revelation God set forth the purpose for His great creative program:

> And *he beheld many lands; and each land was called earth, and there were inhabitants on the face thereof.*
>
> And it came to pass that Moses called upon God, saying: Tell me, I pray thee, why these things are so, and by what thou madest them?

---

[1]Jn. 14:2. Concerning this passage, Joseph Smith said, *"House here named should have been translated kingdom;* and any person who is exalted to the highest mansion has to abide a celestial law, and the whole law too." (HC 6:184. Jan. 21, 1844) On another occasion he taught that "It should be—'In my Father's kingdom are many kingdoms,' in order that ye may be heirs of God and joint heirs with me." (HC 6:365. May 12, 1844)

[2]1 Cor 15:41. See also Ps. 148:1-6.

[3]2 Cor. 12:2. Concerning this passage, Joseph Smith remarked, "Paul saw the third heavens, and I more." (HC 5:392. May 16, 1843)

And behold, the glory of the Lord was upon Moses, so that Moses stood in the presence of God, and talked with him face to face. And the Lord God said unto Moses, *For mine own purpose have I made these things. Here is wisdom and it remaineth in me.*

And by the word of my power, have I created them, which is mine Only Begotten Son, who is full of grace and truth.

And worlds without number have I created; and I also created them for mine own purpose; and by the Son I created them, which is mine Only Begotten.

And the first man of all men have I called Adam, which is many.

But only an account of this earth, and the inhabitants thereof, give I unto you. For behold, *there are many worlds that have passed away by the word of my power. And there are many that now stand, and innumerable are they unto man; but all things are numbered unto me, for they are mine and I know them.*

And it came to pass that Moses spake unto the Lord, saying: Be merciful unto thy servant, O God, and tell me concerning this earth, and the inhabitants thereof, and also the heavens, and then thy servant will be content.

And the Lord God spake unto Moses, saying: *the heavens, they are many, and they cannot be numbered unto man; but they are numbered unto me, for they are mine.*

And as one earth shall pass away, and the heavens thereof even so shall another come; and there is no end to my works, neither to my words.

For behold, this is my work and my glory—to bring to pass the immortality and eternal life of man.[4]

Concerning the many kingdoms which become the eternal rewards of men from these numerous earths, President Brigham Young once remarked,

The kingdoms that God has prepared are innumerable. . . . How many kingdoms there are has not been told to us: they are innumerable. The disciples of Jesus were to dwell with him. *Where will the rest go? Into kingdoms prepared for them, where they will live and endure.*[5]

And on another occasion he commented, concerning the various levels or degrees of glory of these kingdoms,

The celestial is the highest of all. The telestial and terrestrial are also spoken of; and *how many more kingdoms of glory there are is not for me to say. I do not know that they are not innumerable.* This is a source of great joy to me.[6]

---

[4]Moses 1:29-39.

[5]JD 8:154. Aug. 26, 1860.

[6]JD 8:35. Apr. 6, 1860.

Apostle Orson Pratt explained that the many mansions of the Father are worlds of greater and lesser magnitude:

> This earth, this creation, will become a heaven. *The heavens that exist now are innumerable to man. God has from all eternity been organizing, redeeming and perfecting creations in the immensity of space; all of which, when they are sanctified by celestial law, and made new and eternal, become the abode of the faithful former inhabitants, who also become immortal, through and by celestial law.* They are the mansions referred to by the Savior—'In my Father's house are many mansions.' In other words, we may say, in our Father's dominions are many mansions. *They are not like mansions built by men, they are worlds of greater and lesser magnitude.* The first grade are exalted, celestial bodies, from which celestial light will radiate through the immensity of space.[7]

The Lord, while revealing the nature of heavenly law, proclaimed that

> All kingdoms have a law given;
>
> And *there are many kingdoms; for there is no space in the which there is no kingdom; and there is no kingdom in which there is no space, either a greater or a lesser kingdom.*
>
> And unto every kingdom is given a law, and unto every law there are certain bounds also and conditions.
>
> All beings who abide not in those conditions are not justified.[8]

The Lord revealed the role of God in the eternal worlds, showing that He was creator, governor and controller of the heavenly systems:

> *Judgment goeth before the face of him who sitteth upon the throne and governeth and executeth all things.*
>
> He comprehendeth all things, and all things are before him, and all things are round about him; and he is above all things, and in all things, and is through all things, and is round about all things; and *all things are by him, and of him, even God, forever and ever.*
>
> And again, verily I say unto you, *he hath given a law unto all things, by which they move in their times and their seasons;*
>
> *And their courses are fixed, even the courses of the heavens and the earth,* which comprehend the earth and all the planets.
>
> And they give light to each other in their times and in their seasons, in their minutes, in their hours, in their days, in their weeks, in their months, in their years—all these are one year with God, but not with man.
>
> The earth rolls upon her wings, and the sun giveth his light by

---

[7]JD 18:322. Dec. 3, 1876.

[8]D&C 88:36-38.

day, and the moon giveth her light by night, and the stars also give their light, as they roll upon their wings in their glory, *in the midst of the power of God.*[9]

Abraham, by means of the Urim and Thummim, was given a basic understanding of the vast galaxies God has created.

I saw the stars, that they were very great, and that *one of them was nearest unto the throne of God; and there were many great ones which were near unto it;*

And the Lord said unto me: *These are the governing ones; and the name of the great one is Kolob,* because it is near unto me, for I am the Lord thy God: *I have set this one to govern all those which belong to the same order as that upon which thou standest.*

And the Lord said unto me, by the Urim and Thummim, that *Kolob was after the manner of the Lord, according to its time and seasons in the revolutions thereof; that one revolution was a day unto the Lord, after his manner of reckoning, it being one thousand years according to the time appointed unto that whereon thou standest.* This is the reckoning of the Lord's time, according to the reckoning of Kolob.

And the Lord said unto me: *The planet which is the lesser light, lesser than that which is to rule the day, even the night, is above or greater than that upon which thou standest in point of reckoning, for it moveth in order more slow;* this is in order because it standeth above the earth upon which thou standest, therefore the reckoning of its time is not so many as to its number of days, and of months, and of years.

And the Lord said unto me: Now, Abraham, these two facts exist, behold thine eyes see it; it is given unto thee to know the times of reckoning, and the set time, yea, the set time of the earth upon which thou standest, and the set *time of the greater light which is set to rule the day, and the set time of the lesser light which is set to rule the night.*

Now the set time of the lesser light is a longer time as to its reckoning than the reckoning of the time of the earth upon which thou standest.

And where these two facts exist, there shall be another fact above them, that is, *there shall be another planet whose reckoning of time shall be longer still;*

And thus there shall be the reckoning of the time of one planet above another, until thou come nigh unto Kolob, which Kolob is after the reckoning of the Lord's time; which Kolob is set nigh unto the throne of God, to govern all those planets which belong to the same order as that upon which thou standest.[10]

---

[9]D&C 88:40-45.

[10]Abra. 3:2-9. The drawing and the revealed explanation which accompanies the book of Abraham in the Pearl of Great Price reveal additional information.

The Lord, in an effort to show God's relationship to each of His many kingdoms, set forth this parable:

> *Behold, I will liken these kingdoms unto a man having a field, and he sent forth his servants into the field to dig in the field.*
>
> And he said unto the first: Go ye and labor in the field, and in the first hour I will come unto you, and ye shall behold the joy of my countenance.
>
> And he said unto the second: Go ye also into the field, and in the second hour I will visit you with the joy of my countenance.
>
> And also unto the third, saying: I will visit you;
>
> And unto the fourth, and so on unto the twelfth.
>
> And the lord of the field went unto the first in the first hour, and tarried with him all that hour, and he was made glad with the light of the countenance of his lord.
>
> And then he withdrew from the first that he might visit the second also, and the third, and the fourth, and so on unto the twelfth.
>
> *And thus they all received the light of the countenance of their lord, every man in his hour, and in his time, and in his season—*
>
> *Beginning at the first, and so on unto the last, and from the last unto the first, and from the first unto the last;*
>
> *Every man in his own order, until his hour was finished,* even according as his lord had commanded him, that his lord might be glorified in him, and he in his lord, that they all might be glorified.
>
> *Therefore, unto this parable I will liken all these kingdoms, and the inhabitants thereof—every kingdom in its hour, and in its time, and in its season, even according to the decree which God hath made.*[11]

Man Inherits Future Kingdoms According to Law He Abides in Mortality

It appears that the planets which have "passed away" and gained their final status have been classified into three levels: celestial, terrestrial, and telestial. As Paul saw, their respective glories are comparable to the light of the sun, the moon, and the stars[12] as seen by man from the earth. A modern revelation shows that there are varying degrees of glory and reward, even among these three general categories or kingdoms:

> The glory of the celestial is one, even as the glory of the sun is one.
>
> And the glory of the terrestrial is one, even as the glory of the moon is one.

---

[11]D&C 88:51-61.

[12]See 1 Cor. 15:40-41.

> And the glory of the telestial is one, even as the glory of the stars is one, *for as one star differs from another star in glory, even so differs one from another in glory in the telestial world.*[13]

Another revelation also shows that there are sub-degrees in the highest of the three general degrees of glory, for it reports that "In the celestial glory there are three heavens or degrees."[14]

The Lord has revealed that after the final judgment, men will be assigned to live on one of these three levels, with a resurrected body of capabilities appropriate to the assigned level. This assignment will be based on the level of law the individual has lived while on earth:

> It is decreed that the poor and the meek of the earth shall inherit it.
>
> *Therefore, it must needs be sanctified from all unrighteousness, that it may be prepared for the celestial glory;*
>
> For after it hath filled the measure of its creation, it shall be crowned with glory, even with the presence of God the Father;
>
> That bodies who are of the celestial kingdom may possess it forever and ever; for, for this intent was it made and created, and for this intent are they sanctified.
>
> *And they who are not sanctified through the law which I have given unto you, even the law of Christ, must inherit another kingdom, even that of a terrestrial kingdom, or that of a telestial kingdom.*
>
> For he who is not able to abide the law of a celestial kingdom *cannot abide a celestial glory.*
>
> And he who cannot abide the law of a terrestrial kingdom *cannot abide a terrestrial glory.*
>
> And he who cannot abide the law of a telestial kingdom *cannot abide a telestial glory;* therefore he is not meet for a kingdom of glory. Therefore he must abide a kingdom which is not a kingdom of glory.[15]

As Brigham Young understood it, *"All these different glories are ordained to fit the capacities and conditions of men."*[16] And man, in going to his assigned kingdom, will be regaining the company of those with whom he associated while on earth: "The one raised to happiness according to his desires of happiness, or

---

[13]D&C 76:96-98.

[14]D&C 131:1.

[15]D&C 88:17-24. Verses 28-31 show that in the resurrection those who inherit these kingdoms receive comparable celestial, terrestrial, or telestial bodies suitable to their assigned dwelling place.

[16]JD 9:315. July 13, 1862.

good according to his desires of good, and the other to evil according to his desires of evil."[17]

Apostle Orson Pratt was well aware of the manner in which the various kingdoms would be suited to the many levels of man's earthly endeavor and degrees of righteousness. He taught that

> God is the author of many creations besides those that are celestial. *He will prepare a creation just adapted to the condition of such people—those who are not sanctified by the Gospel in all its fullness, and who do not endure faithful to the end, will find themselves located upon one of the lower creations,* where the glory of God will not be made manifest to the same extent. *There they will be governed by laws adapted to their inferior capacity and to the condition which they will have plunged themselves in.* They will not only suffer after this life, but will fail to receive glory and power and exaltation in the presence of God the Eternal Father; they will fail to receive an everlasting inheritance upon this earth, in its glorified and immortal state.[18]

Thus the three general degrees of glory are each adapted to the lesser or greater degree of perfection of its eternal inhabitants. Man may anticipate that his final reward will place him among others of similar character, knowledge, capacity, and degree of advancement. Such an environment may be regarded as being best suited to his eternal felicity.

The key to man's knowledge of the eternal worlds is found in the great series of visions given to Joseph Smith and Sidney Rigdon on February 16, 1832, at Hiram, Ohio. These five remarkable visions are today found recorded as Section seventy-six of the Doctrine and Covenants. They are known collectively as "The Vision." Their greatest value is found in the knowledge and understanding they give to man concerning the three degrees of glory and concerning what manner of individual inherits each degree.[19]

Careful study of "The Vision" shows that the revelation systematically treats each of the three degrees of glory. For each of the three eternal levels of reward it

---

[17]Al. 41:5.

[18]JD 18:323. Dec. 3, 1876.

[19]For the interesting comments of Philo Dibble, who observed Joseph Smith and Sidney Rigdon during and just after "The Vision," see p. 19.

1. tells what type of individual will inherit the kingdom,
2. traces the route of the individual through the eternal plan from mortality until he comes into his assigned glory, and
3. outlines the nature of his final reward.

"The Vision" is best understood when the reader has gained this insight into its organization and presentation.

The Glory of the Telestial, Which Surpasses All Understanding

Although the telestial glory will be reserved for the lowest type of individual here upon the earth, God has seen fit to make it a reward far superior to the life men know upon the earth today. As Joseph Smith recorded after receiving "The Vision," "Thus we saw, in the heavenly vision, *the glory of the telestial, which surpasses all understanding;* And no man knows it except him to whom God has revealed it."[20]

An extensive coverage of the type of individual who will inherit the telestial kingdom is set forth in the revelation. It is here presented in list form with appropriate commentary:

1. *They do not receive the gospel of Christ.* (*D&C 76:82, 101*)
2. *They do not receive the testimony of Jesus.* (*D&C 76:82, 101*)
3. *They do not receive the testimony of the prophets.* (*D&C 76:101*)
4. *They do not receive the everlasting covenant.* (*D&C 76:101*)

Although in the final judgment every man will be compelled to bow before Christ and acknowledge His divinity,[21] this great mass of humanity, *"the inhabitants of the telestial world, . . . as innumerable as the stars in the firmament of heaven, or as the sand upon the seashore,"*[22] will not have yielded obedience to gospel law. Throughout their mortal probation and their stay in the spirit prison, they will refuse the gospel until they re-

[20]D&C 76:89-90.
[21]D&C 76:110.
[22]D&C 76:109.

ject their privilege of hearing it further and are cast down to hell to pay for their sins. Acknowledgement of Christ's divinity at the day of judgment does not imply that they will have accepted the gospel at that time, for knowledge does not mean acceptance.[23] These individuals may have followed other churches or apostate factions while on earth, yet that will be of no avail to them as they are assigned to the telestial glory.[24]

5. *They are liars, who love and make lies.* (*D&C 76:103*)

6. *They are sorcerers.* (*D&C 76:103*)

7. *They are adulterers.* (*D&C 76:103*)

8. *They are whoremongers.* (*D&C 76:103*)

These are they who were vile and abominable while upon the earth, who never rose above the level of the carnal man, but remained an enemy to God in their sins.[25]

9. *They deny not the Holy Spirit.* (*D&C 76:83*)

Just as the vision reveals the greatness of their depravity, it also reveals that these individuals have not committed the unpardonable sin and become sons of perdition. Since they have never completely accepted the gospel and then rebelled against it, they are saved from the worst of all fates and are able to achieve a limited portion of God's eternal rewards.

"The Vision" also identifies the inhabitants of the telestial kingdom by tracing their route through the eternal worlds, saying that

10. *They suffer the wrath of God on earth.* (*D&C 76:104*)

11. *They are thrust down to hell.* (*D&C 76:84, 106*)

12. *They do not resurrect in the first resurrection.* (*D&C 76:102*)

13. *They suffer the wrath of Almighty God in hell until the second resurrection.* (*D&C 76:85, 105-106*)

14. *They are then redeemed from the devil.* (*D&C 76:85*)

15. *They finally bow before Christ, confess, and are assigned their eternal inheritance.* (*D&C 76:110-111*)

[23]As James wrote, "The devils also believe, and tremble." (Jas. 2:19)

[24]See D&C 76:99-101; Mt. 7:21-23.

[25]See Mos. 16:12; 26:3-4; Al. 41:11, 13.

In the great revelation the Lord also outlines the nature of their reward:

1. *The glory of their kingdoms surpasses mortal understanding, though it is less than the glory of the terrestrial.* (*D&C 76:89-90, 81*)
2. *They cannot come to where God and Christ dwell, worlds without end.* (*D&C 76:112*)
3. *They are ministered to by the Holy Ghost and by angels from the terrestrial kingdom.* (*D&C 76:86-88*)

These terrestrial angels are directed, in turn, by celestial beings.[26]

4. *They shall be heirs of salvation.* (*D&C 76:88*)
5. *They shall be servants of the Most High.* (*D&C 76:112*)

Items three, four, and five (above) seem to indicate that these individuals may accept the limited portion of the gospel message available to them while in the telestial kingdom and grow and progress there to some limited degree.

Parley P. Pratt understood their positions as servants to the Most High to be, in reality, servitude to those of the higher kingdoms, writing that "They never can come where God and Christ dwell, *but will be servants in the dominions of the Saints, their former victims.*"[27]

The Terrestrial Glory

In "The Vision," Joseph Smith recorded that "we saw the glory of the terrestrial *which excels in all things the glory of the telestial, even in glory, and in power, and in might, and in dominion.*"[28] This glorious inheritance will be granted to a higher class of people than those consigned to the telestial kingdom. While the inhabitants of the telestial kingdom are to be those who were wicked and corrupt while on earth, the terrestrial kingdom will be inhabited by those who in mortality gave obedience to a higher level of law. Yet even these individuals lacked

[26]D&C 76:87.
[27]Parley P. Pratt, *Key To The Science of Theology, op cit.*, p. 83.
[28]D&C 76:91.

valor in their service to Jesus, "Wherefore, they obtain not the crown over the kingdom of our God."[29]

The revealed keys to their identity and status are:

1. *They are honorable men of the earth.* (*D&C 76:75*)
2. *They are not valiant in the testimony of Jesus.*[30] (*D&C 76:79*)

As is the case with the inhabitants of the telestial and celestial kingdoms, their course through the eternal worlds is traced in "The Vision" as an aid to their identification:

3. *They are honorable men on earth who were blinded by the craftiness of men.*[31] (*D&C 76:75*)
4. *They died without law.*[32] (*D&C 76:72*)
5. *They went into the spirit prison, heard the gospel there, and received it.*[33] (*D&C 76:73-74*)

---

[29]D&C 76:79. Because of their lack of diligence and valor they have failed to prepare and purify themselves by making full use of the gospel program which was available to them. As the Lord revealed, "They who are *not sanctified through the law which I have given unto you,* even the law of Christ, must inherit another kingdom, even that of a terrestrial kingdom, or that of a telestial kingdom." (D&C 88:21)

[30]Some have erroneously taught within the Church that Latter-day Saints, if they gain a kingdom of glory, will go only to the celestial or the telestial kingdoms. It would appear that, contrary to their teaching, many of the saints will inherit the terrestrial glory. As explained by Elder Spencer W. Kimball,

> This is a gospel of individual work. I wish our Latter-day Saints could become more valiant. As I read the seventy-sixth section of the Doctrine and Covenants, the great vision given to the Prophet Joseph Smith, *I remember that the Lord says to that terrestrial degree of glory may go those who are not valiant in the testimony, which means that many of us who have received baptism by proper authority, many who have received other ordinances, even temple blessings, will not reach the celestial kingdom of glory unless we live the commandments and are valiant.*
>
> What is being valiant? . . . There are many people in this Church today who think they live, but they are dead to the spiritual things. And I believe even many who are making the pretenses of being active are also spiritually dead. Their service is much of the letter and less of the spirit. (*Conference Report,* April 1951, pp. 104-105.)

[31]See Mor. 8:28-41; 2 Ne. 28:1-16.

[32]Though many die without law and therefore escape the initial commitment to hell because of Christ's atonement (see 2 Ne. 9:25-27; Mos. 3:11-12; 15:24-25), it does not follow that they will also be resurrected without law in the first resurrection, "For for this cause was the gospel preached also to them that are dead, *that they might be judged according to men in the flesh,* but live according to God in the spirit." (1 Pet. 4:6) The scriptures repeatedly assert that the gospel is eventually to be preached to "every nation, and kindred, and tongue, and people," unto "all people" and "all nations." (See Rev. 14:6; D&C 133:6-9, 37; 42:58; 1:4; 90:11; Al. 30:8; etc.) At some point in his eternal progression (whether in the premortal life, in mortality, or in the spirit world), every man must have the opportunity to hear the gospel and place himself in a position of complete conformity with it, rebellion against it, or acceptance of its precepts but with only limited compliance.

Although the atonement of Christ frees those who died without knowledge of gospel

These five clues are somewhat ambiguous and leave a number of questions unanswered except by private interpretation. As with the inhabitants of the telestial kingdoms, the revealed word stops short of a full explanation concerning the nature of these terrestrial beings.

One conclusion remains predominant, however. Though these people have good intentions while on earth, they will be limited at the last day because their desires were not fully translated into works and service. They may have given lip service to righteous principles but they did not fully apply them in their own lives. They may have carried the banner of Jesus but they have not served Him with valor.

"The Vision" defines the nature of the reward prepared for the inhabitants of the terrestrial kingdom:

1. *Their bodies are terrestrial, not celestial, and differ from celestial bodies in glory as the moon differs from the sun. (D&C 76:71, 78)*

---

law from the sufferings of hell until they have heard the gospel in the spirit world, it does not follow that the great bulk of mankind who are in this category are automatically spared from the dangers of hell and are guaranteed at least a terrestrial resurrection. They must someday make a decision concerning the gospel and then reap the eventual outcome of their decision.

The justice of God does not condemn a man to live in a higher glory than he may truly merit any more than it condemns one to suffer in hell without reason. For example, a person who desires evil things, yet who died without the gospel, would not be happy in the terrestrial glory, where they receive "the presence of the Son" (D&C 76:77). As Moroni taught,

> *Ye would be more miserable to dwell with a holy and just God, under a consciousness of your filthiness before him, than ye would to dwell with the damned souls in hell.*
>
> For behold when ye shall be brought to see your nakedness before God, and also the glory of God, and the holiness of Jesus Christ, it will kindle a flame of unquenchable fire upon you. (Mor. 9:4-5. See also Al. 41:11-13; 42:25-26; Mos. 2:38-39.)

[33]The privilege of coming forth in the first resurrection, at the time of Christ's coming in glory, is promised to this group by the Lord:

> Another trump shall sound, which is the *second* trump; and then cometh the redemption of those *who are Christ's* at his coming; *who have received their part in that prison which is prepared for them, that they might receive the gospel, and be judged according to men in the flesh.* (D&C 88:99)

It may be deduced from the above as well as in D&C 76:73-74, that this group accepted the gospel. How else can they be Christ's? How else can they be just and come forth in the resurrection of the just without coming to Christ? (See D&C 84:50-53; 35:12; Jn. 3:18-21,36. Note John's statement that those who come forth in the first resurrection will be *priests* and will *reign* with Christ, which surely implies gospel acceptance. (Rev. 20:4-6) What purpose would be accomplished by having people who are not useful servants of Christ live on earth as resurrected beings throughout the millennium? The gospel and its ordinances are designed to prepare men for the highest of the three kingdoms, yet many who accept those ordinances will fall below that level and will dwell in the terrestrial world.

2. *They receive of Christ's glory but not of His fulness.* (*D&C 76:76*)

3. *They receive of the presence of the Son, but not the fulness of the Father.* (*D&C 76:77*)

4. *They obtain not the crown over the kingdom of our God.* (*D&C 76:79*)

5. *From among them are appointed ministering angels to govern the telestial kingdoms.* (*D&C 76:86-88*)

6. *Their kingdom excels the telestial in glory, power, might and dominion.* (*D&C 76:91*)

Concerning their reward apostle Orson Pratt explained,

> But how about these terrestrials, can they come up into the celestial? *No, their intelligence and knowledge have not prepared and adapted them to dwell with those who reign in celestial glory, consequently they can not even be angels in that glory. They have not obeyed the law that pertains to that glory, and hence they could not abide it.* But will there be blessings administered to them by those who dwell in celestial glory? *Yes, angels will be sent forth from the celestial world to minister to those who inherit the glory of the moon, bearing messages of joy and peace and of all that which is calculated to exalt, to redeem and ennoble those who have been resurrected into a terrestrial glory.* They can receive the Spirit of the Lord there, and the ministration of angels there.[34]

The Celestial Glory

As was seen earlier in the chapter, "In the celestial glory there are three heavens or degrees."[35] The status of those that inherit the lowest of these degrees will be considered in this section; the condition of those who gain the highest degree, or exaltation, will be the subject of chapter XI. There is, at present, insufficient information to delineate the nature of the middle degree so that subject is not treated in this volume.

The scriptures again set forth the qualifications one must meet to attain this glory:

1. *They have been baptized by immersion.* (*D&C 76:51*)

Baptism is the "strait gate" by which men become eligible to enter the celestial kingdom.[36] To be baptized is essential to

[34] JD 15:322. Jan. 19, 1873.
[35] D&C 131:1.
[36] Mt. 7:13-14.

every man who seeks to "fulfill all righteousness,"[37] for the Savior has commanded that *"except a man be born of water and of the Spirit, he cannot enter into the kingdom of God."*[38] Baptism is to be preceded by certain acts and desires, if it is to be efficacious:

> All those who *humble themselves before God,* and *desire to be baptized,* and come forth with *broken hearts* and *contrite spirits,* and *witness before the church* that they have *truly repented* of all their sins, and are *willing to take upon them the name of Jesus Christ, having a determination to serve him to the end,* and truly manifest by their works that they have received of the Spirit of Christ unto the *remission of their sins, shall be received by baptism into his church.*[39]

2. *They receive the Holy Spirit through the laying on of hands by authorized priesthood members.* (*D&C 76:52*)

3. *They receive the testimony of Jesus.* (*D&C 76:51*)

Not only do they receive the confirmation ordinance; they also seek and receive the guidance of the Holy Ghost. "The testimony of Jesus is the spirit of prophecy,"[40] and that testimony comes only through the Holy Spirit. Jesus taught that "when the Comforter is come, . . . even the Spirit of truth, which proceedeth from the Father, *he shall testify of me:* And ye also shall bear witness."[41] These are individuals who have sought and received divine revelation and guidance and have used it to shape their life's direction.

4. *They have repented of all their sins.* (*Moses 6:57*)

The Lord has revealed that *"all men, everywhere, must repent, or they can in nowise inherit the kingdom of God, for no unclean thing can dwell there."*[42] To the Nephites He proclaimed that *"no unclean thing can enter into his [the Father's] kingdom;* therefore nothing entereth into his rest save it be those who have washed their garments in my blood, because of their faith, and the repentance of *all their sins."*[43] They have made their repentance

[37] 2 Ne. 31:5-9.
[38] Jn. 3:5.
[39] D&C 20:37. See also Mos. 18:8-11.
[40] Rev. 19:10.
[41] Jn. 15:26-27.
[42] Moses 6:57.
[43] 3 Ne. 27:19. See Al. 11:37.

complete, for James warned that *"whosoever shall keep the whole law, and yet offend in one point, he is guilty of all."*[44]

5. *They have kept the commandments.* (*D&C 76:52*)

6. *They are just and true.* (*D&C 76:53*)

They have sought the word of God, learned what He would have them do, and then have diligently sought to comply. They are motivated by a love of God and a desire to come into his kingdom. As the Savior revealed,

> *He that hath my commandments, and keepeth them, he it is that loveth me:* and he that loveth me shall be loved of my Father, and I will love him, and will manifest myself to him. . . .
>
> *It a man love me, he will keep my words:* and my Father will love him, and we will come unto him, and make our abode with him.[45]

7. *They have overcome by faith.* (*D&C 76:53*)

Herein lies the principle of valor that separates the inhabitants of the celestial glory from those who inherit the terrestrial kingdom. The latter were honorable men, with good intentions, yet they failed to exert themselves in the gospel cause. Joseph Smith remarked that "Salvation means a man's being placed beyond the power of all his enemies."[46] That person who desires to enter into the celestial kingdom must diligently overcome every enemy—every flaw and imperfection in his character, every temptation and evil desire—until he is beyond them. He must heed Paul's instruction to "Work out your own salvation with fear and trembling."[47]

8. *They have remained faithful to the end.* (*3 Ne. 27:16-19*)

They have continued to labor in the Lord's work and to strive to keep His commandments throughout their lifetime. As Nephi recorded,

> I heard a voice from the Father, saying: Yea, the words of my Beloved are true and faithful. *He that endureth to the end, the same shall be saved.*
>
> And now, my beloved brethren, I know by this that *unless a*

[44]Jas. 2:10. See Mt. 5:29-30.
[45]Jn. 14:21, 23.
[46]HC 5:392. May 17, 1843.
[47]Phil. 2:12.

> *man shall endure to the end, in following the example of the Son of the living God, he cannot be saved.*[48]

As with each of the other kingdoms, the Lord has helped to identify the recipients of the celestial glory by tracing their course through the various stages of the eternal plan. In addition to their mortal diligence,

9. *They have their names written in the Lamb's book of life in heaven.*[49] (*D&C 76:68*)
10. *At death they go into paradise where they are among the just men made perfect.*[50] (*D&C 76:69*)
11. *They come forth in the resurrection of the just, the first resurrection.* (*D&C 76:50, 63-65*)
12. *They are made perfect through the atonement of Christ.* (*D&C 76:69*)

They come unto Christ, are partakers of His grace and mercy at the judgment day, and the Lord holds them guiltless before the Father.[51]

It is difficult to fully define the reward and final status of these celestial beings using only "The Vision" as a basis, for that view of the celestial glory is actually a glimpse of exaltation, the highest degree of that kingdom. Those who inherit the lower portion of the celestial glory, however, will receive certain blessings which will so far exceed the blessings of the terrestrial inhabitants as the glory of the sun exceeds that of the moon. Their blessings:

1. *Their resurrected bodies will be celestial.* (*D&C 76:70*)
2. *They shall have reigned on earth with Christ during the millennium.* (*D&C 76:63*)
3. *They live in the presence of the Father, the Son, and the Holy Ghost.*[52] (*D&C 76:62*)
4. *They enjoy the company and association of celestial beings.* (*D&C 76:67*)

---

[48] 2 Ne. 31:15-16.
[49] See pp. 283-284.
[50] See pp. 124-125.
[51] See 3 Ne. 27:16.
[52] See pp. 23-25.

5. *They may be assigned to minister to the terrestrial kingdom. (D&C 76:87)*
6. *Their function will be to minister to exalted beings. (D&C 132:16)*

These individuals will be trusted and loyal servants. As capable and chosen ambassadors of the gods they will perform valuable service and reap the joy which it brings throughout all eternity. The Lord has revealed that such individuals

> *Are appointed angels in heaven; which angels are ministering servants,* to minister for those who are worthy of a far more, and an exceeding, and an eternal weight of glory. . . .
>
> They cannot be enlarged, but *remain separately and singly, without exaltation, in their saved condition, to all eternity;* and from henceforth are not gods, but are angels of God forever and ever.[53]

Orson Pratt gave a concise account of the position these beings will fill in the celestial kingdom. He said,

> Those other classes . . . have neglected the new and everlasting covenant of marriage. They can not inherit this glory and these kingdoms—they can not be crowned in the celestial world. What purpose will they serve? *They will be sent on errands—be sent to other worlds as missionaries to minister, they will be sent on whatever business the Lord sees proper; in other words, they will be servants.* To whom will they be servants? To those who have obeyed and remained faithful to the new and everlasting covenant, and have been exalted to thrones; to those who have covenanted before God with wives so that they may raise up and multiply immortal intelligent beings through all the ages of eternity. *Here is the distinction of classes, but all of the same glory, called celestial glory.*[54]

Such celestial beings have been seen in various visions of the heavens. In "The Vision," for instance, Joseph Smith and Sidney Rigdon reported,

> We beheld the glory of the Son, on the right hand of the Father, and received of his fulness;
>
> And *saw the holy angels, and them who are sanctified before his throne, worshiping God, and the Lamb, who worship him forever and ever.*[55]

In his vision of the heavens the prophet Lehi "saw God sitting

---

[53]D&C 132:16-17.
[54]JD 15:321-322. Jan. 19, 1873.
[55]D&C 76:20-21.

upon his throne, surrounded with *numberless concourses of angels in the attitude of singing and praising their God.*"[56]

John the Revelator received several such views of the celestial glory. In one he saw

> A throne was set in heaven, and one sat on the throne. . . .
>
> And round about the throne were *four and twenty seats:* and upon the seats I saw four and twenty elders sitting, *clothed in white raiment; and they had on their heads crowns of gold.* . . .
>
> The four and twenty elders fall down before him that sat on the throne, and worship him that liveth for ever and ever, and cast their crowns before the throne, saying,
>
> Thou art worthy, O Lord, to receive glory and honour and power: for thou hast created all things, and for thy pleasure they are and were created.[57]

Later he saw a numberless concourse of angels or celestial beings who served the Lord and the elders (the elders were, apparently, exalted beings):

> After this I beheld, and, lo, *a great multitude, which no man could number,* of all nations, and kindreds, and people, and tongues, stood before the throne, and before the Lamb, *clothed with white robes, and palms in their hands:*
>
> And cried with a loud voice, saying, Salvation to our God which sitteth upon the throne, and unto the Lamb.
>
> And all the angels stood round about the throne, and about the elders and the four beasts, and fell before the throne on their faces, and worshiped God.
>
> Saying, Amen: Blessing, and glory, and wisdom, and thanksgiving, and honour, and power, and might, be unto our God for ever and ever. Amen.
>
> And one of the elders answered, saying unto me, What are these which are arrayed in white robes? and whence came they?
>
> And I said unto him, Sir, thou knowest. And he said to me, *These are they which came out of great tribulation, and have washed their robes, and made them white in the blood of the Lamb.*
>
> *Therefore are they before the throne of God, and serve him day and night in his temple: and he that sitteth on the throne shall dwell among them.*
>
> They shall hunger no more, neither thirst any more; neither shall the sun light on them, nor any heat.

[56]1 Ne. 1:8.

[57]Rev. 4:2, 4, 10-11. An interpretive revelation given to Joseph Smith revealed that these men "were elders who had been faithful in the work of the ministry and were dead; who belonged to the seven churches, and were then in the paradise of God." (D&C 77:5)

For the Lamb which is in the midst of the throne shall feed them, *and shall lead them unto living fountains of waters: and God shall wipe away all tears from their eyes.*[58]

John the Revelator described yet a third group of celestial beings which he saw in the heavens:

And I heard a voice from heaven, as the voice of many waters, and as the voice of a great thunder: and *I heard the voice of harpers harping with their harps:*

And they sung as it were a new song before the throne, and before the four beasts, and the elders: and no man could learn that song but the hundred and forty and four thousand, which were redeemed from the earth.

These are they which were not defiled with women; for they are virgins. *These are they which follow the Lamb withersoever he goeth. These were redeemed* from among men, being the firstfruits unto God and to the Lamb.

And in their mouth was found no guile: for they are without fault before the throne of God.[59]

From these revelations man can draw at least a limited concept of the life led by these celestial beings and the desirability of their associations.

Damnation Means a Limit to Progression

Those who inherit the telestial glory, the terrestrial glory, and even the lower degrees in the celestial glory will all be damned, for there are boundaries set beyond which they can never pass, throughout all eternity. In the case of the telestial and terrestrial inhabitants, their resurrected bodies are suited to only those degrees of glory and will not allow them to enter a higher kingdom, worlds without end. The law they have chosen to live has fixed their limits, and "he who is not able to abide the law of a celestial kingdom cannot abide a celestial glory."[60]

Man's mortal activity serves to open or close the doors to his eternal progress. Speaking of baptism, the gateway to the celestial kingdom, the Lord warned,

---

[58]Rev. 7:9-17.

[59]Rev. 14:2-5. Some believe that these individuals who were virgins and are without fault are those who died in childhood and have come into the celestial kingdom.

[60]D&C 88:22.

> They who believe not on your words, and are not baptized in water in my name, for the remission of their sins, that they may receive the Holy Ghost, *shall be damned, and shall not come into my Father's kingdom where my Father and I am.*
>
> And this revelation unto you, and commandment, *is in force from this very hour upon all the world.*[61]

The Lord has revealed, concerning those of the lower kingdoms, that *"where God and Christ dwell they cannot come, worlds without end."*[62]

Yet damnation does not refer only to non-members of the Church. A revelation warning the saints of the danger of slothfulness warns that they, through lack of valor, may lose their reward, and implies the damnation which exists to those who inherit the terrestrial glory:

> *It is not meet that I should command in all things;* for he that is compelled in all things, the same is a slothful and not a wise servant; wherefore *he receiveth no reward.*
>
> Verily I say, *men should be anxiously engaged in a good cause, and do many things of their own free will, and bring to pass much righteousness;*
>
> For the power is in them, wherein they are agents unto themselves. *And inasmuch as men do good they shall in nowise lose their reward.*
>
> But he that doeth not anything until he is commanded, and *receiveth a commandment with doubtful heart, and keepeth it with slothfulness, the same is damned.*[63]

Even those who are in the celestial kingdom, if they do not meet the requirements for exaltation, are limited in their progress and are relegated to positions of servitude rather than rulership in that kingdom. Failure to enter into the divine covenant of celestial marriage, for instance, limits them so that "they cannot be enlarged,"[64] and so they "cannot have an increase."[65] And though they partake of a portion of the celestial glory, they cannot experience the full glory of exalted beings, for the Lord has warned that "the angels and the gods are appointed there, by whom they cannot pass; they cannot, therefore, inherit my glory."[66] In revealing the covenant of eternal marriage the Lord commanded the Church,

---

[61]D&C 84:74-75. See also 42:60; 68:9; 112:29; 49:5.
[62]D&C 76:112.
[63]D&C 58:26-29.
[64]D&C 132:17.
[65]D&C 131:4.
[66]D&C 132:18.

> Prepare thy heart to receive and obey the instructions which I am about to give unto you; for all those who have this law revealed unto them must obey the same.
>
> For behold, *I reveal unto you a new and an everlasting covenant; and if ye abide not that covenant, then are ye damned; for no one can reject this covenant and be permitted to enter into my glory.*
>
> *For all who will have a blessing at my hands shall abide the law which was appointed for that blessing, and the conditions thereof,* as were instituted from before the foundation of the world.
>
> And as pertaining to the new and everlasting covenant, it was instituted for the fulness of my glory; and he *that receiveth a fulness thereof must and shall abide the law, or he shall be damned, saith the Lord God.*[67]

While answering a series of questions put to him by various inquirers, Joseph Smith was asked the question, "Will everybody be damned, but the Mormons?" His reply was significant: *"Yes, and a great portion of them, unless they repent, and work righteousness."*[68]

This is not to say that there will be no progress by those who inherit the lesser glories, only that there are limits set beyond which they cannot pass. The passages cited above strongly imply that there is no progression from one kingdom of glory to another kingdom of a higher degree, though the Church has never taken a formal doctrinal stand on this point. It should be recalled that those of the telestial kingdom receive that glory because of their firm refusal to accept the program of growth set forth in the gospel, and that the inhabitants of the terrestrial glory received that kingdom primarily because of their lack of diligence and valor in applying the principles of eternal progression. Progress is not what they sought, and the resurrection restored them to a similar status in the eternal worlds.

---

[67]D&C 132:3-6.

[68]HC 3:28. May 8, 1838. See also JD 9:315. On the theme of sectarian salvation and damnation, President Brigham Young said,

> Sectarians have not the Priesthood; but all of them who live according to the best light and intelligence they can obtain through faithfulness to what they believe, as taught unto them, *will receive a kingdom and glory that will far transcend all their expectations, imaginations, or visions in their most excited moments,* whether in their falling-down power, jumping power, or squawling power. All they have ever desired or anticipated they will receive, and far more; *but they cannot dwell with the Father and Son, unless they go through these ordeals that are ordained for the Church of the Firstborn. The ordinances of the house of God are expressly for the Church of the Firstborn.* (JD 8:154. Aug. 26, 1860)

That progress which is made in the lower kingdoms will be much less than that which can be realized in the celestial glory. There is no scriptural basis whatsoever for the contention that those in the telestial and terrestrial kingdoms may someday progress to the point of development which God now occupies. They are damned, they will never be able to abide celestial law and glory.

Apostle Melvin J. Ballard summarized their situation well when he taught,

> The question is often asked, 'Is it possible for one who attains Telestial Glory in time in the eternal world to live so well that he may graduate from the Telestial and pass into the Terrestrial, and then after a season that he may progress from that and be ultimately worthy of the Celestial Glory?' That is the query that has been asked. *I have just read the answer, so far as the Telestial group is concerned. 'Where God and Christ dwell they cannot come, worlds without end.' I take it upon the same basis, the same argument likewise applies to the Terrestrial World.* Those whose lives have entitled them to Terrestrial Glory can never gain Celestial Glory. *One who gains possession of the lowest degree of the Telestial Glory may ultimately arise to the highest degree of that glory, but no provision has been made for promotion from one glory to another.* Let us be reasonable about it.
>
> I wish to say in illustrating the subject that if three men were starting out on an endless race, one having an advantage of one mile, the other of two miles, and each one could run as fast as the other, when would the last ever catch up to the first? If you can tell me that, I can tell you when candidates for the Telestial Glory will get into the Celestial Glory. *Each will grow, but their development will be prescribed by their environment, and there is a reason for it.*
>
> Applying this illustration to those who are entitled to the different degrees of glory: *He who enters the Celestial Glory has the advantage over all others. He dwells in the presence of the Father and the Son. His teachers are the highest.* The others will receive all they learn from the Celestial to the Terrestrial, from the Terrestrial to the Telestial. *They get it second hand and third hand, and how can they ever hope to grow as fast as those who drink from the fountain head.* Again, those who come forth in the Celestial Glory with Celestial bodies have bodies that are more refined. They are different. *The very fibre and texture of the Celestial body is more pure and holy than a Telestial or Terrestrial body, and a Celestial body alone can endure Celestial Glory.*[69]

[69]N.B. Lundwall, *The Vision, op. cit.*, pp. 48-49.

Christ's parable of the talents should also be recalled in this context. Those who labored diligently for the Master were abundantly rewarded for their valor. But concerning the unprofitable servant the Lord commanded,

> *Take therefore the talent from him,* and give it unto him which hath ten talents.
>
> For unto every one that hath shall be given, and he shall have abundance: but *from him that hath not shall be taken away even that which he hath.*[70]

SUMMARY

1. God has created so many worlds that they are innumerable to man, though He is aware of their progress and visits them in their turn. Many of these worlds have already "passed away" and have reached their eternal glory and condition. It may be presumed that they are now inhabited by resurrected beings.
2. God controls the movement and rotation of the eternal worlds. It has been revealed that a key to the movement of these spheres is the great Kolob, a star near the residence of God. This is, apparently, several galaxies removed from the earth's present position.
3. The eternal worlds are divided primarily into three levels or degrees of glory: telestial, terrestrial, and celestial. Those who inherit these kingdoms will have resurrected bodies of corresponding glory.
4. The three general degrees of glory are each adapted to the lesser or greater degree of perfection of its eternal inhabitants.
5. The law which man abides in mortality determines the kingdom and degree of glory which he will inherit for all eternity. He will dwell in eternity with those having similar desires and capacities to his own.
6. The glory of the telestial world is so great that it surpasses human understanding. Yet it is reserved for the lowest of earth's society other than the sons of perdition. It will be the inheritance of those who have steadfastly refused to accept the gospel and the wicked and sinful who, however, have not become sons of perdition. They will be ministered to by the Holy Ghost and by angels from the terrestrial kingdom.
7. The glory of the terrestrial kingdom far exceeds that of the telestial. It will be the reward of honorable men who have

[70]Mt. 25:28-29.

lacked valor and determination in their compliance to gospel standards and service to Christ and His Church. Though some of them may have rejected the gospel during their mortal probation, it appears that this group will all have had gospel law taught to them in time to come forth in the first resurrection, the resurrection of the just. They will be visited by Christ and ministering angels from the celestial kingdom.

8. The celestial glory exceeds the terrestrial in glory, might and dominion. It is sub-divided into three levels. Admittance to the celestial kingdom is granted only to those who have accepted the gospel through baptism and confirmation, received a testimony through the guidance of the Holy Ghost, and then valiantly overcome their many obstacles and temptations through faith. They received of Christ's mercy and forgiveness so they are able to enter the kingdom without sin. Those who inherit the lowest of the celestial degrees serve as ministers and servants to those who gain exaltation.

9. Damnation means a limit to eternal progression. Every person in the telestial, terrestrial and celestial glories is damned to some degree except those who merit and receive exaltation in the highest level of the celestial glory.

10. Scriptural evidence indicates that those in the lower kingdoms can never graduate upward from one glory to a higher kingdom, nor will the inhabitants of the lower glories ever progress to the point where they are equal to celestial glory and abilities. Indeed, it appears that telestial and terrestrial inhabitants have but little upward motivation and desire to progress.

CHAPTER XI

EXALTATION

Exaltation Is Perfection and Godhood

A FUNDAMENTAL PRINCIPLE OF THE GOSPEL OF JESUS CHRIST is that man may be exalted and attain the highest of all goals: godhood. Without this concept man is unable to comprehend the purposes and scope of the great gospel plan; the divine plan of salvation must needs be unfulfilled. Man's true goal is not merely to "go to heaven," to "enter the celestial kingdom," or "regain the presence of God." He is to meet a higher challenge, that of personal perfection and godhood.

The admonition to seek perfection is not an idle challenge. The goal is not an impossible dream. Rather, it is the guiding principle in the life of everyone who has truly accepted Christ and His gospel. *"Be ye therefore perfect, even as your Father which is in heaven is perfect,"*[1] was the goal Jesus set for mankind. The scriptures often repeat His commandment. Paul taught that the Church was established

> *For the perfecting of the saints. . . .*
>
> Till we all come in the unity of the faith, and of the knowledge of the Son of God, *unto a perfect man, unto the measure of the stature of the fulness of Christ.*[2]

To the Colossians Paul wrote that the goal of their labors was *"to present every man perfect* in Christ Jesus."[3] To Timothy he wrote that the purpose of the scriptures was *"that the man of God may be perfect,* thoroughly furnished unto all good works."[4] To the Hebrews he gave the admonition to progress beyond the fundamental principles to a higher level of life and joined them in the challenge, saying *"let us go on unto perfection."*[5] He

[1]Mt. 5:48.
[2]Eph. 4:12-13.
[3]Col. 1:28.
[4]2 Tim. 3:17.
[5]Heb. 6:1.

knew full well the necessity of setting exaltation as man's true goal and recognized that no other goal would lead to man's perfection. He saw that "the law made nothing perfect, but the bringing in of a better hope did."[6] And he expressed his desire to the Hebrews that God "make you perfect in every good work."[7]

This commandment to seek and achieve perfection is the most difficult of all man's responsibilities, and but few men will have the determination to endure to the end in their quest to fulfill it. As Apostle Melvin J. Ballard explained, "I wish to say that *few men will become what God is. And yet, all men may become what He is if they will pay the price.*"[8] Those who would give up prematurely and relinquish their hope of exaltation would do well to memorize and fully accept Nephi's resolve:

> *I will go and do the things which the Lord hath commanded, for I know that the Lord giveth no commandments unto the children of men, save he shall prepare a way for them that they may accomplish the things which he commandeth them.*[9]

The Rich Blessings of Exaltation

Surely the achievement of perfection, and therefore exaltation and godhood, is the most significant goal man can seek. Exaltation, or eternal life as it is often termed in the scriptures, is the goal God desires all mankind to achieve. Just as every father desires the very best for his children, the Eternal Father in heaven wants man to share His eternal joy. His entire plan of salvation is directed to that end, and He has revealed that *"this is my work and my glory—to bring to pass the immortality and eternal life of man."*[10] Surely the Giver of good gifts[11] knows what is of greatest worth for His children, and He has reserved this reward as the greatest of His gifts[12] unto the most righteous of His loved ones.

---

[6]Heb. 7:19.
[7]Heb. 13:21. See also 1 Pet. 5:10.
[8]N. B. Lundwall, *The Vision, op. cit.*, p. 45.
[9]1 Ne. 3:7.
[10]Moses 1:39.
[11]See. Mt. 7:11.
[12]See 1 Ne. 15:36; D&C 6:13.

Those unaccustomed to the idea may scoff and assume that the Father would never share His dominions with His children. Yet the scriptures testify that God, the Father of the spirits of all mankind,[13] has sought to exalt man and to give him just such dominion. The psalmist recognized this as he queried,

> What is man, that thou art mindful of him? and the son of man, that thou visitest him?
>
> *For thou hast made him a little lower than the angels, and hast crowned him with glory and honour.*
>
> *Thou madest him to have dominion over the works of thy hands;* thou hast put all things under his feet:[14]

And God has revealed His word that "I have said, Ye are gods; and all of you are children of the most High."[15] The Father desires that His children progress to the point that they can share His association, powers and dominion throughout all eternity.

The scriptures reveal a detailed explanation of the nature of exaltation. Those who attain this, the greatest of all rewards, will receive:

Godhood

The recipients of this reward will "have entered into their exaltation, according to the promises, and sit upon thrones, *and are not angels but are gods.*"[16]

According to President Brigham Young, the bestowing of godhood is accomplished through the process of ordination:

> We cannot receive, while in the flesh, the keys to form and fashion kingdoms and to organize matter, for they are beyond our capacity and calling, beyond this world. In the resurrection, men who have been faithful and diligent in all things in the flesh, have kept their first and second estate, and [*are*] *worthy to be crowned Gods, even the sons of God, will be ordained to organize matter.*[17]

---

[13]See Num. 16:22; Heb. 12:9.

[14]Ps. 8:4-6. See also Heb. 1:4-7.

[15]Ps. 82:6.

[16]D&C 132:37. See also 76:58.

[17]JD 15:137. Aug. 24, 1872.

Eternal Association with the Father and Christ

"These shall dwell in the presence of God and his Christ forever and ever."[18] This is not understood as an indication that exalted man will always be in close proximity to their persons, but rather that man will have the privilege of conversing with them even across the immensities of space as the need arises. As Orson Pratt explained,

> What are we to understand by being in the presence of God? *Is it necessary, to do so, that we should be in the same vicinity or within a few yards or feet of him? I think not.* We are now laboring under the imperfections of the fall, and because of that fall a veil shuts us from his presence; but *let the effects of the fall be removed and mankind be able to again look upon the face of their Father and Creator, and they will be in his presence. . . .* There is something more perfect in the construction of the works of the Almighty that lets man into His presence whatsoever part of the universe he may exist in—we may have the veil removed, and His presence become visible.
>
> *Can they converse with Him when situated at these immense distances from His person? Yes. How? Through those more perfect faculties which God will give to immortal man.* It is as easy for His children, when they are perfected and made like him, to converse with Him at these immense distances and for their eyes to pierce all these creations as it is for their Father and God to do so.[19]

Membership in the Church of the Firstborn

A special Church organization exists in the celestial glory, and membership is limited to those who gain exaltation there.[20] While revealing the reward of those who inherit exaltation in the celestial glory the Lord revealed that "they are they who are the church of the Firstborn."[21] There is no scriptural indication that others besides exalted beings participate in this sacred association. To the contrary, the Lord has revealed that participants in this Church have gained the fulness of godhood:

> I give unto you these sayings that you may understand and know how to worship, and know what you worship, that you may come unto the Father in my name, and *in due time receive of his fulness.*

[18]D&C 76:62.
[19]JD 16:364, 367. Jan. 27, 1874.
[20]See D&C 76:71, 94; 88:4-5.
[21]D&C 76:54. See also 76:67, 102; 77:11.

For if you keep my commandments *you shall receive of his fulness, and be glorified in me as I am in the Father;* therefore, I say unto you, you shall receive grace for grace.

And now, verily I say unto you, I was in the beginning with the Father, and am the Firstborn;

And all those who are begotten through me are partakers of the glory of the same, and are the church of the Firstborn.[22]

Joint Inheritance with Christ

Those who achieve exaltation become joint heirs with Jesus Christ in their inheritance of the powers and glory of godhood. Paul taught that

> As many as are led by the Spirit of God, *they are the sons of God.*
>
> For ye have not received the spirit of bondage again to fear; but *ye have received the Spirit of adoption, whereby we cry, Abba, Father.*
>
> The Spirit itself beareth witness with our spirit, that *we are the children of God:*
>
> *And if children, then heirs: heirs of God, and joint-heirs with Christ; if so be that we may suffer with him, that we may be also glorified together.*
>
> For I reckon that the sufferings of this present time are not worthy to be compared with *the glory which shall be revealed in us.*[23]

In the eternal kingdoms all mankind will follow one of two paths, for they will become either servants or joint-heirs with Christ. Only the latter will be able to rule and reign in the heavens. Though they will be joint-heirs with the Savior, having equal power and dominion, the eternal organization will still place man under the jurisdiction of Jesus, for "they are Christ's, and Christ is God's."[24]

The Fulness and Glory of a Celestial Body

While telling of the blessings of exalted beings, the Lord revealed that "They are they into whose hands the Father has

---

[22]D&C 93:19-23.

[23]Ro. 8:14-18. See also Gal. 3:26-29; 4:1-7. The term "son of god," when used in the sense of a joint heirship with Christ, has reference to those who have accepted Christ and His Church on earth. (See D&C 39:4-6; 11:30; 35:2; Mos. 5:7.) Priesthood power is also a seeming prerequisite for those who become "sons of God" in this sense. (See Moses 6:67-68; D&C 45:8.) The implication of these passages is that man, while already a spirit-child of God the Father, may also become a son of Christ in the sense that they are His disciples and may eventually inherit a place in His celestial Church, the Church of the Firstborn. This is called spiritual rebirth. (See Mos. 5:7; 27:24-27; Al. 5:14, 49; 22:15; 36:23-26; 38:6; Jn. 1:12-13; 3:3-6; Tit. 3:5-7.)

[24]D&C 76:59.

given all things . . . who have *received of his fulness, and of his glory.*"[25] God has revealed the nature of the wondrous glory which exalted beings will inherit, saying that *"the glory of God is intelligence, or, in other words, light and truth.*"[26] In "The Vision" it is revealed that "these are they *whose bodies are celestial, whose glory is that of the sun, even the glory of God, the highest of all, whose glory the sun of the firmament* is written of as being typical."[27]

Priesthood Authority

Those who gain exaltation will be "priests of the Most High, after the order of Melchizedek, which was after the order of Enoch, which was after the order of the Only Begotten Son."[28] "The rights of the priesthood are inseparably connected with the powers of heaven,"[29] and priesthood power is the basis for exalted man's activities as a god, for "this greater priesthood administereth the gospel and *holdeth the key of the mysteries of the kingdom, even the key of the knowledge of God.*"[30]

Eternal Companionship of a Beloved Spouse

The Lord has revealed that

> If a man marry a wife by my word, which is my law, and by the new and everlasting covenant, and it is sealed unto them by the Holy Spirit of promise, by him who is anointed, unto whom I have appointed this power and the keys of this priesthood, . . . it shall be done unto them in all things whatsoever my servant hath put upon them, in time, and through all eternity; and *shall be of full force when they are out of the world; and they shall pass by the angels, and the gods, which are set there, to their exaltation and glory in all things, as hath been sealed upon their heads.*[31]

The marriage union, when consummated in God's holy temples by His authorized servants, remains in force in the celestial resurrection. This is basic to God's eternal program. As

[25] D&C 76:55-56.
[26] D&C 93:36. See also Jn. 1:14.
[27] D&C 76:70.
[28] D&C 76:57.
[29] D&C 121:36.
[30] D&C 84:19.
[31] D&C 132:19.

Paul stated the principle, *"Neither is the man without the woman, neither the woman without the man, in the Lord."*[32]

The principle is glorious, for it provides the basis for the Latter-day Saint understanding of the exalted state of womanhood. Without the principle of eternal marriage, woman would be barred from the privilege of exaltation, but as the married partner of an exalted man she can share all the privileges and blessings of godhood. As President John Taylor expressed it,

> *To be a priestess queen upon thy Heavenly Father's throne, and a glory to thy husband and offspring, to bear the souls of men, to people other worlds* (as thou didst bear their tabernacles in mortality) while eternity goes and eternity comes, and if you will receive it, lady, this is eternal life.[33]

And Parley P. Pratt wrote that "I learned that *the highest dignity of womanhood was to stand as a queen and a priestess to her husband, and to reign for ever and ever as the queen mother of her numerous and still increasing offspring.*"[34]

Eternal Powers of Procreation

Exalted beings will enjoy the power of procreation and will continue the process of bearing children which they began on earth during mortality. The Lord has revealed that exalted beings

> Shall pass by the angels, and the gods, which are set there, to their exaltation and glory in all things, as hath been sealed upon their heads, *which glory shall be a fulness and a continuation of the seeds forever and ever.*

---

[32]1 Cor. 11:11. The sectarian world has occasionally advanced their erroneous interpretation of Mt. 22:23-30, (also Mk. 12:18-25; Lk. 20:27-36) in opposition to this teaching. Jesus is quoted as saying, "In the resurrection they neither marry, nor are given in marriage . . .", and this is interpreted as evidence that no one enjoys the marriage relationship in the after life: a false interpretation. To the Latter-day Saints the Lord has revealed that the highest degree of the celestial kingdom can only be achieved through eternal marriage. (See D&C 131:1-4) It is understood, however, that such a marriage can only be consummated while in mortality, or done vicariously in the temples for those in the spirit world. If eternal marriage has not been consummated under these circumstances, it appears that resurrected beings will be unable to attain the highest degree of the celestial kingdom and are limited to angels', or servants', status in the celestial glory or a lesser kingdom. Indeed, this is the intent of the Savior's words when he said, *"In the resurrection,* they neither marry, nor are given in marriage, *but are as the angels of God in heaven."*

[33]N. B. Lundwall, *The Vision, op. cit.*, p. 147.

[34]Parley P. Pratt, *Autobiography of Parley P. Pratt* (sixth edition, Salt Lake City, Utah: Deseret Book Company, 1966), p. 298.

> *Then shall they be gods, because they have no end; therefore shall they be from everlasting to everlasting, because they continue.*[35]

The power to bear children in the resurrected state is fundamental to the eternal plan of salvation, for it is through these children that exalted beings will progress and be glorified. God has revealed that a man's wife or wives

> Are given unto him to multiply and replenish the earth, according to my commandment, and to fulfill the promise which was given by my Father before the foundation of the world, and *for their exaltation in the eternal worlds, that they may bear the souls of men; for herein is the work of my Father continued, that he may be glorified.*[36]

In reality, godhood is eternal parenthood, for the god-man relationship is actually a parent-child relationship. A god rules over his own children, and his kingdom increases as his eternal family is enlarged. As Orson Pratt expressed it,

> Who will be the subjects in the kingdom which they will rule who are exalted in the celestial kingdom of our God? Will they reign over their neighbors' children? Oh, no. Over whom then will they reign? *Their own children, their own posterity will be the citizens of their kingdoms; in other words, the patriarchal order will prevail there to the endless ages of eternity, and the children of each patriarch will be his while eternal ages roll on.*[37]

Just as men were first born as spirit children to their Eternal Father and His companion[38] the children born to resurrected beings are spirit beings[39] and must be sent in their turn to another earth to pass through the trials of mortality and obtain a physical body. A doctrinal statement issued by

---

[35]D&C 132:19-20.

[36]D&C 132:63.

[37]JD 15:319. Jan. 19, 1873.

[38]See Num. 16:22, Heb. 12:9. On this theme President Brigham Young said,

> There is no spirit but what was pure and holy when it came here from the celestial world. There is no spirit among the human family that was begotten in hell; none that were begotten by angels, or by any inferior being. *They were not produced by any being less than our Father in heaven. He is the Father of our spirits;* and if we could know, understand, and do His will, every soul would be prepared to return back into His presence. And when they get there, they would see that they had formerly lived there for ages, that they had previously been acquainted with every nook and corner, with the palaces, walks, and gardens; and they would embrace their Father, and He *would embrace them and say, 'My son, my daughter, I have you again;' and the child would say, 'O my Father, my Father, I am here again.'* (JD 4:268. Mar. 8, 1857)

[39]Spirit beings look exactly like mortal beings, for "the spirit of man [is] in the likeness of his person." (D&C 77:2. See 131:7-8)

the First Presidency of the Church on June 30, 1916, asserted in part,

> So far as the stages of eternal progression and attainment have been made known through divine revelation, we are to understand that *only resurrected and glorified beings can become parents of spirit offspring.* Only such exalted souls have reached maturity in the appointed course of eternal life; and *the spirits born to them in the eternal worlds will pass in due sequence through the several stages or estates by which the glorified parents have attained exaltation.*[40]

According to some Latter-day Saint leaders, the process for procreating spirit beings is identical to the process for conceiving and bringing forth children on earth. A statement by the First Presidency teaches that "*man as a spirit being was begotten and born of heavenly parents,* and reared to maturity in the eternal mansions of the Father, prior to coming upon the earth in a temporal body to undergo an experience in mortality."[41] This process was described by apostle Orson Pratt:

> If we were born in heaven before this world was made, the question might arise as to the nature of that birth. Was it by command that the spiritual substance, scattered through space, was miraculously brought together, and organized into a spiritual form, and called a spirit? Is that the way we were born? Is that the way that Jesus, the firstborn of every creature, was brought into existence? Oh no; *we were all born there after the same manner that we are here, that is to say, every person that had an existence before he came here had a literal father and a literal mother, a personal father and a personal mother;* hence the Apostle Paul, in speaking to the heathen at Ephesus, says, 'We are his offspring.'[42]

Thus the eternal marriage compact and the blessing of eternal increase are the keys to exaltation. Those who gain the celestial kingdom but do not fulfill these obligations are limited to the role of servants, ministering to their exalted brethren. Gods rule over their own progeny, and there is no exaltation without the ability to bring forth spirit children. This law is immutable. Few will be able to receive its blessings rather than its damnation, for the Lord has revealed that

---

[40]James E. Talmage, *Articles of Faith,* (Salt Lake City, Utah: The Church of Jesus Christ of Latter-day Saints), p. 473.

[41]Joseph F. Smith, John R. Winder, Anthon H. Lund (The First Presidency of the Church), "The Origin of Man," *Improvement Era,* Vol. XIII, No. 1, p. 80, November, 1909.

[42]JD 15:246. Dec. 15, 1872. See also Parley P. Pratt, *Key to the Science of Theology, op. cit.,* pp. 56-57, 125; and JD 15:320.

> Strait is the gate, and narrow the way that leadeth unto the exaltation and continuation of the lives, and *few there be that find it,* because ye receive me not in the world neither do ye know me.[43]

Family Relationship with Progenitors and Descendants

A great union of family relationships will be prepared for those who enter into exaltation.[44] All who dwell among the gods will participate in this great patriarchal order, while those who fail to merit exaltation will be excluded from the family order and will exist in a single state.[45] This last dispensation, the dispensation of the fulness of times, is the time for the joining of this patriarchal line:

> *We without them cannot be made perfect; neither can they without us be made perfect.* Neither can they nor we be made perfect without those who have died in the gospel also; for it is necessary in the ushering in of the dispensation of the fulness of times, which dispensation is now beginning to usher in, that *a whole and complete and perfect union, and welding together of dispensations, and keys, and powers, and glories should take place,* and be revealed from the days of Adam even to the present time.[46]

Each man will take his place in the patriarchal order, and will show reverence and respect to those who precede him in the order. As Orson Pratt explained,

> There will never be any such thing there as being from under their father's rule, no matter whether twenty-one or twenty-one thousand years of age, it will make no difference, they will still be subject to the laws of their Patriarch or Father, and they must observe and obey them throughout all eternity.[47]

As each exalted being develops his own kingdoms and exaltation, these many glories will also add to the honor, glory, and joy of his progenitors who stand before him in the patri-

---

[43]D&C 132:22.

[44]This family relationship is discussed on pp. 187-189.

[45]See D&C 132:15-18.

[46]D&C 128:18.

[47]JD 15:320. Jan. 19, 1873. Elder Pratt continued to explain the only alternative to acceptance of patriarchal rule:

> There is only one way by which children can be freed from that celestial law and order of things, and that is by rebellion. They are agents, and they can rebel against God and against the order of things he has instituted there, just as Satan and the fallen angels rebelled and turned away.

archal order. Joseph Smith explained the principle in this fashion:

> What did Jesus do? Why, I do the things I saw my Father do when worlds came rolling into existence. My Father worked out His kingdom with fear and trembling, and I must do the same; and *when I get my kingdom, I shall present it to my Father, so that He may obtain kingdom upon kingdom, and it will exalt Him in glory. He will then take a higher exaltation, and I will take His place, and thereby become exalted myself. So that Jesus treads in the tracks of His Father, and inherits what God Himself did before; and God is thus glorified and exalted in the salvation and exaltation of all His children.* It is plain beyond disputation, and you thus learn some of the first principles of the gospel, about which so much hath been said.[48]

A portion of the line of authority as it will exist in the celestial glory has been revealed. God the Father will stand at the head, and next to Him in authority will stand His Only Begotten Son, Jesus Christ, who testified that "I go unto the Father: *for my Father is greater than I.*"[49] Christ is to perfect his work upon the earth, then "deliver up the kingdom, and present it unto the Father, spotless,"[50] and then be "crowned with the crown of his glory, to sit on the throne of his power to reign forever and ever"[51] over other exalted beings as "King of kings, and Lord of lords."[52]

Next in authority will be Adam, unto whom the Lord promised that "I have set thee to be at the head; a multitude of nations shall come of thee, and *thou art a prince over them forever.*"[53] While speaking of Adam's role in the great last days Council at Adam-ondi-Ahman the prophet Joseph said that *"Adam delivers up his stewardship to Christ, that which was delivered to him as holding the keys of the universe, but retains his standing as head of the human family."*[54] In the same discourse the prophet extended the line of authority another step, to Noah:

> *The Priesthood was first given to Adam; he obtained the First Presidency, and held the keys of it from generation to generation.* He obtained it in the

[48]HC 6:306. April 7, 1844.
[49]Jn. 14:28.
[50]D&C 76:107. See also 1 Cor. 15:22-26, 28.
[51]D&C 76:108.
[52]Rev. 19:16. See also 1:5-6; D&C 130:9.
[53]D&C 107:55. See also 78:15-16.
[54]HC 3:387. July 2, 1839.

> Creation, before the world was formed, as in Genesis 1:26,27,28. He had dominion given him over every living creature. He is Michael the Archangel, spoken of in the Scriptures. *Then to Noah, who is Gabriel; he stands next in authority to Adam in the Priesthood;* he was called of God to this office, and was the father of all living in his day, and to him was given the dominion. These men held keys first on earth, and then in heaven.[55]

Then, as Parley P. Pratt explained, the line of priesthood rule passes to each of the heads of dispensations in turn. Each of them will govern the people who lived in their dispensation or era in mortality. Under their direction the fathers who lived during that period will preside over their families in the patriarchal order:

> Having now established the fact that the celestial order is designed not only to give eternal life, but also to establish an eternal order of family government, founded upon the most pure and holy principles of union and affection, we will take a review of the celestial family of man as it will exist in the restoration of all things spoken of by the holy prophets. First, his most gracious and venerable majesty, *King Adam, with his royal consort, Queen Eve, will appear at the head of the whole great family of the redeemed, and be crowned in their midst, as a king and a priest over them after the Order of the Son of God.* They will then be arrayed in garments as white as snow, and will take their seats on the throne, in the midst of the paradise of God on the earth, to reign forever and ever; while thousands of thousands stand before him and ten thousand times ten thousand minister unto him. And if you will receive it, this is the order of the Ancient of Days.
>
> The kingdom prepared and organized to meet Jesus when He comes. *This venerable patriarch and sovereign will hold lawful jurisdiction over Abel, Noah, Enoch, Abraham, Isaac, Jacob, Joseph, Moses, the prophets, apostles and saints of all ages and dispensations,* who will all reverence and obey him as their venerable father and lawful sovereign. . . . *They will then be organized each over his own department of the government according to their birthright and office,* in their families, generations and nations. . . . Each one will obey and be obeyed according to the connection which he sustains as a member of the great celestial family.[56]

Every man who gains exaltation will take his place in this patriarchal line and will rule and reign in eternity as a part of the patriarchal order.

Participation of parents in the eternal marriage covenant

[55]HC 3:385-86. July 2, 1839.

[56]Lynn A. McKinlay, *Life Eternal, op. cit.*, pp. 173-74.

while in mortality seals the children who result from the union into the family unit for eternity, thereby allowing the family to maintain the same family relationship in the celestial kingdom if all have met the standards of personal worthiness. This seems to be the intent of the statement made by Joseph Smith at the funeral of Judge Higbee:

> Four destroying angels [are] holding power over the four quarters of the earth until the servants of God are sealed in their foreheads, *which signifies sealing the blessing upon their heads, meaning the everlasting covenant, thereby making their calling and election sure. When a seal is put upon the father and mother, it secures their posterity, so that they cannot be lost, but will be saved by virtue of the covenant of their father and mother.*[57]

In contrast, those who have not entered into the eternal marriage covenant will lose the families with whom they dwelled in mortality and will be compelled to live singly. As Orson Pratt explained to women who marry outside of the Church,

> If you marry a man who receives not the Gospel, you lay a foundation for sorrow in this world, besides *losing the society of a husband in eternity. You forfeit your right to an endless increase of immortal lives. And even the children which you may be favored with in this life, will not be entrusted to your charge in eternity, but you will be left in that world, without a husband, without a family, without a kingdom*—without any means of enlarging yourselves, being subject to the principalities and powers who are counted worthy of families, and kingdoms and thrones and increase of dominions forever. To them you will be servants and angels—that is, providing that your conduct should be such as to secure this measure of glory.[58]

[57]HC 5:530. Aug. 13, 1843. According to apostle Melvin J. Ballard, exalted beings may have children who will not merit the celestial kingdom and may choose to visit them in the lesser kingdoms:

> I have several times been asked, how is it possible for those who attain Celestial glory to ever feel happy and satisfied to know that their children are in the Telestial world, and never would have the privilege of coming up with their parents in the Celestial Kingdom.
>
> *We must not overlook the fact that those who attain to the higher glories may minister unto and visit and associate with those of the lesser kingdoms. While the lesser may not come up, they may still enjoy the companionship of their loved ones who are in higher stations.* Also we must not forget that even the last degree of glory, as the Lord has expressed it, is beyond all our present understanding. So that they are in the presence of glorious conditions, even though they attain unto the least place. (N. B. Lundwall, *The Vision, op. cit.*, pp. 49-50)

[58]Orson Pratt, "Marriage," *Millennial Star,* Vo. XV, No. 36, p. 584, Sept. 3, 1853.

Thrones, Kingdoms, Principalities, Powers, and Dominions

From the beginning it has been God's plan that His children will reign with Him. This principle was taught to Abraham when he saw that God stood among the pre-mortal spirits and said of "the noble and great ones," "These I will make my rulers."[59] Those who have already gained exaltation have been awarded their dominions and now sit upon exalted thrones. Speaking of Abraham, Isaac, and Jacob, for instance, the Lord has revealed that "They have entered into their exaltation, according to the promises, and *sit upon thrones,* and are not angels but are gods."[60] The Savior has promised the faithful that "to him that overcometh will I grant to sit with me in my throne, even as I also overcame, and am set down with my Father in his throne."[61] A modern revelation promises that *"all thrones and dominions, principalities and powers, shall be revealed and set forth* upon all who have endured valiantly for the gospel of Jesus Christ . . . when every man shall enter into his eternal presence and into his immortal rest."[62] It would appear that exalted beings may have jurisdiction over lesser kingdoms of glory,[63] but their major responsibility will ultimately lie with the governing of the worlds they have created and upon which they will have placed their offspring.

Admittance to the City of the Living God

God dwells in a glorious city, apart from this earth, to which the inheritors of celestial glory may come. The Lord has revealed that admittance to this celestial city will be limited to exalted beings and certain angels who serve them. Others will discover that "the angels and the gods are appointed there, by whom they cannot pass; they cannot, therefore, inherit my glory; for my house is a house of order; saith the Lord God."[64] Apparently there will be a careful screening

---

[59]Abra. 3:23.

[60]D&C 132:37. See also Rev. 20:4.

[61]Rev. 3:21.

[62]D&C 121:29, 32. See also 132:19, 49.

[63]See D&C 76:87.

[64]D&C 132:18. See also verse 19. The endowment is designed to prepare men to pass these divine sentinels. See pp. 184-185.

of those who are permitted to enter, for the prophet Jacob warned,

> Come unto the Lord, the Holy One. Remember that his paths are righteous. Behold, the way for man is narrow, but it lieth in a straight course before him, *and the keeper of the gate is the Holy One of Israel; and he employeth no servant there; and there is none other way save it be by the gate; for he cannot be deceived, for the Lord God is his name.*
>
> *And whoso knocketh, to him will he open;* and the wise, and the learned, and they that are rich, who are puffed up because of their learning, and their wisdom, and their riches—yea, they are they whom he despiseth; and save they shall cast these things away, and consider themselves fools before God, and come down in the depths of humility, *he will not open unto them.*[65]

Though the Master employs no servant there, it appears that the heads of dispensations will be called upon to verify the worthiness of those who have been under their jurisdiction. Heber C. Kimball told of a vision given to Joseph Smith in which he was shown Adam admitting people one by one to the city:

> He saw the Twelve going forth and they appeared to be in a far distant land. . . . He . . . saw until they had accomplished their work, and *arrived at the gate of the celestial city; there Father Adam stood and opened the gate to them, and as they entered he embraced them one by one and kissed them. He then led them to the throne of God,* and then the Savior embraced each one of them and kissed them, and crowned each one of them in the presence of God. *He saw that they all had beautiful heads of hair and all looked alike.* The impression this vision left on Brother Joseph's mind was of so acute a nature that he never could refrain from weeping while rehearsing it.[66]

Brigham Young taught that Joseph Smith, as head of this dispensation, would have to certify the worthiness of any Latter-day Saint who approaches exaltation:

---

[65]2 Ne. 9:41-42.

[66]Orson F. Whitney, *Life of Heber C. Kimball, op. cit.,* p. 106. This seems to be a reference to the visions Joseph Smith received on January 21, 1836 (See HC 2:380-382) but adds detail which Joseph did not record. On March 17, 1861, President Kimball again described Joseph's vision, as follows:

> This brings to my mind the vision that Joseph Smith had, when *he saw Adam open the gate of the Celestial City and admit the people one by one. He then saw Father Adam conduct them to the throne one by one, when they were crowned Kings and Priests of God.* I merely bring this up to impress upon your mind the principles of order, but it will nevertheless apply to every member of the Church. (JD 9:41. Mar. 17, 1861)

> As I have frequently told them, *no man in this dispensation will enter the courts of heaven, without the approbation of the Prophet Joseph Smith, jun.* Who has made this so? Have I? Have this people? Have the world? No; *but the Lord Jehovah has decreed it. If I ever pass into the heavenly courts, it will be by the consent of the Prophet Joseph.* If you ever pass through the gates into the Holy City, *you will do so upon his certificate that you are worthy to pass. Can you pass without his inspection? No; neither can any person in this dispensation,* which is the dispensation of the fulness of times. In this generation, and in all the generations that are to come, every one will have to undergo the scrutiny of this Prophet.[67]

Heber C. Kimball believed that but few of the Saints would have the opportunity to enter the celestial city:

> Will one out of twenty of those who are here to-day go through the gates into the celestial City? As I told some to-day, when passing through the gate at noon, when you go to the straight gate that we read of, you will not go through there crowding by hundreds as you do now.[68]

Various individuals have been shown the celestial city of God and their accounts are useful to those who attempt to visualize that place of grandeur and beauty. Joseph Smith recorded, for instance,

> The heavens were opened upon us, and I beheld the celestial kingdom of God, and the glory thereof, whether in the body or out I cannot tell. *I saw the transcendent beauty of the gate through which the heirs of that kingdom will enter, which was like unto circling flames of fire;* also *the blazing throne of God,* whereon was seated the Father and the Son. *I saw the beautiful streets of that kingdom, which had the appearance of being paved with gold.*[69]

President David O. McKay may have seen the celestial city on May 10, 1921, on board a ship approaching Apia, Samoa. He recorded in his world tour diary for that date,

> I then fell asleep, and beheld in vision something infinitely sublime. In the distance I beheld a beautiful *white city.* Though far away, yet I seemed to realize that *trees with luscious fruit, shrubbery with gorgeously-tinted leaves, and flowers in perfect bloom abounded everywhere. The clear sky above seemed to reflect these beautiful shades of color.* I then saw a great concourse of people approaching the city. *Each one wore a white flowing robe, and a white headdress.* Instantly my attention seemed

[67]JD 8:224. Oct. 21, 1860.
[68]JD 3:230. Mar. 2, 1856.
[69]HC 2:380. Jan. 21, 1836.

centered upon their Leader, and though I could see only the profile of his features and his body, I recognized him at once as my Savior! The tint and radiance of his countenance were glorious to behold! There was a peace about him which seemed sublime—it was divine!

The city, I understood, was his. *It was the City Eternal;* and the people following him were to abide there in peace and eternal happiness.

But who were they?

As if the Savior read my thoughts, he answered by pointing to a semicircle that then appeared above them, and on which were written in gold the words:

'These Are They Who Have Overcome The World—Who Have Truly Been Born Again!'

When I awoke, it was breaking day over Apia Harbor.[70]

Lorenzo Dow Young was shown a city which conforms to the description of the celestial city of God. After he had been shown the spirit prison and hell he was taken by the heavenly messenger who was conducting him to another area—a place of great beauty:

My guide said, 'Now let us go.'

In a moment we were at the *gate* of a beautiful city. A *porter* opened it and we passed in. The city was *grand and beautiful* beyond anything that I can describe. It was *clothed in the purest light, brilliant but not glaring or unpleasant.*

The people, men and women, in their employments and surroundings, seemed *contented and happy.* I knew those I met without being told who they were. *Jesus and the ancient apostles were there. I saw and spoke with the apostle Paul.*

My guide would not permit me to pause much by the way, but rather hurried me on *through this place to another still higher but connected with it.* It was still more beautiful and glorious than anything I had before seen. To me its extent and magnificence were incomprehensible.

My guide pointed to a mansion which excelled everything else in perfection and beauty. It was clothed with fire and intense light. It appeared a fountain of light, throwing brilliant scintillations of glory all around it, and I could conceive of no limit to which these emanations extended. Said my guide, *'That is where God resides.'* He permitted me to enter this glorious city

[70]Clare Middlemiss (comp.), *Cherished Experiences from the Writings of David O. McKay* (Salt Lake City, Utah: Deseret Book Co., 1955), p. 102.

but a short distance. Without speaking, he motioned that we would retrace our steps.

We were soon in the *adjoining city.* There I met my mother and a sister who died when six or seven years old. These I knew at sight without an introduction.

After mingling with the pure and happy beings of this place a short time, my guide said again, 'Let us go.'

We were soon through the *gate* by which we had entered the city. My guide then said, 'Now we will return.'

I could distinctly see the world from which we had first come. *It appeared to be a vast distance below us. To me, it looked cloudy, dreary and dark.* I was filled with sad disappointment, I might say horror, at the idea of returning there. I supposed I had come to stay in that heavenly place, which I had so long desired to see; up to this time, the thought had not occurred to me that I would be required to return.

I plead with my guide to let me remain. He replied that *I was permitted to only visit these heavenly cities, for I had not filled my mission in yonder world;* therefore I must return and take my body. If I was faithful to the grace of God which would be imparted to me, if I would bear a faithful testimony to the inhabitants of the earth of a sacrificed and risen Savior, and His atonement for man, in a little time I should be permitted to return and remain.[71]

Others have seen specific buildings in the celestial city. President Wilford Woodruff, for instance, recorded that

> I saw a few of the mansions in the Celestial Kingdom of God which were composed of beautiful stones and of materials that were as real as anything on earth, and that the best architects in heaven were employed in the construction of these buildings.[72]

The elder watching by the bedside of Briant Stevens shortly before the latter's death, apparently saw a celestial edifice in an inspired dream:

> The night before Briant died one of the Elders who had attended at the bedside, fell asleep while thinking about the sick child. He

[71]Lorenzo Dow Young, *Fragments of Experience, op cit.*, pp. 28-29.

[72]Matthias F. Cowley, *Wilford Woodruff, op. cit.*, p. 543. This is but the latter portion of a dream which was given to President Woodruff. His journal entry for Dec. 30, 1882, precedes the above with these words:

> I dreamed last night that Captain William H. Hooper was dead. I told my family this morning that when I heard from him I should hear that he was dead. Later, Brother Jacques informed me at the Historian's office that the captain died at twenty minutes past eight. I saw Captain Hooper in the spirit world in my dream.

dreamed that himself and three of his companion Elders, who had also waited on Briant, went upon a journey into a distant and beautiful country. They seemed to have some definite object in view, but during their travel this object was not present to their minds.

When they reached the fair land of their destination, they saw a *superb building, which they at once divined to be a temple of the living God. It was not yet completed; but it had assumed such proportions as to show the utmost grandeur. It was constructed of white, shining stone, seemingly as hard as granite.* Many workmen appeared to be engaged in the building; and one of them, clothed in a white robe, with his head and hands and feet bare, stood upon the ground near the entrance to the structure.

In the *white outer wall, at one side of the mighty arched doorway,* and at the height of a man's head, a monogram seemed to be newly set into the stone. It was composed of three letters; the top one being B, clearly distinguishable; and the other two being fainter. At once the sojourners knew that this was what they had come after. The Elder who dreamed, thought that he reached forward and attempted to take it from its place. But the white robed workman stayed his hand, saying:

'You cannot take it. It has been set here *by order of the Master,* as an ornament to this temple.'

The Elders then walked around the building, and *entered the interior through a magnificent portal, and saw that much workmanship of fine patterns was being used in the adornment of the structure.* They walked out and once more essayed to pluck the monogram from its place in the glittering wall. But again the voice of the guardian workman stayed their hands. For the second time they walked around the temple, entered through the archway and gazed at the magnificent interior. Then they said:

'Let us try once more.'

The third time the Elder stretched out his hand to take the monogram; but, as on the other occasions, he was told to desist. The workman had spoken to him each time in perfect kindness, but in a decided tone. On this final effort a voice sounding like a trumpet descended from the top of the building, saying:

'Brother [calling him by name], you must go back; your wish cannot be granted.'

Then they withdrew. Soon the Elder awoke, and he felt certain that the prayers which had been offered concerning Briant Stevens—though *they had reached the throne of the Eternal Father*—were powerless to change the decree which had been made in heaven concerning the boy, and that Briant must speedily pass from earth.[73]

Inheritance on the Celestialized Earth

The Lord has revealed that this earth will become the final resting place for those who merit exaltation after fulfilling their mortal probation here. In the revelation known as the "Olive Leaf," the teaching is set forth that

> It is decreed that the poor and the meek of the earth shall inherit it.
>
> Therefore, it must needs be sanctified from all unrighteousness, *that it may be prepared for the celestial glory;*
>
> For after it hath filled the measure of its creation, *it shall be crowned with glory, even with the presence of God the Father;*
>
> *That bodies who are of the celestial kingdom may possess it forever and ever;* for, for this intent was it made and created, and for this intent are they sanctified.[74]

John the Revelator saw that the celestial earth would become "a sea of glass like unto crystal,"[75] or "a sea of glass mingled with fire."[76] When the prophet Joseph Smith made inquiry of the Lord concerning the sea of glass seen by John, it was revealed that "it is the earth, in its sanctified, immortal, and eternal state."[77]

The celestial earth will itself serve as a great Urim and Thummim, or revelator, to the exalted beings who will dwell upon it, according to instructions set forth by Joseph Smith:

> This earth, in its sanctified and immortal state, *will be made like unto crystal and will be a Urim and Thummim to the inhabitants who dwell thereon, whereby all things pertaining to an inferior kingdom, or all kingdoms of a lower order,* will be manifest to those who dwell on it; and this earth will be Christ's.[78]

---

[73]Kennon, *Helpful Visions, op. cit.*, pp. 32-33.

[74]D&C 88:17-20.

[75]Rev. 4:6.

[76]Rev. 15:2.

[77]D&C 77:1.

[78]D&C 130:9. Such a change will make the earth similar to the sphere upon which the Father now dwells:

> The angels do not reside on a planet like this earth;
>
> But *they reside in the presence of God, on a globe like a sea of glass and fire,* where all things for their glory are manifest, past, present, and future, and are continually before the Lord.
>
> *The place where God resides is a great Urim and Thummim.* (D&C 130:6-8)

As he visualized the celestial glory of this earth, John reported that "I saw a new heaven and a new earth: for the first heaven and the first earth were passed away; and there was no more sea."[79] In his vision he saw two cities, the new Jerusalem[80] and the holy Jerusalem,[81] "descending out of heaven from God, having the glory of God."[82] This aspect of John the Revelator's vision was carefully explained by apostle Orson Pratt:

> Righteousness will abide upon its face, during a thousand years, and the Savior will bless it with his personal presence: after which the end soon comes, and the *earth itself will die, and its elements be dissolved* through the agency of a fire. . . .
>
> But all mankind are made alive from the first death through the resurrection, so *the earth will again be renewed, its elements will again be collected, they will be recombined and reorganized as when it first issued from the womb of chaos. . . .*
>
> As the earth passes through its great last change, *two of its principal cities—the Old Jerusalem of the eastern continent, and the new Jerusalem of the western continent, will be preserved from the general conflagration, being caught up into heaven. These two cities, with all their glorified throng, will descend upon the redeemed earth, being the grand capitals of the new creation.* 'Without' (or exterior to these holy cities, and upon other creations of an inferior order, far separated from the glorified earth) 'will be dogs, and sorcerers, and whoremongers, and murderers, and idolaters, and whosoever loveth and maketh a lie.' (Rev. xxii. 15.) *These are they who are banished from the presence of God, and from the glory of a celestial earth.*[83]

John the Revelator described the holy Jerusalem he saw descending onto the redeemed earth as a huge city of great beauty:

> Her light was like unto a stone most precious, even like a jasper stone, clear as crystal:
>
> And had a *wall great and high, and had twelve gates,* and at the gates twelve angels, and names written thereon, which are the names of the twelve tribes of the children of Israel:

[79]Rev. 21:1.

[80]Rev. 21:2-7. Latter-day Saints understand this to be the city which is to be built in the last days at Jackson County, Missouri. See D&C 105:5; 133:56; 57:1-5; 84:2-5; 97:10-19; 124:51.

[81]This is understood to be the Jerusalem located in the land of Israel.

[82]Rev. 21:10-11.

[83]JD 1:331-332.

> On the east three gates; on the north three gates; on the south three gates; and on the west three gates.
>
> And the wall of the city had twelve foundations, and in them the names of the twelve apostles of the Lamb.
>
> And he that talked with me had a golden reed to measure the city, and the gates thereof, and the wall thereof.
>
> And *the city lieth four-square, and the length is as large as the breadth: and he measured the city with the reed, twelve thousand furlongs. The length and the breadth and the height of it are equal.*
>
> *And he measured the wall thereof, an hundred and forty and four cubits,* according to the measure of a man, that is, of the angel.
>
> *And the building of the wall of it was of jasper: and the city was pure gold, like unto clear glass.*
>
> *And the foundations of the wall of the city were garnished with all manner of precious stones.* The first foundation was jasper; the second, sapphire; the third, a chalcedony; the fourth, an emerald;
>
> The fifth, sardonyx; the sixth, sardius; the seventh, chrysolite; the eighth, beryl; the ninth, a topaz; the tenth, a chrysoprasus; the eleventh, a jacinth; the twelfth, an amethyst.
>
> And the twelve gates were twelve pearls; every several gate was of one pearl: and the street of the city was pure gold, as it were transparent glass.[84]

An inheritance in the holy city will be awarded to the resurrected beings who are to inherit the earth at the time of Christ's coming in glory:

> *Blessed are the dead that die in the Lord,* from henceforth, when the Lord shall come, and old things shall pass away, and all things become new, they shall rise from the dead and shall not die after, *and shall receive an inheritance before the Lord, in the holy city.*[85]

Though many exalted beings may choose to live in these holy cities, others may receive eternal inheritances in less populated areas. David John, a Welsh convert who later became president of the Utah Stake, was shown in January, 1856, a vision of such an eternal inheritance available to him:

---

[84]Rev. 21:11-21. He described the city as being equal in length, breadth, and height: twelve thousand furlongs. Various sources give the length of a furlong in that day as 200 yards, 202 yards, and 220 yards. Assuming even the smallest length, John is prophesying of an eternal city over 1360 miles long, wide, and high, with walls that stand approximately seventy-seven feet high! Many Bible scholars scoff at his testimony because of the huge size of the dimensions he cites.

[85]D&C 63:49.

> I dremt [sic] that I saw an angel of the Lord. After he had talked a little with me, he placed his right hand on my left shoulder. His eyes were of a dark brown color, but full of glory. His voice was clear, but full of power and authority. . . .
>
> 'Look,' said he, 'on thy right hand.' I looked, and there beheld a *large and very extensive valley—the most beautiful land I ever saw.* We were standing on one side of it, which was flat. *On the side we stood were high and beautiful trees.* Under the shadow of one of them we stood from the heat of the sun, which was very powerful. *On the other side were mountains or hills, but not very high. Those extended to the extremity of the valley. The beauty and glory of the valley, which was from three to four miles wide, was beyond description.* 'Oh, my God,' I exclaimed, 'I never knew that such a beautiful scene as this belonged to our earth.' *'This,' said the angel, 'shall be thy inheritance and thy seed after thee forever, if thou wilt obey the commandments of God and do right in the flesh.* Look, behold thee,' said he. 'I then found myself in a large and beautiful building. There I saw on the stand one that I knew, preaching the principles of life. 'This,' said my guide, *'is the house of the Lord.'* At this I awoke, believing that the spirit of the Lord and angels filled the room.[86]

Ever the analyst, Orson Pratt made this interesting comment on the land available to the righteous for their eternal inheritance:

> It has been conjectured by some, that the earth will not be sufficiently capacious to accommodate the nations of the righteous. But such a conjecture will appear erroneous to anyone who will exercise his reasoning powers sufficient to calculate the superficial contents of our globe, and compare the same with the probable number of inhabitants who are destined for this creation.
>
> In round numbers, *the surface of our terrestrial spheroid contains one hundred and ninety-seven millions of square miles, or over one hundred and twenty-six thousand millions of acres.* Now, if from the creation of the earth, to its final glorification, there should elapse a period of eight thousand years, or eighty centuries, and if we should suppose the population to average one thousand millions per century, (which is probably an average far too great) yet there would be an abundance of room upon the earth for all this vast multitude. *There would be over one acre and a half for every soul.* But when we reflect how few will be saved—how few have received the plan of redemption, even when it has been proclaimed by authority in their ears, and how many generations have passed away unto whom the Almighty has sent no message, *we are compelled to believe that not one out of a hundred will receive*

[86]Andrew Jenson, *Latter-day Saint Biographical Encyclopedia, op. cit.,* 1:489-90.

> *an inheritance upon the new earth.* But even though we suppose one per cent of all this immensity of population shall, through obedience to the gospel, become lawful heirs to the new earth, *then there will be over one hundred and fifty acres for every soul.* If the new earth contains only the same proportion of land as the old, there would still be about forty acres for every redeemed soul. *But the new earth is represented by the Apostle John, as being without any sea, which increases its capacity for inhabitants above the old fourfold.* The farmer who is looking forward to the new earth for his everlasting inheritance need have no fears of being too much limited in his possessions. There will be ample room for the delightful pursuits of the agriculturist. He can have his pleasure grounds—his orchards of the most delicious fruits; his gardens decorated with the loveliest flowers; and still have land enough for the raising of the more staple articles, such as manna to eat, and flax for the making of fine robes, etc.[87]

The Lord has revealed that the earth will be as a land of milk and honey for those who inherit it:

> I have made the earth rich, and behold it is my footstool, wherefore, again I will stand upon it.
>
> *And I hold forth and deign to give unto you greater riches, even a land of promise, a land flowing with milk and honey, upon which there shall be no curse when the Lord cometh;*
>
> *And I will give it unto you for the land of your inheritance,* if you seek it with all your hearts.
>
> And this shall be my covenant with you, ye shall have it *for the land of your inheritance, and for the inheritance of your children forever, while the earth shall stand, and ye shall possess it again in eternity, no more to pass away.*[88]

The inheritance will be available not only to exalted beings, but also to their spirit children until the time comes to send them to other earths. Christ has revealed that "the fatness of the earth shall be theirs . . . And *their generations shall inherit the earth from generation to generation, forever and ever.*"[89] Yet as families grow, it will be necessary to create new earths and send the spirit offspring to pass through the trials of mortality upon them. As Orson Pratt said,

> *The peopling of worlds, or an endless increase, even of one family, would require an endless increase of worlds;* and if one family were to be united in the eternal covenant of marriage, to fulfil that great commandment, to multiply his species, and propogate them; and if there be

87Orson Pratt, *Millennial Star,* Vol. XII, p. 68-72.

88D&C 38:17-20. See also 45:58; 63:20.

89D&C 56:18, 20.

no end to the increase of his posterity, it would call for an endless increase of new worlds. And *if one family calls for this, what would innumerable millions of families call for?* They would call for as many worlds as have already been discovered by the telescope; yea, *the number must be multiplied to infinity in order that there may be room for the inheritance of the sons and daughters of the Gods.*

Do you begin to understand how these worlds get their inhabitants? Have you learned that the sons and daughters of God before me this day, are his offspring—made after his own image: that they are to multiply their species until they become innumerable?[90]

Association with Celestial Beings

The privilege of good friends is a rich blessing on earth; how much greater it will be for exalted beings to rejoice in the companionship of the gods in celestial glory! The Lord has revealed that exalted beings "come to an innumerable company of angels, to the general assembly and church of Enoch, and of the Firstborn."[91] It may be presumed that they will someday take their appointed place or be represented in "the Council of the Eternal God of all other gods,"[92] and find satisfaction therein. And what a privilege it will be to share the companionship of those one has helped along the road to exaltation!

If it so be that you should labor all your days in crying repentance unto this people, and bring, save it be one soul unto me, *how great shall be your joy with him in the kingdom of my Father!*

And now, if your joy will be great with one soul that you have brought unto me into the kingdom of my Father, *how great will be your joy if you should bring many souls unto me!*[93]

It is of interest to note that the inhabitants of celestial glory will be privileged to enjoy not only the companionship of man but also that of the resurrected animal kingdom. Benjamin F. Johnson, an early companion of Joseph Smith, wrote that the latter *"taught that all the animal kingdoms would be resurrected, and made us understand that they would remain in the dominion of those who, with creative power, reach out for dominion,*

---

[90]Orson Pratt, *Millennial Star,* Vol. XV, supplement, p. 23.
[91]D&C 76:67.
[92]D&C 121:32.
[93]D&C 18:15-16. See also 15:6; 16:6.

through the power of eternal lives."[94] Commenting on animal beings seen in heaven by John the Revelator, the prophet Joseph Smith said,

> I suppose John saw beings there of a thousand forms, that had been saved from ten thousand times ten thousand earths like this, *strange beasts of which we have no conception; all might be seen in heaven.* The grand secret was to show John what there was in heaven. John learned that *God glorified Himself by saving all that His hands had made, whether beasts, fowls, fishes or men, and He will gratify Himself with them.*[95]

Perfect Knowledge

The Lord has promised that at the time when "man shall enter into his eternal presence and into his immortal rest," all knowledge which man lacks will be given to him and "nothing shall be withheld." This perfect knowledge forms an important basis for exalted man's work as a god and creator:

> *God shall give unto you knowledge by his Holy Spirit, yea, by the unspeakable gift of the Holy Ghost,* that has not been revealed since the world was until now;
>
> Which our forefathers have awaited with anxious expectation to be revealed in the last times, which their minds were pointed to by the angels, as held in reserve for the fulness of their glory;
>
> *A time to come in the which nothing shall be withheld,* whether there be one God or many gods, they shall be manifest.
>
> All thrones and dominions, principalities and powers, shall be revealed and set forth upon all who have endured valiantly for the gospel of Jesus Christ.
>
> And also, if there be bounds set to the heavens or to the seas, or to the dry land, or to the sun, moon, or stars—
>
> All the times of their revolutions, all the appointed days, months, and years, and all their glories, laws, and set times, shall be revealed in the days of the dispensation of the fulness of times—
>
> According to that which was ordained in the midst of the Council of the Eternal God of all other gods before this world was, *that should be reserved unto the finishing and the end thereof, when every man shall enter into his eternal presence and into his immortal rest.*[96]

When exalted beings partake of Jesus' promise that "he that receiveth my Father receiveth my Father's kingdom;

---

[94]"An Interesting Letter," unpublished letter of Benjamin F. Johnson to George S. Gibbs, 1903. Brigham Young University Library, p. 8.

[95]B. H. Roberts, *The Rise and Fall of Nauvoo, op. cit.*, p. 213. His comment pertained to Rev. 5:13. See also Rev. 4:6-9 and D&C 77:2-4.

[96]D&C 121:26-32.

therefore *all that my Father hath shall be given unto him,*"[97] they will be equal with God in the absolute knowledge of all things which they will possess. Of that knowledge it is revealed that

> *He comprehendeth all things, and all things are before him,* and all things are round about him; and he is above all things, and in all things, and is through all things, and is round about all things; and all things are by him, and of him, even God, forever and ever.[98]

Much of the knowledge may be revealed by the white stone, or Urim and Thummim, which is promised to every exalted being. The Lord made reference to this gift when He revealed to John the Revelator that "to him that overcometh will I give to eat of the hidden manna, and will give him *a white stone, and in the stone a new name written* which no man knoweth saving he that receiveth it."[99] The prophet Joseph, while explaining that the celestialized earth would serve as a Urim and Thummim to reveal the things of the lower kingdoms,[100] taught that

> The white stone mentioned in Rev. 2:17, will become *a Urim and Thummim to each individual who receives one, whereby things pertaining to a higher order of kingdoms will be made known;*
>
> And a white stone is given to each of those who come into the celestial kingdom, whereon is a new name written, which no man knoweth save he that receiveth it. The new name is the key word.[101]

The knowledge which every exalted being will receive is what must have prompted the prophet Joseph Smith to warn that "it is impossible for a man to be saved in ignorance."[102]

Governing and Lawgiving Jurisdiction

Exalted beings are "they into whose hands the Father has given all things."[103] They are to receive governing and law-

---

[97] D&C 84:38.

[98] D&C 88:41. The continual testimony of the scriptures is that God's knowledge is absolute—that he knows *all* things. (See 2 Ne. 9:20; Al. 26:35; D&C 38:1-2; 93:26; Ps. 147:5; etc.) There is no intimation in the scriptures that this knowledge is relative, or limited in its perfection to the things of this earth. God progresses by the "continuation of the lives" and by the expanding of his creations, but not, according to that which He has revealed, in the acquisition of knowledge, wisdom, and power.

[99] Rev. 2:17. See also 3:12; Is. 56:5; 62:2; 65:15.

[100] D&C 130:9.

[101] D&C 130:10-11.

[102] D&C 131:6.

[103] D&C 76:55.

giving power similar to that presently possessed by deity. Of them it will also be said that "judgment goeth before the face of him who sitteth upon the throne and *governeth and executeth all things* . . . he hath given a law unto all things."[104]

The Lord has revealed of him who is thus ordained of God that "he is possessor of all things; for *all things are subject unto him,* both *in heaven and on the earth,* the life and the light, the Spirit *and the power.*"[105] And this ruling power extends over the very angels of heaven, for of those who attain exaltation the Lord has revealed, "Then shall they be above all, *because all things are subject unto them.* Then shall they be gods, because they have all power, and *the angels are subject unto them.*"[106]

The Powers of Godhood

When the time comes that exalted beings receive fulfillment of the promise that "all things are theirs,"[107] they will be blessed with the full array of divine power. As joint-heirs with Christ, they will share the same completeness of power which He has been given, for it is revealed that

> *He received all power, both in heaven and on earth,* and the glory of the Father was with him, for he dwelt in him. . . .
>
> I give unto you these sayings that you may understand and know how to worship, and know what you worship, that *you may come unto the Father in my name, and in due time receive of his fulness.*[108]

To consider what these powers are is to analyze the powers of Christ and the Father. These powers include,

1. *Power to create worlds.* (*Moses 1:33; D&C 93:10*)
2. *Power to make worlds pass through the exaltation process.* (*Moses 1:35-39*)
3. *Power to enumerate His creations.* (*Moses 1:37*)
4. *Power to create mortal bodies for spirit beings.* (*Moses 2:26-27; Abra. 5:7*)
5. *Power over mortal man's life and death.* (*D&C 76:59*)

[104]D&C 88:40, 42.
[105]D&C 50:27.
[106]D&C 132:20.
[107]D&C 76:59.
[108]D&C 93:17, 19.

6. *Power of judgment.* (*Jn. 5:22,27*)
7. *Power to reward and punish.* (*Mt. 25:31-46*)
8. *Power to resurrect.* (*1 Cor. 15:22*)
9. *Power over the elements.* (*Abra. 4:14-18; Mk. 4:39*)
10. *Power to discern man's thoughts and intent.* (*D&C 33:1*)
11. *Power to see all things, past, present and future.* (*D&C* 76:59; *38:1-3*)
12. *Power to know all things.* (*D&C 38:2*)
13. *Power to determine the bounds of man's habitation.* (*Acts 17:26-27*)
14. *Power to forgive and pardon.* (*Mi. 7:18-20; D&C 64:10*)
15. *Power to hear and answer prayers.* (*Mt. 6:6*)
16. *Power to reveal His will.* (*D&C 76:7*)

These are but examples of the powers of godhood. As a god is omnipotent, such a list would have to expand to cover all the powers of eternity, for all of them are God's. When man gains exaltation, certain of these powers will be conferred through ordination. But exalted man will have powers even beyond those conferred upon him, for it is revealed that "the kingdom is given you of the Father, *and power to overcome all things which are not ordained of him.*"[109]

The Plurality of Gods

Thus it becomes obvious that there are now, and will continue to be, many gods who will rule and reign throughout eternity on an ever increasing number of worlds which they will create. This is not in opposition to the Biblical concept of "one God," for an earth serves as the dwelling place for the children of only one God, and He alone reigns over His children there as Father and God. He may seek and use the assistance of others as the Eternal Father of this earth has done with His Only Begotten Son, Jesus, and with the Holy Ghost. Yet He alone reigns as the Father of all mankind upon that earth. The apostle Paul well understood this principle when he wrote,

[109] D&C 50:35.

> Though there be that are called gods, whether in heaven or in earth, (as *there be gods many, and lords many,*)
>
> *But to us there is but one God, the Father,* of whom are all things, and we in him; and one Lord Jesus Christ, by whom are all things, and we by him.[110]

A discourse by Joseph Smith presented on June 16, 1844, just eleven days before the prophet's martyrdom, sheds light on the plurality of Gods. Joseph took as his text Revelation 1:6, *"And hath made us kings and priests unto God and his Father; to him be glory and dominion for ever and ever.* Amen," and then said,

> *It is altogether correct in the translation.* Now, you know that of late some malicious and corrupt men have sprung up and apostatized from the Church of Jesus Christ of Latter-day Saints, and they declare that the Prophet believes in a plurality of Gods, and, lo and behold! we have discovered a very great secret, they cry—'The Prophet says there are many Gods, and this proves that he has fallen.'
>
> It has been my intention for a long time to take up this subject and lay it clearly before the people, and show what my faith is in relation to this interesting matter. I have contemplated the saying of Jesus (Luke 17th chapter, 26th verse) — 'And as it was in the days of Noah, so shall it be also in the days of the Son of Man.' And if it does rain, I'll preach this doctrine, for the truth shall be preached.
>
> I will preach on the plurality of Gods. I have selected this text for that express purpose. *I wish to declare I have always and in all congregations when I have preached on the subject of the Deity, it has been the plurality of Gods. It has been preached by the Elders for fifteen years.*
>
> I have always declared God to be a distinct personage, Jesus Christ a separate and distinct personage from God the Father, and that the Holy Ghost was a distinct personage and a Spirit: and *these three constitute three distinct personages and three Gods.* If this is in accordance with the New Testament, lo and behold! *we have three Gods anyhow, and they are plural: and who can contradict it?*
>
> Our text says 'And hath made us kings and priests unto God and His Father.' The Apostles have discovered that there were Gods above, for Paul says God was the Father of our Lord Jesus Christ. My object was to preach the scriptures, and preach the doctrine they contain, *there being a God above, the Father of our Lord Jesus Christ.* I am bold to declare I have taught all the strong doctrines publicly, and always teach stronger doctrines in public than in private.
>
> John was one of the men, and apostles declare they were made

[110] 1 Cor. 8:5-6.

> kings and priests unto God, the Father of our Lord Jesus Christ. It reads just so in the Revelation. *Hence, the doctrine of a plurity* [sic] *of Gods is as prominent in the Bible as any other doctrine. It is all over the face of the Bible. It stands beyond the power of controversy.* A way-faring man, though a fool, need not err therein.
>
> Paul says there are Gods many and Lords many. I want to set it forth in a plain and simple manner; but to us there is but one God—that is pertaining to us; and he is in all and through all. But if Joseph Smith says there are Gods many and Lords many, they cry, 'Away with him! Crucify him! crucify him!'
>
> Mankind verily say that the scriptures are with them. Search the scriptures, for they testify of things that these apostates would gravely pronounce blasphemy. Paul, if Joseph Smith is a blasphemer, you are. *I say there are Gods many and Lords many, but to us only one, and we are to be in subjection to that one, and no man can limit the bounds or the eternal existence of eternal time.* Hath he beheld the eternal world, and is he authorized to say that there is only one God? He makes himself a fool if he thinks or says so, and there is an end of his career or progress in knowledge. He cannot obtain all knowledge, for he has sealed up the gate to it.
>
> Some say I do not interpret the scripture the same as they do. They say it means the heathen's gods. Paul says there are Gods many and Lords many; and that makes a plurality of Gods, in spite of the whims of all men. Without a revelation, I am not going to give them the knowledge of the God of heaven. *You know and I testify that Paul had no allusion to the heathen gods. I have it from God, and get over it if you can. I have a witness of the Holy Ghost, and a testimony that Paul had no allusion to the heathen gods in the text.*[111]

Though man has received fleeting glimpses of the relationship enjoyed by the gods,[112] yet God has chosen to limit their knowledge while in mortality to the things of this earth. Even Moses, who was shown the many kingdoms created by the Father, was limited in his knowledge by God. When he asked about the other worlds, the Lord God said, "Here is wisdom and it remaineth in me. . . . *only an account of this earth,* and the inhabitants thereof, give I unto you."[113] Man must wait until he gains his own exaltation to know fully of the exalted hosts.[114]

---

[111]HC 6:473-475. June 16, 1844.
[112]See Abra. 5:2-3; D&C 121:32.
[113]Moses 1:31, 35.
[114]See D&C 121:28, 32.

God the Father Was Once as Man Is Now

Latter-day Saints realize that they are limited in the knowledge which has been revealed concerning the Gods in heaven. They know little beyond the limitations of this earth and do not yet envision the entire panorama of eternity. Yet certain clues are available to them through the sermons and teachings of their inspired prophets. In his sermon of June 16, 1844, Joseph Smith made it clear that there are other Gods who precede the Eternal Father of this earth and His Son, Jesus Christ, in the patriarchal order of the Gods:

> *If Jesus Christ was the Son of God, and John discovered that God the Father of Jesus Christ had a Father, you may suppose that He had a Father also.* Where was there ever a son without a father? And where was there ever a father without first being a son? Whenever did a tree or anything spring into existence without a progenitor? And everything comes in this way. Paul says that which is earthly is in the likeness of that which is heavenly. *Hence if Jesus had a Father, can we not believe that He had a Father also? I despise the idea of being scared to death at such a doctrine, for the Bible is full of it.*
>
> I want you to pay particular attention to what I am saying. *Jesus said that the Father wrought precisely in the same way as His Father had done before Him. As the Father had done before. He laid down His life, and took it up the same as His Father had done before.* He did as He was sent, to lay down His life and take it up again; and then was committed unto Him the keys, &c.[115]

In the same sermon, while discussing the meaning of Gen. 1:1, the Prophet asserted that other Gods hold jurisdiction over the God and Father of this earth:

> In the very beginning the Bible shows there is a plurality of Gods beyond the power of refutation. It is a great subject I am dwelling on. The word *Eloheim* ought to be in the plural all the way through—Gods. *The heads of the Gods appointed one God for us;* and when you take [that] view of the subject, it sets one free to see all the beauty, holiness and perfection of the Gods. All I want is to get the simple, naked truth, and the whole truth.[116]

---

[115]HC 6:476-77. June 16, 1844.

[116]HC 6:476. June 16, 1844. In his King Follett discourse Joseph Smith also discussed the translation of this passage and said,

> *The head God brought forth the Gods in the grand council. . . .*
>
> *The head God called together the Gods and sat in grand council to bring forth the world.* The grand councilors sat at the head in yonder heavens and contemplated the creation of the worlds which were created at the time. . . .

The prophet Joseph Smith did not teach that the God of this earth has always been an exalted being. On the contrary, he said that "I am going to tell you how God came to be God. We have imagined and *supposed that God was God from all eternity. I will refute that idea,* and take away the veil, so that you may see."[117]

Joseph Smith explained that the Eternal Father of this earth passed through a mortal probation on another earth just as Jesus Christ did here:

> It is the first principle of the gospel to know for a certainty the character of God, and to know that we may converse with Him as one man converses with another, and that *He was once a man like us; yea, that God himself, the Father of us all, dwelt on an earth, the same as Jesus Christ Himself did;* and I will show it from the Bible.[118]

Jesus, while debating with the Jews, told them that

> *The Son can do nothing of himself, but what he seeth the Father do:* for what things soever he doeth, these also doeth the Son likewise.
>
> For the Father loveth the Son, and *sheweth him all things that himself doeth.*[119]

While apparently using this text as his basis, the prophet Joseph taught,

> What did Jesus do? Why, I do the things I saw my Father do when worlds came rolling into existence. *My Father worked out His kingdom with fear and trembling, and I must do the same. . . .* So that Jesus treads in the tracks of His Father, and inherits what God did before.[120]

Jesus had taught that "as the Father hath life in himself;

In the beginning, *the head of the Gods called a council of the Gods; and they came together and concocted [prepared] a plan to create the world and people it.* When we begin to learn this way, we begin to learn the only true God, and what kind of a being we have got to worship. Having a knowledge of God, we begin to know how to approach Him, and how to ask so as to receive an answer.

When we understand the character of God, and know how to come to Him, he begins to unfold the heavens to us, and to tell us all about it. When we are ready to come to him, he is ready to come to us. (HC 6:307, 308. April, 7, 1844)

The reader would do well to compare the similarities and parallels between the two discourses given by Joseph Smith April 7th and June 16th, 1844.

[117]HC 6:305. April 7, 1844.

[118]*Ibid.*

[119]Jn. 5:19-20.

[120]HC 6:306. April 7, 1844.

so hath he given to the Son to have life in himself."[121] Joseph Smith saw that the process by which Christ was able to raise himself from the dead as a resurrected being was a duplication of the experience God the Father had previously undergone, and that the Father had previously passed from His mortal probation into immortality:

> The scriptures inform us that Jesus said, as the Father hath power in himself, even so hath the Son power—to do what? *Why, what the Father did. The answer is obvious—in a manner to lay down his body and take it up again. Jesus, what are you going to do? To lay down my life as my Father did, and take it up again.* Do you believe it? If you do not believe it you do not believe the Bible. The scriptures say it, and I defy all the learning and wisdom and all the combined powers of earth and hell together to refute it.[122]

President Brigham Young also taught that God the Father of this earth passed through a mortal probation and has walked the path which man must yet walk today:

> *The Father, after He had once been in the flesh, and lived as we live, obtained His exaltation, attained to thrones, gained the ascendancy over principalities and powers, and had the knowledge and power to create*—to bring forth and organize the elements upon natural principles. *This He did after His ascension, or His glory, or His eternity, and was actually classed with the Gods, with the beings who create,* with those who have kept the celestial law while in the flesh, and again obtained their bodies. Then He was prepared to commence the work of creation, as the Scriptures teach.[123]

Thus the Eternal Father of this earth is regarded as having been sent by His Father, another exalted being, to another earth, sometime in the past, to pass through a mortal probation. He was able to abide a celestial law and to win exaltation for Himself. As Joseph Smith put it, *"God himself was once as we are now, and is an exalted man, and sits enthroned in yonder heavens!"*[124]

Four years earlier, Elder Lorenzo Snow had received the revealed impressions which caused him to express the doctrine

---

[121]Jn. 5:26.
[122]HC 6:305-306. April 7, 1844.
[123]JD 4:217. Feb. 8, 1857.
[124]HC 6:305. April 7, 1844.

in the well-known couplet, "As man now is, God once was; As God now is, man may be."[125]

Though God has not revealed the full details of the past or future of the eternal worlds, man is able to more fully comprehend the past and future of this earth. He can grasp his role as a participant in the eternal pattern, and he knows the goal which he is to seek. There is no cause for uncertainty—the path he is to follow is clear. As the prophet Joseph Smith summarized it,

> Here, then, is eternal life—to know the only wise and true God; and *you have got to learn how to be gods yourselves, and to be kings and priests to God, the same as all gods have done before you, namely, by going from one small degree to another, and from a small capacity to a great one; from grace to grace, from exaltation to exaltation, until you attain to the resurrection of the dead, and are able to dwell in everlasting burnings, and to sit in glory, as do those who sit enthroned in everlasting power.* And I want you to know that God, in the last days, while certain individuals are proclaiming His name, is not trifling with you or me.[126]

---

[125]LeRoi C. Snow, "Devotion to a Divine Inspiration." *Improvement Era,* Vol. XXII, No. 8, p. 656, June, 1919. The circumstance in which this teaching was revealed are interesting:

> In May, 1836, after a blessing meeting, to which he had been invited, in the Kirtland Temple, the Patriarch, Father Joseph Smith, said to Lorenzo Snow: 'You will soon be convinced of the truth of the latter-day work, and be baptized, and you will become as great as you can possibly wish—even as great as God, and you cannot wish to be greater.'
>
> What a remarkable promise! It astonished the young man and awakened thoughts in his mind of which he had never before dreamed. Two weeks later, in June, 1836, at the age of twenty-two, he was baptized by Apostle John Boynton. . . . In the spring of 1840, just before leaving on his first mission to England, Lorenzo Snow spent an evening in the home of his friend, Elder H. G. Sherwood, in Nauvoo. Elder Sherwood was endeavoring to explain the parable of the Savior about the husbandman who sent forth servants at different hours of the day to labor in the vineyard. While thus engaged in thought this most important event occurred, as told by President Snow himself:
>
> 'While attentively listening to his (Elder Sherwood's) explanation, the Spirit of the Lord rested mightily upon me—the eyes of my understanding were opened, and I saw as clear as the sun at noonday, with wonder and astonishment, the pathway of God and man. I formed the following couplet which expresses the revelation, as it was shown to me, and explains Father Smith's dark saying to me at a blessing meeting in the Kirtland temple, prior to my baptism, as previously mentioned in my first interview with the Patriarch:
>
> As man now is, God once was;
> As God now is, man may be.
>
> I felt this to be a sacred communication which I related to no one except my sister Eliza, until I reached England, when in a confidential, private conversation with President Brigham Young, in Manchester, I related to him this extraordinary manifestation.' (*Ibid.*)

[126]HC 6:306. April 7, 1844.

SUMMARY

1. The fundamental principle of the gospel of Jesus Christ is that man may be exalted and gain godhood. Man's true goal must be complete perfection.
2. It appears that few men will achieve exaltation, yet every individual may do so if he will but pay the price by living celestial law.
3. God desires that man achieve exaltation. His work and glory is to bring to pass the immortality and eternal life of man.
4. Exaltation consists of
   - A. Godhood,
   - B. Eternal association with the Father and Christ,
   - C. Membership in the Church of the Firstborn,
   - D. Joint inheritance with Christ,
   - E. The fulness and glory of a celestial body,
   - F. Priesthood authority,
   - G. Eternal companionship of a beloved spouse,
   - H. Eternal powers of procreation,
   - I. Family relationship with progenitors and descendants,
   - J. Thrones, kingdoms, principalities, powers, and dominions,
   - K. Admittance to the city of the Living God,
   - L. Inheritance on the celestialized earth,
   - M. Association with celestial beings,
   - N. Perfect knowledge,
   - O. Governing and lawgiving jurisdiction, and
   - P. The powers of godhood.
5. The key difference between those who become servants in the celestial kingdom and those who are exalted there lies in the fulfillment of and faithfulness to the temple ordinances and covenants.
6. Godhood is parenthood, for the god-man relationship is actually a parent-child relationship. A god presides over the children which result from his eternal marriage union. Resurrected beings beget spirit children, whom they send to pass through mortality on the earths they create.

7. Spirit children are begotten and born just as mortal children are procreated.

8. Latter-day Saints believe in a plurality of Gods. They believe God the Father, Jesus Christ, and the Holy Ghost to be separate and distinct Beings. They also believe that others have become gods and that man can attain godhood today.

9. Latter-day Saints believe that God the Father was once a man who dwelt upon an earth. "As man now is, God once was . . ." God the Father had a father who also passed through the process of mortal probation.

10. Man knows little about the other gods and their creations, for God has chosen to give man only an account of this earth and that which relates to it.

11. It is man's purpose and responsibility to learn how to be a god himself, as other gods have done before him, by progressing from one small degree to another, until he attains to the celestial resurrection and is able to dwell in eternal burnings.

BIBLIOGRAPHY

Latter-day Saint Scriptures

The Book of Mormon. trans. Joseph Smith. Salt Lake City, Utah: The Church of Jesus Christ of Latter-day Saints, 1949.

The Doctrine and Covenants of The Church of Jesus Christ of Latter-day Saints. Salt Lake City, Utah: The Church of Jesus Christ of Latter-day Saints, 1948.

The Holy Bible. King James Version; Salt Lake City, Utah: The Church of Jesus Christ of Latter-day Saints, 1950.

The Pearl of Great Price. Salt Lake City, Utah: The Church of Jesus Christ of Latter-day Saints, 1950.

Latter-day Saint Historical and Doctrinal Books and Pamphlets

A Book of Remembrance — A Lesson Book for First Year Junior Genealogical Classes. Salt Lake City, Utah: The Genealogical Society of Utah, 1936.

Bennett, Archibald F. *Saviors on Mount Zion.* Salt Lake City, Utah: The Deseret News Press, 1950.

Cowley, Matthias F. *Wilford Woodruff — History of His Life and Labors.* Salt Lake City, Utah: Bookcraft, Inc., 1964.

Crowther, Duane S. *Gifts of the Spirit.* Salt Lake City, Utah: Bookcraft, Inc., 1965.

Crowther, Duane S. *Prophecy — Key to the Future.* Salt Lake City, Utah: Bookcraft, Inc., 1962.

Crowther, Duane S. *Prophets and Prophecies of the Old Testament.* Salt Lake City, Utah: Deseret Book Company, 1966.

Crowther, Duane S. *The Prophecies of Joseph Smith.* Salt Lake City, Utah: Bookcraft, 1963.

Dibble, Philo. "Philo Dibble's Narrative," *Early Scenes in Church History.* Salt Lake City, Utah: Juvenile Instructor Office, 1882.

The Forefather Quest — A Lesson Book for Third Year Junior Genealogical Classes. Salt Lake City, Utah: The Genealogical Society of Utah, 1936.

Hackworth, Dorothy South. *The Master's Touch.* Salt Lake City, Utah: Bookcraft, Inc., 1961.

The Handbook for Genealogy and Temple Work. Salt Lake City, Utah: Genealogical Society of The Church of Jesus Christ of Latter-day Saints, 1956.

Hinckley, Bryant S. *The Faith of Our Pioneer Fathers.* Salt Lake City, Utah: Deseret Book Co., 1959.

Hinckley, Bryant S. *Heber J. Grant, Highlights in the Life of a Great Leader.* Salt Lake City, Utah: Deseret Book Co., 1951.

Hinckley, Bryant S. *Sermons and Missionary Services of Melvin J. Ballard.* Salt Lake City, Utah: Deseret Book Co., 1949.

Jenson, Andrew. *Latter-day Saint Biographical Encyclopedia.* 4 vols. Salt Lake City, Utah: Published by the Andrew Jensen History Company and printed by the Deseret News, 1901.

Journal of Discourses. 26 vols. Los Angeles: General Printing and Lithograph Co., 1961. (Photo lithographic reprint of exact original edition published in 1882.)

Kennon. "Briant S. Stevens," *Helpful Visions.* Salt Lake City, Utah: Juvenile Instructor Office, 1887.

Kimball, Abraham A. "Finding a Father," *Gems For the Young Folks.* Salt Lake City, Utah: Juvenile Instructor Office, 1881.

Kimball, Spencer W. *Tragedy or Destiny.* Address to the Brigham Young University studentbody at Provo, Utah, December 6, 1935. Provo, Utah: BYU Extension Division.

Lambert, George C. "A Modern Stoic," *Treasures In Heaven.* Salt Lake City, Utah: by the author, 1914.

Life Story of Parley Thomas Richins and Fannie Judd. Published by their family. (No publication data given.)

Little, James A. *Jacob Hamblin.* Salt Lake City, Utah: Juvenile Instructor Office, 1881.

Ludlow, Daniel H. *Latter-day Prophets Speak.* Salt Lake City, Utah: Bookcraft.

Lundwall, N. B. (comp.) *Faith Like the Ancients.* Salt Lake City, Utah: Paragon Printing Co., 1950.

Lundwall, N. B. (comp.) *Temples of the Most High.* 10th ed. Salt Lake City, Utah: Bookcraft.

Lundwall, N. B. (comp.) *The Vision.* Salt Lake City, Utah: Bookcraft Publishing Co.

McConkie, Bruce R. (comp.) *Doctrines of Salvation — Sermons and Writings of Joseph Fielding Smith.* 3 vols. Salt Lake City, Utah: Bookcraft, 1954-1956.

McKinlay, Lynn A. *Life Eternal.* By the author, 1950.

Middlemiss, Clare (comp.) *Cherished Experiences from the Writings of David O. McKay.* Salt Lake City, Utah: Deseret Book Co., 1955.

Nibley, Preston (comp.) *Sharing the Gospel with Others, Excerpts from the Sermons of President Smith.* Salt Lake City, Utah: Deseret Book Co., 1948.

Parley P. Pratt. *Autobiography of Parley P. Pratt.* 6th ed. Salt Lake City, Utah: Deseret Book Company, 1966.

Pratt, Parley P. *Key to The Science of Theology.* 9th ed. Salt Lake City, Utah: Deseret Book Co.

Richards, Franklin D. and Little, James A. *A Compendium of the Doctrines of the Gospel.* Salt Lake City, Utah: Geo. Q. Cannon & Sons Co., Printers, 1898.

Richards, Le Grand. *A Marvelous Work And a Wonder.* Salt Lake City, Utah: Deseret Book Company, 1953.

Roberts, B. H. *The Rise and Fall of Nauvoo.* Salt Lake City, Utah: Bookcraft, Inc., 1965.

Shreeve, Thomas A. "Finding Comfort," *Helpful Visions.* Salt Lake City, Utah: Juvenile Instructor Office, 1887.

Smith, Joseph. *History of the The Church of Jesus Christ of Latter-day Saints.* 7 vols., 2nd ed. Salt Lake City, Utah: Deseret Book Company, 1959.

Smith, Joseph F. *Gospel Doctrine.* Salt Lake City, Utah: Deseret Book Co., 1919.

Smith, Joseph Fielding (comp.) *Teachings of the Prophet Joseph Smith.* Salt Lake City, Utah: The Deseret News Press, 1938.

Smith, Joseph F., Jr. *Blood Atonement and The Origin of Plural Marriage.* Salt Lake City, Utah: The Deseret News Press.

Smith, Lucy Mack. *History of Joseph Smith by His Mother.* Salt Lake City, Utah: Bookcraft, Inc., 1958.

Sperry, Sidney B. *Doctrine and Covenants Compendium.* Salt Lake City, Utah: Bookcraft, Inc., 1960.

Stokes, Jeremiah. *Modern Miracles.* Salt Lake City, Utah: Bookcraft, Inc., 1945.

Tagg, Melvin S. *The Life of Edward James Wood.* Master's Thesis, College of Religious Instruction, Brigham Young University (published by the author).

Talmage, James E. *Articles of Faith.* Salt Lake City, Utah: The Church of Jesus Christ of Latter-day Saints, 1952.

Tyler, Daniel. "Incidents of Experience," *Scraps of Biography.* Salt Lake City, Utah: Juvenile Instructor Office, 1883.

Whitney, O. F. "A Terrible Ordeal," *Helpful Visions.* Salt Lake City, Utah: Juvenile Instructor Office, 1887.

Whitney, Orson F. *Life of Heber C. Kimball.* Salt Lake City, Utah: Published by the Kimball family; printed at the Juvenile Instructor Office, 1888.

Whitney, Orson F. *Through Memory's Halls.* Independence, Mo.: Zion's Printing and Publishing Co., 1930.

Woodruff, Wilford. *Leaves From My Journal.* 4th ed. Salt Lake City, Utah: The Deseret News, 1909.

Young, Lorenzo Dow. "Lorenzo Dow Young's Narrative," *Fragments of Experience.* Salt Lake City, Utah: Juvenile Instructor Office, 1882.

Periodicals

Carpenter, J. Hatton. *Utah Genealogical and Historical Magazine.* Salt Lake City, Utah: The Genealogical Society of Utah, vol. XI (July, 1920).

"Discourse Delivered at the Weber Stake Conference, Ogden, Monday, October 19th, 1896, by Prest. Wilford Woodruff," *The Deseret Weekly,* vol. 53, no. 21 (November 7, 1896).

Huntington, O. B. "The Prophet on Old Houses," *Young Woman's Journal,* vol. II (July, 1891).

Johnson, Peter E. "A Testimony," *The Relief Society Magazine,* vol. VII, no. 8 (August, 1920).

"Manifestation About Building of Temples," *Deseret Evening News,* May 18, 1918.

"Many Remarkable Cures and Other Instances of God's Power Attest That His Spirit Attends Church." Address delivered in the Tabernacle, Salt Lake City, Sunday, February 29, 1920, by President Heber J. Grant, *Deseret News,* April 24, 1920.

Penrose, Charles W. "The Witch of Endor," *Improvement Era,* vol. I, no. 7, (May, 1898).

Pomeroy, F. T. "A Genealogical Development and Testimony," *The Genealogical and Historical Magazine.* Mesa, Arizona, vol. VII, no. 3 (July, 1935).

Pratt, Orson. "Celestial Marriage," *The Seer,* vol. I, no. 9 (September, 1853).

Pratt, Orson. "Celestial Marriage," *The Seer,* vol. I, no. 10 (October, 1853).

Pratt, Orson. "Marriage," *Millennial Star,* vol. XV, no. 36 (September 3, 1853).

Pratt, Orson. "Questions and Answers," *Millennial Star,* vol. I.

"Prophecy of Heber C. Kimball," Church Section, *The Deseret News,* May 23, 1931.

Smith, Joseph F.; Winder, John R.; and Lund, Anthon H. "The Origin of Man," *Improvement Era,* vol. XIII, no. 1 (November, 1909).

Snow, LeRoi C. "Devotion to a Divine Inspiration," *Improvement Era,* vol. XXII, no. 8 (June, 1919).

Snow, LeRoi C. "Raised From the Dead," *Improvement Era,* vol. XXXII, no. 12 (October, 1929).

Taylor, John. "The Mormon." New York City, August 29, 1857.

" 'Unseen Force' Even Moves His Furniture," *The Herald Journal.* Logan, Cache County, Utah, October 11, 1966.

Wilson, Lerona A. "My Testimony Concerning Temple Work," *Relief Society Magazine,* vol. III, no. 2 (February, 1916).

Woodruff, Wilford. "Obtaining the Spirit of God," *Millennial Star,* vol. 67, no. 39.

Young, Brigham. "Preaching to Spirits in Prison," *The Contributor.* Salt Lake City, Utah: The Deseret News Company, vol. X, no. 9 (July, 1889).

Unpublished Materials

"An Interesting Letter." Unpublished letter of Benjamin F. Johnson to George S. Gibbs, 1903. (typewritten copy in the B.Y.U. Library)

"A Testimony Received by John Mickelson Lang in the St. George Temple in the Year 1928." (mimeographed)

Brooks, David Lynn. "Personal Records of David Lynn Brooks, Morgan, Utah." (mimeographed)

Crowther, Duane S. "Personal History." (manuscript)

Hale, Heber Q. "A Heavenly Manifestation by Heber Q. Hale, President of Boise Stake of The Church of Jesus Christ of Latter-day Saints." (mimeographed)

LeSueur, James W. "A Peep into The Spirit World." (mimeographed)

"Personal Records of Fern R. Morgan." (manuscript)

Peterson, Cora Anna Beal. "Biography of William Beal." (mimeographed)

Weiss, Marie W. "The Hearts of the Fathers." (mimeographed)

Zollinger, Henry. "My Experience in the Spirit World." (manuscript)

LIST OF QUOTATIONS

SUMMARY OF SUPERNATURAL MANIFESTATIONS CITED

This is a listing and summary of the supernatural manifestations cited in the book. The incidents are listed under the name of the dead individual who was seen in the spirit world or who returned to mortality. The listing also includes the mortal beings who were recipients of the manifestations cited in cases where this seems necessary for identification. An identifying phrase is given for most of the individuals listed, together with the year of the manifestation or experience when it is known.

1. **Abraham**
   A. Was shown Kolob and the Lord's other creations. 312
2. **Adam**
   A. Was seen admitting the saints through the gates of the celestial city. 347
3. **Albert (Indian helper of Jacob Hamblin)**
   A. Knew of his approaching death and future mission. Saw vision of himself preaching to a multitude of his people. 27-28
4. **Alma**
   A. Was taught about the spirit world by an angel. 23
   B. Was racked with the pains of hell. 170-171
5. **Alma the younger**
   A. Was translated? 123
6. **Angel who appeared at Kirtland Temple dedication**
   A. Was tall, with black eyes, white hair, stoop-shouldered, dressed in white. 82
7. **Angel who appeared to Adam**
   A. Said "Why dost thou offer sacrifices unto the Lord?" 122
8. **Ballard, Melvin J. (Apostle)**
   A. Saw his son, who had died at age six, as a man in the spirit world, and he saw he had agency and would be able to choose and be sealed to a companion. 200
9. **Barber, ... (Killed by anti-Mormon mob in 1833)**
   A. Saw the room was full of angels as he was dying. Others could not see them. 29
10. **Beal, Clarissa Allen (Mother of Harriet Salvina Beal)**
    A. Told her daughter Joseph Smith was preparing genealogy work. 102
    B. Went to work in a spirit world kitchen. 102
11. **Beal, Harriet Salvina (16-year old Utah Pioneer, 1852)**
    A. Was taken by her deceased mother into the spirit world. 6
    B. Saw a beautiful but unfinished building, bedroom, and beds in the spirit world. 77-78
    C. Was told by her mother that her new dress had been given to her by the Lord. 80
    D. Saw Joseph Smith supervising a large group of men who were writing. 102
    E. Learned that Joseph Smith, Hyrum Smith and others were preparing genealogy so that work can be done on the earth. 102
    F. Learned that her mother took her turn working in the kitchen. 102
12. **Brooks, David Lynn, Wife of (1947)**
    A. Appeared to her husband in a time of his sorrow. She showed her husband a vision of people in the spirit world to whom she was teaching the gospel. 59-60
13. **Burt, Keith (Missionary from Alberta Stake)**
    A. Appeared to his father in the Canadian temple and told him not to grieve. As a sign, he told him Edward J. Wood would call on him to bear his testimony. 134-135
14. **Cannon, George (Father of George Q., who was a member of the First Presidency)**
    A. Was told in a dream of the death of his wife before he even married her and fifteen years prior to her passing. 27

89. **Roskelley, Bishop (Bishop of Smithfield, Utah; before 1881)**
A. Was visited and interviewed by Peter Maughan but not called into the spirit world. 53-54

90. **Shreve, Sophia (8½-year-old sister of Thomas A. Shreeve)**
A. Appeared to Thomas, told him she would warn him of danger, kissed him, and disappeared behind a hand holding a torch. 137-138

91. **Shreeve, Thomas A. (L.D.S. missionary, 1878)**
A. Was visited by his brother, Teddy, then dead for twenty years, who appeared as a child. He could feel Teddy. His brother had not seen Heavenly Father yet. 23-24, 84-85
B. Saw a personage dressed in white enter the room. 82
C. Was visited by a messenger who had him report the activity of the Sydney Branch. 135-136
D. Was visited by his sister Sophia, who promised to warn him of danger. 137-138

92. **Shunammite, Son of the**
A. Was restored to mortality by Elisha. 4

93. **Smith, ... (Youngest daughter of Joseph F. Smith)**
A. Told her father "I'll sleep today" the day she died. 30

94. **Smith, Alvin (Brother of Joseph the prophet)**
A. Was visited by the angel of the Lord in his last moments. 146

95. **Smith, George A. (Member of First Presidency)**
A. Recorded that on the evening after the dedication of the Kirtland Temple, hundreds of the brethren received the ministering of angels..... 107
B. Appeared to Wilford Woodruff. 112
C. Was attacked by evil spirits in England. He was saved by three messengers. 140

96. **Smith, George Albert (President of the Church)**
A. Saw a beautiful lake, a forest, and a path obscured by grass in the spirit world. 75
B. Circumstances of his sickness in St. George, Utah are given. 75
C. Met his grandfather, saw his whole life in retrospect. 111-112
D. Said "everything I had ever done passed before me, as though it were a flying picture on a screen." 270

97. **Smith, Hyrum (Church patriarch, brother of Joseph Smith)**
A. Was seen by Wilford Woodruff in the spirit world. 81
B. Was seen in the spirit world by Harriet Salvina Beal. 102
C. Appeared to Wilford Woodruff while he was traveling by sea to England. 113

98. **Smith, Joseph F. (President of the Church)**
Vision of the Redemption of the Dead (1918)
A. Said that the dead had looked upon the long absence of their spirits from their bodies as a bondage. 22
B. Saw Joseph Smith, Hyrum Smith, Brigham Young, John Taylor, Wilford Woodruff and other choice spirits, but in a meredian of time context. 93
C. Saw that the Savior taught the faithful that they might carry the message of redemption unto all the dead. 95-96
D. Saw that righteous and wicked were separated; Christ went to the righteous, but did not visit the wicked who were in darkness. 155
E. Saw that the missionaries went forth to proclaim the gospel to all who would repent. Said that the dead who repent will be redeemed, through obedience to temple ordinances, and after paying for their sins, they will receive their reward. 186-187
F. Saw that the Lord did not go in person among the wicked but he commissioned messengers to preach to them. 202
Dream during his mission to Hawaii (1854)
A. Saw Joseph Smith, Hyrum Smith, Brigham Young, Heber C. Kimball, Willard Richards, his mother, and a small baby. He touched and felt Joseph Smith. 93-95
B. Described the circumstances of his dream. 95

99. **Smith, Joseph, Jr. (President of the Church)**
A. Recorded instances of angels appearing in the Kirtland temple. Others saw the face of the Savior. 107
B. Was seen by Wilford Woodruff in the spirit world. 81
C. Was seen in the spirit world by Harriet Salvina Beal. 102
D. Visited Wilford Woodruff in dreams and while Elder Woodruff was on the sea going on a mission to England. He taught him the work the Twelve had to perform. 112, 113
E. Appeared to Brigham Young at Winter Quarters and told him to tell the people to labor to obtain the Spirit of God. 113, 114
F. Was seen by Wilford Woodruff at the door of the temple in heaven..... 113
G. Has been handled and afflicted by the devil, face to face. 114
H. Contended with the devil face to face over control of a house at Far West. 165
I. Saw a vision of men arising from the grave in the resurrection. 241-242
J. Saw Satan fall from heaven in the "Vision." 290-291
K. Saw God the Father, the Son, and angels. 325
L. Saw Adam admitting the saints through the gate of the celestial city..... 347
M. Saw the celestial kingdom, the gate, the Father and Son on thrones of fire, and streets of gold. 348

100. **Smith, Joseph Sr. (Father of the prophet Joseph)**
A. Was seen by Wilford Woodruff at the door of the temple in heaven.... 113

101. **Smith, Sylvester (President in First Quorum of Seventy)**
A. Saw the horsemen and chariots of Israel in the Kirtland temple. 115

102. **Smoot, Brigham (Missionary to Samoa)**
A. Drowned; inspired Edward J. Wood to administer to him and restore him to life by touching Elder Wood on the shoulder and telling him to use his priesthood. 47-48

103. **Snow, Eliza R. (Author, 1836)**
A. Was seen teaching children in the spirit world. 85, 100
B. Heard the singing of heavenly choirs at the dedication of the Kirtland temple. 101

104. **Snow, Lorenzo (President of the Church)**
A. Describes his baptism of the spirit. 295
B. Was shown the pathway of God and man and formed the couplet "As man now is, God once was; As God now is, man may become." 366-367

105. **Stevens, Briant S. (Boy of 13, 1887)**
A. Moved without effort, projected body by inclining head, as a spirit being after death. 15
B. Returned to his father in white robes. 82
C. Elders were prompted to give him the Melchizedek Priesthood before his death. 88-89
D. Returned to visit his friend Fred J. Bluth. 130-131
E. An Elder watching at his bedside dreamed that he came to the temple of the living God and the throne of the Eternal Father. He tried to take down a monogram representing Briant. 350-352

106. **Stiff, Grandmother (Great-grandmother of Merrill Neville, 1917)**
A. Appeared to Eliza Neville. Told her that none can do the work for those who have had the privilege of doing it for themselves here—it's got to be done on this earth—it cannot be done hereafter. Showed Eliza a group of people for whom she was working. 213

107. **Tabitha**
A. Was restored to mortality by Peter. 3

108. **Tyler, Daniel, Grandfather of**
A. Was visited by an angel who told him his sickness was unto death. 26-27

109. **Ure, James W. (Salt Lake temple worker, 1897)**
A. Saw a group of spirits in a large building who were called out one by one to witness their baptisms and then walked away joyfully. 200

110. **Warburton, Joseph, Daughter of (1898)**
A. Saw three couples in the Salt Lake temple as she and her father were sealed vicariously for them. 223-224

DOCTRINAL INDEX

This index is a supplement to the table of contents and omits items which can be readily located through its use. This index serves to correlate many less important doctrines of which mention is made throughout the book.

ALPHABETICAL INDEX

Y

Z